HOUGHTON MIFFLIN

Reading
★ California ★

The Time Is Right

for
Houghton Mifflin
Reading

Give your students the gift of literacy—the gift that lasts forever.

Give yourself the gift of time.

Time to teach.

Time for standards success!

Time
to Teach

You have the literature students love in a program that fully integrates the California standards.

Everything you need for success!

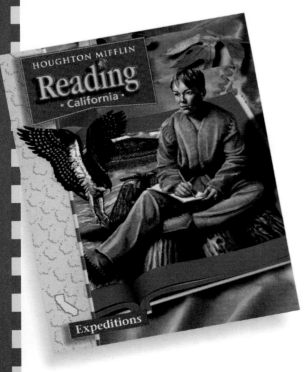

Outstanding literature

Award-winning read-alouds and anthology literature, decodable text, content-area selections, and a wide range of paperbacks—all with proven student appeal.

Clear and organized instruction

Lessons are thorough and easy to follow.
You know what to do, how to do it, and when.

Time-saving plans

Day to day, you have what you need at your fingertips:

- Easy-to-use daily lessons
- Management support to get students working independently

Time to Achieve the Standards

Houghton Mifflin Reading makes the California standards visible, accessible, and achievable for all students.

This is the very best curriculum for meeting every standard.

• California standards are built into daily instruction. You have the standards in the right place at the right time.

• With the convenient Pacing Chart at the end of this section, you know you have the right emphasis on all the standards.

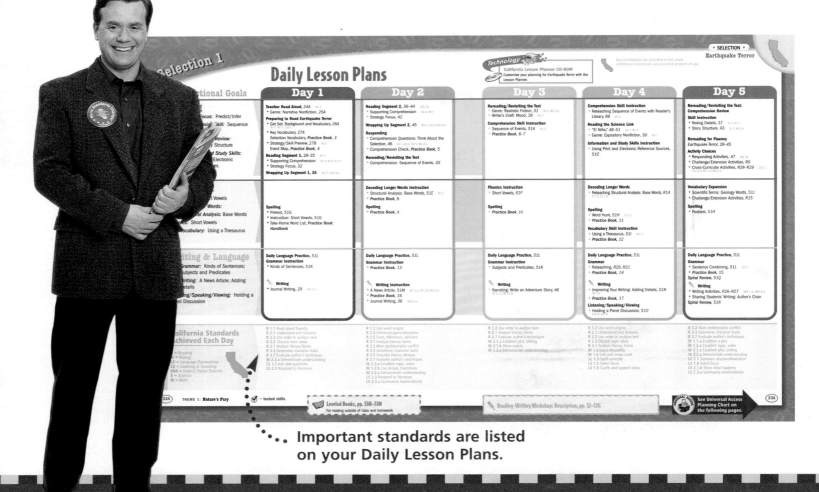

Important standards are listed on your Daily Lesson Plans.

Standards in student books help students take charge of their learning.

Get Set to Read

Volcanoes

California Standards

Standards to Achieve

Reading

- Understand text features (R2.1)
- Use order to analyze text (R2.2)
- Discern main ideas (R2.3)

The World of Volcanoes

From Hawaii to the Pacific Northwest, from Guatemala to Iceland, Seymour Simon's *Volcanoes* will take you on a world tour. You'll see more than mountain peaks. The heart of the story is about the part of the earth that's deep underground, where the heat turns the earth's crust into molten rock.

Mauna Loa
Molten rock erupts as flowing **lava** from Hawaii's Mauna Loa.

Mount St. Helens
One of many volcanoes in the Pacific Northwest, Mount St. Helens cooled down to form a hard lava dome in its **crater**.

Surtsey
An undersea volcano near Iceland created a new island, Surtsey.

Fuego and Acatenango
These volcanoes in Guatemala are built of **cinders** and ash.

Time to Manage

Your students work well independently, so you have time to ensure that each one is successful.

From the beginning, *Houghton Mifflin Reading* and the *Classroom Management Handbook* provide management plans and assignable work. You have the guidance you need to organize your classroom for the best possible results.

In the handbook you'll find:

- Flexible grouping and differentiated instruction strategies

- Independent activities

- Five-step plan for student independence

- Efficient planning for assignments

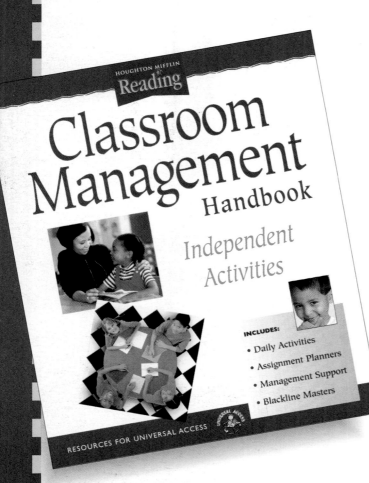

HOUGHTON MIFFLIN
Reading

Classroom Management Handbook

Independent Activities

INCLUDES:
- Daily Activities
- Assignment Planners
- Management Support
- Blackline Masters

RESOURCES FOR UNIVERSAL ACCESS

Linking
It All Together

We're making great connections to all subjects.

Content-area links and activities help you and your students achieve the standards for science, history and social science, and math.

Maximize your time!

Outstanding selections include how-to lessons to build real-world reading skills.

Reaching
All Students

With engaging Universal Access resources, all students can achieve the California standards!

We've got high standards and we're all meeting them.

Extra Support, English Language Development, and Challenge lessons are linked to daily lesson plans. You have meaningful independent activities and challenge projects, giving you the time to reach all students.

Complete and easy planning

- **preteaching and reteaching support**

- **constructive learning opportunities for advanced learners**

- **diagnostic and ongoing assessments to support your planning**

- **a wealth of literature for a wide range of reading abilities**

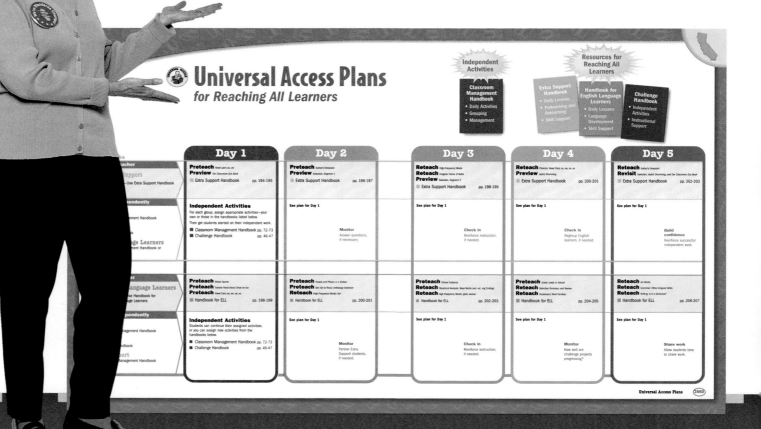

Universal Access Plans

Time to Shine!

You have confidence in the materials you're using. Your students love reading, they're meeting the standards, and test scores are up.

Time to share your success!

It's **Time** for *Houghton Mifflin Reading.*

California Standards Pacing Chart - Grade 5

This chart shows the California standards and the themes in which each standard is taught or reviewed or practiced. Some standards are taught throughout the year. Others are taught explicitly in one or two themes, with ongoing practice or review in other themes. Standards also taught in a previous year may be reviewed throughout this year. You can use this chart to adjust the pacing of instruction to make sure you cover all the standards during the year, or by a certain point in the year.

KEY

- ● taught in this theme
- ◑ review and practice
- ○ ongoing practice

GRADE 5 English–Language Arts Standards		Theme 1	Theme 2	Theme 3	Theme 4	Theme 5	Theme 6
READING							
R1.1	Read aloud fluently	◑	○	○	○	●	○
R1.2	Use word origins	●	●	◑	◑	●	●
R1.3	Understand synonyms/antonyms	●	●	●	●	◑	◑
R1.4	Use roots and affixes	●	●	●	●	●	●
R1.5	Figurative language	●	○	○	○	○	●
R2.1	Understand text features	●	●	●	●	●	●
R2.2	Use order to analyze text	●	●	●	●	●	
R2.3	Discern main ideas	●	●	●	●	●	●
R2.4	Inferences/generalizations	●	●	●	●	●	●
R2.5	Facts, inferences, opinions	●	●	●	●	○	●
R3.1	Analyze literary forms	●	●	●	●	●	●
R3.2	Main problem/plot conflict	●	●	●	●	●	◑
R3.3	Determine character traits	●	◑	○	●	●	○
R3.4	Understand theme	○	○	●	○	○	○
R3.5	Describe literary devices	●	●	●	●	●	●
R3.6	Evaluate patterns/symbols	●		○	○		
R3.7	Evaluate author's techniques	●	●	●	●	●	●

GRADE 5 English-Language Arts Standards	Theme 1	Theme 2	Theme 3	Theme 4	Theme 5	Theme 6
WRITING						
W1.1 Create a narrative	●		●	●		○
W1.1.a Establish a plot	●	○	●	●		○
W1.1.b Describe setting	●	○	●	●		○
W1.1.c Present ending	●	○	●	●	●	○
W1.2 Create an exposition	○	○	●	○	●	●
W1.2.a Establish topic, order	●	●	●	●	○	○
W1.2.b Use details, transitions	●	●	●	●	○	○
W1.2.c Conclude with a summary	●	◐	●	●		
W1.3 Locate information	●	●	◐			◐
W1.4 Use electronic media	●	○	○	○	●	○
W1.5 Use a thesaurus	●	○	○			◐
W1.6 Edit and revise work	●	●	●	●	●	●
W2.1 Write narratives	●		●	●		
W2.1.a Establish plot, setting	●	○	●	●	●	○
W2.1.b Show events	○		○	●	●	○
W2.2 Write responses to literature	●	○	●	○		◐
W2.2.a Demonstrate understanding	●	●	●	◐	◐	◐
W2.2.b Support judgments	◐	●	●	◐		◐
W2.2.c Develop interpretations	◐	●	●	○		◐
W2.3 Write research reports					●	
W2.3.a Frame questions	◐		●	○	●	
W2.3.b Establish focused topic	◐		●	○	●	
W2.3.c Develop topic	◐		●	○	○	
W2.4 Write persuasive compositions	●	●	◐		○	●
W2.4.a State a clear position	◐	●	◐			●
W2.4.b Support position with facts	◐	●	◐			●
W2.4.c Use organizational pattern	◐	●	◐			●
W2.4.d Address reader concerns		●	◐			●

continue

California Standards Pacing Chart - Grade 5

GRADE 5 English–Language Arts Standards	Theme 1	Theme 2	Theme 3	Theme 4	Theme 5	Theme 6
LANGUAGE CONVENTIONS						
LC1.1 Sentence structure/transitions	●	◐	◐	◐		●
LC1.2 Verbs, modifiers, pronouns	◐	◐	●		●	●
LC1.3 Colons and quotation marks		◐	●	●	◐	○
LC1.4 Use correct capitalization	●	◐	◐		◐	◐
LC1.5 Spell correctly	◐	●	●	●	●	●
LISTENING AND SPEAKING						
LS1.1 Ask new questions	●	○	◐	◐	●	○
LS1.2 Verbal, nonverbal messages	◐		●	○	●	
LS1.3 Inferences and conclusions		◐	○	○	●	◐
LS1.4 Select focus	●	○	●	●	●	○
LS1.5 Clarify and support ideas	●		●	●	●	○
LS1.6 Verbal and nonverbal cues	○	○	○			
LS1.7 Analyze persuasive techniques		●	●	●	●	
LS1.8 Analyze media		●	●	◐	◐	●
LS2.1 Make narrative presentations	◐	●			○	
LS2.1.a Establish situation	○	●	○	○	●	
LS2.1.b Show what happens	○	●	○	◐	●	
LS2.2 Informative presentations	◐	○		●	○	○
LS2.2.a Frame questions		●	○	●		●
LS2.2.b Establish controlling idea		●		●		●
LS2.2.c Develop topic		●		○		●
LS2.3 Respond to literature	◐	◐	○	○	●	○
LS2.3.a Summarize events/details	●	◐	◐	○	◐	◐
LS2.3.b Understand ideas/images	●	○	○	○	○	○
LS2.3.c Use examples	●	●	○	○		○

Other Content Standards

Some content standards for History-Social Science, Science, and Mathematics are addressed in Reading/Language Arts instruction at this level. Use this chart for your cross-curricular planning.

GRADE 5 Standards Addressed for History-Social Science, Science, Mathematics		Theme 1	Theme 2	Theme 3	Theme 4	Theme 5	Theme 6
HSS5.1.1	Indians adapt to nature					✔	
HSS5.1.2	Varied customs/traditions					✔	
HSS5.3.1	Conflict among settlers/Indians			✔		✔	
HSS5.3.2	Colonists coexist with Indians			✔			
HSS5.3.5	Indians compete with others					✔	
HSS5.4.1	Location of 13 colonies			✔			
HSS5.4.3	Religion in early colonies			✔			
HSS5.5.1	Causes of the Revolution			✔			
HSS5.6	Understand the Revolution			✔			
HSS5.6.2	Other people affect Revolution			✔			
HSS5.6.4	Impact of the Revolution			✔			
HSS5.8	U.S. migration to mid-1800s					✔	
HSS5.8.4	Settlers move to West					✔	
HSS5.8.5	Mexican migration					✔	

We're Standards Champs!
California Standards

continued

California Standards Pacing Chart - Grade 5

GRADE 5 Standards Addressed for History-Social Science, Science, Mathematics		Theme 1	Theme 2	Theme 3	Theme 4	Theme 5	Theme 6
S1.c	Properties of metals			✔			
S3.a	Water covers most of Earth		✔				
S4.b	Oceans and weather patterns	✔					
S4.c	Severe weather	✔					
S4.d	Weather forecasts	✔					
S6.a	Classify objects		✔		✔		
MNS1.1	Estimate large/small numbers				✔		
MNS2.1	Calculate with decimals			✔			
MMG2.3	Draw solid objects					✔	
MSDP1.2	Display data in graphs					✔	✔
MMR2.1	Use estimation	✔					
MMR2.6	Make, check calculations		✔				

Looking Ahead Many standards build throughout the grade levels. Look ahead to the standards you are teaching this year that your students will be expected to achieve next year. Use these to provide a challenge for all your students.

Grade 6 Standards Addressed in Grade 5

R1.1	Read aloud fluently
R1.2	Figurative language
R1.3	Recognize foreign words
R2.3	Connect/clarify main ideas
R2.7	Make reasonable assertions
R3.1	Identify forms of fiction
R3.6	Identify and analyze themes
W1.2	Create expository compositions
W1.5	Format documents
W1.6	Revise; improve organization
W2.1	Write narratives
W2.2	Write expository compositions
W2.3	Write research reports
W2.4	Write responses to literature
W2.5	Persuasive compositions
LC1.1	Compound/complex sentences
LC1.3	Colons, semicolons, commas
LC1.4	Correct capitalization
LS1.1	Verbal/nonverbal messages
LS1.4	Focus and structure
LS1.6	Support opinions
LS2.1	Narrative presentations
LS2.2	Informative presentations
LS2.3	Oral responses to literature

We're Standards Champs!
California Standards

Teacher's Notes

California Teacher's Edition

Grade 5

Expeditions

▶ Back to School
▶ **Theme 1** **Nature's Fury**
Focus On **Tall Tales**

Theme 2 **Give It All You've Got**
Focus On **Poetry**

Theme 3 **Voices of the Revolution**

Theme 4 **Person to Person**
Focus On **Plays**

Theme 5 **One Land, Many Trails**
Focus On **Autobiography**

Theme 6 **Animal Encounters**

Senior Authors J. David Cooper, John J. Pikulski

Authors Patricia A. Ackerman, Kathryn H. Au, David J. Chard, Gilbert G. Garcia, Claude N. Goldenberg, Marjorie Y. Lipson, Susan E. Page, Shane Templeton, Sheila W. Valencia, MaryEllen Vogt

Consultants Linda H. Butler, Linnea C. Ehri, Carla B. Ford

HOUGHTON MIFFLIN   BOSTON • MORRIS PLAINS, NJ

California • Colorado • Georgia • Illinois • New Jersey • Texas

Literature Reviewers

Consultants: **Dr. Adela Artola Allen**, Associate Dean, Graduate College, Associate Vice President for Inter-American Relations, University of Arizona, Tucson, Arizona; **Dr. Manley Begay**, Co-director of the Harvard Project on American Indian Economic Development, Director of the National Executive Education Program for Native Americans, Harvard University, John F. Kennedy School of Government, Cambridge, Massachusetts; **Dr. Nicholas Kannellos**, Director, Arte Publico Press, Director, Recovering the U.S. Hispanic Literacy Heritage Project, University of Houston, Texas; **Mildred Lee**, author and former head of Library Services for Sonoma County, Santa Rosa, California; **Dr. Barbara Moy**, Director of the Office of Communication Arts, Detroit Public Schools, Michigan; **Norma Naranjo**, Clark County School District, Las Vegas, Nevada; **Dr. Arlette Ingram Willis**, Associate Professor, Department of Curriculum and Instruction, Division of Language and Literacy, University of Illinois at Urbana-Champaign, Illinois

Teachers: **Midge Anuson**, Ridge Hall Lutheran School, Rodona Beach, California; **Sue Hooks**, Lebanon Road Elementary School, Charlotte, North Carolina; **Anatia Gayle Mills**, Cranberry-Prosperity School, Beckley, West Virginia; **Tom Torres**, Elaine Wynn Elementary School, Las Vegas, Nevada; **Celeste Watts**, Meadow Hill Magnet Elementary School, Newburgh, New York

Program Reviewers

California Reviewers: **Maureen Carlton**, Barstow, California; **Karen Cedar**, Gold River, California; **Karen Ciraulo**, Folsom, California; **Marilyn Crownover**, Tustin, California; **Cheryl Dultz**, Citrus Heights, California; **Beth Holguin**, San Jose, California; **Sandi Maness**, Modesto, California; **Muriel Miller**, Simi Valley, California; **Jean Nielson**, Simi Valley, California; **Sue Patton**, Brea, California; **Jennifer Rader**, Huntington, California; **Bea Tamo**, Huntington, California

Supervisors: **Judy Artz**, Middletown Monroe City School District, Ohio; **James Bennett**, Elkhart Schools, Elkhart, Indiana; **Kay Buckner-Seal**, Wayne County, Michigan; **Charlotte Carr**, Seattle School District, Washington; **Sister Marion Christi**, St. Matthews School, Archdiocese of Philadelphia, Pennsylvania; **Alvina Crouse**, Garden Place Elementary, Denver Public Schools, Colorado; **Peggy DeLapp**, Minneapolis, Minnesota; **Carol Erlandson**, Wayne Township Schools, Marion County, Indianapolis; **Brenda Feeney**, North Kansas City School District, Missouri; **Winnie Huebsch**, Sheboygan Area Schools, Wisconsin; **Brenda Mickey**, Winston-Salem/Forsyth County Schools, North Carolina; **Audrey Miller**, Sharpe Elementary School, Camden, New Jersey; **JoAnne Piccolo**, Rocky Mountain Elementary, Adams 12 District, Colorado; **Sarah Rentz**, East Baton Rouge Parish School District, Louisiana; **Kathy Sullivan**, Omaha Public Schools, Nebraska; **Rosie Washington**, Kuny Elementary, Gary, Indiana; **Theresa Wishart**, Knox County Public Schools, Tennessee

Teachers: **Carol Brockhouse**, Madison Schools, Wayne Westland Schools, Michigan; **Eva Jean Conway**, R.C. Hill School, Valley View School District, Illinois; **Carol Daley**, Jane Addams School, Sioux Falls, South Dakota; **Karen Landers**, Watwood Elementary, Talladega County, Alabama; **Barb LeFerrier**, Mullenix Ridge Elementary, South Kitsap District, Port Orchard, Washington; **Loretta Piggee**, Nobel School, Gary, Indiana; **Cheryl Remash**, Webster Elementary School, Manchester, New Hampshire; **Marilynn Rose**, Michigan; **Kathy Scholtz**, Amesbury Elementary School, Amesbury, Massachusetts; **Dottie Thompson**, Erwin Elementary, Jefferson County, Alabama; **Dana Vassar**, Moore Elementary School, Winston-Salem, North Carolina; **Joy Walls**, Ibraham Elementary School, Winston-Salem, North Carolina; **Elaine Warwick**, Fairview Elementary, Williamson County, Tennessee

English Language Learners Reviewers: **Maria Arevalos**, Pomona, California; **Manuel Brenes**, Kalamazoo, Michigan; **Susan Dunlap**, Richmond, California; **Tim Fornier**, Academia de Español Elementary School, Grand Rapids, Michigan; **Connie Jimenez**, Los Angeles, California; **Diane Bonilla Lether**, Pasadena, California; **Anna Lugo**, Patrick Henry School, Chicago, Illinois; **Marcos Martel**, Hayward, California; **Carolyn Mason**, Yakima School District, Yakima, Washington; **Jackie Pinson**, Moorpark, California; **Jerilyn Smith**, Salinas, California; **Noemi Velazquez**, Jersey City, New Jersey; **Dr. Santiago Veve**, JM Ullom School, Las Vegas, Nevada

Printed in the U.S.A.

ISBN: 0-618-13821-8

4 5 6 7 8 9 10 WC 11 10 09 08 07 06 05 04 03 02

Credits

Front Cover Photography
by Tony Scarpetta

Front Cover Illustration
by Gary Aagaard

Photography
CA9 (Hat) The Purcell Team/CORBIS. (Astronaut) © 2003 PhotoDisc. (Liberty Bell) Leif Skoogfors/CORBIS. (Flag) Owen Franken/CORBIS. (Earth) Reuters NewMedia Inc./CORBIS.

Corbis Royalty Free
p. 51C

Mark Epstein/DRK photo
p. 53U

Bob Barbour/AllStock/PictureQuest
p. 81W

Assignment Photography
CA1 Jade Albert. **CA2** Allan Landau. **CA3** Jade Albert. **CA4–CA6** Allan Landau. **CA7** Joel Benjamin. **CA8** (t) Allan Landau. (b) Joel Benjamin. **CA9** (b) Joel Benjamin. **CA10** (t) Allan Landau. (b) Joel Benjamin. **CA11** Jade Albert. **CA12** (t) Allan Landau. **CA13** Allan Landau. **CA17** Joel Benjamin. **CA18** Tony Scarpetta. **CA19** Joel Benjamin.

Tony Scarpetta
pp. BTS 16, BTS 18

Parker/Boon Productions
pp. BTS 1, 51D

Illustration
Nancy Carpenter, pp. BTS5, BTS9, BTS13

Acknowledgments

Grateful acknowledgment is made for permission to reprint copyrighted material as follows:

Theme 1
"The Pumpkin Box" from MANIAC MONKEYS ON MAGNO-LIA STREET, by Angela Johnson, illustrated by John Ward. Text copyright © 1999 by Angela Johnson. Illustrations copyright © 1999 by John Ward. Reprinted by permission of Alfred A. Knopf, a division of Random House, Inc.

"Making Waves" from the October 1999 issue of *Contact Kids*. Copyright © 1999 by the Children's Television Workshop. Reprinted by permission of the Children's Television Workshop.

"The Wreck of the E.S. Newman," by Ruth Ewers, from the December 1995 issue of *Cricket* magazine. Copyright © 1995 by Ruth L. Ewers. Reprinted by permission of the Carus Publishing Company.

Student Writing Model Feature

Special thanks to the following teachers whose students' compositions appear as Student Writing Models: **Cindy Cheatwood**, Florida; **Diana Davis**, North Carolina; **Kathy Driscoll**, Massachusetts; **Linda Evers,** Florida; **Heidi Harrison**, Michigan; **Eileen Hoffman**, Massachusetts; **Julia Kraftsow**, Florida; **Bonnie Lewison**, Florida; **Kanetha McCord**, Michigan

Introducing the California Standards

Your students are about to begin a year-long journey in Reading, experiencing rich literature and achieving the standards set for them by the Reading/Language Arts Framework for California Public Schools.

For a positive, motivating introduction to the standards, "walk through" the opening pages of *Expeditions* with your students.

Before you begin, notice the placement of standards on pages throughout the student book:
- before and after the selections on Get Set to Read, Strategy Focus, and Responding pages
- on cross-curricular Links and "Focus on..." genre pages
- on Student Writing Model and Taking Tests pages

Reading the Anthology

Explain to students that together you will read the first pages of Expeditions *because the California standards are so important to learning.*

Welcome to Reading!
Have students follow along as you read aloud the first page.

Meet the Standards Along the Way
These pages show one way in which standards are posted in the student book. After you or a student reads aloud the left page, explain that standards are shown so that students will better understand what skills they are learning in reading, writing, grammar, and in listening and speaking.

Hold up a student book and point out placements of standards throughout the book. Explain that the standards on the red panel on Get Set to Read pages relate to the whole selection, not just to what students will learn on that page. Likewise, the Link standards relate to the entire content of the Link.

After reading aloud the right page, explain that achieving the standards for Grade 5 is like taking a trip. Say: *You can't get where you want to go all of a sudden. It takes time. Standards are the same way. You don't have to achieve them all at once. You'll learn the right ones at the right time as you go along.*

History–Social Science and Science Come Alive!
Before reading aloud, call on students to talk about what they see on these pages. Point out that as students read selections throughout the year, they will be learning about topics in science, history and social science, and they will be practicing math. This will help them achieve state standards for those subject areas as well.

You may want to post the standards for Grade 5 in your classroom and refer to them frequently during the year. This can help students understand and take responsibility for their learning goals.

Key to California Standards in Back to School

Reading

1.0 Word Analysis, Fluency, and Systematic Vocabulary Development

R1.1 Read aloud narrative and expository text fluently and accurately and with appropriate pacing, intonation, and expression.

2.0 Reading Comprehension

R2.3 Discern main ideas and concepts presented in texts, identifying and assessing evidence that supports those ideas.

R2.4 Draw inferences, conclusions, or generalizations about text and support them with textual evidence and prior knowledge.

3.0 Literary Response and Analysis

R3.7 Evaluate the author's use of various techniques (e.g., appeal of characters in a picture book, logic and credibility of plots and settings, use of figurative language) to influence readers' perspectives.

Writing

2.0 Writing Applications

W2.2 Write responses to literature:

   W2.2a. Demonstrate an understanding of a literary work.

Listening and Speaking

1.0 Listening and Speaking Strategies

LS1.1 Ask questions that seek information not already discussed.

LS1.5 Clarify and support spoken ideas with evidence and examples.

2.0 Speaking Applications

LS2.3 Deliver oral responses to literature:

   LS2.3a. Summarize significant events and details.

Back to School

Get your students off to a good start with reading strategies . . . and diagnostic planning resources for you.

Strategy Workshop

Reading Strategies

- Predict/Infer
- Phonics/Decoding
- Monitor/Clarify
- Question
- Evaluate
- Summarize

Diagnostic Planning

Assessing Students Needs

- Informal Observation
- Using Diagnostic Instruments
- Oral Reading Fluency

Planning Instruction

- Customizing Instruction

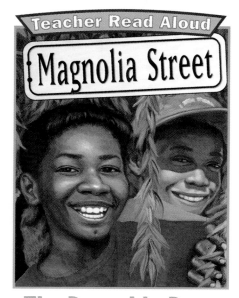

Teacher Read Aloud

Magnolia Street

The Pumpkin Box
by Angela Johnson

A short story from *Magnolia Street*

Using Reading Strategies

Predict/Infer, Phonics/Decoding, Monitor/Clarify, Question, Evaluate, Summarize

Discuss with students what good readers do when they read. Talk about the following points:

- Good readers use strategies whenever they read.

- Different strategies are used before, during, and after reading.

- As readers learn to use strategies, they must think about how each strategy will help them.

Then display the strategies using **Transparencies BTS–A1-A2**. Talk about the different reading strategies students are familiar with. Tell them that before they begin reading this school year, you will review with them each of the strategies that will help them be successful readers.

Tell students that you will read aloud the story "The Pumpkin Box" and help them use strategies with each segment of the story. They will respond in their **Practice Books** to each strategy. Then you will model for them how to use this strategy and discuss how it is helpful. Transparencies BTS–B through BTS–G will enable you to display the appropriate passages of text for modeling.

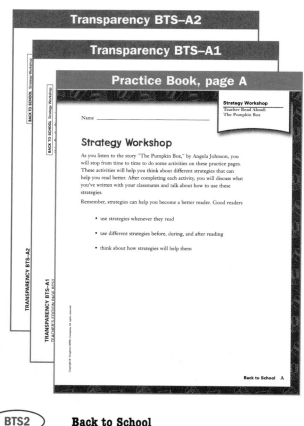

Transparency BTS–A2

Transparency BTS–A1

Practice Book, page A

Strategy Workshop
Teacher Read Aloud:
The Pumpkin Box

Name _____

Strategy Workshop

As you listen to the story "The Pumpkin Box," by Angela Johnson, you will stop from time to time to do some activities on these practice pages. These activities will help you think about different strategies that can help you read better. After completing each activity, you will discuss what you've written with your classmates and talk about how to use these strategies.

Remember, strategies can help you become a better reader. Good readers

- use strategies whenever they read

- use different strategies before, during, and after reading

- think about how strategies will help them

Back to School   A

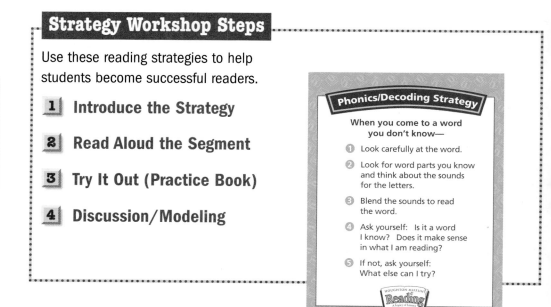

Strategy Workshop Steps

Use these reading strategies to help students become successful readers.

1 Introduce the Strategy

2 Read Aloud the Segment

3 Try It Out (Practice Book)

4 Discussion/Modeling

Phonics/Decoding Strategy

When you come to a word you don't know—

1 Look carefully at the word.

2 Look for word parts you know and think about the sounds for the letters.

3 Blend the sounds to read the word.

4 Ask yourself: Is it a word I know? Does it make sense in what I am reading?

5 If not, ask yourself: What else can I try?

Reading

California Standards pp. BTS2–BTS3

R 1.1   Read aloud fluently
W 2.2.a Demonstrate understanding
LS 2.3   Respond to literature

R 1.1
W 2.2.a
LS 2.3

Strategy: Predict/Infer

1 Introduce the Strategy

Have students open to **Practice Book** page B and read aloud the steps for the Predict/Infer Strategy.

2 Read Aloud

Invite students to listen as you read aloud the title and the first paragraph of "The Pumpkin Box."

3 Try It Out

Practice Book Now have students return to **Practice Book** page B and write what they think the pumpkin box is.

4 Discussion/Modeling

Have students model how to use the Predict/Infer Strategy. Have them discuss their predictions and whether or not their predictions are based on what you have read so far and on their own background information.

If students need help modeling the strategy, use the following Think Aloud.

Think Aloud

I can see from the title that this story will be about a pumpkin box. I wonder what a pumpkin box might be. The girl in the story says she's a digger. I bet it's something she buries or digs up. I'll start reading to see if I'm right.

What to Notice

If students have difficulty making reasonable predictions, guide them in looking for clues in the title and in the beginning text. Tell them that thinking about what they have just read and about any background knowledge they have will help them think about what will happen next.

The Pumpkin Box

Read Aloud, *Segment 1*

It all started because I'm a digger.

Digging is something that I can't help. I have done it since I was a little baby. Dad says I used to try to dig my way out of the playpen.

I don't talk about my digging too much 'cause every time I dig it usually gets me in trouble.

Billy understands about my digging. He says that he knows how hard it can be to break a habit like that. He has a nosy problem and that is pretty hard for him.

When we moved to Magnolia Street, one of the first things I noticed was a vacant lot that looked like the perfect place to dig.

So —

I had been trying not to dig for a long time. But a few nights ago, I dreamed I was in a cave that had treasures and fossils. I woke up digging in my sleep. It was time to do something about this digging problem.

When I asked Billy what I should do about it, he blew a big bubble and spun around on his skates.

"Dig!"

So what was I going to do?

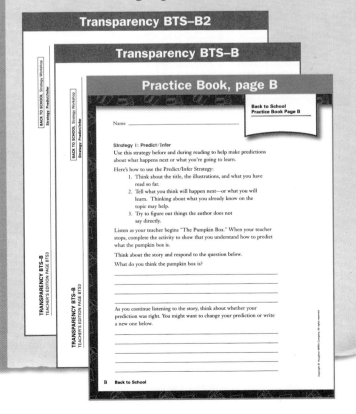

Strategy: Phonics/Decoding

1 Introduce the Strategy

Tell students that as they are reading they will use the Phonics/Decoding Strategy to help them read new words. Have them open to **Practice Book** page C; read and discuss the steps of the strategy.

2 Read Aloud the Segment

Continue reading the story, stopping at the word *munching*. Then print the word *munching* on the chalkboard.

3 Try It Out

Practice Book Now have students return to **Practice Book** page C and write the words in the blanks to complete the steps of the Decoding Strategy. Discuss the decoding steps.

4 Discussion/Modeling

Have students model how to use the Phonics/Decoding Strategy. Have them discuss the steps they find most helpful as they read.

If students need help modeling the strategy, use the following Think Aloud.

Think Aloud

First, I look carefully at the word; I want to see if there are any word parts I know. I see munch, which I think is a word that means "chew," but I'm not sure about that. I know the m sound, and un probably rhymes with "fun." I know the ch sound is often /ch/ as in change. When I blend all those together /m-un-ch/, add the familiar -ing ending, and look at the word in the sentence, I see that Billy is munching on an apple. That makes sense.

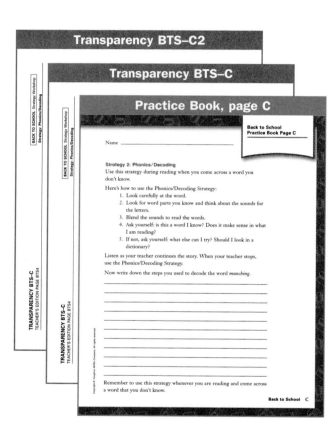

What to Notice

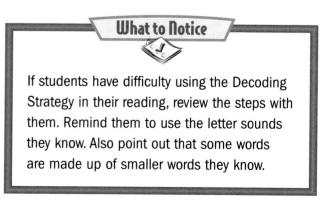

If students have difficulty using the Decoding Strategy in their reading, review the steps with them. Remind them to use the letter sounds they know. Also point out that some words are made up of smaller words they know.

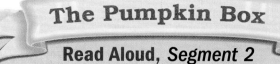

The Pumpkin Box

Read Aloud, *Segment 2*

I'd been looking at the empty place across the street from my house for a long time. I decided to drag Billy away from his skating. I had to tell him I was pretty sure that there was a sabertooth tiger or something just waiting for us to dig up.

"Okay, Charlie, where is it?" Billy said, munching on an apple and looking real unhappy.

I had expected more from Billy, even though I know that everybody is not a digger. But I figured that Billy should have been a little happier that I was sharing with him.

"Billy?"

"What?"

"Guess what?"

"What, Charlie?"

"What are you going to do with your part of the sabertooth tiger bones you find?"

"Well, I guess I'll put them together with yours."

"Then you'll help me dig?"

Well, I can say this about Billy, and it's probably why we're friends, if you bug him enough, he'll join in sooner or later. He even looked like he might be getting excited about the sabertooth across the street.

While we were both hanging upside down in Miss Marcia's apple tree, Billy asked, "What do we need to dig? You know we have to be careful. We don't want to break any sabertooth bones or anything."

I thought for a while.

"A shovel might be too much. Anyway, my mom won't let me use it after that flower-digging accident I had."

Billy swung by his legs faster.

"What flower-digging accident?"

Strategy: Monitor/Clarify

1 Introduce the Strategy

Remind students that good readers ask themselves if what they are reading makes sense. Tell them when they are confused by what they are reading they can reread or read ahead. Have them open to **Practice Book** page D and read aloud the steps for the Monitor/Clarify Strategy.

2 Read Aloud the Segment

Invite students to listen as you read aloud Segments 3 and 4 of "The Pumpkin Box."

3 Try It Out

Practice Book Have students open their **Practice Books** to page D and answer the questions about the pumpkin box.

4 Discussion/Modeling

Have students model how to use the Monitor/Clarify Strategy and discuss how it helps them understand what they are reading. Remind them that when they're confused by what they're reading, they can reread or read ahead.

If students need help modeling the strategy, use the following Think Aloud.

Think Aloud

After I read the part about finding the pumpkin box, I was confused about how it got there and what it might be. What was a box doing under the ground? I reread the last few paragraphs to see if I had missed something. But I didn't find anything that told me why it was there. I have read other stories about buried treasure, or about people burying valuable things, so maybe it's something like that. I will now read ahead to see if there's something later that will tell me why the box was buried—and who buried it!

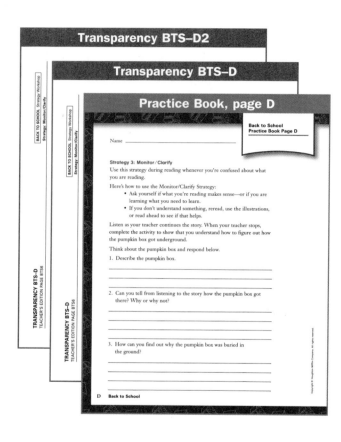

What to Notice

If students have difficulty monitoring as they read, tell them to stop and think about the story as you continue reading. Tell them that thinking about how well they understand what they are reading will help them understand and enjoy the story more.

The Pumpkin Box

Read Aloud, *Segment 3*

I closed my eyes, remembering all the dirt and flowers lying around the backyard. I only meant to move the different flowers around so all the colors would be lined up together. Well, I got kind of tired and there was this funny movie on television that Sid was watching.

Mom wasn't happy.

So I just said, "Nothing."

Billy jumped down from the tree.

"My dad has digging tools he uses for the garden out back. They're small, and I'm sure he won't miss them."

"Yeah, he probably won't miss them. I'll get some bags to keep the bones and other stuff we find."

Me and Billy were set.

The digging was hard in the beginning. An old house used to be there, but the only thing left from it was part of the chimney. You wouldn't believe the things we started to find underneath the dirt. I just knew that there had to be a sabertooth or something there.

The first thing we dug up was spoons.

Billy said, "We could clean these things up. They probably are gold!"

Billy put the gold spoons in the bag that was for everything else but bones.

After a while it started getting real hot. I could almost make believe that me and Billy were digging way off in a desert somewhere. We were far away from home with only a little water. We were famous archaeologists.

I would find bones.

Billy would find gold spoons.

I would find fossils.

Billy would find gold spoons.

I would find a whole city buried way down underneath the desert.

And there, Billy would find more gold spoons.

R 1.1
W 2.2.a

Strategy: Question

1 Introduce the Strategy

Remind students that good readers ask themselves questions about important ideas as they read. Tell them that by asking questions they will understand and enjoy the story more. Have them open to **Practice Book** page E; read and discuss the steps of the strategy.

2 Read Aloud the Segment

Invite students to listen as you reread aloud Segment 4 of "The Pumpkin Box."

3 Try It Out

Practice Book Now have students return to **Practice Book** page E and write down a question they might ask themselves at this point.

4 Discussion/Modeling

Have students model how to use the Question strategy and discuss how asking about something they want to know more about will help them understand what they are reading. Have students discuss the questions they've written.

If students need help modeling the strategy, use the following Think Aloud.

Think Aloud

In the story, the things inside the pumpkin box cause the narrator to feel that to be a digger is very exciting. I wonder why.

Discuss with students what information in the story would explain why the things in the pumpkin box make the narrator excited about being a digger. Compare what they already know about the narrator and what they learn about the things in the box in Segment 5.

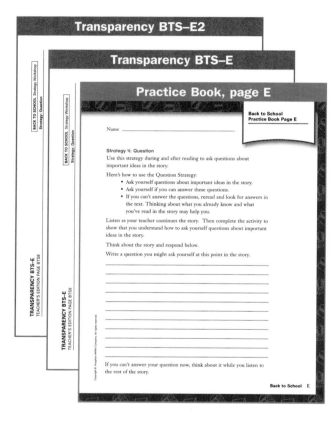

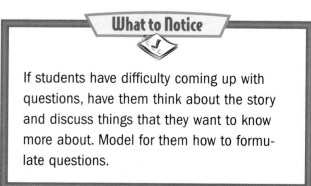

What to Notice

If students have difficulty coming up with questions, have them think about the story and discuss things that they want to know more about. Model for them how to formulate questions.

California Standards pp. BTS8–BTS9

R 1.1   Read fluently
W 2.2.a Demonstrate understanding

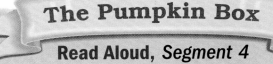

The Pumpkin Box

Read Aloud, *Segment 4*

Me and Billy didn't even talk to each other while we dug. We were too busy finding all kinds of treasures.

Billy found a cracked mirror.

I found a scrub brush.

Billy found a bottle with a metal top on it, and I found an old can.

The non-bone bag was filling up, and I noticed that Billy was smiling. Sometimes you just have to bring out the digger in some people.

Just as I was starting to get a little worried 'cause we hadn't run into any bones yet, I hit something with the little hand shovel I had. I took a while to dig it up 'cause I didn't want to wreck any of it.

I'd found something better than a sabertooth.

It was a pumpkin box.

It was metal and square, and somebody had pasted paper pumpkins all over it.

Billy said, "Can we open it?"

"I don't know"

"Try."

So I did. I just wiggled the lock a little and it opened right up.

And the things inside. I knew then that to be a digger was probably to be one of the most exciting things in the world.

Me and Billy sat side by side and stared at the pumpkin box. Most of the pumpkins had fallen off, but there were a couple left. Inside, there was magic.

Billy looked at me and smiled.

I looked at him and smiled.

R 1.1
R 3.7
W 2.2.a

Strategy: Evaluate

1 Introduce the Strategy

Remind students that good readers should always think about their reactions to what they are reading and why they are reacting that way.

Tell them that they can *evaluate* a story in many different ways:

• How well the author writes

• What the story is about

• Their reaction to the story

Have students open to **Practice Book** page F; read and discuss the steps of the strategy.

2 Read Aloud the Segment

Read aloud the next segment of "The Pumpkin Box."

3 Try It Out

Practice Book Now have students return to **Practice Book** page F and respond to one of the prompts.

4 Discussion/Modeling

Have students model how to use the Evaluate strategy and discuss how following the steps can help them understand the story.

If students need help modeling the strategy, use the following Think Aloud.

Think Aloud

The author gets me interested in the story right from the beginning. I liked the way she tells the story from her own point of view. It made it that much more interesting to me. It made me want to read it to see what happened to the characters.

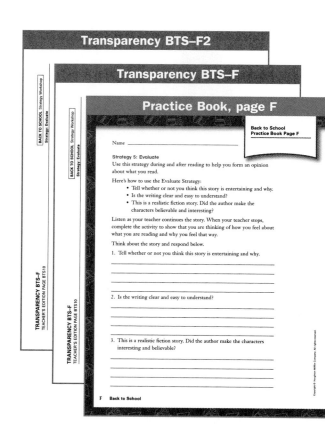

Transparency BTS–F2

Transparency BTS–F

Practice Book, page F

What to Notice

If students have difficulty evaluating the story, guide them with questions that require students to give opinions about the story. Explain that when giving opinions, they are evaluating the story.

California Standards pp. BTS10–BTS11

R 1.1   Read aloud fluently
R 3.7   Evaluate author's techniques
W 2.2.a Demonstrate understanding

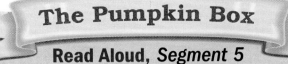

The Pumpkin Box

Read Aloud, *Segment 5*

The first thing we found in the box was a yo-yo.

It was red and wooden.

We laid it out beside the pumpkin box. We didn't want to put it in the non-bone bag.

Next we found three nickels tied up in a handkerchief. They had buffaloes on them.

After that, we found an old watch. It didn't run.

The only way you could tell we liked everything we found was when we'd say, "Wow." And we said that a lot.

Underneath that, we found a book. It had cowboys on the front of it. The pages were falling apart and we were afraid to open it too much, so we laid it down gently beside the other stuff.

The next thing we found was a note. It was wrapped in wax paper. Billy handed it to me to read, since I was the main digger. The note said:

Whoever finds this box must share it. It doesn't matter who you share it with. When you have shared the things in this box, you must put your own treasures in it and bury it again.

Signed,

Tracy and David

The note was brown and falling apart.

And in the bottom of the box was a picture of two kids dressed in funny clothes. The picture was old and a little blurry, but you could still see the kids, and they were smiling.

Billy pointed at the picture, then pointed at my house across the street. Sure enough, there was my tree and house right there in the picture. There is nothing like digging . . .

R 1.1
W 2.2.a
LS 2.3.a

Strategy: Summarize

1 Introduce the Strategy

Explain to students that summarizing means telling the most important parts of a story in a quick way. Remind students that thinking about the following story elements can help them summarize a story:

- Who the main character is

- Where the story takes place

- What the problem is

- What happens in the beginning, middle, and end

Have them open to **Practice Book** page G; read and discuss the steps of the strategy.

2 Read Aloud the Segment

Invite students to listen as you read aloud the last segment of "The Pumpkin Box."

3 Try It Out

Practice Book Now have students return to **Practice Book** page G and respond to the three prompts.

4 Discussion/Modeling

Have students model how to use the Summarize Strategy by telling in their own words

- Who the main character is

- What the character's problem is

- How the character's problem is solved

If students need help modeling the strategy, use the following Think Aloud.

Think Aloud

The main character in the story is Charlie, who is a digger. Charlie's problem is deciding what to do with the things she finds in the pumpkin. She solves the problem by thinking of the right people to receive the items in the box.

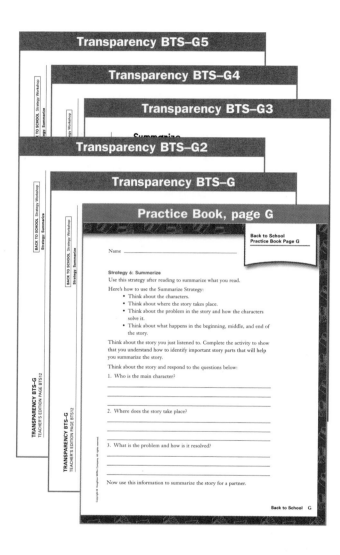

What to Notice

If students have difficulty summarizing the story, then use a graphic organizer to chart where the story takes place, who the main characters are, what the problem is, and what happens in the beginning, middle, and end. Then have students use the information on the chart to summarize the story.

California Standards pp. BTS12–BTS13

R 1.1   Read aloud fluently
W 2.2.a Demonstrate understanding
LS 2.3.a Summarize events/details

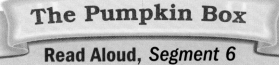

The Pumpkin Box

Read Aloud, *Segment 6*

We put all the pumpkin box stuff back in the box and loaded up to go home.

Billy thought I should keep the pumpkin box and he should keep the spoons until we figured out what we should do with them.

I slept that night with the pumpkin box right beside my turtle night light.

I dreamed of Tracy and David. I dreamed that they liked the things that me and Billy liked and did the things that me and Billy did.

Maybe they were diggers too. One of them must have been, because the box was buried to be dug up. In my dreams, they ran alongside me and Billy. We ate ice cream at Mo's and played and raced around the block for hours. They also got separated a lot and had to go to porch time-out for the whole afternoon.

The next morning, Billy was at my door.

"So who have you been thinking about giving the pumpkin box stuff to?"

I stuffed a doughnut in my mouth and handed Billy one, too. We munched and thought.

It was going to take us a while to think.

We decided to walk around with the box and figure it out. We walked up and down Magnolia Street. We looked at the street like we never had before. Who would we give the pumpkin box treasures to?

I said, "Magnolia Street must have been here a long time. My mom says that the picture in the box is probably sixty years old."

Billy said, "I don't think I know anybody that old. Do I?"

All of a sudden Billy got a big smile on his face, grabbed my hand, and started running toward Mr. Pinkton's. Mr. Pinkton was out in his yard with his roses.

Billy took the watch out of the pumpkin box and handed it to Mr. Pinkton.

"For you," Billy said, and then grabbed me by the hand and ran away. Then he stopped and called to Mr. Pinkton, "So you'll have more time with your fish."

When we got to Billy's yard, I smiled at him.

I dreamed of Tracy and David again that night, and when I woke up the next morning, I knew who we could give the yo-yo to.

The sun was shining real bright out back when Sid sprayed me with the hose. He laughed for a long time.

Mom called from the window, "Sid!"

Sid said, "I didn't do it," like he always does when he's been caught.

I made my mind up then. I went to the pumpkin box and handed the yo-yo to Sid. And the look on his face made me so happy. He was real surprised and said, "Why?"

I said, "'Cause I like you sometimes, and you're a yo-yo, too."

I skipped away to Billy's.

The pumpkin box was great.

When I got to Billy's house, his mom was on the phone.

Billy said, "Mom's calling the library. She says the book in the box is real old and the library may want it."

We smiled at each other.

R 2.3
R 2.4
R 3.7
W 2.2.a
LS 1.5

Reading Strategies Evaluation

Discuss with students the strategies that they have used in listening to this story. Have students respond to the following prompts:

1 What strategies were the most helpful to you in understanding this story?

2 What strategies do you use when you are reading? Why do you find them helpful?

Encourage students to be strategic readers as they begin reading this year. Discuss from time to time what strategies students are using and what strategies would be helpful to use. Remind students that the opening page of their **Practice Book** provides a quick reference to using strategies.

Comprehension: Story Response

1 What habit did the narrator have that caused everything to happen? (She was a digger.)

2 What did the kids do with the things inside the pumpkin box? Why? (They gave them to people in the neighborhood because the note told them to.)

3 Why do you think that the people who buried the pumpkin box wanted the finders to put other treasures in it and bury it again? (Answers will vary.)

4 What do you think the kids will put in the pumpkin box? (Answers will vary.)

California Standards pp. BTS14–BTS15

R 2.3 Discern main ideas
R 2.4 Inferences/generalizations
R 3.7 Evaluate author's techniques

W 2.2.a Demonstrate understanding
LS 1.5 Clarify and support ideas

The Pumpkin Box

(Read Aloud, *Segment 6 continued*)

The next night, Billy said he dreamed of Tracy and David, too.

While Billy skated behind me, I rode my bike to Mo's. I walked up to the counter and handed Mo the nickels. The whole store smelled like cookies and French fries.

Mo looked confused when I said, "For you."

Mo said, "I used to collect these when I was your age."

He wiped his eyes, smiled, and said, "Thanks, kid."

Being a digger must be the best thing you could ever be in this world. You can find things that nobody ever thought could be found again.

Being a digger helps people remember gone things.

Me and Billy have decided to keep the picture of Tracy and David. He will keep it for a week, then I will have it for a week. We will always think about them running and playing on Magnolia Street like us.

We were swinging from the tree in my front yard, wondering what to put back into the pumpkin box.

Billy said, "Why do you think they put what they put in the pumpkin box, Charlie?"

"I don't know. Maybe it was stuff that they found. But it was probably stuff that made them happy."

Billy said, "I figure we can take a little time and think about the stuff that makes us happy before we put it in the pumpkin box."

And because a serious digger understands these things, I thought Billy was right.

Responding Activities

■ Ask students to list the kinds of things they would put in a pumpkin box of their own. Discuss the objects and why students chose them.

■ Have students gather things from the class that they would want to bury for future diggers. Gather the things together, put them in a container, and bury them in an appropriate part of the school grounds.

R 1.1   W 2.2.a
R 2.3   LS 1.1
R 2.4   LS 2.3.a
R 3.7

Assessing Student Needs

During the first few weeks of school, take time to observe and evaluate students' skill development and their instructional strengths and needs. This information can be gathered through informal assessment and through formal test instruments. Your diagnosis can help in planning instruction and customizing your teaching to meet students' individual needs.

▶ Informal Assessment

For many students, much can be learned through informal observation of students' reading and writing. Students' work in the Strategy Workshop can provide clues to how well they understand reading strategies and to their writing ability. As students begin work in Theme 1, you may want to make some of the observations listed below. Additional suggestions for Informal Assessment are in Planning for Assessment at the start of each theme.

- Listen to students read aloud to observe fluency, decoding, and expression.

- To note students' comprehension of Anthology selections, observe answers to Comprehension/Critical Thinking and Think About the Selection questions, or use the Selection Test.

- Observe students' writing in the Reading-Writing Workshop or in Quick Writes, Practice Book pages, Journals, or other writing assignments.

- Note students' interest in and motivation for reading.

▶ Diagnosing Needs

In addition to informal assessment, you may wish to use one or more diagnostic instruments to assess students' strengths and needs.

Baseline Group Test The **Baseline Group Test** can be used to evaluate students' reading level and comprehension. See the annotated **Baseline Group Test.**

Leveled Reading Passages For a more detailed diagnosis of individual students, the **Leveled Reading Passages** can be used to take an Oral Reading Record. This individual assessment can provide information about the student's reading level, phonics and decoding skills, comprehension, use of strategies, and fluency.

California Standards pp. BTS16–BTS17

R 1.1 Read aloud fluently
R 2.3 Discern main ideas
R 2.4 Inferences/generalizations

R 3.7   Evaluate author's techniques
W 2.2.a Demonstrate understanding
LS 1.1   Ask new questions

Assessing Phonics For students who appear to be having difficulty reading grade-level materials, you can use the **Lexia Quick Phonics Assessment CD-ROM** or the **Phonics-Decoding Screening Test** to assess the need for phonics instruction.

The chart below summarizes the diagnostic tests that are included in *Houghton Mifflin Reading: A Legacy of Literacy.*

Test	Assesses	Administration
Baseline Group Test	Comprehension Reading Level Writing	Group
Leveled Reading Passages	Reading Level Decoding Comprehension Strategies Oral Reading Fluency	Individual
Lexia Quick Phonics Assessment CD-ROM	Phonemic Awareness Phonics	Individual (with Computer)
Phonics/Decoding Screening Test	Phonics Structural Analysis	Individual

▶ **Estimating Fluency**

An estimate of oral reading fluency can help determine whether students can automatically and quickly decode words, which is important for effective comprehension. Oral reading rates vary depending on the content and difficulty of text. Oral fluency can be estimated using selections identified in the Theme Assessment Wrap-Up. Students can check their own fluency by timing themselves reading easier texts.

For students who are unable to read grade-level texts with 90% accuracy, you can use easier texts in the **Leveled Reading Passages.** English language learners especially may show inconsistencies between reading rate and comprehension. For detailed information and procedures for estimating oral reading fluency, see the **Teacher's Assessment Handbook.**

Oral Reading Fluency

Early Grade 5	106–132 words correct per minute*
Mid Grade 5	118–143 words correct per minute*
Late Grade 5	128–151 words correct per minute*

To estimate oral reading fluency, ask the student to read aloud with expression from an appropriate independent level text (90% accuracy or better). Note misreadings or self-corrections. Record the word the student is reading at the end of one minute, and allow the student to read to the end of the sentence or paragraph. Count the number of words read correctly in the timed minute. Count self-corrections or repeated words as correct. Do not count misreadings. The resulting measure is words correct per minute. Fluency measures should be interpreted in conjunction with comprehension and not used as a sole measure of reading progress.

*These rates are approximate.

Planning Instruction

Diagnostic assessment can be used to help plan appropriate instruction for each student. Instructional support to meet a variety of individual needs is included in this **Teacher's Edition** and in other components of *Houghton Mifflin Reading: A Legacy of Literacy.* The chart below suggests the appropriate instructional emphasis and resources for students with different individual needs.

Customizing Instruction

Student Performance Shows:	Modifications to Consider:
Difficulty with Decoding or Word Skills	• **Emphasis:** Word skills, phonics, reading for fluency; check for phonemic awareness • **Resources:** Teacher's Edition: *Phonics Review, Decoding Longer Words Reteaching lessons;* Lexia Phonics CD-ROM: Intermediate Intervention
Difficulty with Oral Fluency	• **Emphasis:** Reading and rereading of independent level text; vocabulary development • **Resources:** Teacher's Edition: *Leveled Books;* Reader's Library; Theme Paperbacks; Literature Resources; Book Adventure Website
Difficulty with Comprehension	• **Emphasis:** Oral comprehension; strategy development; story comprehension; vocabulary development • **Resources:** Teacher's Edition: *Teacher Read Alouds, Strategies, Extra Support notes, Comprehension Reteaching lessons, Vocabulary Skills;* Get Set for Reading CD-ROM; Extra Support Handbook
Overall High Performance	• **Emphasis:** Independent reading and writing; vocabulary development; critical thinking • **Resources:** Teacher's Edition: *Think About the Selection questions, Challenge notes;* Theme Paperbacks; Literature Resources; Book Adventure Website; Education Place Website; Challenge Handbook

Key to California Standards in Theme 1

Reading

1.0 Word Analysis, Fluency, and Systematic Vocabulary Development

R1.1 Read aloud narrative and expository text fluently and accurately and with appropriate pacing, intonation, and expression.

R1.2 Use word origins to determine the meaning of unknown words.

R1.3 Understand and explain frequently used synonyms, antonyms, and homographs.

R1.4 Know abstract, derived roots and affixes from Greek and Latin and use this knowledge to analyze the meaning of complex words (e.g., *controversial).*

R1.5 Understand and explain the figurative and metaphorical use of words in context.

2.0 Reading Comprehension

R2.1 Understand how text features (e.g., format, graphics, sequence, diagrams, illustrations, charts, maps) make information accessible and usable.

R2.2 Analyze text that is organized in sequential or chronological order.

R2.3 Discern main ideas and concepts presented in texts, identifying and assessing evidence that supports those ideas.

R2.4 Draw inferences, conclusions, or generalizations about text and support them with textual evidence and prior knowledge.

R2.5 Distinguish facts, supported inferences, and opinions in text.

3.0 Literary Response and Analysis

R3.1 Identify and analyze the characteristics of poetry, drama, fiction, and nonfiction and explain the appropriateness of the literary forms chosen by an author for a specific purpose.

R3.2 Identify the main problem or conflict of the plot and explain how it is resolved.

R3.3 Contrast the actions, motives (e.g., loyalty, selfishness, conscientiousness), and appearances of characters in a work of fiction and discuss the importance of the contrasts to the plot or theme.

R3.4 Understand that theme refers to the meaning or moral of a selection and recognize themes (whether implied or stated directly) in sample works.

R3.5 Describe the function and effect of common literary devices (e.g., imagery, metaphor, symbolism).

R3.6 Evaluate the meaning of archetypal patterns and symbols that are found in myth and tradition by using literature from different eras and cultures.

R3.7 Evaluate the author's use of various techniques (e.g., appeal of characters in a picture book, logic and credibility of plots and settings, use of figurative language) to influence readers' perspectives.

Writing

1.0 Writing Strategies

W1.1 Create multiple-paragraph narrative compositions:

    W1.1a. Establish and develop a situation or plot.

    W1.1b. Describe the setting.

    W1.1c. Present an ending.

W1.2 Create multiple-paragraph expository compositions:

    W1.2a. Establish a topic, important ideas, or events in sequence or chronological order.

    W1.2b. Provide details and transitional expressions that link one paragraph to another in a clear line of thought.

    W1.2c. Offer a concluding paragraph that summarizes important ideas and details.

W1.3 Use organizational features of printed text (e.g., citations, end notes, bibliographic references) to locate relevant information.

W1.4 Create simple documents by using electronic media and employing organizational features (e.g., passwords, entry and pull-down menus, word searches, the thesaurus, spell checks).

W1.5 Use a thesaurus to identify alternative word choices and meanings.

W1.6 Edit and revise manuscripts to improve the meaning and focus of writing by adding, deleting, consolidating, clarifying, and rearranging words and sentences.

2.0 Writing Applications

W2.1 Write narratives:

    W2.1a. Establish a plot, point of view, setting, and conflict.

    W2.1b. Show, rather than tell, the events of the story.

W2.2 Write responses to literature:

    W2.2a. Demonstrate an understanding of a literary work.

    W2.2b. Support judgments through references to the text and to prior knowledge.

    W2.2c. Develop interpretations that exhibit careful reading and understanding.

W2.3 Write research reports about important ideas, issues, or events by using the following guidelines:

    W2.3a. Frame questions that direct the investigation.

    W2.3b. Establish a controlling idea or topic.

    W2.3c. Develop the topic with simple facts, details, examples, and explanations.

W2.4 Write persuasive letters or compositions:

    W2.4a. State a clear position in support of a proposal.

    W2.4b. Support a position with relevant evidence.

    W2.4c. Follow a simple organizational pattern.

    W2.4d. Address reader concerns.

continued

Written and Oral English Language Conventions

1.0 Written and Oral English Language Conventions

LC1.1 Identify and correctly use prepositional phrases, appositives, and independent and dependent clauses; use transitions and conjunctions to connect ideas.

LC1.2 Identify and correctly use verbs that are often misused (e.g., *lie/lay, sit/set, rise/raise*), modifiers, and pronouns.

LC1.3 Use a colon to separate hours and minutes and to introduce a list; use quotation marks around the exact words of a speaker and titles of poems, songs, short stories, and so forth.

LC1.4. Use correct capitalization.

LC1.5 Spell roots, suffixes, prefixes, contractions, and syllable constructions correctly.

Listening and Speaking

1.0 Listening and Speaking Strategies

LS1.1 Ask questions that seek information not already discussed.

LS1.2 Interpret a speaker's verbal and nonverbal messages, purposes, and perspectives.

LS1.3 Make inferences or draw conclusions based on an oral report.

LS1.4 Select a focus, organizational structure, and point of view for an oral presentation.

LS1.5 Clarify and support spoken ideas with evidence and examples.

LS1.6 Engage the audience with appropriate verbal cues, facial expressions, and gestures.

LS1.7 Identify, analyze, and critique persuasive techniques (e.g., promises, dares, flattery, glittering generalities); identify logical fallacies used in oral presentations and media messages.

LS1.8 Analyze media as sources for information, entertainment, persuasion, interpretation of events, and transmission of culture.

2.0 Speaking Applications

LS2.1 Deliver narrative presentations:

LS2.1a. Establish a situation, plot, point of view, and setting with descriptive words and phrases.

LS2.1b. Show, rather than tell, the listener what happens.

LS2.2 Deliver informative presentations about an important idea, issue, or event by the following means:

LS2.2a. Frame questions to direct the investigation.

LS2.2b. Establish a controlling idea or topic.

LS2.2c. Develop the topic with simple facts, details, examples, and explanations.

LS2.3 Deliver oral responses to literature:

LS2.3a. Summarize significant events and details.

LS2.3b. Articulate an understanding of several ideas or images communicated by the literary work.

LS2.3c. Use examples or textual evidence from the work to support conclusions.

Content Area Standards

Science

S4.b Students know the influence that the ocean has on the weather and the role that the water cycle plays in weather patterns.

S4.c Students know the causes and effects of different types of severe weather.

S4.d Students know how to use weather maps and data to predict local weather and know that weather forecasts depend on many variables.

Math

MMR2.1 Use estimation to verify the reasonableness of calculated results.

Nature's Fury

OBJECTIVES

Reading Strategies predict/infer; question; monitor/clarify; phonics/decoding

Comprehension sequence of events; text organization; categorize and classify

Decoding Longer Words base words; syllabication; word roots *struct* and *rupt*; short vowels; long vowels /ā/,/ē/,/ī/; long vowels /ō/,/ōō/,/yōō/

Vocabulary using a thesaurus; dictionary: alphabetical order and guide words; dictionary: definitions

Spelling short vowels; /ā/,/ē/, and /ī/ sounds; /ō/,/ōō/, and /yōō/ sounds

Grammar kinds of sentences; subjects and predicates; conjunctions; compound sentences; singular and plural nouns; more plural nouns

Writing news article; response to a prompt; paragraph of information; process writing: description

Listening/Speaking/Viewing panel discussion; literature discussion; effective conversations

Information and Study Skills using print and electronic reference sources; using print and electronic card catalogs; using graphic aids: maps, globes, charts, tables, and graphs

Theme 1

Nature's Fury
Literature Resources

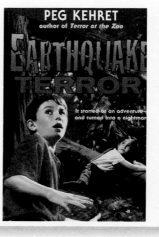
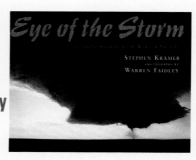

Theme Writing Process: Description

Student Writing Model

By the Sea

a description by Dena S.
page 52

Reading-Writing Workshop

Description

pages 52–53G

Leveled Books

See Cumulative Listing of Leveled Books.

Reader's Library

Theme Paperbacks

Very Easy

- **Riding Out the Storm**
- **White Dragon: Anna Allen in the Face of Danger**
- **Floods**

Lessons, pages R2–R7

Easy

If You Lived at the Time of the Great San Francisco Earthquake

by Ellen Levine
Lesson, page 53I

On Level

Drylongso

by Virginia Hamilton
Lesson, page 53K

Challenge

Hurricanes: Earth's Mightiest Storms

by Patricia Lauber
Lesson, page 53M

📼 **Audiotape and Selection Summary Masters**

Nature's Fury
Earthquake Terror
Eye of the Storm
Volcanoes

Literature Resources

Grade 5

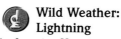

Theme 1

Bibliography

Books for Independent Reading

Choose books from this list for students to read, outside class, for at least thirty minutes a day.

Key

🔬 Science

🌐 Social Studies

🌍 Multicultural

🎸 Music

📦 Math

⭐ Classic

🎨 Art

Very Easy

Hurricane!
by Corinne Demas Bliss
Cavendish 2000 (32p)
A family rides out the storm when Hurricane Bob strikes Cape Cod.

The Blizzard's Robe
by Robert Sabuda
Atheneum 1999
(32p)
In this Arctic tale, a young girl makes a robe for Blizzard, who then creates the Northern Lights.

Anna, Grandpa, and the Big Storm
by Carla Stevens
Puffin 1985 (64p) paper
Anna is determined to get to school, despite a major snow storm.

Birdie's Lighthouse
by Deborah Hopkinson
Atheneum 1997
(32p)
Young Birdie is the only one who can tend the lighthouse in the midst of a violent storm.

Storm on the Desert
by Carolyn Lesser
Harcourt 1997 (40p)
This poetic description tells what happens when a storm strikes a desert in the Southwest.

Easy

 Rain Player
by David Wisniewski
Clarion 1991 (32p)
Pik hopes to save the people of his Mayan village from a drought.

 Wild Weather: Lightning
by Lorraine Hopping
Scholastic 1999 (48p)
The author explains the power of lightning and its positive and negative effects.

 Rocking and Rolling
by Philip Steele
Candlewick 1997
(24p)
Volcanologists and other scientists study volcanoes, tsunami, geysers, and glaciers.

🔬 **Wildfire**
by Patrick Cone
Carolrhoda 1997 (48p)
Learn how destructive wildfires are also a part of nature's cycle of growth.

🔬 **Tornadoes**
by Seymour Simon
Morrow 1999 (32p)
Simon explains how tornadoes are formed and how we can protect ourselves from them.

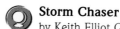 **Storm Chaser**
by Keith Elliot Greenberg
Blackbirch 1997 (32p)
NOAA pilot Brian Taggart flies into the eye of a hurricane to study it and report its progress.

Tornado
by Betsy Byars
Harper 1996 (49p)
A farmhand tells how a dog, complete with doghouse, blew into his life during a tornado.

On Level

🌐 **Trial by Ice**
by K. M. Kostyal
Nat'l Geo 1999 (64p)
This photobiography of explorer Ernest Shackleton is introduced by his granddaughter.

The Volcano Disaster
by Peg Kehret
Minstrel 1998 (136p) also paper
Warren and Betsy get more than they expect when they research Mount St. Helens.

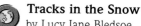 **Tracks in the Snow**
by Lucy Jane Bledsoe
Holiday 1997 (96p)
Erin and Tiffany struggle to survive a snowstorm in the Sierras.

Earthquake at Dawn
by Kristiana Gregory
Harcourt 1992 (192p)
This story of the 1906 earthquake is based on an actual letter and on photographs.

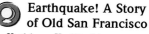 **Earthquake! A Story of Old San Francisco**
by Kathleen Kudlinski
Puffin 1995 (64p)
Philip must save his horses during the San Francisco earthquake.

🔬 **Volcano: The Eruption and Healing of Mount St. Helens**
by Patricia Lauber
Aladdin 1993 (60p)
The devastating 1980 eruption was followed by the return of life to the area.

 Flood
by Mary Calhoun
Morrow 1997 (40p)
Sarajean and her family are forced to leave their home during the devastating Midwest floods of 1993.

Shock Waves Through Los Angeles

by Carole G. Vogel
Little 1996 (32p)
Causes of the 1994 earthquake, its devastation, and heroic rescues it inspired are recounted here.

Blizzards! And Ice Storms

by Maria Rosada
Simon 1999 (64p) paper
This informative book contains meteorological information, as well as safety tips and interesting facts.

El Niño! And La Niña

by Sally Rose
Simon 1999 (64p) paper
Facts are presented about these two worldwide weather phenomena.

Night of the Twisters

by Ivy Ruckman
Harper 1986 (159p) paper
A boy and his family struggle to survive a series of devastating tornadoes.

Fire in Their Eyes

by Karen Magnuson Beil
Harcourt 1999 (64p)
The author explores the training and dangers faced by people who fight wildfires.

Missing in the Mountains

by T. S. Fields
Rising Moon 1999 (136p)
A brother and sister fight for their lives when they are caught in a sudden avalanche.

Blizzard: Estes Park, Colorado, 1886

by Kathleen Duey
Aladdin 1998 (64p)
Maggie must try to save her cousin who is lost in a sudden blizzard.

SOS Titanic

by Eve Bunting
Harcourt 1996 (256p) paper
Fifteen-year-old Barry on board the ill-fated *Titanic* finds his personal problems no longer matter.

El Niño

by Caroline Arnold
Clarion 1999 (48p)
Learn more about the wild weather phenomenon that's been making headlines around the world.

No Way Out

by Ivy Ruckman
Harper 1988 (160p) also paper
A flash flood traps a group of hikers in a narrow canyon.

Books for Teacher Read Aloud

The Long Winter

by Laura Ingalls Wilder
Harper 1961 (334p) paper
After a blizzard, Almanzo must try to save the village from starvation.

I Am Lavina Cumming

by Susan Lowell
Milkweed 1993 (200p) paper
Lavina visits her grandmother and learns of her ordeal during the 1906 San Francisco earthquake.

Computer Software Resources

- **Get Set for Reading CD-ROM**
  Nature's Fury
  Provides background building, vocabulary support, and selection summaries in English and Spanish.

Video Cassettes

- **El Niño.** *Filmic Archives*
- **Can't Drown This Town.** *Nat'l Geo*
- **After the Hurricane.** *Nat'l Geo*
- **When the Earth Quakes.** *Nat'l Geo*
- **Volcano: Nature's Inferno.** *Nat'l Geo*
- **Eyewitness: Volcanos.** *Filmic Archives*
- **Eyewitness: Natural Disasters.** *Filmic Archives*
- **The Eruption of Mount St. Helens.** *Filmic Archives*

Audio Cassettes

- **El Niño: Stormy Weather for People and Wildlife** *by Caroline Arnold. Recorded Books*
- **Keep the Lights Burning, Abbie** *by Peter and Connie Roop. Audio Bookshelf*
- **The Rain Player** *by David Wisniewski. Houghton Mifflin Company*
- **I Am Lavina Cumming** *by Susan Lowell. Recorded Books*
- **Audiotapes for *Nature's Fury*.** *Houghton Mifflin Company*

  Technology Resources addresses are on page R31.

Education Place
www.eduplace.com *Log on to Education Place for more activities relating to* Nature's Fury.

Book Adventure
www.bookadventure.org *This Internet reading incentive program provides thousands of titles for students to read.*

Theme at a Glance

Theme Concept: *Nature is powerful, and people must cope with its challenges.*

✅ **Indicates Tested Skills**
See page 20G for assessment options.

	Reading		Word Work
	Comprehension Skills and Strategies	**Information and Study Skills**	**Decoding Longer Words** Structural Analysis/Phonics
Anthology Selection 1: **Earthquake Terror** Science Link	✅ Sequence of Events, *27C, 33, 51A* R2.2 **Genre:** Realistic Fiction, *31;* Expository Nonfiction, *50;* **Comprehension:** Noting Details, *37;* Story Structure, *43;* How to Read a Science Article, *48;* **Writer's Craft:** Mood, *39* ✅ Strategy Focus: Predict/Infer, *27B, 32, 42*	✅ Using Print and Electronic Reference Sources, *51C* R2.1 R2.3 R3.1 R3.2 R3.3 R3.7	✅ **Structural Analysis:** Base Words, *51E* R1.2 **Phonics:** Short Vowels, *51F*
Anthology Selection 2: **Eye of the Storm: Chasing Storms with Warren Faidley** Career Link	✅ Text Organization, *55C, 73, 81A* R 2.2, R 2.3 **Writer's Craft:** Suspense, *61;* **Visual Literacy:** Photographs, *63;* Communicating Information, *80;* **Comprehension:** Fact and Opinion, *65;* Sequence of Events, *71;* How to Read a Sequence Chart, *78* **Spiral Review,** *81Q* **Strategy Focus:** Question, *55B, 64, 72*	Using Print and Electronic Card Catalogs, *81C* R1.4 R2.1 R2.2 R2.5 R3.7 LS1.2	✅ **Structural Analysis:** Syllabication, *81E* LC1.5 **Spiral Review,** *81R* R1.4 **Phonics:** Long Vowel Sounds /ā/,/ē/,/ī/, *81F*
Anthology Selection 3: **Volcanoes** Folktale Link	✅ Categorize and Classify, *83C, 97, 105A* **Comprehension:** Topic, Main Idea, and Details, *89;* Text Organization, *95;* How to Read a Folktale, *102* R2.2, R2.3, R3.6 **Strategy Focus:** Monitor/Clarify, *83B, 88, 96*	✅ Using Graphic Aids: Maps, Globes, Charts, Tables, and Graphs, *105C* R2.1, R2.2 **Spiral Review,** *105Q* W2.3.a, W2.3.b, W2.3.c, LS2.3, LS2.3.c	✅ **Structural Analysis:** Word Roots *struct* and *rupt, 105E* R1.2, R1.4 **Phonics:** Long Vowel Sounds /ō/, /o͞o/, and /yo͞o/, *105F*
Theme Resources	**Reteaching:** Comprehension, *R8, R10, R12* R2.1, R2.2, R2.3 **Challenge/Extension:** Comprehension, *R9, R11, R13* W1.2.a, W1.2.b, LS2.1.a, LS2.1.b		**Reteaching:** Structural Analysis, *R14, R16, R18* R1.2, R1.4, LC1.5

California Standards

R = Reading
W = Writing
LC = Language Conventions
LS = Listening & Speaking   **Sci** = Science
HSS = History/Social Studies   **M** = Math

Test Preparation

Taking Tests: Choosing the Best Answer
- Anthology, *106*
- Teacher's Edition, *106* R 2.1
- Practice Book, *53–54*

Spelling

Additional Lessons:
- Frequently Misspelled Words
- Spelling Review/Assessment

Pacing	Multi–age Classroom	Technology
• This theme is designed to take approximately 4 to 6 weeks, depending on your students' needs.	**Related themes—** • **Grade 4:** *Nature: Friend and Foe* • **Grade 6:** *New Frontiers: Oceans and Space*	**Education Place: www.eduplace.com** Log on to Education Place for more activities relating to *Nature's Fury*. **California Lesson Planner CD-ROM** Customize your planning with the Lesson Planner.

Writing & Language / Cross-Curricular

Spelling	Vocabulary Skills, Vocabulary Expansion	Grammar, Usage, and Mechanics	Writing	Listening/ Speaking/Viewing	Content Area
✓ Short Vowels, *51G*	✓ Using a Thesaurus, *51I* R1.3, W1.5 Scientific Terms: Geology Words, *51J*	✓ Kinds of Sentences, *51K* ✓ Subjects and Predicates, *51K* **Spiral Review, *51Q*** R3.3, LC1.2	A News Article, *51M* W1.2.a, W1.2.b, W1.2.c Adding Details, *51N* W1.6 **Spiral Review, *51R*** R1.2, LC1.2	Holding a Panel Discussion, *51O* LS1.4, LS1.5	**Responding:** Health and Safety, Listening and Speaking, Internet, *47* R2.1, W2.4, LS2.2 **Theme Resources:** *R28–R29* R1.1, W1.1.a, W1.1.b, W1.1.c, W2.2.a, LS1.1, LS2.3.a, LS2.3.b, LS2.3.c
✓ The /ā/, /ē/, and /ī/ Sounds, *81G*	✓ Dictionary: Alphabetical Order and Guide Words, *81I* **Spiral Review, *81R*** R1.4 Words from Many Languages: Weather Words, *81J*	✓ Conjunctions, *81K* LC1.1 ✓ Compound Sentences, *81K* LC1.1	A Response to a Prompt, *81M* W2.1, W2.2, W2.3, W2.4 ✓ Capitalizing and Punctuating Sentences, *81N* W1.6, LC1.3, LC1.4	Having a Literature Discussion, *81O* LS1.1, LS2.3.a, LS2.3.b, LS2.3.c	**Responding:** Math, Viewing, Internet, *77* R2.0, MMR 2.1 **Theme Resources:** *R28–R29* LS1.1, LS2.1, W2.2.a
✓ The /ō/, /o͞o/, and /yo͞o/ Sounds, *105G*	✓ Dictionary: Definitions, *105I* **Spiral Review, *105R*** R1.3 Words from Mythology, *105J* R1.2, R1.4	✓ Singular and Plural Nouns, *105K* ✓ More Plural Nouns, *105L*	A Paragraph of Information, *105M* W1.2.a ✓ Correcting Sentence Fragments, *105N* W1.6	Having Effective Conversations, *105O* LS1.1, LS1.2	**Responding:** Science, Social Studies, Internet, *100* R2.3, R2.4 **Theme Resources:** *R28–R29* LS1.1, LS2.1, W2.2.a
	Challenge/Extension: Vocabulary Activities, *R15*, *R17*, *R19* R 3.5, W 1.5, LS 2.3.b, LS 2.3.c	Reteaching: Grammar, *R20–R25* LC1.1	**Writing Activities, *R26–R27*** W2.1.a, W2.1.b, W2.2, W2.2.a, W2.3.a, W2.3.b, W2.3.c, LS1.4, LS1.5		**Cross-Curricular Activities, *R28–R29*** W2.2.a, LS1.1, LS2.1

• Teacher's Edition, *53F, 107* LC 1.5
• Practice Book, *20–22, 55–57*

Reading-Writing Workshop: Description
• Anthology: Student Writing Model, *52–53*
• Practice Book, *18, 19*

• Teacher's Edition, *52–53G* R 1.5, R 2.3, R 2.4, R 3.1, R 3.5, R 3.7, R 3.7, W 1.2.a, W 1.2.b, W 1.2.c
Writing Process
Using Sensory Language
Organizing Details
Writing Complete Sentences

Planning for Assessment

Use these resources to meet your assessment needs. For additional information, see the **Teacher's Assessment Handbook**.

Baseline Group Test

Phonics/Decoding Screening Test

Lexia Quick Phonics Assessment CD-ROM

Diagnostic Planning

During the first few weeks of school, assess students' abilities and needs in order to plan instruction. Recommended options: Administer the **Baseline Group Test** to screen for students who are below level. Use the **Leveled Reading Passages** to determine reading level and assess comprehension development. Use the **Phonics/Decoding Screening Test** or the **Lexia Quick Phonics Assessment CD-ROM** to gather more information about skill levels and instructional needs. Check individual students' oral reading fluency, using the **Leveled Reading Passages** or other texts (see the Theme Assessment Wrap-Up or the **Teacher's Assessment Handbook,** page 25). Begin extra support with students who need it.

Baseline Group Test
- Indicates the amount of reading support individual students will need

Houghton Mifflin Phonics/Decoding Screening Test
- Assesses a student's use of phonics to decode and spell one- to three-syllable words

Lexia Quick Phonics Assessment CD-ROM
- Identifies students who need more help with phonics

Leveled Reading Passages Assessment Kit
- Can be used to determine reading level and instructional needs

Theme Skills Test
- Various subtests can be used as a pretest to find which skills students know prior to instruction and to plan levels of support for meeting individual needs.

Comprehension Checks

Selection Tests

Reading-Writing Workshop

Ongoing Informal Assessment

Day-to-day informal measurement of your students' progress should be performed as an integral part of your instructional plan. Your observations, recorded on checklists and in anecdotal records, will complement the informal measures listed below.

Comprehension
- Selection Comprehension Checks, **Practice Book,** pp. 5, 25, 40
- Selection Tests, **Teacher's Resource Blackline Masters**

Writing
- Reading-Writing Workshop: Description, pp. 52–53G
- Other student writing samples for portfolios

Ongoing Informal Assessment *continued*

Observation Checklist

Other Informal Assessment

- Diagnostic Checks, pp. 35, 45, 51B, 51F, 51L, 68, 75, 81B, 81F, 81L, 90, 99, 105B, 105F, 105L, R3, R5, R7–R8, R10, R12, R14, R16, R18, R20–R25
- Student Self-Assessment, pp. 47, 53G, 77, 101
- Reading Fluency, p. 107A
- Observation Checklist, **Teacher's Resource Blackline Masters**

End-of-Theme Assessment

Integrated Theme Test

Theme Skills Test

Use the following formal assessments to help you measure student progress in attaining the theme's instructional goals.

Integrated Theme Test

- Tests in a format that reflects instruction
- Tests comprehension strategies and skills, word skills, spelling, grammar, and writing

Theme Skills Test

- Tests discrete skills: comprehension skills, word skills, spelling, grammar, writing, and information and study skills

Periodic Progress Assessment

Benchmark Progress Test

Periodically throughout the year, evaluate your students' progress compared to other students at the same grade level.

Benchmark Progress Test

- Assesses overall student progress in reading and writing, two to four times a year

Assessment Management

Learner Profile™ CD-ROM by Sunburst Technology

This software can help you record, manage, and report your assessment of student progress.

Learner Profile™ CD-ROM

- Records students' achievement of the California English/Language Arts Standards and other instructional goals
- Has companion software, **Learner Profile to Go™**, that allows you to record student information on a handheld computer device

Theme 1

Theme Resources

Houghton Mifflin Reading includes a wide variety of resources for meeting the needs of all students. The chart below indicates features and components of the program and the students for whom they are most appropriate.

Universal Access: Reaching All Students

	On Level Students	English Language Learners	Challenge Students	Extra Support Students	Inclusion/ Special Needs
Anthology					
Get Set to Read	★	★	○	★	★
Content Links	★	★	★	★	★
Education Place	★	○	★	○	★
Student Writing Model	★	★	○	★	★
Taking Tests	★	★	○	★	★
Audiotape	○	★		★	★
Teacher's Edition					
Teacher Read Aloud	★	★	○	★	★
Universal Access notes		★	★	★	★
Theme Resources	★		★	★	★
Selection Summaries	○	★		★	★
Theme Project	★	○	★	○	○
Reading-Writing Workshop	★	★	★	★	★
Practice Book	★	★	★	★	★
Leveled Books					
Reader's Library `Decodable`	○	○		★	★
Theme Paperback `Easy`		★		★	★
Theme Paperback `On Level`	★		○		
Theme Paperback `Challenge`	○	○	★		
Literature Resources	★	○	★	○	○
* **Challenge Handbook**	○	○	★		
* **Extra Support Handbook**		○		★	★

* See Universal Access Plans, pp. 23B–23C, 53S–53T, 82E–82F

KEY: ★ = highly appropriate ○ = appropriate

	On Level Students	English Language Learners	Challenge Students	Extra Support Students	Inclusion/ Special Needs
* Classroom Management Handbook	★	★	★	★	○
* Handbook for English Language Learners		★		○	○
Home/Community Connections	★	★	★	★	★

Technology

	On Level Students	English Language Learners	Challenge Students	Extra Support Students	Inclusion/ Special Needs
Education Place	★	○	★	○	○
Get Set for Reading CD-ROM	★	★	○	★	★
Lexia Quick Phonics Assessment CD-ROM				★	★
Lexia Phonics CD-ROM: Intermediate Intervention				★	★
Published by Sunburst Technology*					
• Tenth Planet™: Blends and Digraphs	○	○		★	★
• Tenth Planet™: Word Parts	○	○		★	★
• Reading Who? Reading You!	○	○		★	★
• EasyBook Deluxe	★	★		○	○
• Writer's Resource Library	★	★	○	○	○
• Media Weaver™ (Sunburst/Humanities Software)	★	★	★	○	

Theme 1

Launching the Theme
for *Nature's Fury*

▷ Using the Theme Opener

Read aloud the theme title and the poem on Anthology page 20. Explain that "Wind Song" comes from the Native American Pima tribe. Use questions like these to prompt discussion:

- What do you think is the meaning of the theme title *Nature's Fury*? (extremely large-scale, violent, or powerful acts of nature)
- In what ways does the passage from "Wind Song" express nature's fury? (It describes powerful forces of nature, such as wind and thunder, and uses strong words such as *roaring* to describe them.)
- Can you think of some examples of nature's fury that have happened in this region? elsewhere? (natural disasters, storms, hurricanes, earthquakes, floods, volcanoes, tornadoes, etc.)
- What are some things people can do to cope with nature's fury? (People can learn about the powerful natural forces that affect the area they live in and plan for safety before an event occurs; they can organize to help victims of natural disaster.)

Multi-age Classroom

Related Themes:

Grade 6 . . . New Frontiers: Oceans and Space

◆ Grade 5 . . . Nature's Fury ◆

Grade 4 . . . Nature: Friend and Foe

California Standards pp. 20K–21A

R 1.1 Read aloud fluently
R 3.1 Analyze literary forms
R 3.4 Understand theme

R 3.5 Describe literary devices
R 3.6 Evaluate patterns/symbols

▶ Theme Connections

Introduce Selection Connections on **Practice Book** pages 1–2. Explain that students will add to these pages after each selection and at the end of the theme to build their understanding of *Nature's Fury*.

⭐ **Connecting/Comparing** questions in Responding (Anthology pages 46, 76, 100) help students focus on relationships among selections and between individual selections and the theme overall.

Poetry Project

✎ **Writing** Using the passage from "Wind Song" as an example, have students compose their own poetry. Have them recall a time when they personally witnessed severe weather. Tell them each to brainstorm a list of words and phrases that describe the furious movements, sounds, and sights created by nature. Then have them use their lists to compose a short poem.

Challenge Explain to students that poems are not always written from the point of view of a person. Often the poet will try to imagine what it is like to write from the point of view of an animal, an object, or something in nature. Explain to them that the *I* in the passage from "Wind Song" is actually the wind. Have them use this as an example to write their own poems from the point of view of an element of nature.

windy	dark clouds
noisy	lightning
deafening	boots
pounding rain	gloves
thunder	twisted umbrellas
drenching	whistling
frigid	

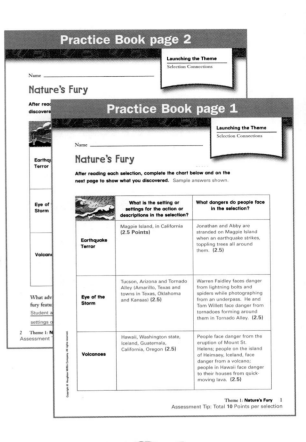

R 3.1
R 3.5
R 3.6

Practice Book page 2

Practice Book page 1

Technology

Education Place
www.eduplace.com

Log on to **Education Place** for more activities relating to *Nature's Fury*.

California Lesson Planner CD-ROM

Customize your planning for *Nature's Fury* with the Lesson Planner.

Home Connection

Send home the theme letter for *Nature's Fury* to introduce the theme and suggest home activities. See **Teacher's Resource Blackline Masters**.

For other suggestions relating to *Nature's Fury*, see **Home/Community Connections**.

Earthquake Terror
Different texts for different purposes

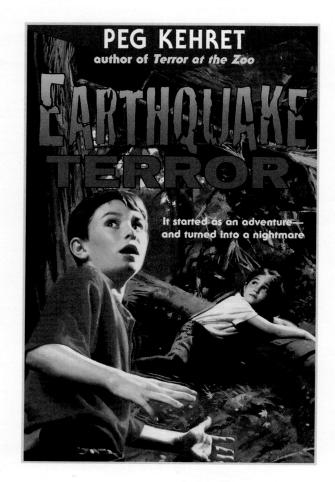

PEG KEHRET
author of *Terror at the Zoo*

EARTHQUAKE TERROR

It started as an adventure— and turned into a nightmare

Anthology: Main Selection

Purposes

- strategy focus: predict/infer
- comprehension skill: sequence of events
- vocabulary development
- critical thinking, discussion

Genre: Realistic Fiction

Realistic characters and events come to life in a fictional plot.

Awards

- ★ IRA/CBC Children's Choice
- ★ Texas Bluebonnet Award
- ★ Garden State Children's Book Award
- ★ William Allen White Award Master List

Selection Summary

While on a camping trip in California, Jonathan confronts nature's fury as he struggles to save his sister and himself from a dangerous earthquake.

Teacher's Edition: Read Aloud

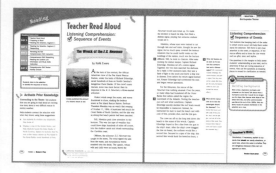

Purposes

- listening comprehension: sequence of events
- vocabulary development
- critical thinking, discussion

Anthology: Get Set to Read

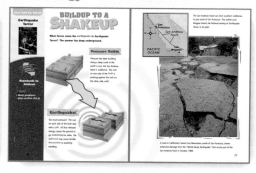

Purposes

- background building: earthquakes
- developing key vocabulary

Anthology: Content Link

Purposes

- content reading: science
- skill: how to read a science article
- critical thinking, discussion

Leveled Books and Resources

Use these resources to ensure that students read, outside of class, at least thirty minutes a day. See also Cumulative Listing of Leveled Books.

Reader's Library

Very Easy

Riding Out the Storm
by **Kathryn Snyder**

(Also available on blackline masters)

Purposes

- fluency practice in below-level text
- alternate reading for students reading significantly below grade level
- strategy application: predict/infer
- comprehension skill application: sequence of events
- below-level independent reading

Lesson Support

- Lesson Plan, page R2
- Alternate application for Comprehension Skill lesson on sequence of events, page 51A
- Reteaching for Comprehension Skill: sequence of events, page R8

Selection Summary Masters

Audiotape

Earthquake Terror
Audiotape for
Nature's Fury

Earthquake Terror
Teacher's Resource Blackline Masters

UNIVERSAL ACCESS

Reaching All Students
Inclusion Strategy

Significantly Below-level Readers

R 1.1

Students reading so far below level that they cannot read *Earthquake Terror* even with the suggested Extra Support should still participate with the class whenever possible.

- Include them in the Teacher Read Aloud (p. 24A) and Preparing to Read (pp. 26A–27C).

- Have them listen to *Earthquake Terror* on the audiotape for *Nature's Fury* and read the Selection Summary while others read Segment 1 of the selection.

- Have them read "Riding Out the Storm" in the Reader's Library collection for *Nature's Fury* while others read Segment 2 of *Earthquake Terror*.

- Have all students participate in Wrapping Up Segment 2 (p. 45) and Responding (p. 46).

Theme Paperbacks

Easy

If You Lived at the Time of the Great San Francisco Earthquake
by **Ellen Levine**

Lesson, TE page 53I

On Level

Drylongso
by **Virginia Hamilton**

Lesson, TE page 53K

Challenge

Hurricanes: Earth's Mightiest Storms
by **Patricia Lauber**

Lesson, TE page 53M

Technology

Get Set for Reading CD-ROM
Earthquake Terror
Provides background building, vocabulary support, and selection summaries in English and Spanish.

Education Place
www.eduplace.com
Log on to Education Place for more activities relating to *Earthquake Terror*.

Book Adventure
www.bookadventure.org
This Internet reading incentive program provides thousands of titles for students to read.

Daily Lesson Plans

Instructional Goals

Day 1

Day 2

Reading

60–80 minutes

- ✓ **Strategy Focus:** Predict/Infer
- ✓ **Comprehension Skill:** Sequence of Events

Comprehension Skill Review:
Noting Details; Story Structure

- ✓ **Information and Study Skills:** Using Print and Electronic Reference Sources

Day 1

Teacher Read Aloud, *24A*   R2.2
- Genre: Narrative Nonfiction, *25A*

Preparing to Read *Earthquake Terror*
- Get Set: Background and Vocabulary, *26A*
- Key Vocabulary, *27A*   R1.1, R2.1, LS2.3
  Selection Vocabulary, *Practice Book, 3*
- Strategy/Skill Preview, *27B*   R2.2
  Event Map, *Practice Book, 4*

Reading Segment 1, *28–35*   R1.1
- Supporting Comprehension   R2.3, R3.3, R 3.7
- Strategy Focus, *32*

Wrapping Up Segment 1, *35*   LS1.1, LS2.3.a

Day 2

Reading Segment 2, *36–44*   LS2.3.a
- Supporting Comprehension   R2.4, R3.7
- Strategy Focus, *42*

Wrapping Up Segment 2, *45*   R2.5, LS2.3 LS2.3.a

Responding
- Comprehension Questions: Think About the Selection, *46*   R3.1–R3.3, R3.5, W2.2.a
- Comprehension Check, *Practice Book, 5*

Rereading/Revisiting the Text
- Comprehension: Sequence of Events, *33*

Word Work

30–40 minutes

- ✓ **Spelling:** Short Vowels

Decoding Longer Words:
- ✓ **Structural Analysis:** Base Words

Phonics: Short Vowels
- ✓ **Vocabulary:** Using a Thesaurus

Spelling
- Pretest, *51G*
- Instruction: Short Vowels, *51G*
- Take-Home Word List, *Practice Book: Handbook*

Decoding Longer Words Instruction
- Structural Analysis: Base Words, *51E*   R1.2
- *Practice Book, 8*

Spelling
- *Practice Book, 9*

Writing & Language

30–40 minutes

- ✓ **Grammar:** Kinds of Sentences; Subjects and Predicates
- ✓ **Writing:** A News Article; Adding Details

Listening/Speaking/Viewing: Holding a Panel Discussion

Daily Language Practice, *51L*
Grammar Instruction
- Kinds of Sentences, *51K*

✏ **Writing**
- Journal Writing, *29*   W2.2.a

Daily Language Practice, *51L*
Grammar Instruction
- *Practice Book, 13*

✏ **Writing Instruction**
- A News Article, *51M*   W1.2.a, W1.2.b, W2.2.a
- *Practice Book, 16*
- Journal Writing, *36*   W2.2.a

California Standards Achieved Each Day

R = Reading
W = Writing
LC = Language Conventions
LS = Listening & Speaking
HSS = History/Social Science
S = Science
M = Math

R 1.1 Read aloud fluently
R 2.1 Understand text features
R 2.2 Use order to analyze text
R 2.3 Discern main ideas
R 3.1 Analyze literary forms
R 3.3 Determine character traits
R 3.7 Evaluate author's techniques
W 2.2.a Demonstrate understanding
LS 1.1 Ask new questions
LS 2.3 Respond to literature

R 1.2 Use word origins
R 2.4 Inferences/generalizations
R 2.5 Facts, inferences, opinions
R 3.1 Analyze literary forms
R 3.2 Main problem/plot conflict
R 3.3 Determine character traits
R 3.5 Describe literary devices
R 3.7 Evaluate author's techniques
W 1.2.a Establish topic, order
W 1.2.b Use details, transitions
W 2.2.a Demonstrate understanding
LS 2.3 Respond to literature
LS 2.3.a Summarize events/details

THEME 1: **Nature's Fury**   ✓ = tested skills

📖 **Leveled Books, pp. 53H–53N**
For reading outside of class and homework

Technology

California Lesson Planner CD-ROM
Customize your planning with the Lesson Planner.

Key correlations are provided in this chart.
Additional correlations are provided at point of use.

Day 3

Rereading/Revisiting the Text
- Genre: Realistic Fiction, *31*   R3.1, W2.2.a
- Writer's Craft: Mood, *39*   R3.7

Comprehension Skill Instruction
- Sequence of Events, *51A*   R2.2
- *Practice Book, 6–7*

Phonics Instruction
- Short Vowels, *51F*

Spelling
- *Practice Book, 10*

Daily Language Practice, *51L*

Grammar Instruction
- Subjects and Predicates, *51K*

✎ **Writing**
- Narrating: Write an Adventure Story, *46*
  W 2.1.a, W 2.1.b

Day 4

Comprehension Skill Instruction
- Reteaching Sequence of Events with Reader's Library, *R8*   R2.2

Reading the Science Link
- "El Niño," *48–51*   R2.1, R2.3
- Genre: Expository Nonfiction, *50*   R3.1

Information and Study Skills Instruction
- Using Print and Electronic Reference Sources, *51C*

Decoding Longer Words
- Reteaching Structural Analysis: Base Words, *R14*
- Challenge/Extension Activities, *R15*   R 1.2, LC 1.5

Spelling
- Word Hunt, *51H*   LC1.5
- *Practice Book, 11*

Vocabulary Skill Instruction
- Using a Thesaurus, *51I*   W1.5
- *Practice Book, 12*

Daily Language Practice, *51L*

Grammar
- Reteaching, *R20, R21*
- *Practice Book, 14*

✎ **Writing**
- Improving Your Writing: Adding Details, *51N*   W 1.6
- *Practice Book, 17*

Listening/Speaking/Viewing
- Holding a Panel Discussion, *51O*
  LS1.4, LS1.5

Day 5

**Rereading/Revisiting the Text:
Comprehension Review**

Skill Instruction
- Noting Details, *37*   R3.3, R3.7
- Story Structure, *43*   R3.2, W2.2.a

Rereading for Fluency
Earthquake Terror, 28–45

Activity Choices
- Responding Activities, *47*   W2.2.a
- Challenge/Extension Activities, *R9*
- Cross-Curricular Activities, *R28–R29*   LS1.1, LS2.3.a, W1.1.a, W2.2.a

Vocabulary Expansion
- Scientific Terms: Geology Words, *51J*

Spelling
- Posttest, *51H*

Daily Language Practice, *51L*

Grammar
- Sentence Combining, *51L*   LC1.1
- *Practice Book, 15*

Spiral Review, *51Q*

✎ **Writing**
- Writing Activities, *R26–R27*   W2.1.a, W2.2.a
- Sharing Students' Writing: Author's Chair

Spiral Review, *51R*

R 2.2 Use order to analyze text
R 3.1 Analyze literary forms
R 3.7 Evaluate author's techniques
W 2.1.a Establish plot, setting
W 2.1.b Show events
W 2.2.a Demonstrate understanding

R 1.2 Use word origins
R 2.1 Understand text features
R 2.2 Use order to analyze text
R 2.3 Discern main ideas
R 3.1 Analyze literary forms
W 1.5 Use a thesaurus
W 1.6 Edit and revise work
LC 1.5 Spell correctly
LS 1.4 Select focus
LS 1.5 Clarify and support ideas

R 3.2 Main problem/plot conflict
R 3.3 Determine character traits
R 3.7 Evaluate author's techniques
W 1.1.a Establish a plot
W 1.2.a Establish topic, order
W 2.1.a Establish plot, setting
W 2.2.a Demonstrate understanding
LC 1.1 Sentence structure/transition
LS 1.4 Select focus
LS 2.1.b Show what happens
LS 2.3.a Summarize events/details

✎ *Reading-Writing Workshop: Description, pp. 52–53G*

**See Universal Access
Planning Chart on
the following pages.**

Universal Access Plans
for Reaching All Learners

Grouping for Instruction

30–45 minutes

	Day 1	Day 2
With the Teacher		
Extra Support Teach—Use Extra Support Handbook	**Preteach** Base Words **Preview** Selection, Segment 1 ■ Extra Support Handbook pp. 14–15	**Preteach** Sequence of Events **Preview** Selection, Segment 2 ■ Extra Support Handbook pp. 16–17
Working Independently		
On Level Use Classroom Management Handbook **Challenge** Use Challenge Handbook **English Language Learners** Use Classroom Management Handbook or Challenge Handbook	**Independent Activities** For each group, assign appropriate activities—your own or those in the handbooks listed below. Then get students started on their independent work. ■ Classroom Management Handbook pp. 4–5 ■ Challenge Handbook pp. 2–3	See plan for Day 1 **Monitor** Answer questions, if necessary.

30–45 minutes

	Day 1	Day 2
With the Teacher		
English Language Learners Teach—Use Handbook for English Language Learners	**Preteach** Describing Earthquakes **Preteach** Get Set to Read; Selection, Segment 1 **Preteach** Structural Analysis: Base Words ■ Handbook for ELL pp. 18–19	**Preteach** Camping **Preteach** Selection, Segment 2 **Reteach** Grammar: Kinds of Sentences ■ Handbook for ELL pp. 20–21
Working Independently		
On Level Use Classroom Management Handbook **Challenge** Use Challenge Handbook **Extra Support** Use Classroom Management Handbook	**Independent Activities** Students can continue their assigned activities, or you can assign new activities from the handbooks below. ■ Classroom Management Handbook pp. 4–5 ■ Challenge Handbook pp. 2–3	See plan for Day 1 **Monitor** Partner Extra Support students, if needed.

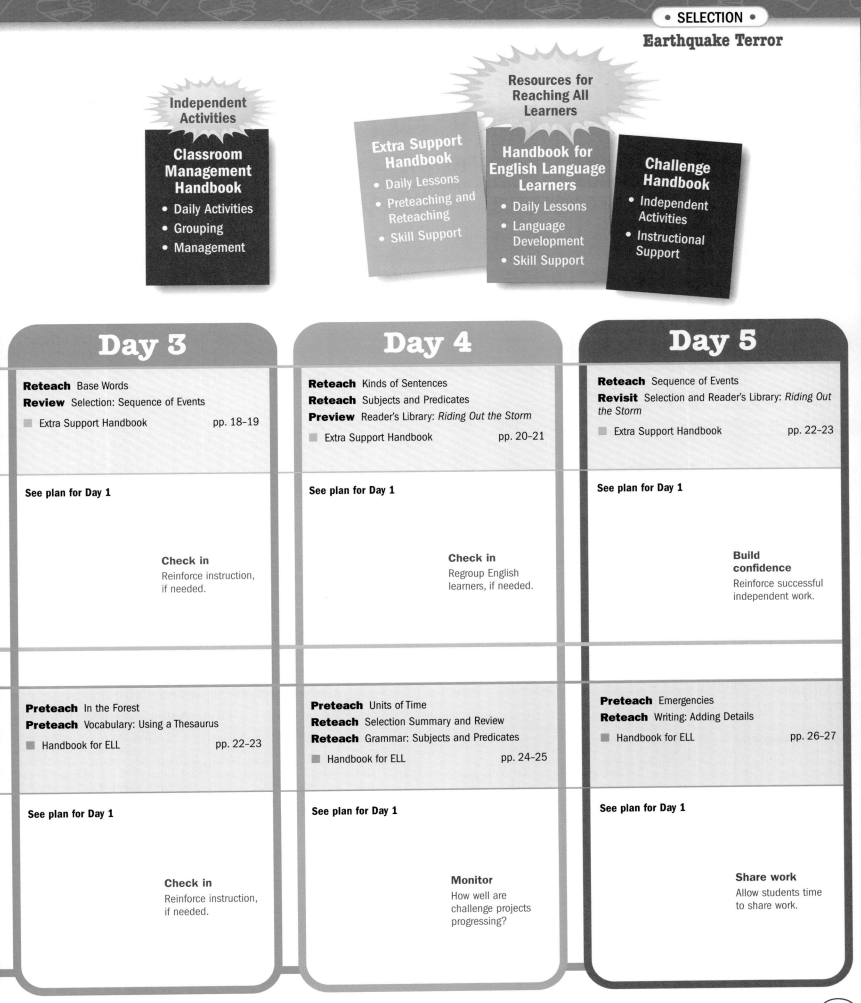

Independent Activities

Classroom Management Handbook
- Daily Activities
- Grouping
- Management

Resources for Reaching All Learners

Extra Support Handbook
- Daily Lessons
- Preteaching and Reteaching
- Skill Support

Handbook for English Language Learners
- Daily Lessons
- Language Development
- Skill Support

Challenge Handbook
- Independent Activities
- Instructional Support

Day 3

Reteach Base Words
Review Selection: Sequence of Events
- Extra Support Handbook   pp. 18–19

See plan for Day 1

Check in
Reinforce instruction, if needed.

Preteach In the Forest
Preteach Vocabulary: Using a Thesaurus
- Handbook for ELL   pp. 22–23

See plan for Day 1

Check in
Reinforce instruction, if needed.

Day 4

Reteach Kinds of Sentences
Reteach Subjects and Predicates
Preview Reader's Library: *Riding Out the Storm*
- Extra Support Handbook   pp. 20–21

See plan for Day 1

Check in
Regroup English learners, if needed.

Preteach Units of Time
Reteach Selection Summary and Review
Reteach Grammar: Subjects and Predicates
- Handbook for ELL   pp. 24–25

See plan for Day 1

Monitor
How well are challenge projects progressing?

Day 5

Reteach Sequence of Events
Revisit Selection and Reader's Library: *Riding Out the Storm*
- Extra Support Handbook   pp. 22–23

See plan for Day 1

Build confidence
Reinforce successful independent work.

Preteach Emergencies
Reteach Writing: Adding Details
- Handbook for ELL   pp. 26–27

See plan for Day 1

Share work
Allow students time to share work.

Reading Instruction

DAY 1	• Teacher Read Aloud • Preparing to Read • Reading the Selection, Segment 1
DAY 2	• Reading the Selection, Segment 2 • Responding
DAY 3	• Revisiting the Text • Comprehension Skill Instruction
DAY 4	• Comprehension Skill Reteaching • Reading the Content Link • Information and Study Skills Instruction
DAY 5	• Comprehension Skill Review • Activity Choices

OBJECTIVES

Students listen to the selection
to identify the sequence of events.

▶ Activate Prior Knowledge

R 2.4

Connecting to the Theme Tell students
that you are going to read aloud an exciting
true story about a very difficult rescue in
stormy weather.

Help students connect the selection with
what they know, using these suggestions:

■ Ask students to mention any shipwrecks
they know of.

■ Display a map of the United States, and
help students locate the Outer Banks of
North Carolina. Explain to students that the
men at the rescue station on Pea Island in
the Outer Banks saved hundreds of lives.

Teacher Read Aloud

Listening Comprehension:
✔ Sequence of Events

The Wreck of the *E.S. Newman*

by Ruth Ewers

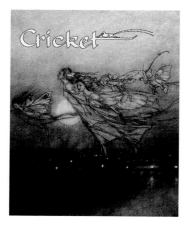

*Cricket published this account
of a historic rescue at sea.*

At the turn of the century, the African
American crew of the Pea Island Rescue
Station, under the helm of Richard Etheridge,
saved hundreds of lives on North Carolina's
dangerous Outer Banks. Of the crew's many
rescues, none was more heroic than its
response to the *E. S. Newman*, a three-masted
schooner.

Violent winds swept the ocean, and waves
thundered to shore, shaking the lookout
tower at Pea Island Rescue Station. Surfman
Theodore Meekins was on watch that evening
of October 11, 1896. A hurricane had struck the
Outer Banks of North Carolina, and the tide was
so strong that beach patrols had been canceled.

Still, Meekins paid close attention to the
horizon. This was the type of weather that
could blow ships hundreds of miles off course,
into the shallow sands and shoals surrounding
the Carolina coast.

Offshore, the schooner *E.S. Newman* was
caught in the storm. The wind ripped the sails
from the masts, and mountainous waves
smashed onto the decks. The captain, whose
wife and child were on board, feared the

California Standards pp. 24A–24B

R 2.2 Use order to analyze text
R 2.4 Inferences/generalizations
LS 1.1 Ask new questions

Newman would soon break up. He made the decision to beach his ship, then fired a distress signal, praying that someone onshore would see it.

Meekins, whose eyes were trained to cut through rain and surf mists, thought he saw the signal, but so much spray covered the lookout windows that he could hardly make out the buildings of the station, much less the horizon offshore. Still, he took no chances. After summoning the station keeper, Captain Richard Etheridge, Meekins set off a coston signal. Together, the two men searched the darkness for a reply. A few moments later, they saw a flash of light to the south and knew a ship was in distress. Even before the return signal burned out, Keeper Etheridge had summoned his men and begun rescue operations.

For the lifesavers, the rescue of the *Newman* was nothing unusual. Over the years, so many ships had foundered off the Outer Banks that sailors called the region the Graveyard of the Atlantic. Noting the treacherous surf and wind conditions, Captain Etheridge quickly decided the surf boats would be impossible to maneuver. Instead, he instructed his men to load the beach cart with coils of line, powder, shot, and the lyle gun.

The crew set off on the long trek down the beach to the scene of the wreck. Captain Etheridge hoped to fire a line from the gun to the ship's mast. After the ship's crew dragged the line on board, the surfmen would fire a second line. Secured to a spar of the ship, this second line would hold the breeches buoy, a

1 What did Meekins do as soon as he realized that someone had sent a distress signal? (He summoned Captain Etheridge, the station keeper, and sent a signal. Then they waited for a reply. After they got the reply, the keeper called his men and started the rescue effort.)

2 What did the rescue crew do to save the passengers aboard the *Newman*? (They loaded the beach cart with coils of line, powder, shot, and the lyle gun, and set off to the scene of the wreck. They crossed three miles of sand and foam to reach the stranded ship.)

Listening Comprehension: ✓ Sequence of Events

Tell students that keeping track of the order in which events occur will help them understand the selection. Tell them to pay close attention to the order, or sequence, of the rescue efforts and to listen for clue words such as *after*, *later*, and *before*.

Use questions in the margins to help assess students' understanding as you read, and to determine if they are noting sequence of events. Also use the questions as stopping places to reread for clarification as needed.

UNIVERSAL ACCESS
Reaching All Students
English Language Learners

Building Background

Write *wreck*, *shipwreck*, *hurricane*, and *schooner* on the board. Talk about what a *hurricane* is and why it would be so dangerous for ships. Also discuss what ships of the times were like, and what communication was like at the end of the 1800s. Help students locate the places mentioned in the selection on a map.

📎 **Teacher's Note**

Vocabulary If necessary, explain to students that **shoals** are sandy elevations, or sand bars, where the water is shallow. They are dangerous because ships can run aground on them.

(**Teacher Read Aloud,** *continued*)

Genre Lesson
Narrative Nonfiction

OBJECTIVES

Students identify elements of narrative non-fiction in the selection.

Explain the characteristics of narrative nonfiction:

- tells about real people, animals, places, or events

- is told in story form

- gives facts about the subject

- usually describes events in chronological order

- may include the author's opinions and feelings

- may include photographs, captions, illustrations, and graphic aids to communicate information

Point out that this selection tells the story of a rescue that really happened, in the order in which events happened, and of real people who were rescued. Ask students to identify other characteristics that make this a narrative nonfiction piece.

Teacher's Note

Reading Tip Preview the story so that when you read it aloud to students, your voice conveys the danger of the situation and stresses the courage and determination of the rescuers.

R 2.3
R 3.1

harness for carrying survivors safely to shore. Struggling with the weight of the 185-pound gun, the surfmen crossed three miles of sand and boiling foam to reach the stranded ship. The water was freezing, and the men often sank up to their knees in sand. Captain Etheridge noted in his logbook that "the voice of gladden hearts greeted the arrival of the station crew," but that "it seemed impossible under such circumstances to render any assistance. The team was often brought to a standstill by the sweeping current," and the *Newman* was "rolling and tossing well upon the beach with head sails all blown away."

Even when the rescue equipment proved useless, Etheridge refused to give up. Choosing two of his strongest surfmen, he tied rope lines around their waists and sent them into the surging water. The two men, lashed together

California Standards pp. 25A–25B

R 2.2 Use order to analyze text	**R 3.7** Evaluate author's techniques
R 2.3 Discern main ideas	**LS 2.3** Respond to literature
R 3.1 Analyze literary forms	**LS 2.3.a** Summarize events/details
R 3.3 Determine character traits	**LS 2.3.b** Understand ideas/images

and holding a line from shore, waded as far as they could before diving through the waves. Nearly worn out by the exertion of swimming against the tide, they finally made it to the vessel.

3 The first to be rescued were the captain's wife and child. With the two passengers tied to their backs, the surfmen fought their way back to shore. Taking turns, Etheridge and his crew made ten trips to the *Newman*, saving every person on board. It was 1:00 A.M. when the crew and survivors finally made it back to the station. That night, as the exhausted survivors lay sleeping and his lifesaving crew rested, Captain Etheridge picked up his pen, and in the flickering light of an oil lantern, wrote with satisfaction that all the people on board had been saved and were "sheltered in this station" — words he would write for many years to come.

LS 2.3
LS 2.3.a
LS 2.3.b
LS 2.3.c

R 2.2

3 What did Captain Etheridge do next to rescue the passengers? (When the rescue equipment proved useless, he chose two of his strongest surfmen, tied ropes around their waists, and sent them into the surging waters. After ten trips to the *Newman*, they saved all the passengers.)

R 3.3
R 3.7

R 3.3

▶ **Discussion**

Summarize After reading, discuss any parts that could still be confusing to students. Then ask them to summarize the selection.

Listening Comprehension:
☑ **Sequence of Events** Ask students to list the order in which the rescue efforts occurred. Write their responses on the chalkboard.

Personal Response Ask students to evaluate the personal traits of the characters that made the rescue possible and successful.

★ **Connecting/Comparing** Ask students to discuss how the people in the selection coped with nature's fury.

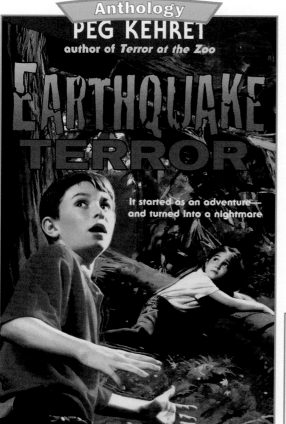

Reading

Anthology
PEG KEHRET
author of *Terror at the Zoo*

EARTHQUAKE TERROR

It started as an adventure— and turned into a nightmare

Technology

Get Set for Reading CD-ROM

Earthquake Terror

Provides background building, vocabulary support, and selection summaries in English and Spanish.

Preparing to Read

▶ Using *Get Set* for Background and Vocabulary

Connecting to the Theme Remind students that this theme is about the power and challenges of nature. You have just read aloud a story about a terrible storm at sea. Next they will read a story called *Earthquake Terror*.

Discuss with students the kinds of challenges an earthquake might bring. Then use the Get Set to Read on pages 26–27 to explain what causes an earthquake.

- Have someone read aloud "Buildup to a Shakeup."

- Go over the map of California, the setting of the story. Trace the San Andreas fault and discuss how it might affect the story plot.

- Ask students to explain the meaning of the Key Vocabulary: *fault, jolt, undulating, upheaval,* and *devastation.* Then have them use those words as they talk about earthquake damage.

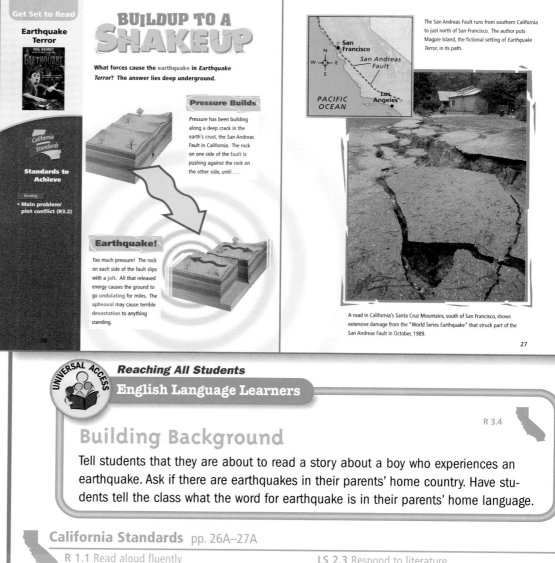

Get Set to Read

Earthquake Terror

California Standards

Standards to Achieve

Reading
- Main problem/ plot conflict (R3.2)

26

BUILDUP TO A SHAKEUP

What forces cause the earthquake in *Earthquake Terror*? The answer lies deep underground.

Pressure Builds

Pressure has been building along a deep crack in the earth's crust, the San Andreas Fault in California. The rock on one side of the fault is pushing against the rock on the other side, until . . .

Earthquake!

Too much pressure! The rock on each side of the fault slips with a jolt. All that released energy causes the ground to go undulating for miles. The upheaval may cause terrible devastation to anything standing.

The San Andreas Fault runs from southern California to just north of San Francisco. The author puts Magpie Island, the fictional setting of *Earthquake Terror*, in its path.

PACIFIC OCEAN

San Francisco

San Andreas Fault

Los Angeles

A road in California's Santa Cruz Mountains, south of San Francisco, shows extensive damage from the "World Series Earthquake" that struck part of the San Andreas Fault in October, 1989.

27

Reaching All Students
English Language Learners

UNIVERSAL ACCESS

R 3.4

Building Background

Tell students that they are about to read a story about a boy who experiences an earthquake. Ask if there are earthquakes in their parents' home country. Have students tell the class what the word for earthquake is in their parents' home language.

California Standards pp. 26A–27A

R 1.1 Read aloud fluently
R 2.1 Understand text features
R 3.4 Understand theme

LS 2.3 Respond to literature

Vocabulary

▶ Developing Key Vocabulary

Use **Transparency 1–1** to introduce additional earthquake-related words from *Earthquake Terror*.

■ Model how to figure out the meaning of the word *debris* from clues in the sentence.

■ For each remaining sentence, ask students to use what they know to figure out the Key Vocabulary word. Have students explain how they figured out each word.

Remind students that it's helpful to use the Phonics/Decoding Strategy when they read. For students who need more help with decoding, use the review below.

Practice/Homework **Practice Book** page 3.

UNIVERSAL ACCESS

Strategy Review
Phonics/Decoding

Modeling Write this sentence from *Earthquake Terror* on the board, and point to *thundering*.

> "Mommy!" Abby's shrill cry rose above the <u>thundering</u> noise.

Think Aloud

To figure out this word, I'll start by dropping the -ing. Maybe I can break the word that's left into syllables. I see the VCCV pattern, so I'll break it between the n and d. The word starts with t-h followed by un. That syllable might sound like thuhn. The letters in the second syllable probably sound like der. If I blend all the sounds together, I'll say THUHN der ing. That word makes sense in the sentence.

Skill Finder

| • Decoding Longer Words, pp. 51E–51F | • Vocabulary Expansion, p. 51J |

Key Concept
causes and effects of earthquakes

Key Vocabulary

debris: the remains of something broken or destroyed

devastation: destruction or ruin

fault: a break in a rock mass caused by a shifting of the earth's crust

impact: the striking of one body against another

jolt: a sudden jerk or bump

shuddered: shook, vibrated, or quivered

susceptible: easily affected

undulating: moving in waves or with a smooth, wavy motion

upheaval: a lifting or upward movement of the earth's crust

See Vocabulary notes on pages 30, 32, 34, 36, 38, and 40 for additional words to preview.

Practice Book page 3

Name _____

A Sci...

Use the w...
on the Mo...

NATURE'S FURY Earthquake Terror
Key Vocabulary

fault...
the re...
report...
jolt...
shake...
shudd...
to fall...
its pe...
in a c...

devast...
Debri...
uphea...

Transparency 1–1

Earthquake Words

Interviewer: Today I am happy to welcome Isaac Ramstein, an expert on earthquakes. Mr. Ramstein, help readers of the *California Daily* understand why earthquakes leave so much <u>debris</u> in their wake.

Mr. Ramstein: Earthquakes cause a tremendous amount of <u>devastation</u> because of the great <u>upheaval</u> of the ground itself.

Interviewer: Tell us what it feels like to be in an earthquake.

Mr. Ramstein: First, you may sense that the ground has <u>shuddered</u> ever so slightly beneath your feet. Next, you may feel a powerful <u>jolt</u> that can knock you down with a terrific <u>impact</u> if the quake is forceful enough. As the quake builds, the ground can feel like it is <u>undulating</u> up and down.

Interviewer: Why is California so <u>susceptible</u> to earthquakes?

Mr. Ramstein: A major <u>fault</u> runs through California, so when the crust of the earth shifts, it often shifts along that crack. Residents of the state should take precautions so they are not caught unprepared.

Interviewer: We appreciate your talking with us today, Mr. Ramstein. I'm sure our readers will take your suggestion to heart.

TRANSPARENCY 1–1
TEACHER'S EDITION PAGE T27A

Reading Strategy

✓ Strategy Focus:
Predict/Infer

> ### Strategy Focus
>
> Think about the selection, title and cover illustration. What do you **predict** Jonathan will do to protect himself and his younger sister when a powerful earthquake strikes?

Have students turn to page 28 as you read the title and author of the selection. Ask someone to read the Strategy Focus. Give students a chance to read the introduction on page 29 and to think about the Strategy Focus question. Then ask them for their predictions and record their responses.

Teacher Modeling Review how to make a good prediction or inference. (Think of a possibility based on text clues and personal information.) Then model the strategy.

Think Aloud

From the title and cover, I predict that the two children will get caught in an earthquake. From the introduction, I can make an inference about Jonathan. It says he's looking after his sister and he feels very alone. He must feel that he has too much responsibility.

Ask students to work in pairs or individually to make other predictions and inferences about Jonathan and to record them in their journals. Then remind students to keep their predictions and inferences in mind and to change them or make new ones as they read the story. Also remind students to use their other reading strategies as they read the selection.

Teacher's Note

Strategy/Skill Connection For a better understanding of *Earthquake Terror,* students can use the

- Predict/Infer Strategy
- Sequence of Events Comprehension Skill

Anticipating possible story events will help students focus on the sequence, which lays the groundwork for later skill instruction.

As students fill in their *Earthquake Terror* Event Map (**Practice Book** page 4 and **Transparency 1–2**), they can use their answers to decide if their predictions were correct or need to be revised.

THEME 1: **Nature's Fury**

California Standards pp. 27B–27C

R 2.2   Use order to analyze text
R 2.4   Inferences/generalizations
W 2.2.a Demonstrate understanding

Comprehension Skill

✓ **Comprehension Skill Focus:**
Sequence of Events

Event Map Explain that students will focus on the sequence of events, or the order of the story events, in *Earthquake Terror*. To develop the skill, students will record the main story events in the order they occur on an event map. Display **Transparency 1–2,** and demonstrate how to use this graphic organizer.

■ Begin by asking someone to read aloud pages 29–30, stopping after *"I'm hot," Abby said. "It's too hot to eat."*

■ Have a student read the first box on the Event Map. Model how to complete the sentence and record the answer.

■ Ask students to complete the first box on **Practice Book** page 4 with the same answer.

■ As they read, have students complete the other boxes of the Event Map. Monitor their work, or have students check each other's maps.

Graphic Organizer: Event Map

Page 30 At first Moose listens. Then he barks and paces back and forth as if he senses *that something is wrong.*

Page 30–31 After Jonathan puts the leash on Moose, they all slowly start to *walk back to the camper.*

Page 32–33 Jonathan and Abby hear a strange noise. At first Jonathan thinks it is thunder or hunters. Then suddenly he realizes *they are caught in an earthquake.*

Page 35 Abby screams and falls. As Jonathan lunges forward, he tries to catch Abby. Then he shouts *"Stay where you are. I'm coming."*

Page 36–37 Jonathan sees the huge redwood tree sway back and forth. Then *he scrambles away from it as it falls.*

Transparency 1–2

Event Map

Page 30
At first Moose listens. Then he barks and paces back and forth as if he senses

Pages 30–31
After Jonathan puts the leash on Moose, they all slowly start to

Pages 32–33
Jonathan and Abby hear a strange noise. At first Jonathan thinks it is thunder or hunters. Then suddenly he realizes

Page 35
Abby screams and falls. As Jonathan lunges forward, he tries to catch Abby. Then he shouts,

Pages 36–37
Jonathan sees the huge redwood tree sway back and forth. Then

TRANSPARENCY 1–2
TEACHER'S EDITION PAGES T27C AND T51A

NATURE'S FURY *Earthquake Terror*
Graphic Organizer Event Map

Practice Book page 4

Earthquake Terror
Graphic Organizer Event Map

Name _____

Event Map

Record in this Event Map the main story events in the order in which they occurred.

Page 30
At first Moose listens. Then he barks and paces back and forth as if he senses that something is wrong. **(2 points)**

Pages 30–31
After Jonathan puts the leash on Moose, they all slowly start to walk back to the camper. **(2)**

Pages 32–33
Jonathan and Abby hear a strange noise. At first Jonathan thinks it is thunder or hunters. Then suddenly he realizes they are _____ caught in an earthquake. **(2)**

Page 35
Abby screams and falls. As Jonathan lunges forward, he tries to catch Abby. Then he shouts, "Stay where you are, I'm coming." **(2)**

Pages 36–37
Jonathan sees the huge redwood tree sway back and forth. Then he scrambles away from it as it falls. **(2)**

4   Theme 1: **Nature's Fury**
Assessment Tip: Total **10** Points

Focus Questions

Have students turn to Responding on page 46. Read the questions aloud and tell students to keep them in mind as they read *Earthquake Terror.*

Reading

R 1.1

Options for Reading

▶ **Reading in Segments** Students can read *Earthquake Terror* in two segments (pages 28–35 and 36–44) or in its entirety.

▶ **Deciding About Support** Action and suspense make *Earthquake Terror* exciting to read.

■ Because of the familiar genre (realistic fiction) and predictable plot, most students should be able to follow On Level reading instruction.

■ For students who might have difficulty with vocabulary or the use of flashbacks, use the Extra Support notes.

■ Significantly below-level readers can listen to the **Audiotape** and read the Selection Summary for *Earthquake Terror,* and then read "Riding Out the Storm" in the **Reader's Library.**

▶ **Universal Access** Use the notes at the bottom of the pages.

PEG KEHRET
author of *Terror at the Zoo*

EARTHQUAKE TERROR

It started as an adventure—
and turned into a nightmare

Strategy Focus

Think about the selection, title and cover illustration. What do you **predict** Jonathan will do to protect himself and his younger sister when a powerful earthquake strikes?

Reading   Inferences/generalizations (R2.4)

28

Reaching All Students

Classroom Management

UNIVERSAL ACCESS

On Level

Reading Cards 1-2

While Reading: Reading Card 1; Event Map (**Practice Book** p. 4); generate questions

After Reading: Discussion Group (Reading Card 2); Wrapping Up Segment 1 (p. 35) and Segment 2 (p. 45)

Challenge

Reading Cards 1-4

While Reading: Event Map (**Practice Book** p. 4); Character's Perspective (p. 33, Reading Card 3); Similes (p. 40, Reading Card 4)

After Reading: Discussion Group (Reading Card 2); Wrapping Up Segment 1 (p. 35) and Segment 2 (p. 45)

English Language Learners

Intermediate and Advanced Fluency
Have students read with partners. Remind students to use the illustrations and context clues to help them figure out the meanings of unfamiliar words.

R 2.1

For English language learners at other proficiency levels, use the **Handbook for English Language Learners.**

California Standards pp. 28–29

R 1.1 Read aloud fluently
R 2.1 Understand text features
R 2.3 Discern main ideas

R 2.4   Inferences/generalizations
W 2.2.a Demonstrate understanding

A family vacation begins peacefully in the woods of Magpie Island. Then Jonathan and Abby's mom breaks her ankle, and their dad has to rush her to the hospital. He promises to return in three hours, leaving Jonathan, age twelve, in charge of his six-year-old sister, whose legs are partially paralyzed. Moose, the family's dog, is with them. But Jonathan is uneasy.

In his mind, Jonathan could see his father unhitching the small camping trailer. He pictured the car going along the narrow, winding road that meandered from the campground through the woods. He saw the high bridge that crossed the river, connecting the island campground to the mainland.

He imagined his father driving across the bridge, faster than usual, with Mom lying down in the back seat. Or maybe she wouldn't lie down. Maybe, even with a broken ankle, she would wear her seat belt. She always did, and she insisted that Jonathan and Abby wear theirs.

29

Reading Segment 1
pages 28–35

Purpose Setting Have students recall the predictions they made for the Strategy Focus on Anthology page 28. Have them read to confirm or change their predictions as the story unfolds.

 Journal Writing Students can use their journal to record their original predictions and to add new ones.

Reinforcing Comprehension and Strategies

■ Remind students to use Predict/Infer and other strategies as they read and to add to their Event Map (**Practice Book** page 4).

■ Use the Strategy Focus notes on pages 32 and 42 to reinforce Predict/Infer.

■ Use Supporting Comprehension questions beginning on page 30 to help students develop higher-level understanding of the text.

Before each segment, preview the text, using the notes below and on page 36. **While** reading, model strategies (pages 31, 38, and 41). **After** reading, review each segment (pages 34 and 44) before students join the Wrapping Up discussion.

pages 29–31 Jonathan and Abby start back to their campsite, but their dog, Moose, begins to act strangely, as if he senses danger. Why might Moose act that way?

pages 32–33 Jonathan hears loud noises and feels a sudden jolt. He doesn't know what's happening at first, but we know it's an earthquake! What's Jonathan doing in the picture?

pages 34–35 By now Jonathan knows they're caught in an earthquake. He's practiced what to do in school, but they're outdoors. What's happening in the picture? What do you think the children will do?

▶ Supporting Comprehension

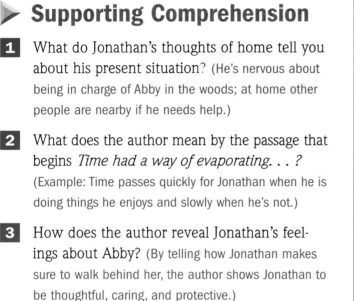

1 What do Jonathan's thoughts of home tell you about his present situation? (He's nervous about being in charge of Abby in the woods; at home other people are nearby if he needs help.)

R 2.3
R 3.3

2 What does the author mean by the passage that begins *Time had a way of evaporating. . . ?* (Example: Time passes quickly for Jonathan when he is doing things he enjoys and slowly when he's not.)

R 3.7

3 How does the author reveal Jonathan's feelings about Abby? (By telling how Jonathan makes sure to walk behind her, the author shows Jonathan to be thoughtful, caring, and protective.)

R 3.3
R 3.7

Vocabulary *(page 30)*
isolated: separated from others

Moose cocked his head, as if listening to something. Then he ran toward the trail, sniffing the ground.

"Moose," Jonathan called. "Come back."

Moose paused, looked at Jonathan, and barked.

"Come!"

Moose returned but he continued to smell the ground and pace back and forth.

"Moose wants Mommy," Abby said.

Moose suddenly stood still, his legs stiff and his tail up. He barked again.

"Silly old dog," Abby said.

He knows something is wrong, Jonathan thought. Dogs sense things. He knows I'm worried about Mom. Jonathan patted Moose's head. "It's all right, Moose. Good dog."

Moose barked again.

"I'm hot," Abby said. "It's too hot to eat."

"Let's start back. It'll be cooler in the shade and we can finish our lunch in the camper."

Maybe he could relax in the camper. Here he felt jumpy. He didn't like being totally out of communication with the rest of the world. Whenever he stayed alone at home, or took care of Abby, there **1** was always a telephone at his fingertips or a neighbor just down the street. If he had a problem, he could call his parents or Mrs. Smith next door or even nine-one-one.

Here he was isolated. I wouldn't do well as a forest ranger, Jonathan thought. How do they stand being alone in the woods all the time?

He rewrapped the uneaten food, buckled the backpack over his shoulders, and put the leash on Moose. The goofy way Moose was acting, he might bolt down the trail and not come back.

30

Demonstration

R 2.3

Place two paperback books flat on a desk next to each other so their pages touch and their spines face outward. Push on the spines until the books shift or buckle. Explain that a similar thing happens along a fault line.

California Standards pp. 30–31

R 2.3 Discern main ideas	R 3.3 Determine character traits
R 2.4 Inferences, generalizations	R 3.7 Evaluate author's techniques
R 3.1 Analyze literary forms	W 2.2.a Demonstrate understanding

Jonathan helped Abby stand up and placed her walker in position. Slowly, they began the journey across the sand and into the woods, to follow the trail through the trees.

Jonathan wished he had worn a watch. It seemed as if his parents had been gone long enough to get partway to town, but it was hard to be sure. Time had a way of evaporating instantly when he was engrossed in an interesting project, such as cataloging his baseball cards, or reading a good mystery. But time dragged unbearably when he was in the dentist's office or waiting for a ride. It was hard to estimate how much time had passed since his parents waved good-bye and walked away. Forty minutes? An hour?

2

Abby walked in front of him. That way he could see her and know if she needed help, and it kept him from going too fast. When he was in the lead, he usually got too far ahead, even when he tried to walk slowly.

3

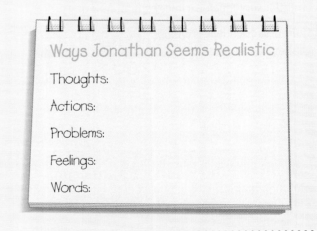

31

Reaching All Students

Extra Support

Strategy Modeling

R 2.4

Predict/Infer If students are having difficulty modeling the strategy, use this example to model it for them.

I can use clues to help figure out what might happen later. On page 31, I see that Jonathan walks behind his sister so he can see if she needs help. I can infer that he does this because he cares for Abby. I predict that if Abby runs into trouble later in the story, Jonathan will try to help her.

R 3.1
W 2.2.a

Revisiting the Text

Genre Lesson
Realistic Fiction

OBJECTIVES

Students identify elements of realistic fiction in the selection.

Explain the characteristics of realistic fiction:

■ The story problem and solution are realistic. Story events could happen in real life, even though the author created them.

■ The story characters speak, think, feel, and act as real people do and have the same problems real people might have.

Point out how Jonathan's worries about being far from neighbors and a phone make him seem like a real person. Then ask students to identify other details that make *Earthquake Terror* a piece of realistic fiction. (Examples: the setting; Jonathan and Abby's reaction to the earthquake)

Have small groups create a chart showing examples of how Jonathan behaves like a real person. Allow time for groups to compare their work.

Ways Jonathan Seems Realistic

Thoughts:

Actions:

Problems:

Feelings:

Words:

▶ Strategy Focus: Predict/Infer

R 2.4

Teacher/Student Modeling Discuss clues on page 32 that can help students predict that trouble is on the way. (Example: From the sentence *Jonathan noticed again how quiet it was* the reader can infer that the quiet is not normal.)

Ask students what predictions they can make from these sentences: *Jonathan listened. He heard a deep rumbling sound in the distance. . . Hunters! he thought.* (Example: Jonathan is wrong, and the noise is probably an earthquake.)

▶ Supporting Comprehension

R 2.3

4 Why does the author say that Jonathan *felt as if he were on a surfboard... ?* (to help us understand what it feels like to be in an earthquake)

Vocabulary (pages 32–33)

stifling: very hot or stuffy; suffocating

frantic: very much excited, as from fear or worry

jolt: a sudden jerk or bump

Cross-Curricular Connection

Science Dogs howl; snakes leave their burrows; zoo animals refuse to go inside—for centuries people have reported unusual animal behavior before earthquakes. Scientists think changes to the earth's crust before a quake create sudden changes in sound vibrations or electro-magnetic fields, which act as danger signals to many creatures.

While they walked Jonathan planned what he would do when they got back to the camper. As soon as he got Abby settled on her bed, he would turn on the radio and listen to the ball game. That would give him something to think about. The San Francisco Giants were his favorite baseball team and he hoped they would win the World Series.

Jonathan noticed again how quiet it was. No magpies cawed, no leaves rustled overhead. The air was stifling, with no hint of breeze.

Moose barked. Jonathan jumped at the sudden noise. It was Moose's warning bark, the one he used when a stranger knocked on the door. He stood beside Jonathan and barked again. The dog's eyes had a frantic look. He was shaking, the way he always did during a thunderstorm.

"What's wrong, boy?" Jonathan asked. He reached out to pet Moose but the dog tugged toward Abby and barked at her.

"Hush, Moose," Abby said.

Jonathan looked in all directions. He saw nothing unusual. There were still no people and no animals that would startle Moose and set him off. Jonathan listened hard, wondering if Moose had heard something that Jonathan couldn't hear.

Abby stopped walking. "What was that?" she said.

"What was what?"

Jonathan listened. He heard a deep rumbling sound in the distance.

Thunder? He looked up. The sky was bright and cloudless. The noise came closer; it was too sharp to be thunder. It was more like several rifles being fired at the same time.

Hunters! he thought. There are hunters in the woods and they heard us move and they've mistaken us for deer or pheasant. Moose must have seen them or heard them or possibly smelled them.

32

Reaching All Students
English Language Learners

Intermediate and Advanced Fluency   LS 2.3.a

Summarize

After they read page 32, ask students to summarize what has happened so far. As needed, guide them with questions such as "What is the boy's name? What is the girl's name? Where are they? What are they doing? Why aren't their parents there? What has just happened?" Ask students to guess what the sound really is.

California Standards pp. 32–33

R 2.2 Use order to analyze text
R 2.3 Discern main ideas
R 2.4 Inferences/generalizations

R 3.7 Evaluate author's techniques
LS 2.3 Respond to literature
LS 2.3.a Summarize events/details

"Don't shoot!" he cried.

As he yelled, Jonathan felt a jolt. He stumbled forward, thrusting an arm out to brace himself against a tree. Another loud noise exploded as Jonathan lurched sideways.

He dropped the leash.

Abby screamed.

A bomb? Jonathan thought. Who would bomb a deserted campground?

The noise continued, and the earth moved beneath his feet. As he felt himself lifted, he knew that the sound was not hunters with guns. It was not a bomb, either.

Earthquake! The word flashed across his brain as if he had seen it blazing on a neon sign.

He felt as if he were on a surfboard, catching a giant wave, rising, cresting, and sliding back down again. Except he was standing on dry land.

4

33

R 2.2

Revisiting the Text

Tested Skill

Comprehension Skill Lesson
Sequence of Events

OBJECTIVES

Students

- determine the sequence (or order) of story events
- identify words that signal sequence

Review sequence of events by writing these events from page 32 on the board: First Jonathan noticed how quiet it was, and then Moose barked.

■ Point out which event happened first and how the words *first* and *then* signal when each event happened.

■ Ask students to name other story events from pages 32 and 33; list them in order on the board. Note any words students use to signal sequence. (Samples: *before, after, next*)

■ Tell students that sometimes two or more story events happen at the same time.

■ Read aloud the first sentence on page 32. Explain how the word *while* signals that two events happen at the same time; they walked and Jonathan planned.

■ Have students identify simultaneous events in the second paragraph on page 33 and the signal word. (Jonathan yells and feels a jolt and another noise explodes as he lurches sideways; *as*.)

■ Have partners find other story events happening at the same time. (Example: page 35; As Abby fell, her walker flew sideways.)

Skill Finder

- **Instruction,** pp. 51A–51B
- **Reteaching,** p. R8
- **Review,** p. 71; Theme 2

Reading Card 3

Reaching All Students
Challenge

UNIVERSAL ACCESS

R 3.7   LS 2.3

Character's Perspective

This story is told from Jonathan's perspective. The reader experiences the same sounds, smells, memories, and sensations as Jonathan. Have students discuss how the story might be different if it were told from the perspective of Abby or Moose.

- For Abby, consider her age, her physical limitations, and her feelings toward her brother.

- For Moose, consider his extrasensitive senses of smell and hearing, and his inability to speak to Abby and Jonathan.

Supporting Comprehension

R 2.3

5 Why do you think the author includes Jonathan's memories about school earthquake drills? (to tell Jonathan's previous knowledge about earthquakes; to explain that Jonathan learned earthquake safety procedures in school)

6 What does the author mean in the passage, *That was school. This was Magpie Island?* (The action moves from Jonathan's memory back to the present; he only knows what to do inside the school, not out in open woods.)

Vocabulary *(page 35)*

fault: a break in a rock mass caused by a shifting of the earth's crust

susceptible: easily affected

34

 **Reaching All Students**
Extra Support

W 2.2.a

Segment 1: Review

Before students join the whole class for Wrapping Up on page 35, have them

- check predictions
- take turns modeling Predict/Infer and other strategies they used
- add to **Transparency 1–2**, check and revise their Event Map on **Practice Book** page 4, and use it to summarize

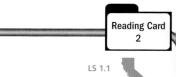 **Reaching All Students**
On Level Challenge

Reading Card 2

LS 1.1

Literature Discussion

In mixed-ability groups of five or six, students can discuss their own questions and the discussion prompts on Reading Card 2.

- How does the story remind you of any real-life experiences?
- How is Jonathan protective of Abby?

California Standards pp. 34–35

R 1.4 Use roots and affixes	LS 1.1 Ask new questions
R 2.3 Discern main ideas	LS 2.3.a Summarize events/details
W 2.2.a Demonstrate understanding	

"Jonathan!" Abby's scream was lost in the thunderous noise. He saw her fall, her walker flying off to one side as she went down. Jonathan lunged forward, arms outstretched, trying to catch Abby before she hit the ground. He couldn't get there fast enough.

The ground dropped away beneath his feet as if a trapdoor had opened. His legs buckled and he sank to his knees. He reached for a tree trunk, to steady himself, but before his hand touched it, the tree moved.

Jonathan's stomach rose into his throat, the way it sometimes did on a fast elevator.

Ever since first grade, when the Palmers moved to California, Jonathan had practiced earthquake drills in school each year. He knew that most earthquakes occur along the shores of the Pacific Ocean. He knew that the San Andreas <u>fault</u> runs north and south for hundreds of miles in California, making that land particularly <u>susceptible</u> to earthquakes. He knew that if an earthquake hit while he was in school, he was supposed to crawl under his desk or under a table because injury was most likely to be caused by the roof caving in on him.

5

That was school. This was Magpie Island. How should he protect himself in the woods? Where could he hide?

6

He struggled to his feet again. Ahead of him, Abby lay whimpering on the ground. Moose stood beside her, his head low.

"Put your hands over your head," Jonathan called.

The ground shook again, and Jonathan struggled to remain on his feet.

"I'm coming," he shouted. "Stay where you are. I'm coming!"

But he did not go to her. He couldn't.

He staggered sideways, unable to keep his balance. He felt as if he were riding a roller coaster standing up, except the ground rocked back and forth at the same time that it rolled up and down.

End of Segment 1:
pages 28–35

English Language Learners

Intermediate and Advanced Fluency   R 1.4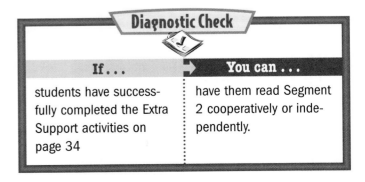

Prefix *un-*

Have students locate the word *unable* in the last paragraph on page 35. Tell students to place their finger over the letters *un*. Remind them that *able* means "can." Say that *un-* is a prefix that means "not." Write *important* and *comfortable* on the board. Write *un-* before each word. Ask students to give the meanings of these words.

Wrapping Up Segment 1
pages 28–35

First, provide Extra Support for students who need it (page 34). Then bring all students together.

■ **Review Predictions/Purpose** Discuss which predictions were accurate and which needed to be revised. Record any changes and new predictions.

■ **Model Strategies** Refer students to the Strategies Poster and have them take turns modeling Predict/Infer and other strategies they used as they read. Provide models if needed (page 31).

■ **Share Group Discussions** Have students share their questions and literature discussions.

LS 1.1

■ **Summarize** Help students use the transparency and their event map to summarize what has happened to Jonathan and Abby so far.

LS 2.3.a

Comprehension/Critical Thinking

1 Using Jonathan's experience, describe how it feels to be in an earthquake. (like being on a surfboard; a trapdoor opening; being on a fast elevator) **Making Generalizations**

2 Will Jonathan be able to use what he learned in school earthquake drills? Explain. (No; he learned to protect himself from a roof cave-in, but now he is in the open.) **Predicting Outcomes**

Diagnostic Check

If . . .	You can . . .
students have successfully completed the Extra Support activities on page 34	have them read Segment 2 cooperatively or independently.

Reading Segment 2
pages 36–44

Purpose Setting Have students summarize the story so far and predict what will happen to Jonathan and Abby. Then ask students to read pages 36–44 to check their predictions.

LS 2.3.

Journal Writing Students can record any revisions they made to their predictions and explain what made them change their minds.

Vocabulary *(pages 36–37)*

impact: the striking of one body against another

shuddered: shook, vibrated, or quivered

A clump of small birch trees swayed like dancers and then fell.

The rumbling noise continued, surrounding him, coming from every direction at once. It was like standing in the center of a huge orchestra, with kettle drums pounding on all sides.

Abby's screams and Moose's barking blended with the noise.

Although there was no roof to cave in on him, Jonathan put his arms over his head as he fell. The school's earthquake drills had taught him to protect his head and he did it the only way he could.

Earthquake.

He had never felt an earthquake before and he had always wondered how it would feel. He had questioned his teacher, that first year. "How will I know it's an earthquake?" he asked. "If it's a big one," the teacher said, "you'll know."

His teacher had been right. Jonathan knew. He knew with a certainty that made the hair rise on the back of his neck. He was in the middle of an earthquake now. A big one.

The ground heaved, pitching Jonathan into the air.

Jonathan hit the ground hard, jarring every bone in his body. Immediately, the earth below him moved, tossing him into the air again.

As he dropped back down, he saw the trunk of a giant redwood tree tremble. The huge tree swayed back and forth for a few moments and then tilted toward Jonathan.

Frantically, he crawled to his left, rushing to get out of the tree's path.

The roots ripped loose slowly, as if not wanting to relinquish their century-long hold on the dirt.

As Jonathan scrambled across the unsteady ground, he clenched his teeth, bracing himself for the impact.

36

Reaching All Students

Extra Support: Previewing the Text

Before reading Segment 2, preview the text, using the notes below. **While** reading, model strategies (pages 38 and 41). **After** reading, review the segment (page 44) before students join the Wrapping Up discussion.

pages 36–38 As the quake continues, a huge redwood tree crashes to the ground near Jonathan. He remembers seeing pictures of terrible earthquake damage. How might he feel now?

pages 39–40 In this picture Jonathan and Abby are protecting themselves under a fallen tree trunk. Jonathan wonders if they are still in danger. Will they be safe there? What might happen?

pages 41–44 The ground stops shaking, and the woods are silent. Jonathan wonders if the quake's really over. You'll have to read the story to find out how it ends.

California Standards pp. 36–37

R 3.3   Determine character traits
R 3.7   Evaluate author's techniques
LS 2.3.a Summarize events/details

The tree fell. Air whizzed across Jonathan as the tree trunk dropped past, and branches brushed his shoulder, scratching his arms. The redwood crashed beside him, missing him by only a few feet. It thudded down, landing at an angle on another fallen tree. Dirt and dry leaves whooshed into the air, and then settled slowly back down.

The earth shuddered, but Jonathan didn't know if it was from the impact of the tree or another jolt from the earthquake.

With his heart in his throat, Jonathan crept away from the redwood tree, toward Abby. Beneath him, the ground swelled and retreated, like ocean waves. Twice he sprawled facedown in the dirt, unable to keep his balance. The second time, he lay still, with his eyes closed. How much longer would this go on? Maybe he should just lie there and wait until this earthquake was over.

37

R 3.3
R 3.7

Revisiting the Text · · · · · · · · · · · · · **Spiral Review**

Comprehension Skill Lesson
Noting Details

OBJECTIVES

Students identify important details about the story characters, events, and setting.

Explain that details are important to a story because they help readers

- understand important information about characters and events

- see, hear, and feel what the characters experience

- picture the story setting and sense the mood an author creates

Point out how the author describes what happens to Jonathan on page 36. After the quake pitches Jonathan into the air, he hits the ground so hard that he *jar[s] every bone in his body.* Those words help the reader picture exactly what happens to him.

Have students identify other story details that help them understand the children's terror, experience the earthquake, and visualize the setting. (Example: Jonathan's attempts to scramble away from the falling tree)

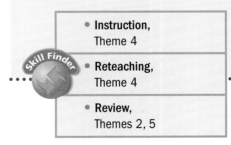

Skill Finder

- **Instruction,** Theme 4

- **Reteaching,** Theme 4

- **Review,** Themes 2, 5

Reading

▶ Supporting Comprehension

R 2.3
R 2.4

7 Why do you think Jonathan tells Abby, *"It's only an earthquake"?* (He doesn't want Abby to worry; he does not want her to know he is afraid; he is trying to convince himself they'll be okay.)

8 Why do you think the author describes Jonathan's memory about earthquakes here? (to emphasize that the danger is serious; to connect the story to real life; to show that Jonathan is very worried about their safety)

9 Describe how the fallen tree provides shelter for Jonathan and Abby. (When the giant redwood falls, it lands on the trunk of another fallen tree, creating a space beneath it which the children use for shelter.)

Vocabulary *(page 38)*

devastation: destruction or ruin

debris: the remains of something broken or destroyed

undulating: moving in waves or with a smooth, wavy motion

"Mommy!" Abby's shrill cry rose above the thundering noise.

Jonathan struggled toward her again, his heart racing. When he finally reached her, he lay beside her and wrapped his arms around her. She clung to him, sobbing.

7 "We'll be okay," he said. "It's only an earthquake."

Only an earthquake. He remembered magazine pictures of terrible <u>devastation</u> from earthquakes: homes toppled, highways **8** buckled, cars tossed upside down, and people crushed in <u>debris</u>. Only an earthquake.

"We have to get under shelter," he said. "Try to crawl with me." Keeping one arm around Abby's waist, he got to his hands and knees and began crawling forward on the <u>undulating</u> ground.

"I can't!" Abby cried. "I'm scared. The ground is moving."

Jonathan tightened his grip, dragging her across the ground. A small tree crashed beside them. Dust rose, filling their noses.

"I want Mommy!" Abby shrieked.

He pulled her to the trunk of the huge redwood tree that had uprooted.

9 "Get under the tree," he said, as he pushed her into the angle of space that was created because the center of the redwood's trunk rested on the other tree.

When Abby was completely under the tree, Jonathan lay on his stomach beside her, with his right arm tucked beneath his stomach and his left arm thrown across Abby. He pulled himself in as close as he could so that both he and Abby were wedged in the space under the big tree.

"What's happening?" Abby sobbed. Her fingernails dug into Jonathan's bare arm.

"It's an earthquake."

"I want to go home." Abby tried to push Jonathan away.

"Lie still," Jonathan said. "The tree will protect us."

38

Reaching All Students

Extra Support

R 2.4

Strategy Modeling

Predict/Infer If students need help modeling the strategy, use this example to model it for them.

Jonathan says that it's "only an earthquake." But he remembers seeing pictures of the devastation that earthquakes can cause. In spite of what Jonathan tells Abby, I predict that this earthquake will cause a great deal of damage and make it very hard for the children to reach a safe place.

California Standards pp. 38–39

R 2.3 Discern main ideas
R 2.4 Inferences/generalizations
R 3.7 Evaluate author's techniques

LC 1.2 Verbs, modifiers, pronouns

Writer's Craft Lesson
Mood

OBJECTIVES

Students

* identify the mood of a story scene
* find other scenes having a similar mood

Explain that writers deliberately use words, details, and descriptive language to create the mood, or emotional tone, in a scene or story.

Model by reading aloud the following from page 38:

Jonathan struggled toward her again, his heart racing.

"I want Mommy!" Abby shrieked.

Her fingernails dug into Jonathan's bare arm.

Point out that the words *his heart racing* and *shrieked* and the image of Abby's nails digging into Jonathan's arm convey a mood of fear, alarm, and panic. Then have students identify other scenes having a similar mood. (Examples: page 36, when Jonathan realizes they're caught in a quake; page 37, right after the redwood tree falls)

Ask students to name other moods an author may want to create. (Examples: humorous, mysterious, sad, peaceful)

Reaching All Students

English Language Learners

Intermediate and Advanced Fluency

Action Verbs

LC 1.2

Have students look for action verbs on page 38. List them on the board; call on volunteers to demonstrate as many as possible. For additional practice, have students find ten to fifteen action verbs up to this point in the selection.

► Supporting Comprehension

10 What does the sentence *Anxiety tied a tight knot in Jonathan's stomach* say about Jonathan's situation? (Jonathan is nervous and worried that the quake may cause the tree to slip and crush them.)

R 2.3
R 2.4

11 What does the author mean by *the silence seemed both comforting and ominous?* (The silence means that the quake has ended for now, but because the regular forest noises have not returned, Jonathan wonders if the quake will start again.)

R 3.7

12 Why do you think the author includes Jonathan's memory of Grandma Whitney? (Jonathan is still thinking about his parents; he realizes that his parents might know nothing about the quake or the danger their children are in.)

R 2.4
R 3.7

Vocabulary *(page 40)*

upheaval: a lifting or upward movement of the earth's crust

ominous: threatening

The dry forest floor scratched his cheek as he inhaled the pungent scent of dead leaves. He felt dwarfed by the enormous redwood and tried not to imagine what would have happened if it had landed on him.

"Moose!" he called. "Come, Moose."

Beneath him, the ground trembled again. Jonathan tightened his grip on Abby and pushed his face close to hers. A sharp crack rang out beside them as another tree hit the ground. Jonathan turned his head enough to peer out; he saw the redwood branches quivering from the impact.

What if the earthquake caused the redwood to move again? What if it slipped off the tree it rested on and crushed them beneath it? **10** Anxiety tied a tight knot in Jonathan's stomach.

The earth shuddered once more. Abby buried her face in Jonathan's shoulder. His shirt grew wet from her tears. The jolt did not seem as severe this time, but Jonathan thought that might be because he was lying down.

Moose, panting with fear, huddled beside Jonathan, pawing at Jonathan's shoulder. Relieved that the dog had not been injured, Jonathan put his right arm around Moose and held him close.

As suddenly as it had begun, the <u>upheaval</u> stopped. Jonathan was unsure how long it had lasted. Five minutes? Ten? While it was happening, time seemed suspended and Jonathan had thought the shaking might go on for days.

The woods were quiet.

He lay motionless, one arm around Abby and the other around Moose, waiting to see if it was really over. The air was completely still. After the roar of the earthquake, the silence seemed both **11** comforting and <u>ominous</u>.

Earlier, even though there were no other people in the area, he'd heard the magpies cawing, and a squirrel had complained when Jonathan tossed a rock.

40

Reaching All Students

English Language Learners

Intermediate and Advanced Fluency

Helping Verb *had*

LC 1.2

Read aloud this phrase on page 40: *a squirrel had complained.* Remind students that the squirrel complained before the earthquake happened. Tell students that *had* as a helping verb means *before something else* in the past. Ask students what else had happened before the earthquake.

California Standards pp. 40–41

R 1.1 Read aloud fluently
R 2.3 Discern main ideas
R 2.4 Inferences/generalizations
R 3.7 Evaluate author's techniques

LC 1.2 Verbs, modifiers, pronouns

Now he heard nothing. No birds. No squirrels. Not even wind in the leaves.

He wondered if his parents had felt the quake. Sometimes, he knew, earthquakes were confined to fairly small areas.

Once Grandma Whitney had called them from Iowa. She had seen news reports of a violent California earthquake less than one hundred miles from where the Palmers lived.

12

"Are you all right?" Grandma cried, when Mrs. Palmer answered the phone. "Was anyone hurt?"

Grandma had been astonished when none of the Palmers knew anything about an earthquake.

After several minutes of quiet, Jonathan eased out from under the tree. He sat up and looked around. Moose, still trembling, licked his hand.

41

Reaching All Students

Extra Support

Strategy Modeling

Phonics/Decoding If students need help modeling the strategy, use this example to model it for them.

On page 41 is a word I'll try sounding out. (Point to *violent.*) *First, I'll look for the parts I know. I see* vi *and the letter* o. *I also see the part* lent. *I'll try blending the sounds together:* VY o lehnt. *Now I'll check to see if it makes sense in the sentence. . . I see, if something is* violent, *it must be something that has great power or force.*

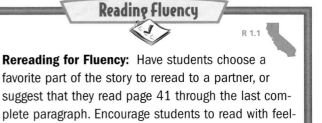

Reading Fluency

R 1.1

Rereading for Fluency: Have students choose a favorite part of the story to reread to a partner, or suggest that they read page 41 through the last complete paragraph. Encourage students to read with feeling and expression.

Assessing Fluency: See guidelines in the Theme Assessment Wrap-Up, page 107A.

▶ Strategy Focus: Predict/Infer

R 2.4

Student Modeling Ask students to model their predictions about what Jonathan and Abby will do after the quake stops. If necessary, use the following prompt: *Based on Jonathan's actions and decisions so far, what might he need to do to get Abby and himself to safety?*

▶ Supporting Comprehension

R 2.4

13 Why do you think the author includes Jonathan's memories of Moose? (Moose brings comfort to Jonathan now in the same way he did after Abby's accident; Jonathan is glad Moose is safe because he has been an important part of Jonathan's life for a long time.)

42

Cross-Curricular Connection

Science Since the 1940s, scientists and engineers have been studying earthquakes to improve the way buildings are constructed. Today, sophisticated instruments in houses, highways, schools, hospitals, and bridges measure how well these structures tolerate each tremor. Their objective is to reduce the loss of life and property damage.

Reaching All Students

English Language Learners

Intermediate and Advanced Fluency

W 2.2.a

Camping

Some students may be unfamiliar with camping as a cultural pastime. Explain that camping means spending time away from home outdoors. As they read, ask them to make note of words relating to camping.

California Standards pp. 42–43

R 1.5 Figurative language
R 2.4 Inferences/generalizations
R 3.2 Main problem/plot conflict

W 2.2.a Demonstrate understanding

Jonathan put his cheek on the dog's neck and rubbed his ears. He had chosen Moose at the animal shelter, more than six years ago. The Palmers had planned to get a small dog but the moment Jonathan saw the big golden retriever, who was then one year old, he knew which dog he wanted.

13

Mrs. Palmer had said, "He's too big to be a house dog."

Mr. Palmer said, "I think he's half moose."

Jonathan laughed and said, "That's what I'll name him. Moose."

His parents tried unsuccessfully to interest Jonathan in one of the other, smaller dogs, before they gave in and brought Moose home.

Despite his size, Moose was a house dog from the start, and he slept beside Jonathan's bed every night. They played fetch, and their own version of tag, and Jonathan took Moose for long walks in the county park. In the summer, they swam whenever they had a chance.

When Abby had her accident and Jonathan's parents focused so much of their attention on her, Moose was Jonathan's comfort and companion.

Now, in the devastation of the earthquake, Jonathan again found comfort in the dog's presence. He let go of Moose and looked around. "Wow!" he said, trying to keep his voice steady. "That was some earthquake."

"Is it over?" Abby's voice was thin and high.

"I think so."

He grasped Abby's hand and pulled her out from under the tree. She sat up, apparently uninjured, and began picking leaves out of her hair.

"Are you okay?" he asked.

"My knee is cut." She touched one knee and her voice rose. "It's bleeding," she said, her lip trembling. "You pushed me under the tree too hard."

43

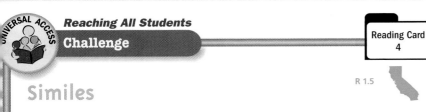

Reaching All Students

Challenge

Reading Card 4

R 1.5

Similes

Sometimes, in order to describe an object, person, or event, an author compares it to something else, using the word *like* or *as*. This comparison is called a simile. For example, the simile the *ground swelled and retreated, like ocean waves* creates a vivid picture of the earth's movement.

• Have students find examples of similes in the story.

• For fun, have students change a simile. For instance, what picture is created if *the ground swelled and retreated, like ripples on a pond*?

Comprehension Skill Lesson
Story Structure

OBJECTIVES

Students use a story map to identify the story structure.

Review how to identify the five elements of a story—setting, characters, problem, main events, and outcome. Explain that together these parts make up the structure of a story.

Point out the words *woods* and *island* and other details from page 29 that provide clues about the setting of *Earthquake Terror.* Then begin a story map similar to the one below by writing *Setting: island campground* on the board. List the other story elements, and ask students to give story details to complete other parts of the map.

Story Map for *Earthquake Terror*

Setting	island campground (p. 29)
Characters	Jonathan, Abby, Moose
Problem	Jonathan must find protection from the earthquake. (pp. 33–40)
Events	He dodges a falling tree, finds shelter, and helps Abby. (pp. 33–41)
Outcome	The earthquake ends and everyone is safe. (p. 40)

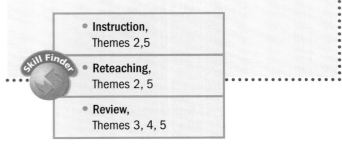

Skill Finder

• **Instruction,** Themes 2,5

• **Reteaching,** Themes 2, 5

• **Review,** Themes 3, 4, 5

Supporting Comprehension

R 2.3

14 What does the author mean by saying that Abby will get upset if Jonathan makes a fuss about her cut? (Abby reacts hysterically if he shows concern, so Jonathan must act as if it's no big deal in order to keep her calm.)

15 How has the author solved the story problem for Jonathan and Abby? What new problems do they face? (The earthquake seems to have stopped, but Jonathan isn't sure if it has ended for good. They don't know when or how their parents will reach them, so they must take care of themselves until help arrives.)

14 Jonathan examined her knee. It was a minor cut. He knew that if he made a fuss over it, Abby would cry. He had seen it happen before; if his mother showed concern about a small injury, Abby got practically hysterical, but if Mom acted like it was no big deal, Abby relaxed, too. It was as if she didn't know whether she hurt or not until she saw how her parents reacted.

"It's all right," he said. "If that tiny little scrape is all you got, you are lucky, and so am I. We could have been killed."

"We could?" Abby's eyes grew round.

15 Quickly Jonathan said, "But we weren't, and the earthquake is over now."

44

End of Segment 2:
pages 36–44

Reaching All Students
Extra Support

Segment 2 Review

R 2.4

Before students join in Wrapping Up on page 45, have them

- review and discuss the accuracy of their predictions
- take turns modeling the reading strategies they used
- help you complete **Transparency 1–2** and their Event Map on **Practice Book** page 4, and use it to summarize

---

Reaching All Students
On Level Challenge

Literature Discussion

LS 1.1

Have small groups of students discuss the story, using their own questions or the questions in Think About the Selection on Anthology page 46.

California Standards pp. 44–45

R 1.5 Figurative language
R 2.3 Discern main ideas
R 2.4 Inferences/generalizations
R 2.5 Facts, inferences, opinions

LS 1.1 Ask new questions
LS 2.3.a Summarize events/details
LS 2.3.c Use examples

Meet the Author
Peg Kehret

Favorite outfit: Jeans and sweatshirt
Favorite dish: Spaghetti
When not writing: Reads, plays her player piano, bakes bread, volunteers at The Humane Society
Home: An eighty-year-old house in the state of Washington with apple and pear trees, blueberry and blackberry bushes, and a big vegetable garden
Popularity: Kehret has won children's choice awards in fifteen states. Twice a year she and her husband travel across the country in their motor home so that she can speak in schools and meet her readers.

More Kehret books: *Volcano Disaster, Blizzard Disaster, Nightmare Mountain, The Richest Kids in Town, Shelter Dogs: Amazing Stories of Adopted Strays*

Meet the Illustrator
Phil Boatwright

Lone Star boyhood: Boatwright grew up in Mesquite, Texas, a suburb of Dallas.
Favorite children's book: *Treasure Island,* by Robert Louis Stevenson
Favorite illustrators: Gennady Spirin, Jerry Pinkney, John Collier, and N. C. Wyeth
Tips for success: "You have to love to draw, take all the art classes possible, read all the art books available, and study the artists you admire."

For more information about Peg Kehret and Phil Boatwright, visit Education Place. **www.eduplace.com/kids**

45

Idioms

Some students may be unfamiliar with the expression *make a fuss over* on page 44. Ask students if Abby's cut was big or small. Explain that because her cut was small, Jonathan didn't worry or act frightened—he didn't make a fuss over it.

Wrapping Up Segment 2
pages 36–44

Provide Extra Support for students who need it (page 44). Then bring all students together.

■ **Review Predictions/Purpose** Discuss reasons why students' predictions were or were not accurate.

■ **Model Strategies** Have students tell how they used the Predict/Infer Strategy, and then have them take turns modeling it. Ask what other strategies they found helpful while reading.

R 2.4
R 2.5

■ **Share Group Discussions** Have students share their reactions to Jonathan's predicament and problem-solving abilities.

■ **Summarize** Ask students to summarize the main events of the story, using their Event Map.

LS 2.3.a

Comprehension/Critical Thinking

1 In your opinion, is it a good idea for Jonathan to take Abby and crawl under the redwood tree? Explain. (Yes, it protects them from other falling things; no, the tree might fall on them.) **Making Judgments**

R 2.3

2 How do Jonathan's memories help him during the earthquake? (Sample answers: He uses what he has already learned about earthquakes to figure out how to protect Abby and himself; memories of earlier experiences with Moose bring him comfort.) **Cause and Effect**

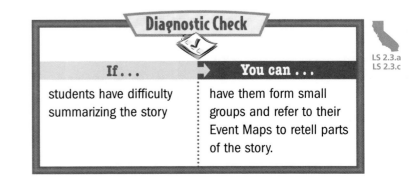

Diagnostic Check

LS 2.3.a
LS 2.3.c

If...	You can ...
students have difficulty summarizing the story	have them form small groups and refer to their Event Maps to retell parts of the story.

Reading

Responding

▶ Think About the Selection

Discuss or Write Have students discuss or write their answers. Sample answers are provided; accept reasonable responses that are supported with evidence from the story.

1 **Drawing Conclusions** Moose seems to sense something long before the children do. On page 30 Moose cocks his head, paces, and sniffs; on page 32 he uses his warning bark.

R 3.7

2 **Summarizing** Jonathan puts his hands over his head to protect himself and tells Abby to do the same; he finds shelter in the space beneath a fallen tree for Abby and himself.

R 3.2
W 2.2.a

3 **Making Judgments** yes, because they explain Jonathan's past; no, because they take away from the story suspense

4 **Noting Details** The San Andreas Fault runs north and south for hundreds of miles along the California coastline, so the area is likely to be affected by earthquakes.

5 **Making Generalizations** Jonathan is caring, considerate, and protective of Abby; he assists her to safety during the earthquake. Abby relies on her older brother for help and comfort.

R 3.3

6 **Compare and Contrast** Accept responses that reflect an understanding of Jonathan's thoughts.

7 **Connecting/Comparing** Making Judgments yes, because an earthquake is a violent, uncontrollable natural occurrence

---

Responding

Think About the Selection

1. How does the author create suspense before the earthquake hits? Find examples from the story.

2. Summarize what Jonathan does to protect himself and Abby from the earthquake.

3. Sometimes the author interrupts the action with events that happened earlier. Do you think this adds to the story? Why or why not?

4. What did you learn about the fault that runs through the island?

5. How would you describe Jonathan's relationship with his sister? Give examples from the selection that show how they feel about each other.

6. Jonathan thinks about how time goes fast when he's excited or interested, and slowly when he's not. Give examples of that from your own life.

7. **Connecting/Comparing** Do you think *Earthquake Terror* is a good way to begin a theme called *Nature's Fury*? Why or why not?

Narrating

Write an Adventure Story

Use what you learned about Jonathan and Abby in *Earthquake Terror* to write an adventure story with them as characters. Your story can tell how they escape from another natural disaster, such as a fire, a flood, or a storm.

Tips
- Begin by thinking about the problem the characters face and write down details.
- Show how the characters feel.
- Include details of the setting.

Reading Determine character traits (R3.3)
Writing Write narratives (W2.1)

46

Reaching All Students
English Language Learners

Intermediate and Advanced Fluency

W 2.1.a
W 2.1.b

Writing Support

Use pictures to identify other types of natural disasters (hurricane or typhoon, tornado, blizzard, fire, flood). Ask students to choose one of these disasters as a topic for their adventure story. Tell them to begin by creating a list of words appropriate to their topic. Have students who have chosen the same disaster work together. Assist with vocabulary.

California Standards pp. 46–47

R 2.1 Understand text features
R 2.3 Discern main ideas
R 3.2 Main problem/plot conflict
R 3.3 Determine character traits

W 2.1.a Establish plot, setting
W 2.1.b Show events
W 2.2.a Demonstrate understanding
LS 1.1 Ask new questions

46 THEME 1: **Nature's Fury**

Demonstrate Earthquake Safety

On pages 35 and 36 of the selection, Jonathan remembers what he learned in school about earthquake safety. Use that information to demonstrate for classmates what to do in case an earthquake strikes.

Deliver a Newscast

With a partner, present a newscast about the earthquake on Magpie Island. You might wish to take on the roles of a television anchorperson and an on-the-scene reporter. Use information from the selection to give details.

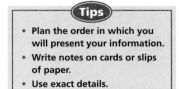

Tips
- Plan the order in which you will present your information.
- Write notes on cards or slips of paper.
- Use exact details.

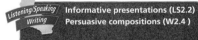

Post a Review

Write a review of *Earthquake Terror*. Tell others what you liked or didn't like about it. Visit Education Place. **www.eduplace.com/kids**

47

Personal Response

Invite volunteers to share their personal responses to *Earthquake Terror*. As an alternative, ask students to write in their journals or to respond in their own way.

W 2.2.a

Comprehension Check

Assign **Practice Book** page 5 to assess students' understanding of the selection.

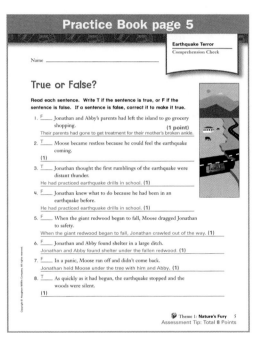

Practice Book page 5

Earthquake Terror
Comprehension Check

Name _____

True or False?

Read each sentence. Write T if the sentence is true, or F if the sentence is false. If a sentence is false, correct it to make it true.

1. F ___ Jonathan and Abby's parents had left the island to go grocery shopping. **(1 point)**
   Their parents had gone to get treatment for their mother's broken ankle.

2. T ___ Moose became restless because he could feel the earthquake coming.
   (1)

3. T ___ Jonathan thought the first rumblings of the earthquake were distant thunder.
   He had practiced earthquake drills in school. **(1)**

4. F ___ Jonathan knew what to do because he had been in an earthquake before.
   He had practiced earthquake drills in school. **(1)**

5. F ___ When the giant redwood began to fall, Moose dragged Jonathan to safety.
   When the giant redwood began to fall, Jonathan crawled out of the way. **(1)**

6. F ___ Jonathan and Abby found shelter in a large ditch.
   Jonathan and Abby found shelter under the fallen redwood. **(1)**

7. F ___ In a panic, Moose ran off and didn't come back.
   Jonathan held Moose under the tree with him and Abby. **(1)**

8. T ___ As quickly as it had begun, the earthquake stopped and the woods were silent.
   (1)

Theme 1: **Nature's Fury** 5
Assessment Tip: Total 8 Points

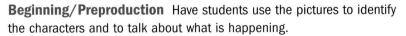

Reaching All Students

English Language Learners

R 2.1
R 2.3
LS 1.1

Before assigning the Responding activities on page 47, use these suggestions.

Beginning/Preproduction Have students use the pictures to identify the characters and to talk about what is happening.

Early Production and Speech Emergence Have students ask each other questions about the story. Then encourage students to tell the story in their own words.

Intermediate and Advanced Ask students to imagine an earthquake in a city. *How would the story have been different?*

End-of-Selection Assessment

Selection Test Use the test in the **Teacher's Resource Blackline Masters** to assess selection comprehension and vocabulary.

Student Self-Assessment Have students assess their reading with additional questions such as

- What parts of this selection were difficult for me? Why?

- What strategies helped me understand the story?

- Would I recommend this story to my friends? Why?

Science Link

pages 48–51

R 2.1
R 2.3
R 2.4

▶ Skill: How to Read a Science Article

Read aloud the title and author. Point out that "El Niño" is a nonfiction science article from *Muse* magazine. Since it differs from a fictional story like *Earthquake Terror*, students should read to understand facts and ideas, not a story plot.

Before you read Have students read and discuss steps 1–3 under "Before you read."

Help students scan the article, pointing out the kinds of information that the subtitles, captions, and graphics provide. Note especially the world map on page 50 and the separate section about La Niña (page 51).

Have them identify the topic of the article. (El Niño and bad weather)

Ask students what they already know about El Niño and what they predict they will learn.

While you read Explain that science articles are often organized in paragraphs with main ideas and supporting details. Have students read and discuss steps 1–2 under "While you read." Ask students how step 2 is like the Monitor/Clarify Strategy.

R 2.1

Vocabulary *(page 48)*

drought: a long period of time with little or no rainfall

Science Link

Skill: How to Read a Science Article

Before you read . . .

❶ Look at the title, captions, and illustrations.

❷ Identify the **topic** and ask what you already know.

❸ Predict what you will learn.

While you read . . .

❶ Find **main idea** and **supporting details** in each paragraph.

❷ When you don't understand something, ask questions and reread.

California Standards

Standards to Achieve

Science

• Oceans and weather patterns (S4.b)

48

El Niño

by Fred Pearce

In the winter of 1998, heavy rains caused mudslides in California that washed houses off cliffs. Ice storms on the eastern seaboard from Maine to Quebec downed so many power lines that thousands of people had to live in the dark and cold for weeks. Indonesia's rain forests got no rain, and the months of dry weather turned the forests into the world's largest pile of firewood. At the same time, the worst drought in a hundred years hit neighboring New Guinea, killing crops and leaving some of the most isolated people on Earth starving. On the other side of the globe, lack of rain left the water level in the Panama Canal so low that large ships couldn't make it through.

Mudslides in California

Reaching All Students

Classroom Management

All Students

Reading the Article Involve all students in the activities under How to Read a Science Article, K-W-L Chart, Genre Lesson, and Comprehension Check. Pair students needing extra reading support with more proficient partners to read the article. Remind them to get as much information as they can from the photos, captions, and map.

California Standards pp. 48–49

R 2.1 Understand text features   W 2.2.a Demonstrate understanding
R 2.3 Discern main ideas
R 2.4 Inferences/generalizations

Early 1998 also saw intense storms in places not used to them. Kenya suffered the worst floods in 40 years — in the middle of the *dry* season. Neighboring Uganda was cut off for several days, when both road and rail links were washed away. In South America, floods made half a million Peruvians homeless along a coastline that often has no rain for years at a time. Neighboring Ecuador said it would take 10 years to repair the damage. And in northern Tibet, the worst snow in 50 years starved or froze to death hundreds of Mongol tribesmen.

Was it just bad luck that there was so much bad weather in so many parts of the world at around the same time? Fifty years ago, most people would have said yes.

Flash floods in Ecuador, South America

Floods in Kenya, East Africa

Forest fires in Indonesia, Southeast Asia

49

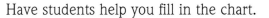

▶ K-W-L Chart

R 2.3
R 2.4
W 2.2.a

Draw a K-W-L chart on the board. Explain how using the chart will help students follow the steps for reading a science article. The steps correspond to various parts of the chart.

Have students help you fill in the chart.

- Begin by writing *Topic: El Niño and bad weather* above the chart.

- In the K column write the ideas students gathered from scanning the selection.

- Use student predictions to fill in the W column.

- Explain that after students have read the selection, they can use the main ideas they found to fill in the L column.

K	W	L
What I Know	**What I Want to Learn**	**What I Learned**
Stormy weather from El Niño caused landslides in California.	How often does El Niño occur?	
El Niño caused forest fires in Indonesia.	What causes El Niño?	

Purpose Setting Have students read "El Niño" to find answers to the questions in the W column. Also remind them to try to identify the main ideas and supporting details in the paragraphs and to use Monitor/Clarify and other strategies as they read.

R 2.3

Intermediate and Advanced Fluency   R 2.1

Skill Practice

Have students work with partners or in small groups to practice the skill. First, have them look at the title, captions, and illustrations. Remind them to use the photos and illustrations to help figure out the meaning of unfamiliar words in the captions as well as the reading itself. Ask students what this article is about. Then ask: *Have you heard of El Niño?* Ask Spanish speakers: *What does El Niño mean?*

Science Link *continued*

pages 48–51

R 3.1

Genre Lesson
Expository Nonfiction

OBJECTIVES

Students identify elements of expository nonfiction in the article.

Explain to students that "El Niño" is an example of expository nonfiction. Tell them that this type of selection

■ explains the way things are, what they mean, how they work, and why they are important

■ gives information about real topics

■ often is organized by main ideas and supporting details

Ask students to identify these elements in the selection.

Vocabulary (pages 50–51)

equator: the imaginary line that circles the earth halfway between the North and South poles, dividing the earth into the Northern and Southern hemispheres *(Show on a globe if there is one available in the classroom.)*

pollen: the fine powderlike material produced by flowering plants

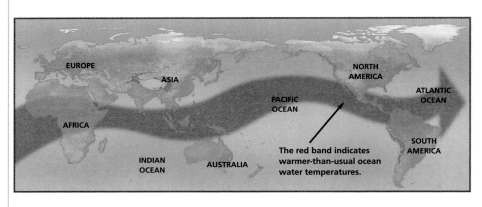

The red band indicates warmer-than-usual ocean water temperatures.

But today, meteorologists (scientists who study weather) blame most of 1998's weather disasters on a giant blip in the weather system called *El Niño*. Many years ago, Spanish-speaking Peruvian fishermen noticed that the fish suddenly disappeared whenever warm waters flowed in from the west. They called the warming El Niño (Spanish for "the child") because it usually happened around Christmas. El Niño is caused by a sudden shift in the winds and ocean currents in the Pacific Ocean that pushes a layer of warm water across the ocean, taking weather systems with it.

El Niño is rather like a wave in your bathtub, only the tub is huge and the wave takes months to go from one end to the other. The huge bathtub in this case is the Pacific, the world's largest ocean.

Most of the time, winds and ocean currents at the equator move from east to west across the Pacific — from the Americas to Asia. The winds and currents push the ocean's water toward Asia. After a few years of this, the sea level around the islands of Indonesia is actually over a foot higher than on the American side. This can't go on forever. And it doesn't. Eventually, like a wave reaching the far end of your bathtub, the water bounces back, moving toward the Americas. Scientists have clocked this wave moving about 125 miles a day.

The water around Indonesia is the hottest in the world — usually warmer than 80° F, which is as warm as many swimming pools. As the wave moves toward the Americas, it spreads a layer of the warm Indonesian water across the

50

Reaching All Students

Extra Support

Demonstration

To help students understand the explanation on page 50, fill a plastic dishpan with water, and use your hand to slowly move the water from one side of the pan to the other. Remove your hand from the dishpan, and allow the water to return to the other side. Refer to the map on page 50, and point to the location of both coasts of the Pacific Ocean. Explain to students that El Niño has a similar effect in the Pacific, causing a huge wave of warm water to move from one coast to the other.

California Standards pp. 50–51

R 1.1 Read aloud fluently
R 2.3 Discern main ideas
R 2.4 Inferences/generalizations

R 3.1 Analyze literary forms
W 1.4 Use electronic media
S 4.c Severe weather

ocean. And because ocean currents and winds are connected, the Indonesian weather follows, too. This means that the heavy rains that normally hit Indonesia for most of the year get moved thousands of miles east, soaking the Pacific Islands and normally dry coastlands from Peru to California. Meanwhile, normally wet Indonesia and its surrounding areas suffer drought.

No one is really sure how long El Niño has been around. Dan Sandweiss of the University of Maine has found telltale signs of sudden El Niño-style floods in old *sediments* in Peru. (Sediments are the solid stuff that settles out of water at places like the mouth of a river.) When it doesn't rain, few plants grow, and there isn't much pollen in the sediments. But when El Niño occurs in these normally dry regions, more plants grow and more pollen shows up. From the amount of pollen in the sediments, Sandweiss can tell that "El Niño has been around for at least 5000 years. Before that there seems to have been a gap."

El Niño isn't just about some rainstorm in California in 1998; it's about wild weather around the world through recorded history.

Episode Two: La Niña Strikes Back!

El Niño typically lasts some 18 months, and usually returns every three to seven years, probably when enough warm water has built up again in the western Pacific. But when El Niño's warm water retreats, it's sometimes followed by a *cool* water wave. Scientists call this cooling of the Pacific *La Niña*. La Niña's effect on the weather is harder to predict than El Niño's. But during La Niña years, the normal weather in some regions becomes *exaggerated*: it gets extra wet in wet Indonesia, extra dry in dry Peru. That's also when we get big droughts in the American Midwest. The great Dust Bowl drought of 1930s America is thought to have been caused by a decade of La Niña-like conditions.

Photo by Arthur Rothstein,
Dust Storm, Cimarron County, 1936.

51

Science/Math

W 1.4
S 4.c

Have volunteers use electronic or print encyclopedias, other reference books, or the Internet to collect, compare, and display facts that relate to weather extremes in their region, the nation, and the world. Suggest that they include facts such as highest and lowest recorded temperatures, most or least amounts of rain, and wind velocities.

Skill Finder

• **Information and Study Skills,** Using Print and Electronic Reference Sources, pp. 51C–51D

▶ Comprehension Check

K-W-L Chart Finish the K-W-L chart by having volunteers fill in the L column on the chalkboard.

Comprehension/Critical Thinking Ask students to read aloud the parts of the selection that support answers to these questions.

R 1.1
R 2.3
R 2.4

1 What causes El Niño? a giant "wave" that creates a shift in ocean and air currents in the Pacific Ocean, which pushes warmer-than-normal water and weather thousands of miles eastward **Cause and Effect**

2 How does El Niño create weather extremes? The warm tropical weather is pushed farther east, so heavy rains occur over areas that are usually dry, producing floods. Areas of normally high rainfall are left without the storms that produce rain, so they experience drought. **Cause and Effect**

3 How are scientists able to draw conclusions about how long El Niño has been affecting the weather? They study sediments and the concentration of pollen in the sediments. **Making Generalizations; Making Inferences**

4 **Connecting/Comparing** How are earthquakes and El Niño alike? How are they different? Both are natural disasters that can cause destruction to large areas. Earthquakes are caused by pressure on the earth's crust, while El Niño is caused by warmer-than-normal water and weather. **Compare and Contrast**

R 2.2
W 2.2.a

Comprehension Skills
✓ Sequence of Events

▶ **Teach**

Review the sequence of events in *Earthquake Terror.* Use **Transparency 1–2** to discuss

■ the main story events and their sequence

■ words that signal sequential order *(at first, then)*

■ words that signal events happening at the same time *(as, while)*

Students can refer to the selection and to **Practice Book** page 4.

Page 30 At first Moose listens. Then he barks and paces back and forth as if he senses that something is wrong.

Page 30–31 After Jonathan puts the leash on Moose, they all slowly start to walk back to the camper.

Page 32–33 Jonathan and Abby hear a strange noise. At first Jonathan thinks it is thunder or hunters. Then suddenly he realized they are caught in an earthquake.

Modeling Tell students that the author sometimes shifts from the present or main action of the story to events that happen in the past. Readers know when a time shift occurs by recognizing time order signal words. Have students reread aloud the last three complete paragraphs on page 30 to find where events shift to the past. Have them frame the point they selected with their fingers and consider their answer as you think aloud.

Think Aloud

The author begins in the present by telling how Jonathan feels in the woods. (Here he felt jumpy.) *Then she tells how he remembers feeling in the past.* (whenever he stayed alone at home) *Later, the word* here *signals to me that Jonathan's thoughts shift back to the present.* (Here he was isolated.)

Explain that authors use time shifts to give readers extra information such as thoughts, feelings, and history of a character or situation.

OBJECTIVES

Students

• identify order of story events

• identify words that signal sequence

• identify when an author shifts from the present action to past events

• learn academic language: **signal words, sequential order**

Practice Book page 4

Earthquake Terror
Graphic Organizer Event Map

Name _____

Event _____

Record in

| Page : |
| At first |
| senses |

| Pages |
| After J |
| walk ba |

| Pages |
| Jonatha |
| thunder |
| caught |

| Page : |
| Abby so |
| Abby. |

| Pages |
| Jonatha |
| he scra |

4 Theme 1: N
Assessment T

Transparency 1–2

NATURE'S FURY Earthquake Terror
Graphic Organizer Event Map

Event Map

Page 30
At first Moose listens. Then he barks and paces back and forth as if he senses

↓

Pages 30–31
After Jonathan puts the leash on Moose, they all slowly start to

↓

Pages 32–33
Jonathan and Abby hear a strange noise. At first Jonathan thinks it is thunder or hunters. Then suddenly he realizes

↓

Page 35
Abby screams and falls. As Jonathan lunges forward, he tries to catch Abby. Then he shouts,

↓

Pages 36–37
Jonathan sees the huge redwood tree sway back and forth. Then

TRANSPARENCY 1–2
TEACHER'S EDITION PAGES 51A AND 51B

Copyright © Houghton Mifflin Company. All rights reserved.

California Standards pp. 51A–51B

R2.2 Use order to analyze text
W2.2.a Demonstrate understanding

▶ Practice

Have students work individually or in small groups to find examples of past and present events on pages 35, 36, 38, 41, and 43. Tell them to also identify words and phrases that signal the time shifts between past and present. Have them record their answers on a chart similar to the one below.

Page	Main Action	Past Event	Words That Signal Time Shift
35	The ground drops away beneath Jonathan's feet.	He practiced earthquake drills in school.	Ever since first grade... That was school. This was Magpie Island.
36	Jonathan scrambles to get away from a falling tree.	He asked his teacher how he'd recognize an earthquake.	that first year

▶ Apply

Use **Practice Book** pages 6–7 to diagnose whether students need Reteaching. Students who do not need Reteaching may work on Challenge/Extension activities, page R9. Students who need easier text to apply the skill can use the **Reader's Library** selection, "Riding Out the Storm," and its Responding activity.

Skill Finder	
• Review, p. 71; Theme 2	• Reteaching, p. R8

Practice Book page 7

Earthquake Terror
Comprehension Skill
Sequence of Events

Name _____

Map...

Write eac...
map belo...

▶ Alison...
▶ Anush...
▶ The r...
▶ Anush...
▶ Alison...

Alison'...	
Anushk...	
Anushk...	
The ra...	
Alison ...	

Now go t...
understa...
▶ when ...
▶ when ...
▶ when a...
▶ wheth...
set of r...

Practice Book page 6

Earthquake Terror
Comprehension Skill
Sequence of Events

Name _____

Mapping the Sequence

Read this passage. Then complete the activity on page 7.

Rapids Ahead!

Alison scanned the river nervously. She had already endured two sets of violent rapids. Each time, she had grasped the ropes of the raft so hard that her knuckles turned white. Luckily, the guide on her raft was strong and skilled. "Relax, Alison," Anushka had smiled when the trip had begun three hours earlier. "Rafting is a blast, once you get the hang of it."

During the first hour on the river, Anushka had taught Alison how to paddle on one side to make the raft go in the opposite direction. She had instructed Alison on what to do if the raft flipped or if she were tossed out. "Don't fight the current," Anushka had said. "Let it carry you downstream as you swim for the shore."

Six months earlier, when Alison's parents had proposed a whitewater rafting trip down the Snake River, Alison said, "No way." Her brother Zack was thrilled, though, so Alison's parents signed all four of them up for a seven-day run. So far, the trip was as bad as Alison had expected.

"Rapids ahead. Hold on!" Anushka said. Alison's stomach knotted as the raft pitched forward with the current. "Paddle left!" Anushka shouted. As Alison's paddle hit the water, the bow of the raft hit a boulder and shot into the air. Alison shut her eyes as icy water drenched her.

When she opened her eyes, Anushka was gone. In a panic, Alison scanned the rapids. "Anushka!" she screamed. Then she saw her. Anushka was making her way to shore, feet first, letting the current do the work. "It's up to me now," Alison said to herself. She paddled left, then right, steering between the rocks. She was amazed that she could control it. Left. Right. Left again. Now Anushka was on the bank, shouting directions over the roar of the river. Alison managed to nose the raft into an eddy and a moment later, onto the shore.

"Great job, Alison!" Anushka grinned. "You really kept your head out there!" Alison beamed. Maybe this trip would be all right after all.

6   Theme 1: **Nature's Fury**

Reaching All Students

Extra Support

• Reteaching, page R8

• **Reader's Library:** *Nature's Fury,* "Riding Out the Storm"

Diagnostic Check

If...	You can...
students need extra help to identify the order of story events	use the Reteaching lesson on page R8.
students have successfully met the lesson objectives	have them do the Challenge/Extension activities on page R9.

Comprehension Skills   51B

Information & Study Skills

✓ *Using Print and Electronic Reference Sources*

▶ Teach

Familiarize students with the variety of available print and electronic information-gathering resources by leading them on a tour of your library media center. Make the following points:

- The library media center contains a variety of tools for finding information.

- Many reference sources, including encyclopedias, dictionaries, thesauruses, and atlases, are available both in print and electronically on CD-ROM.

- A computer with Internet access brings a world of information to users' fingertips.

Print Encyclopedias Display a volume of an encyclopedia and explain that encyclopedias are usually divided into volumes that list subjects alphabetically. To find information on a specific topic, students identify the letters with which the topic begins and look it up in the appropriate volume. Guide words at the top of each page indicate what subjects the page contains. Cross-references list related subjects that may be looked up elsewhere in the encyclopedia. For example, at the end of the information on Indonesia, the encyclopedia may refer students to "Southeast Asia."

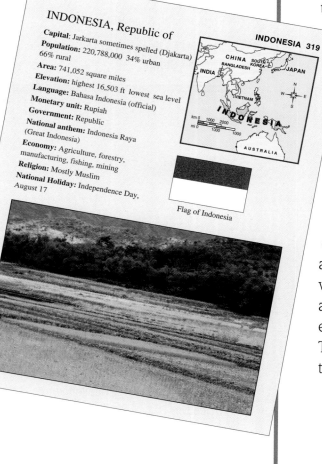

INDONESIA, Republic of

Capital: Jakarta sometimes spelled (Djakarta)
Population: 220,788,000 34% urban 66% rural
Area: 741,052 square miles
Elevation: highest 16,503 ft lowest sea level
Language: Bahasa Indonesia (official)
Monetary unit: Rupiah
Government: Republic
National anthem: Indonesia Raya (Great Indonesia)
Economy: Agriculture, forestry, manufacturing, fishing, mining
Religion: Mostly Muslim
National Holiday: Independence Day, August 17

INDONESIA 319

Flag of Indonesia

Electronic Encyclopedias Tell students that electronic encyclopedias often have a listing of general information categories, such as "Art," "History," and "Science." When students open a category, they will find an alphabetical listing of subcategories. For instance, "Science" might contain "Biology," "Chemistry," and "Meteorology." Explain that they could open "Meteorology" to find information about the subject *weather.* An alternate way for students to locate information about weather is to type the word into the electronic encyclopedia's Search feature. The encyclopedia will display information about weather on the screen.

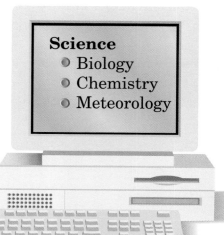

Science
- Biology
- Chemistry
- Meteorology

California Standards pp. 51C–51D

R 2.0 Read/understand grade-level material
W 1.5 Use a thesaurus

Modeling Model selecting a reference source to answer questions.

> **Think Aloud**
>
> *Let's say I want to find out what causes hurricanes. Since an encyclopedia contains general information about a great many topics, I should look up* hurricanes, *either in the* H *volume of a printed encyclopedia or by typing the word* hurricane *into the Search feature of an electronic encyclopedia. If I want to find out about hurricanes that are occurring right now, I'd have better luck searching the Internet, since the Internet contains up-to-the-minute information about current events. If I want a simple definition of the word* hurricane, *or want to know how to pronounce the word, I should look in a print or electronic dictionary.*

▶ Practice

Have pairs of students demonstrate how to use an encyclopedia or other reference source to answer the following questions:

- Where would you find out what a *monsoon* is?

- If you want information on weather instruments, where would you start?

- How would you find information to compare the weather in two different states?

- How could you find out the weather forecast for tomorrow?

▶ Apply

Tell students to use a printed or electronic reference source to find the answer to a question that interests them. Have them share with the class their information and how they located it.

Word Work

Word Work Instruction

DAY 1	• Spelling Pretest • Spelling Instruction
DAY 2	• Structural Analysis Instruction • Spelling Practice
DAY 3	• Phonics Instruction • Spelling Practice
DAY 4	• Structural Analysis Reteaching • Vocabulary Skill Instruction • Spelling Game
DAY 5	• Expanding Your Vocabulary • Spelling Test

OBJECTIVES

Students

- read words that have base words and inflected forms
- read words and syllables that have a short vowel sound
- use the Phonics/Decoding Strategy to decode longer words
- learn academic language: **base word, prefix, suffix**

Decoding Longer Words

✓ Structural Analysis: Base Words

▶ Teach

Write this sentence on the board. Point to the words *crossed* and *connecting.* Explain that each word contains a base word, a word that can stand alone or to which endings and other word parts such as prefixes and suffixes can be added. Identify the base words *cross* and *connect,* and their endings *-ed* and *-ing.*

> He saw the high bridge that <u>crossed</u> the river, connecting the island to the mainland.

Write another sentence: *Jonathan was <u>worried</u> by the way Moose was <u>shaking</u>.* Identify the base words *worry* and *shake* in *worried* and *shaking.* Point out that the spelling of a base word sometimes changes when an ending is added.

Modeling Explain that recognizing base words can help students figure out unfamiliar words. Model how to use the Phonics/Decoding Strategy to identify a base word in the following sentence: *Time seemed to go faster while Jonathan was <u>cataloging</u> his baseball cards.*

Think Aloud

At first I don't recognize the underlined word. I'll try removing the ending -ing. Then I'll try breaking it into syllables. Now I recognize the word catalog, *which means "a book where things are listed." So* cataloging *must mean "putting in a catalog." That makes sense in the sentence.*

▶ Practice

Write this sentence on the board. Have students copy the underlined words and write down the base word and ending for each. *Air <u>whizzed</u> across Jonathan as the tree trunk <u>dropped</u> past, and <u>branches</u> <u>brushed</u> his shoulder.* Then have students work in pairs to find other base words and endings in the selection.

▶ Apply

Have students complete **Practice Book** page 8.

Skill Finder	• Strategy Review: Phonics/Decoding, p. 27A	• Reteaching, p. R14

California Standards pp. 51E–51F

R 1.2 Use word origins
W 2.2 Write responses to literature

Phonics

Spelling Connection

Short Vowels

▶ Teach

Tell students that understanding short vowel sounds can help them use the Phonics/Decoding Strategy to decode the underlined word. Explain:

- Short vowel sounds are usually spelled with a vowel followed by a consonant.

- When a syllable ends with a vowel followed by a consonant, the syllable usually has a short vowel sound.

Modeling Write this sentence and model how to decode *frantically*: _Frantically he crawled to his left, trying to get out of the tree's path._

Think Aloud

I see a short vowel pattern in the first syllable, fran. *The next part could either be* tihk *or* tyk. FRAN tyk *doesn't sound like anything I've heard. Let's try* FRAN tihk. *Oh! I've heard that — frantic. That leaves* -ally. *I've seen that in* finally *and* practically. *So, I'll put all the parts together:* FRAN tihk lee. *I'll read this word in the sentence to see if it makes sense. It does.*

▶ Practice

Write these sentences and have students copy the underlined words:

> The rumbling came from every _direction_; A branch fell and smashed on _impact_; Finding shelter was a _problem_.

Have pairs of students circle the short vowel pattern(s) in each underlined word, pronounce the word, and check to see if it makes sense in the sentence. Call on individuals to model at the board.

▶ Apply

Tell students to decode the following words from *Earthquake Terror* and discuss their meanings: *communication,* page 30; *cataloging,* page 31; *thunderous,* page 35; *inhaled,* page 40; *unsuccessfully,* page 43.

Practice Book page 8

Earthquake Terror
Structural Analysis
Base Words

Name _____

Getting to Base

Read the sentences. For each underlined word, identify the base word. Write the base word and the ending.

Example: shake + -ing

1. Magpie Island was a popular place for <u>hiking</u>. hike + -ing **(1 point)**
2. Jonathan was nervous about staying in such an <u>isolated</u> place. isolate + -ed **(1)**
3. He thought it would be <u>safer</u> to go back to their trailer. safe + -er **(1)**
4. Jonathan and Abby followed the trail past blackberry <u>bushes</u>. bush + -es **(1)**
5. Neither of them had the <u>slightest</u> idea how the day would end. slight + -est **(1)**
6. Moose cocked his head and began <u>sniffing</u>. the ground. sniff + -ing **(1)**
7. At first the earthquake was a <u>thunderous</u> noise in the distance. thunder + -ous **(1)**
8. Trees <u>swayed</u> all around Jonathan and Abby. sway + -ed **(1)**
9. The ground began rising and falling like ocean <u>waves</u>. wave + -s **(1)**
10. Abby <u>cried</u> for Jonathan to come help her. cry + -ed **(1)**

8   Theme 1: **Nature's Fury**
Assessment Tip: Total **10** Points

Phonics/Decoding Strategy

When you come to a word you don't know—

1. Look carefully at the word.

2. Look for word parts you know and think about the sounds for the letters.

3. Blend the sounds to read the word.

4. Ask yourself: Is it a word I know? Does it make sense in what I am reading?

5. If not, ask yourself: What else can I try?

HOUGHTON MIFFLIN
Reading
A Legacy of Literacy

Diagnostic Check

If...	You can...
students need help reading words with base words	use the Reteaching lesson on page R14.

Decoding Longer Words

Word Work

Students write spelling words with short vowel patterns.

Spelling Words

Basic Words

bunk	fond
staff	crush*
dock	grasp*
slept*	dwell
mist	fund
bunch	ditch
swift	split
stuck	swept
breath	deaf
tough	rough

Review Words	Challenge Words
trunk*	trek
skill	frantic*
track	summit
fresh	rustic
odd	mascot

Forms of these words appear in the literature.

Reaching All Students

Extra Support

Basic Word List You may want to use only the left column of Basic Words with students who need extra support.

Spelling

 *Short Vowels*

Day 1   Teaching the Principle

Pretest Use the Day 5 Test sentences. Say each underlined word, read the sentence, and then repeat the word. Have students write only the underlined word.

Teach Write *staff, slept, mist, dock, bunk, breath,* and *tough* on the board. Say each word and have students repeat it. Point to each word, say it, and ask students to name its vowel sound. Underline the single vowel in *staff, slept, mist, dock,* and *bunk* and explain that a short vowel sound is usually spelled by a single vowel and followed by a consonant sound. Then underline the *ea* in *breath* and point out that this is a less common spelling pattern for the short *e* sound. Underline the *ou* in *tough* and explain that this is a less common spelling pattern for the short *u* sound.

Erase the board. Write these symbols on it as column heads: /ă/, /ĕ/, /ĭ/, /ŏ/, and /ŭ/. Point to each symbol and ask students to identify the sound it represents. Then say each Basic Word and ask a student to name its vowel sound. Write the word below the appropriate phonetic symbol.

Practice/Homework Assign **Practice Book** page 407. Tell students to use this Take-Home Word List to study the words they missed on the Pretest.

Day 2   Reviewing the Principle

Practice/Homework Review the spelling principle and assign **Practice Book** page 9.

Day 3   Vocabulary

Definitions Assign a different Basic Word to each student. Tell them to take turns looking up their assigned word's meaning in a dictionary. Then list each Basic Word on the board and ask the appropriate student to add the word's meaning.

Next, have students use each Basic Word from the board orally in a sentence.

Practice/Homework For spelling practice, assign **Practice Book** page 10.

Day 4 W**O**RD HUNT

Have students do a word hunt. Set a time limit of 5–10 minutes and provide books, magazines, and newspapers. Then have students form small groups and follow these steps:

■ Each student hunts for words with short vowel patterns and lists the words.

■ When time is called, each group meets to pool and record its words.

■ Each group makes certain that all words have short vowel patterns.

■ The groups save words that do not have short vowel patterns in a special list.

Select students to list each group's words on the board or on a chart. Give a prize for the most words with short vowel spelling patterns.

Practice/Homework For proofreading and writing practice, assign **Practice Book** page 11.

Day 5 Spelling Assessment

Test Say each underlined word, read the sentence, and then repeat the word. Have students write only the underlined word.

Basic Words

1. I will sleep on the top <u>bunk</u>.

2. The <u>staff</u> welcomed the new campers.

3. The boat was left at the <u>dock</u>.

4. Have you ever <u>slept</u> in a tent?

5. The <u>mist</u> changed to rain.

6. Ann picked a <u>bunch</u> of flowers.

7. The <u>swift</u> runner won the race.

8. The car is <u>stuck</u> in the mud.

9. I took a <u>breath</u> of air.

10. Outdoor clothing must be <u>tough</u>.

11. Maria is <u>fond</u> of her dog.

12. Do not <u>crush</u> the bug with your foot.

13. Please <u>grasp</u> the rope tightly.

14. Do bears <u>dwell</u> in your state?

15. Is there any money in the birthday <u>fund</u>?

16. The car slid into the <u>ditch</u>.

17. Can we <u>split</u> that sandwich in two?

18. He <u>swept</u> the floor with a broom.

19. The <u>deaf</u> cat cannot hear the bell.

20. Today the sea is too <u>rough</u> for sailing.

Challenge Words

21. Our hike turned into a long <u>trek</u>.

22. The dog had a <u>frantic</u> look in its eyes.

23. We saw the sunset from the <u>summit</u>.

24. The <u>rustic</u> house was built from wood.

25. The <u>mascot</u> attends every game.

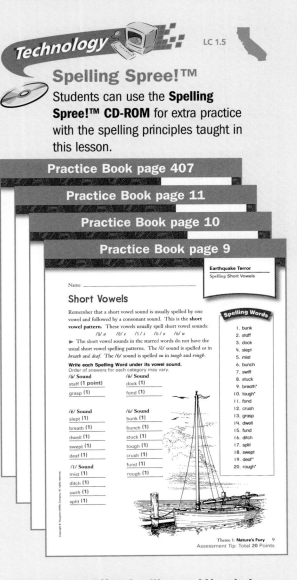

Technology LC 1.5

Spelling Spree!™
Students can use the **Spelling Spree!™ CD-ROM** for extra practice with the spelling principles taught in this lesson.

Practice Book page 407
Practice Book page 11
Practice Book page 10
Practice Book page 9

Houghton Mifflin Spelling and Vocabulary
Correlated instruction and practice, pp. 12, 26

Reaching All Students
UNIVERSAL ACCESS
Challenge

Challenge Word Practice Students can use the Challenge Words to create crossword puzzles. Have them draw the puzzle, write clues, and trade with a partner.

R 1.3
W 1.5

Vocabulary Skills

✓ Using a Thesaurus

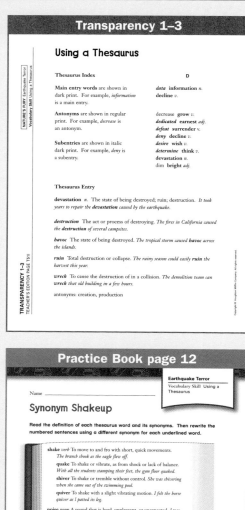

Transparency 1–3

Using a Thesaurus

Thesaurus Index　　　　　D

Main entry words are shown in dark print. For example, *information* is a main entry.

data **information** *n.*
decline *v.*

Antonyms are shown in regular print. For example, *decrease* is an antonym.

decrease **grow** *v.*
dedicated **earnest** *adj.*
defeat **surrender** *v.*
deny **decline** *v.*

Subentries are shown in italic dark print. For example, *deny* is a subentry.

desire **wish** *v.*
determine **think** *v.*
devastation *n.*
dim **bright** *adj.*

Thesaurus Entry

devastation *n.* The state of being destroyed; ruin; destruction. *It took years to repair the devastation caused by the earthquake.*

destruction The act or process of destroying. *The fires in California caused the destruction of several campsites.*

havoc The state of being destroyed. *The tropical storm caused havoc across the islands.*

ruin Total destruction or collapse. *The rainy season could easily ruin the harvest this year.*

wreck To cause the destruction of in a collision. *The demolition team can wreck that old building in a few hours.*

antonyms: creation, production

Practice Book page 12

Synonym Shakeup

Read the definition of each thesaurus word and its synonyms. Then rewrite the numbered sentences using a different synonym for each underlined word.

shake *verb* To move to and fro with short, quick movements. *The branch shook as the eagle flew off.*
quake To shake or vibrate, as from shock or lack of balance. *With all the students stamping their feet, the gym floor quaked.*
shiver To shake or tremble without control. *She was shivering when she came out of the swimming pool.*
quiver To shake with a slight vibrating motion. *I felt the horse quiver as I patted its leg.*

noise *noun* A sound that is loud, unpleasant, or unexpected. *I was awakened by a noise in the alley.*
crash A loud noise, as of a sudden impact or collapse. *They heard a crash of thunder.*
racket A loud, unpleasant noise. *The students made a racket while tuning their instruments.*
thud A heavy, dull sound. *Jeff dropped his books with a thud.*

1. Soon after the ground began to <u>shake</u>, the children heard the <u>noise</u> of a deer leaping from the bushes.
   Soon after the ground began to quake, the children heard the crash of a deer leaping from the bushes. **(4 points)**
2. Jonathan began to <u>shake</u> from cold and fear, listening to the <u>noise</u> of the crows.
   Jonathan began to shiver from cold and fear, listening to the racket of the crows. **(4)**
3. Abby's lip began to <u>shake</u> as she heard the <u>noise</u> of running footsteps.
   Abby's lip began to quiver as she heard the thud of running footsteps. **(4)**

12　Theme 1: **Nature's Fury**
Assessment Tip: Total **12** Points

▶ Teach

Explain to students that a thesaurus is a reference tool that helps writers make their writing clearer and more interesting. It is used to find a word to replace an overused word or to find a word with a more precise meaning.

Explain that a thesaurus lists synonyms (words with similar meanings) and antonyms (words with opposite meanings). It may list words alphabetically, or it may have an index to direct users to more information. Display the top of **Transparency 1–3** and explain that this is part of an index for the second type of thesaurus. Help students identify the main entry words, subentry words, and antonyms.

Then uncover the rest of the transparency. Point to and describe these features of a main entry:

- **Main entry words** are in alphabetical order.

- Each main entry word is followed by the **part of speech**, a **definition**, and a **sample sentence.**

- Several subentry words that could be used in place of the main entry word are given, with a definition and sample sentence for each one.

Write the following sentence on the board: *He remembered magazine pictures of terrible <u>devastation</u> from earthquakes.*

Modeling Model using a thesaurus to find synonyms for *devastation*.

💭 Think Aloud

I have looked up devastation *in the index of my thesaurus. I find that it is a main entry word. I find several subentries with similar meanings, including* destruction, havoc, ruin, *and* wreck.

Explain that all the synonyms for *devastation* have slightly different meanings and it is important to check their definitions before choosing a replacement. Discuss the shades of meaning in *destruction, havoc, ruin,* and *wreck.*

California Standards pp. 51I–51J

R 1.3 Understand synonyms/antonyms	**W 1.5** Use a thesaurus
R 1.4 Use roots and affixes	**LC 1.5** Spell correctly

► Practice

Have students work in groups to use a thesaurus to look up the following words and their synonyms: *evaporating, engrossed, cataloging.* Ask students to rewrite the sentence below using the synonyms they have found.

> *Time had a way of evaporating instantly when he was engrossed in an interesting project, such as cataloging his baseball cards, or reading a good mystery.*

Have them check the exact meanings of the synonyms they chose for their rewrites.

► Apply

Have students complete **Practice Book** page 12.

Expanding Your Vocabulary
Scientific Terms: Geology Words

Explain that *geologists* are scientists who study the earth and the structure of its crust. They use specialized terms to identify and describe features, processes, equipment, and concepts related to their field of expertise. Then begin a word web that shows the technical vocabulary related to earthquakes, similar to the following:

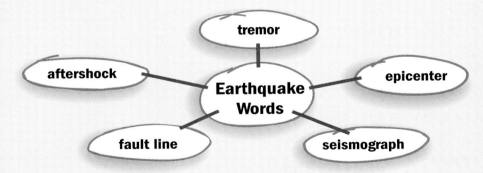

Have students work with partners to find additional earthquake words, along with their meanings. Add the additional words to the word web.

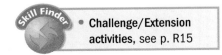

Skill Finder
• Challenge/Extension activities, see p. R15

📎 Teacher's Note

Word Histories Explain that the prefix *seismo-* comes from a Greek word that means "shaking; earthquake." Then ask students to give the meanings of the bold-faced words below. As needed, supply the hints provided.

R 1.4

seismology Think of *biology,* "the science or study of living things."
("the study of earthquakes")

seismologist Think of *geologist,* "a scientist who studies the earth."
("a scientist who studies earthquakes")

seismogram Think of *telegram,* "a message or record made by a telegraph."
("the record of an earthquake")

···· **Houghton Mifflin Spelling and Vocabulary** ····
Correlated instruction and practice, pp. 22, 28

Reaching All Students

English Language Learners

W 1.5

Thesaurus

Show a thesaurus. Write and say the word; have students repeat after you. Talk about how this reference tool is organized and how it is helpful. Work with students in a group, or pair English language learners with English speakers to help them determine nuances in meaning.

Writing & Language

Writing & Language

Writing and Language Instruction

DAY 1	• Daily Language Practice • Grammar Instruction • Journal Writing
DAY 2	• Daily Language Practice • Writing a News Article • Journal Writing • Grammar Practice
DAY 3	• Daily Language Practice • Grammar Instruction • Writing an Adventure Story
DAY 4	• Daily Language Practice • Listening/Speaking/Viewing • Writing: Improving Your Writing • Grammar Practice
DAY 5	• Daily Language Practice • Grammar: Improving Your Writing

OBJECTIVES

Students

• identify the four kinds of sentences

• identify complete and simple subjects and complete and simple predicates

• proofread and correct sentences with grammar and spelling errors

• combine subjects and combine predicates to improve writing

• learn academic language: **declarative, interrogative, imperative, exclamatory**

Technology

Wacky Web Tales

Students may use the **Wacky Web Tales** floppy disk to create humorous stories and review parts of speech.

Grammar Skills

✓ *Kinds of Sentences; Subjects and Predicates*

Day 1   Kinds of Sentences

Display the first four sentences on **Transparency 1–5**.

> An earthquake can be very dangerous.
> Have you ever felt the ground move?
> Stay calm during an earthquake.
> What a scary feeling that must be!

Identify each sentence type. (declarative, interrogative, imperative, exclamatory) Go over the following definitions and rules with students:

■ A declarative sentence tells something. It ends with a period.

■ An interrogative sentence asks a question. It ends with a question mark.

■ An imperative sentence gives a request or an order. It usually ends with a period.

■ An exclamatory sentence expresses strong feeling. It ends with an exclamation mark.

Ask students to look at *Earthquake Terror* to find examples of the different types of sentences and to share the examples they've found. Tell students to write down, on a separate sheet of paper, the sentence type for each of the remaining sentences on **Transparency 1–5**.

Day 2

Practice/Homework Assign **Practice Book** page 13.

Day 3   Subjects and Predicates

Display the first sentence on **Transparency 1–6**.

> *The earthquake caused a great deal of damage.*

Draw a line between *earthquake* and *caused.* Explain to students that the first part of the sentence is the subject and the second part of the sentence is the predicate.

California Standards pp. 51K–51L

LC 1.1 Sentence structure/transition

Day 3 *continued...*

Go over these rules and definitions with students:

- The subject tells whom or what the sentence is about.

- The predicate tells what the subject is or does.

- The complete subject includes all the words in the subject. The simple subject includes just the main word or words.

- The complete predicate includes all the words in the predicate. The simple predicate includes just the main word or words.

Using the sentence on the board, point out the complete subject (The earthquake) and the simple subject (earthquake), and the complete predicate (caused a great deal of damage) and the simple predicate (caused). Have students identify the complete and simple subjects and complete and simple predicates in the rest of the sentences on **Transparency 1–6.**

Day 4

Practice/Homework Assign **Practice Book** page 14.

Day 5 — Improving Your Writing

Sentence Combining: Compound Subjects and Compound Predicates

Tell students that a good writer avoids using too many short, choppy sentences. Model combining subjects and combining predicates:

Combining Subjects to Form a Compound Subject

Jonathan saw the high bridge.	Improved: <u>Jonathan and Abby</u>
Abby saw the high bridge.	saw the high bridge.

Combining Predicates to Form a Compound Predicate

The bridge crossed the river.	Improved: The bridge <u>crossed</u>
The bridge connected the	<u>the river and connected the</u>
island to the mainland.	<u>island to the mainland</u>.

Have students review a piece of their own writing to see if they can improve it by combining sentences.

Practice/Homework Assign **Practice Book** page 15.

Practice Book page 15
Practice Book page 14
Practice Book page 13

Transparency 1–6
Transparency 1–5
Transparency 1–4

Daily Language Practice

Correct two sentences each day.

1. Did you tie the boat to the doct
2. take a deep breeth before you begin.
3. The mayor will set up a fuhnd for the flood victims!
4. watch out for that dich!
5. The two boys sleept until noon?
6. Who swepped the leaves under the fence.
7. Be careful not to cresh your fingers in the car door?
8. Justin and amanda shared a buhch of bananas.
9. Did the staf tell you when your puppy could come home
10. is she fonde of chocolate chip cookies?

Daily Language Practice

·········· **Houghton Mifflin English** ··········

Correlated instruction and practice, pp. 32–41, 68

Diagnostic Check

If...	➤ You can ...
students need extra help with kinds of sentences or subjects and predicates	use the Reteaching lessons on pages R20 and R21.

W 1.2.a
W 1.2.b

Students

- identify the characteristics of a news article
- write a news article
- add details to improve their writing

Transparency 1–8

Adding Details

Transparency 1–7

A News Article

The Dog Days of Summer

When Roberto Garrigues and Robin Foster became firefighters, little did they know what creative thinking skills they would be called upon to use. For on October 11, a small puppy managed to fall into a storm drain on Main Street. How the puppy got into the drainpipe is not clear. It was even less clear how to get it out. But Roberto and Robin were assigned to solve the problem, and solve it they did.

The pipe was too small for either firefighter to crawl into. Likewise, the puppy wouldn't come when it was called, so the firefighters could not lift a storm grate and grab the puppy from above as it approached. Finally, Robin had an idea. "I realized that if we cut a puppy-sized hole in the side of the pipe," she said, "the dog would probably come out on its own." The clever solution worked. With the added incentive of a bowl of puppy food near the hole, the hungry puppy eventually poked its head out, and the firefighters grabbed it.

Within an hour, the puppy was reunited with its grateful owner. "I didn't even know Tornado was missing," said owner Jerry Emerson of his aptly named pup, who had just caused a whirlwind of trouble. "Somehow Tornado must have slipped out when I was carrying in my groceries. I'm certainly glad he had a dog license, so he could be quickly returned. And I'll be forever grateful to the firefighters for their ingenious rescue."

Writing Skills

A News Article

▶ Teach

Explain to students that a powerful earthquake such as the one Jonathan, Abby, and Moose experienced in the woods is a very newsworthy event. Because Jonathan had a unique perspective on the earthquake, a news article based on Jonathan's eyewitness account would indeed be a "scoop."

▶ Practice

Display **Transparency 1–7.** Have students read the news article. Ask:

- What is the news article about? (the rescue of a puppy)

- What basic facts are given in the first paragraph that answer the questions Who?, What?, When?, Where?, Why?, and How?

Who?	What?	When?	Where?	Why?	How?
firefighters, puppy	rescue of a trapped puppy	October 11	storm drain on Main St.	puppy fell into drain opening	firefighters cut into drain pipe

- Did the beginning of the article capture your interest? Why or why not?

- What kinds of information are found in the other paragraphs?

- Did the headline grab your attention? Why or why not?

Discuss with students the guidelines for writing a news article.

Guidelines for
Writing a News Article

- Write a beginning that captures the reader's attention.
- Use facts to answer Who?, What?, When?, Where? Why?, How?
- Write the most important facts at the beginning of the article.
- Use quotations to make the article come alive.
- Write a short, attention-grabbing headline for the article.

California Standards pp. 51M–51N

W 1.2.a Establish topic, order
W 1.2.b Use details, transitions
W 1.6   Edit and revise work

▶ Apply

Have students write a news article about an interesting or unusual event at school, in their neighborhood, or in their town. Remind students to focus on the five *Ws* and *How.* Students can use **Practice Book** page 16 to help plan and organize their news articles. Remind students that a news article should contain only facts, not opinions. Have them check their facts and write quotations exactly. Collect articles into a class newspaper.

Improving Your Writing
Adding Details

W 1.6

Teach Discuss with students the fact that a news article's purpose is to inform. Point out that specific details are included in a news article in order to hold the reader's interest, to give a clearer picture of what took place, and to make the people involved in the event real to the reader.

Practice To model how to add specific details to improve a draft news article, display **Transparency 1–8.**

Ask volunteers to underline any new details added to the original passage. (Jonathan and Abby Palmer, on a camping trip, fallen redwood, during yesterday's quake) Help students understand that each detail was added to the original passage to satisfy the reader's curiosity about who was involved in the event, when and where it took place, what caused it, and how it occurred. Remind students that people who write news articles have a responsibility not to misinform the reader by including inaccurate details or opinions rather than facts.

Apply Assign **Practice Book** page 17. Then have students review their news articles and add details where needed to improve their writing.

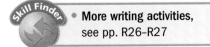

• More writing activities, see pp. R26–R27

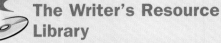

The Writer's Resource Library

Students may use this set of reference tools as they work on their own writing.
©*Sunburst Technology Corporation, a Houghton Mifflin Company. All Rights Reserved.*

Type to Learn™

Students may use **Type to Learn™** to learn proper keyboarding technique.
©*Sunburst Technology Corporation, a Houghton Mifflin Company. All Rights Reserved.*

Portfolio Opportunity

Save students' news articles as samples of their writing development.

Practice Book page 17

Earthquake Terror
Writing Skill Improving Your Writing

Name _____

Addi

A good re
and to bri
article tha
Then rewr
list to imp

A p
campgro
were rep
was dest
Jonathan
quake.
"I y
glad no
Th
debris is

A pow
California
one-hund
mainland
Jonathan
fallen redw
"I wa
sister only
The c
is cleared

Practice Book page 16

Earthquake Terror
Writing Skill News Article

Name _____

Writing a News Article

Jonathan and Abby Palmer experience firsthand an unforgettable event — the terror of an earthquake. Imagine you are a reporter for the *Daily Gazette*. Use the chart below to gather details for a news article about an interesting or unusual event at your school, in your neighborhood, or in your town. Answer these questions: What happened? Who was involved? When, where, and why did this event occur? How did it happen?

Who? (2 points)	
What? (2)	
When? (2)	
Where? (2)	
Why? (2)	
How? (2)	

Now use the details you gathered to write your news article on a separate sheet of paper. Include a headline and a beginning that will capture your reader's attention. Present facts in order of importance, from most to least important. Try to use quotations from eyewitnesses to bring this news event to life. (3)

16   Theme 1: **Nature's Fury**
Assessment Tip: Total 15 Points

•••••••• **Houghton Mifflin English** ••••••••••

Correlated instruction and practice, pp. 430–431

W 2.2.a
W 2.2.b
W 2.2.c
LS 1.4
LS 1.5

OBJECTIVES

Students

- identify the characteristics of a good discussion
- plan and hold a panel discussion

Listening/Speaking/Viewing
Holding a Panel Discussion

► Teach

Ask students what they think a discussion is. Point out that in a discussion two or more people talk about a topic to gain a better understanding of it. Have students brainstorm tips for a good discussion. List their ideas on the chalkboard. Guide students to include the following.

> Stick to the topic of discussion.
> Give reasons for your opinions.
> Listen carefully to what others say.
> Speak clearly.
> Allow others to speak without interrupting them.
> Respect the opinions of others.

Tell students that a panel discussion usually consists of at least three people talking about a topic. One of the people is usually a moderator, who keeps the discussion on track.

Reaching All Students
English Language Learners

LS 1.4
LS 1.5
LS 1.6

Panel Discussion

English language learners will need models and guidance to figure out how to interact with others in a panel discussion. Allow them to observe English speakers to see the panelists' body language and eye contact, how they interrupt and disagree with each other, and what type of language to use. If possible, use video. Later, have small groups discuss their observations.

California Standards pp. 510–51P

W 2.2.a Demonstrate understanding
W 2.2.b Support judgments
W 2.2.c Develop interpretations

LS 1.4 Select focus
LS 1.5 Clarify and support ideas
LS 1.6 Verbal and nonverbal cues

▶ Practice

Tell students that a panel of three students will discuss how Jonathan handled the earthquake emergency. Ask students to find examples from the text that show Jonathan's leadership abilities. Help them to develop a list of the qualities of a good leader. Write their ideas on the chalkboard.

▶ Apply

Now ask for three volunteers to take part in the panel discussion before the class. Ask one of the three to act as moderator to be sure that the panelists follow the tips that they have set up and that they stay with the topic.

Improving Presentation Skills
Speaking to an Audience

LS 1.4
LS 1.5
LS 1.6

- Encourage students to arrange themselves before their audience so that each member of the panel is clearly visible.

- Model how gestures and movements help make a point. Examples:

  You can help! *(Point to audience.)*
  All of you are involved. *(Sweep one arm across audience.)*
  Are we really helpless? *(Shrug.)*

- Demonstrate the way changing volume when you speak alerts the audience to a special point. (Speaking more loudly or more softly will make listeners notice.)

- Tell students to speak more slowly to signal an important point.

Skill Reminder

R 3.3

Compare and Contrast

Remind students that when they compare and contrast, they look for similarities and differences in characters,
places, and events. Have students turn to
page 38 of *Earthquake Terror* and read
the first three paragraphs. Ask them to
describe how Abby and Jonathan's feelings are similar and different.

(Similar: Abby and Jonathan were both
very frightened. Different: Jonathan felt
responsible for Abby's safety, so he tried
to stay calm.)

Taught: *Grade 4, Theme 3*
Reviewed: *Grade 4, Theme 6*

California Standards pp. 51Q–51R

R 1.2   Use word origins
R 3.3   Determine character traits
LC 1.1   Sentence structure/transition
LC 1.2   Verbs, modifiers, pronouns
LC 1.5   Spell correctly

Spiral Review

LC 1.2

Grammar: *Subject, Object, Singular, and Plural Possessive Pronouns*

▶ Review

Remind students that a pronoun is a word that replaces one or more nouns.
Review with students what they have learned about pronouns.

■ Subject pronouns replace the subject of a sentence. For example, *He heard a
noise.*

■ Object pronouns come after action verbs and words such as *to, with, for,* and *at.*
For example, *Jonathan grabbed it. Jonathan wanted to go with them.*

■ Possessive pronouns show ownership and can be singular or plural. For example,
His heart pounded in his chest. Moose is our dog.

Write the pronouns on the board as shown below.

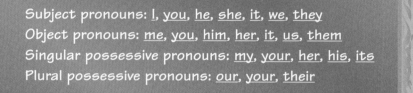

> Subject pronouns: I, you, he, she, it, we, they
> Object pronouns: me, you, him, her, it, us, them
> Singular possessive pronouns: my, your, her, his, its
> Plural possessive pronouns: our, your, their

▶ Apply

Have small groups find sentences in *Earthquake Terror* that contain subject pronouns, object pronouns, singular possessive pronouns, and plural possessive
pronouns. Give each group four sentence strips. Ask students to write four sentences, one sentence for each type of pronoun, on the sentence strips. Have
students underline the pronouns. Then have groups exchange sentence strips
and identify the type of pronoun in each sentence. Have them write their
answers on the other side of each sentence strip.

- **Subject Pronouns** Grade 4, Theme 5, p. 555K; Grade 5, Theme 5, p. 491K-L
- **Object Pronouns** Grade 4, Theme 5, p. 581K; Grade 5, Theme 5, p. 491K-L
- **Singular and Plural Possessive Pronouns** Grade 4, Theme 5, p. 607K; Grade 5,
  Theme 5, p. 519K-L

LC 1.1
LC 1.2

Writing: *Combining Sentences with Subject, Object, and Possessive Pronouns*

▶ Review

Review that writers can use subject, object, and possessive pronouns to combine sentences and make their writing more interesting. The conjunctions *and* and *but* can be used to combine sentences. Write the following example on the board:

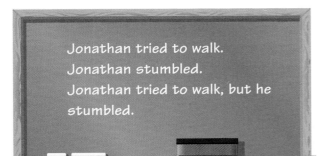

Jonathan tried to walk.
Jonathan stumbled.
Jonathan tried to walk, but he stumbled.

▶ Apply

Have students write two sentences about what a friend or family member does on Saturdays. The first sentence should be about something that person likes to do. The second sentence should be about another thing that person likes to do or about something that person doesn't like to do. Ask students to use the person's name in each sentence. For example: *My friend Jen likes to watch cartoons on Saturday. Jen doesn't like to clean her room.* Have partners exchange sentences. Ask students to combine the sentences on their partner's list with the conjunction *and* or *but* and replace the person's name in the second sentence with a pronoun. Also have students identify any possessive pronouns in the sentences. For example, in the sentence *My friend Jen likes to watch cartoons on Saturday, but she doesn't like to clean her room,* the words *My* and *her* are possessive pronouns. Have students take turns reading their partner's sentences aloud to the class and identifying any possessive pronouns.

Skill Finder

- **Combining Sentences with Pronouns** Grade 4, Theme 5, p. 581N; Grade 5, Theme 5, p. 519N
- **Combining Sentences with Possessive Pronouns** Grade 4, Theme 5, p. 607N

Skill Reminder

R 1.2   LC 1.5
LC 1.2

Base Words, Inflected Forms, and Word Families

Write the word *walked* on the board. Point out that it has the inflected ending *-ed.* Review that in a dictionary they would find *walked* under its base word, *walk.* Circle *walk* and explain that it is the base word for a word family. Make *walk* the center of a word web. Ask students for other words that contain the base word *walk.* Have them look in a dictionary for suggestions. Examples may include *walking, walkie-talkie,* and *walkway.*

Taught: *Grade 4, Theme 4*
Reviewed: *Grade 4, Theme 6*

Reading-Writing Workshop

Description

What Makes a Great Description? Review with students these characteristics of a description.

A description is a picture in words that helps the reader see, hear, taste, smell, or feel something that the writer has experienced.

When you write a description, remember to

- start with a high-interest beginning that grabs the reader's attention

- make crisp and vivid descriptions using sensory language

- provide details in a meaningful order

- use complete sentences

- conclude the description in a satisfying manner

Have students read the Student Writing Model. Then discuss with them what the student writer did to make her writing interesting to read.

A Description

A description is a picture in words that helps the reader share the writer's experience. Use this student's writing as a model when you write a description of your own.

By the Sea

> The **beginning** tells what the description is about.

My grandfather has an apartment that we visit every summer for a few days. My favorite place is a beach where my family goes to play and walk along the shore.

> **Imagery** lets readers visualize how something looks, sounds, smells, tastes, and feels.

When the weather is nice, the sky is blue and the clouds are pure white. The ocean is greenish blue and when the waves crash, the foam is white. Along the water's edge, there are clam shells, crabs, baby shrimp, and once my brother found a starfish! The seagulls walk around like scavengers, looking for clams and crabs to eat. Sometimes I feel like a seagull, because we are both walking around trying to find something special. The seaweed washes up along the shore. It's green and long, and when it wraps around your leg it is ticklish. When we play in the

> **Similes** give the reader a clear mental picture.

Reading / Writing — Figurative language (R1.5)
Establish topic, order (W1.2.a)

52

Skill Finder

Theme Writing Skills

- **Adding Details**, p. 51N
- **Capitalizing and Punctuating Sentences**, p. 81N
- **Correcting Sentence Fragments**, p. 105N

LC 1.4

Theme Grammar Skills

- **Combining Sentences**, p. 51L
- **Correcting Run-on Sentences**, p. 81L
- **Using Exact Nouns**, p. 105L

California Standards pp. 52–53

R 2.4 Inferences/generalizations
R 3.1 Analyze literary forms
W 1.2 Create an exposition

LC 1.1 Sentence structure/transition
LC 1.4 Use correct capitalization
LC 1.5 Spell correctly

water, we are always careful of the jellyfish. Some are red and some are clear, but they all sting.

When the weather is cloudy and stormy, the skies are gray and the waves crash along the shore. It sounds like thunder or like a roaring lion. We don't walk along the shore during a storm, but we can watch from the boardwalk.

The prettiest part of the day is when the sun sets over the bay. It seems as if every time we look up, the colors in the sky change. At first, there is pink, blue, and some green. Then the colors darken to red, orange, blue-gray, and purple. Finally the sky goes dark blue and the sun sets.

I love my grandfather's beach house!

> A good description puts **details** in time order, in spatial order, or in order of importance.

> A good **ending** wraps up the description.

Meet the Author

Dena S.
Grade: five
State: New York
Hobbies: ice skating, singing, and basketball
What she'd like to be when she grows up: a singer

Writing — Use details, transitions (W1.2.b)
Conclude with a summary (W1.2.c)

53

Reading as a Writer
R 2.4

1. What scene does this writer paint a description of? (the beach near her grandfather's apartment)

2. Which of the five senses does the writer focus most on: sight? hearing? taste? touch? smell? Give some examples of this sense. (Answers will vary. Most students will say sight is emphasized most. Examples: blue sky, pure white clouds, greenish blue ocean, white foam)

3. What is the single most vivid feeling that you get from reading this description? (Answers will vary. Typical response: the "ticklish" feel of the seaweed)

4. How does the writer sum up her description at the end? (She says she loves her grandfather's beach house.)

Skill Finder

LC 1.5

Theme Spelling Skills
- Short Vowels, p. 51G
- The / ā /,/ ē /,/ ī / Sounds, p. 81G
- The / ō /,/ o͞o /,/ yo͞o / Sounds, p. 105G

Workshop Focus Skills
- Using Sensory Language, p. 53C
- Organizing Details, p. 53D
- Writing Complete Sentences, p. 53E
- Frequently Misspelled Words, p. 53F

LC 1.1

Description, continued

Houghton Mifflin English

Correlated instruction and practice, pp. 9–27

Technology

Type to Learn™

Students may use **Type to Learn™** to learn proper keyboarding technique.

©Sunburst Technology Corporation, a Houghton Mifflin Company. All Rights Reserved.

The Writer's Resource Library

Students may use this set of reference tools as they work on their own writing.

©Sunburst Technology Corporation, a Houghton Mifflin Company. All Rights Reserved.

Choosing a Topic

W 1.2.a
W 1.2.b
W 1.2.c

Tell students they are going to write their own description of a person, place, or thing that they know about. Have students answer these questions, either in a writing journal or on a sheet of paper:

■ Whom do you see as your audience: classmates? friends? people who share your enthusiasm for your topic?

■ What is your purpose for writing: to inform people about an important matter? to explain your point of view? to entertain? to persuade?

■ How will you publish your description: on the Internet? in a live reading? in a letter that you will send?

Have students generate three or more ideas for descriptions that they could write. Offer the following prompts if students are having trouble getting started.

■ Where would you take a visitor from another country who wanted to learn what your community was like? Is it something you could describe?

■ What person do you admire the most in the world?

■ What is the most amazing new thing that you have seen lately?

Have students work with a partner or in small groups to decide which topic would be the best one to write about.

Tips for
Getting Started

- Browse through magazines for articles about interesting people, places, and ideas.
- Surf the Internet to find web sites about interesting people, places, or things.
- Ask friends to describe the most exciting thing they've done lately.
- Imagine a filmmaker wants to make a documentary film of your topic. How would the filmmaker begin the film? What would be shown on the screen in the film's first scene?

California Standards pp. 53A–53B

W 1.2.a Establish topic, order
W 1.2.b Use details, transitions
W 1.2.c Conclude with a summary

Organizing and Planning

W 1.2.a
W 1.2.b

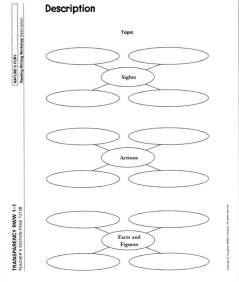

Remind students that good descriptions use colorful language and sharp imagery to paint a vivid picture of the person, place, or thing that they describe. Go over these tips for organizing a description.

- Focus on the "big picture" first, giving a general impression of your topic. Then move on to details that support your general impression.

- Delete any details, no matter how interesting, that are not directly related to your topic.

- Function as your reader's eyes and ears. Record sights, sounds, impressions, sensations, and other sensory information to help the reader visualize the scene.

Display **Transparency RWW1–1**. Show how to describe any topic—person, place, or thing—in terms of its sights (physical appearance), actions (activities, behavior, etc.), and facts and figures (relevant data). Model describing someone or something familiar to students.

Distribute copies of Transparency RWW1–1 for students to use to plan their descriptions.

Tips for
Organizing a Description

- Picture what you are going to describe.
- Make a list of your topic's key features.
- Record sights, sounds, and other sensations that are associated with your topic.

Description, *continued*

R 1.5
R 3.5

Focus Skill

Using Sensory Language

Tell students that a good writer uses sensory language to communicate sights, sounds, feelings, tastes, and smells to readers. Review these features and characteristics of sensory language.

- Sensory language includes any descriptions that appeal to the senses, including words that describe such things as color, speed, texture, sweetness and tartness, fragrance, melody, and so on. Good writers strive to make their descriptions as vivid as possible.

- Use sensory language to help readers get a first-hand experience of what is being described.

- Sensory words create a sharp picture in the reader's mind.

- Use comparisons to heighten the intensity of sensory language. For example, *the duck's feathers were as white as snow.* Or: *My uncle's cheeks were rough, like sandpaper.*

Display **Transparency RWW1–2**, and read the first phrase aloud. Go over the sample response. Then ask the students to come up with their own sensory words that might describe a bouquet of flowers. Have them write a sentence that uses these words. Then instruct students to complete the page on a sheet of paper in a similar manner. Encourage students to use sensory language in their own writing whenever it is appropriate.

Transparency RWW1–2

Using Sensory Language

NATURE'S FURY
Reading-Writing Workshop Using Sensory Language

1. a bouquet of flowers
   Sensory words: pink, fragrant, brilliant, yellow, just-picked
   Sentence: She gave me a just-picked bouquet of brilliant pink and yellow flowers.

2. a swamp
   Sensory words:
   Sentence:

3. a party
   Sensory words:

   Sentence:

4. a Social Studies test
   Sensory words:
   Sentence:

5. a rodeo rider on a bull
   Sensory words:
   Sentence:

TRANSPARENCY RWW 1-2
TEACHER'S EDITION PAGE T273C

Tips for
Using Sensory Language

- List sensory words that are linked to your topic. Think of words that bring to mind tastes, smells, sights, sounds, and feelings.
- Make vivid comparisons using sensory language so the reader can relate to what you're describing.

California Standards pp. 53C–53D

R 1.5 Figurative language
R 3.5 Describe literary devices
W 1.2.a Establish topic, order

W 1.2.b Use details, transitions

Organizing Details

W 1.2.a
W 1.2.b

Remind students that good writers take special care in organizing the details that they use. Review these points for organizing details.

- List your details before you order them. Include only relevant details. If a detail doesn't add to your main point in some way, then leave it out.

- Before choosing an organization scheme, take a moment to consider the main point of what you are trying to communicate. Choose a scheme that suits your purpose.

- Organization schemes can be by order of importance, size, position, and so on.

Display **Transparency RWW1–3**. Go over the first exercise. Have students suggest possible orders. Point out that these exercises are open-ended with no single correct order. Have students give reasons to justify each order they choose.

Instruct students to complete Transparency RWW1–3 on a sheet of paper. Discuss how students can use the strategies presented here in the descriptions that they will write.

Tips for
Organizing Details

- Determine exactly what you are trying to communicate.
- Choose an order that suits your purpose.
- Organize according to such characteristics as importance, size, position, number, color, and so on.

Transparency RWW1–3

Organizing Details

1. Topic: The Big Hockey Game
   a. how long the game lasted
   b. who scored goals in the game
   c. the final score of the game
   d. a player who got injured
   e. when the next game will be played
   f. who scored the winning goal

   Order: _____

   Why I ordered it this way:
   _____

2. Topic: Uncle Daniel
   a. always cracking jokes
   b. once played a joke on my dad
   c. my favorite uncle
   d. introduced me to jazz
   e. married to my dad's older sister
   f. plays the jazz clarinet

   Order: _____

   Why I ordered it this way:
   _____

NATURE'S FURY
Reading-Writing Workshop Organizing Details

TRANSPARENCY RWW 1–3
TEACHER'S EDITION PAGE T273D

Reading-Writing Workshop

Description, *continued*

Practice Book page 19

Practice Book page 18

Transparency RWW1–4

Writing Complete Sentences

1. My family saw the new movie *President Pooch.*
2. A brown and white beagle named Looie.
   Looie is a brown and white beagle.
3. Looie, the President of the United States.

4. Runs all over the White House.

5. Most of the people.

6. The angry vice president and Congress.

7. The scrappy and smart pooch.

8. Slowly shows his marvelous talents.

9. In the end, the great dog-president.

Revising

Once students have finished their drafts, have them evaluate them, using Revising Your Description on **Practice Book** page 18.

Students may want to evaluate their drafts with a partner in a Writing Conference. Once students have evaluated and discussed their drafts, have them go back and revise any parts they feel still need work.

Improving Your Writing
GRAMMAR LINK ▶ Writing Complete Sentences

Tell students that good writers use complete sentences. Review the characteristics of a complete sentence:

- A complete sentence must express a complete thought and have a *subject* and a *predicate*.

- The *subject* is the person, place, or thing that the sentence is about. Example: The big dog ate dinner. (subject: The big dog)

- The *predicate* contains the verb, or action word, and the words that go with the verb, such as the object. Example: The big dog ate dinner. (predicate: ate dinner)

Model writing complete sentences for students, using **Transparency RWW1–4.** Read the first two sentences aloud. Show that the first sentence is complete because it has both a subject (My family) and a predicate (saw the new movie *President Pooch*). Then show that the second sentence is not complete because it does not have a subject. Read the suggested answer. Have students suggest other acceptable answers. Have students complete the remaining sentences.

Assign **Practice Book** page 19. After completing their Practice Book page, encourage students to examine their own descriptions to make sure that they use only complete sentences.

California Standards pp. 53E–53F

W 1.6 Edit and revise work
LC 1.4 Use correct capitalization
LC 1.5 Spell correctly

Proofreading

W 1.6
LC 1.4

Have students proofread their papers carefully to correct any capitalization, punctuation, and spelling errors. Students can use the chart on **Practice Book** page 432 to help them with their proofreading marks.

Practice Book

Spelling Practice: pp. 20–22
Take-Home Word List: p. 407

5-Day Spelling Plan

See p. 51G

Improving Your Writing

Spelling Connection Frequently Misspelled Words

Write the Spelling Words on the board or distribute the Take-Home Word List on **Practice Book** page 407. Read the words aloud, and have students repeat them. Help students identify the part of the word likely to be misspelled.

Spelling Assessment

Pretest

1. I can never do <u>enough</u> hiking.
2. I <u>caught</u> poison ivy on a hike.
3. I <u>brought</u> medicine on the hike.
4. I <u>thought</u> I might have to go home.
5. I put cream on <u>every</u> two hours.
6. Sometimes, I only waited <u>ninety</u> minutes.
7. I used <u>their</u> shower to clean up.
8. <u>They're</u> afraid of bears.
9. <u>There</u> are some bears up here.
10. If you're careful, <u>there's</u> nothing to be afraid of.
11. I <u>know</u> the best hikes in the county.
12. I <u>knew</u> someone who hiked across the state.
13. At six <u>o'clock</u> we turned for home.
14. <u>We're</u> not worried about bears.
15. Bears generally leave <u>people</u> alone.

Test: Use the Pretest sentences.

Challenge Words

16. A <u>decent</u>-sized hike lasts four hours.
17. I even bought some hiking <u>stationery</u>.
18. When I can't hike I ride a <u>stationary</u> bike.
19. I <u>correspond</u> with other hikers on the Internet.
20. Remember to wear a <u>reversible</u>, waterproof jacket.

Challenge Word Practice

Have students use the Challenge Words to write an advertisement for a hiking equipment store.

Spelling Words

LC 1.5

enough	knew
caught	o'clock
brought	we're
thought	people
every	
ninety	**Challenge Words**
their	
they're	decent
there	stationery
there's	stationary
know	correspond
	reversible

Reading-Writing Workshop

Description,
continued

Publishing and Evaluating

Have students make a final copy of their descriptions. Have them look back at the publishing ideas they noted while choosing a topic. Tell them to decide if that's still the way they want to share their writing. If students need help deciding how to share their writing, try these ideas:

■ Publish your description in a letter to a friend or relative.

■ Publish your description on a web site on the Internet.

The Scoring Rubric is based on the criteria in this workshop. It reflects the criteria students used in the Revising Your Description on **Practice Book** page 18. A six-point rubric can be found in the **Teacher's Assessment Handbook.**

Portfolio Opportunity

Save students' final copies of their descriptions as examples of the development of their writing skills.

Student Self-Assessment

- What do you think was the strongest part of your description? the weakest part?

- How clear a picture did your description make in your readers' minds?

- How well did you communicate a sense of the person, place, or thing that you were describing?

- What methods of organizing details did you use in your description? How effective were these methods?

- How would you change your description if you were to write it all over again?

Scoring Rubric

4

The description meets all the evaluation criteria. It is vivid and well organized. It uses sensory language in an imaginative way. Details are organized and give the reader a clear picture of the topic. The writer uses complete sentences and a lively writing style. There are almost no usage, mechanics, or spelling errors.

3

The description has strong points, but could be more effective. The writer uses sensory language well in some places. The organization of details needs improvement. Sentence structure is generally good, but there are some incomplete sentences. There are some usage, mechanics, and spelling errors.

2

The work minimally meets the standards for a description. It uses little sensory language. It is confusing and has an inconsistent point of view. The organization of details is unclear. The description has a number of incomplete sentences. There are many usage, mechanics, and spelling errors.

1

The work does not meet the criteria for a description. There is no use of sensory language. Details are few and misleading. There are few complete sentences. Many mistakes interfere with comprehension.

Using Leveled Books

Paperbacks for *Nature's Fury*

Leveled Theme Paperbacks provide varying levels of reading difficulty—Easy, On Level, and Challenge—to meet all students' needs.

Options for Reading
Students may

- begin reading the Theme Paperbacks at the start of the theme, after the class has read the first Anthology selection, or at any point in the theme

- read the books at their levels independently or with appropriate teacher support

- finish an Easy or On Level book before the completion of the theme and move on to the book at the next difficulty level

- move to an easier book if appropriate, based on your observation. If a student is struggling with the Easy book, have that student read the Very Easy Reader's Library book for this theme.

Theme Paperbacks

Easy	**On Level**	**Challenge**

See Cumulative Listing of Leveled Books.

Reader's Library Very Easy

Reader's Library Books offer stories related by skill and topic to the Anthology stories at a difficulty level approximately two grades below grade level.

Reader's Library

Literature Resources

Literature Resources, Grade 5

Easy

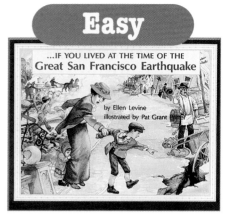

Key Vocabulary

cobblestones, p. 18: rounded stones used for paving streets

terror, p. 25: an extreme, overpowering fear

inspector, p. 50: a person whose job is to carefully review or examine

recover, p. 60: to restore or regain a normal state

committee, p. 63: a group of people brought together for a special purpose

UNIVERSAL ACCESS

If You Lived at the Time of the Great San Francisco Earthquake

by Ellen Levine

▶ Preparing to Read

R 2.4

Building Background Ask students to describe what they know about earthquakes. Be sure they understand that earthquakes are caused by shifts in the earth's crust and can vary greatly in severity. Tell them that this book answers many questions about what happened to people during the 1906 San Francisco earthquake. Remind students to use their reading strategies.

Developing Key Vocabulary Preview with students the meanings of the Key Vocabulary words listed at the left. Also have students pay attention to the many verbs that describe how things looked, sounded, and felt.

▶ Previewing the Text

R 2.1
R 2.4

If You Lived at the Time of the Great San Francisco Earthquake may be read in its entirety or in three segments, pages 4–25, pages 26–45, and pages 46–64. Have students look at the table of contents and the illustrations and ask them what they expect to find out as they read. Remind students to monitor their comprehension as they read.

▶ Supporting the Reading

R 2.5
R 3.7 *pages 4–25*

- Why did many people run outside in their pajamas when the earthquake struck? (Most people had been asleep and quickly ran outside because they were afraid.)

- What steps did Gloria Hansen follow to determine how many people died in the disaster? (First she read the 1906 newspapers, magazines, and official city books. Then she created her own list of the people who had died. Then she sent letters to newspapers, magazines, and clubs to ask if anyone knew someone who had been in the quake.)

California Standards pp. 53I–53J

R 2.1 Understand text features
R 2.4 Inferences/generalizations
R 2.5 Facts, inferences, opinions
R 3.7 Evaluate author's techniques

W 2.2.a Demonstrate understanding

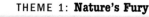

- How does the author help you understand how the earthquake sounded, looked, and felt? (She includes the words of people who were actually there.)

- What words does the author use to describe the sounds and sights? (Sounds: *rumbling, roaring, stampede, thunder, a loud clap, firecrackers;* Sights: *streets splitting open, buildings shook and swayed, cobblestones jumping, treetops touching the ground, ground rolled like ocean waves*)

pages 26–45

- Why do you think the author describes actual attempts to rescue people, property, and animals? (These descriptions give an idea of the events and what being in the earthquake was like; they make the disaster seem more real to the reader.)

- What kinds of things did the people of San Francisco try to save during the earthquake? (Examples: things for sleeping, clothing, pets, household items)

- Describe the kinds of shelters people used after the earthquake. (Be sure students understand the terms *refugee camps, tents, barracks, cottages.*)

pages 46–64

- What kinds of things were sent to help the people of San Francisco after the earthquake? (Examples: money, food, clothing, medicine)

- What caused the fires that burned in the city for three days and nights? (damaged gas pipes, water pipes, and electrical systems; no fire alarms or water)

- What sources of heat did people use for cooking after the earthquake? (stoves, circles of stones, metal garbage cans, cooking shacks)

- What human qualities helped people survive after the earthquake? (sense of humor, sense of helping others, support from around the world)

- Why do you think the author begins each section of the book with a question? (This type of organization helps the reader see the big picture by understanding small parts at a time; it also helps the reader locate specific information.)

▶ Responding

Have students tell whether their predictions were accurate and have them tell how they used reading strategies, such as Monitor/Clarify or Question. Then have students summarize the key ideas of *If You Lived at the Time of the Great San Francisco Earthquake.*

Activity Have students reread the description of what San Francisco looked like after the earthquake, and draw a picture of the image they find most striking or amazing.

W 2.2.a

Reaching All Students

English Language Learners

Be sure students understand the comparisons the author uses to help readers understand what the earthquake felt like, including *an elevator going down fast, sinking, "danced" as she was trying to get dressed, two invisible giants wrestling under the hotel,* and felt *"like corn in a popper."*

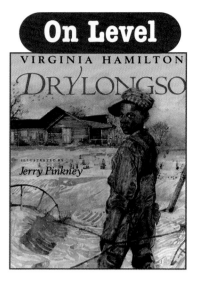

On Level

Drylongso
by Virginia Hamilton

▶ Preparing to Read

R 2.4

Building Background Discuss briefly with students what they know about droughts and explain that this book tells the story of a family trying to farm during a drought. Be sure that students understand the long-term nature of a drought and the damage it can cause. Remind students to use their reading strategies as they read this book.

Developing Key Vocabulary Preview with students the meanings of the Key Vocabulary words listed at the left for each segment of the book, pages 1–28 and pages 29–54.

▶ Previewing the Text

R 2.1
R 2.4

Drylongso may be read in its entirety or in two segments, pages 1–28 and pages 29–54. Encourage students to read the first page and look at the illustrations. Ask them to predict what the story might be about. Explain to students that characters in the story sometimes speak in dialect, or a form of language that is spoken in a particular place or by a particular group of people. For example, Lindy and her father work in his *garden-a-chance* on page 2. Other examples include *drylongso, rain-fella*, and *rag-a-wet*. Encourage students to use context to help them understand how these words and phrases help describe objects, situations, and people in the story.

▶ Supporting the Reading

R 2.5
R 3.7 *pages 1–28*

- Why did the author choose to begin the story with a description of Lindy and her father planting a tomato plant in the dust? (Possible response: to emphasize the dryness of the land and the difficulty the farmers faced, but also their hope and optimism.)

- How long has there been a drought? How does it affect Lindy? (The drought has been going on for three years. It is a part of Lindy's everyday life; she can't even imagine a heavy rain.)

- What happens just before the dust storm to indicate it is approaching? (Lindy

California Standards pp. 53K–53L

R 2.1 Understand text features   W 2.2.a Demonstrate understanding
R 2.4 Inferences/generalizations
R 2.5 Facts, inferences, opinions
R 3.7 Evaluate author's techniques

and her father see the dancing grit, the flock of birds squawking by, and then a sudden quiet. All are clues to an abrupt change in the weather.)

■ What words and phrases does the author use to describe the dryness caused by the drought? (*trail of dust; dirt was fine as powder; dry, packed ground; jumping dirt; grit; brown high wall; bits of dusty ground; misty-dusty; red mist; hazy with a rusty fog*)

■ What reason does Drylongso give about being alone? (He tells Lindy and her family that he got separated from his family during the dust storm.)

pages 29–54

■ When does Lindy's father decide to plant in the streambed? (After Drylongso's dowsing indicates water is present, Lindy's father decides he trusts him enough to plant there.)

■ For people living through a drought, the possibility of finding water is exciting. What words and phrases does the author use to describe water? (*streambed, spring, once-a-stream, flood, faint moisture, a trickling steadying stream, springwater, cross canals, the sweetest water, rain, cloudburst*)

■ What does Drylongso do that makes him seem like a hero? (his survival in the dust storm, his discovery of the dowser, his ability to find water when no one else could)

■ How does Drylongso's departure affect Lindy? (Because she considers him to be like a brother, Lindy misses Drylongso, but she comes to accept that he has to move on and she feels certain that she will meet up with him again.)

■ Why does the author say, "It was as if the forked stick knew there was something underground"? (Possible response: The author wanted to emphasize that it was the stick, rather than Drylongso, that seemed to have a special power.)

▶ Responding

Have students tell whether their predictions were or were not accurate and have them tell how they used the Predict/Infer or Question strategies as they read. Then have students share their reaction to *Drylongso*. Finally, have students summarize the main events of the book. Take this opportunity to observe how well students are using strategies and comprehending the book.

W 2.2.a

UNIVERSAL ACCESS

Reaching All Students

English Language Learners

Be sure students understand the metaphorical reference to the approaching dust storm as "a wall." Discuss the image the author created by describing it in this way. Follow a similar pattern as you point out other figurative language in the selection, including *gravy* (page 2), *whistling in the wind* (page 6), *I'm a baked potato* (page 10), and *plants "grow when your back is turned"* (page 48).

Challenge

Selection Summary

The nonfiction book *Hurricanes: Earth's Mightiest Storms* gives an in-depth look at hurricanes, from the no-name storm that engulfed New England in 1938 to Hurricane Andrew in 1993. The book explains how these powerful storms begin, how scientists have learned to track them, and their devastating effect on the areas they strike.

Key Vocabulary

mooring, p. 7: a place to which a boat or ship can be secured

condense, p. 19: to reduce the volume of

air pressure, p. 20: the amount of air that presses onto the earth's surface

dome, p. 23: a bulge, or rounded extension

cycle, p. 55: a sequence of events that repeats regularly over time

sea level, p. 59: the level at the ocean's surface

UNIVERSAL ACCESS

Hurricanes: Earth's Mightiest Storms
by Patricia Lauber

▶ Preparing to Read

R 2.4 **Building Background** Discuss briefly with students what they know about hurricanes. Tell them that this book describes how hurricanes are formed and traces the paths of several significant hurricanes. Remind students to use their reading strategies as they read this book.

Developing Key Vocabulary Technical terms are introduced with clear explanations in this book. Preview with students the meanings of the Key Vocabulary words listed at the left. Point out the Greek root *meter,* meaning "measure," in the names of the instruments shown on page 26. A *baro<u>meter</u>,* for example, measures air pressure, while a *thermo<u>meter</u>* measures temperature.

▶ Previewing the Text

R 2.1
R 2.4 *Hurricanes: Earth's Mightiest Storms* may be read in its entirety or in two segments, pages 7–27 and pages 28–61. You may have students look at the section titles and photographs and have them make predictions about what each section will describe.

▶ Supporting the Reading

R 2.5
R 3.7 *pages 7–27*

■ Point out that a *breakwater* is land that slows the force of a hurricane. A *storm surge* is a sudden rise in the water level during a hurricane. *Typhoon* and *cyclone* are the names given to hurricanes in some parts of the world.

■ Why were people unprepared for the "monster" storm of September, 1938? (They didn't know the storm was coming. There were no weather satellites at that time, and no ships were near the storm as it was developing.)

■ What is the order in which events happen when conditions are right to start a hurricane? (First, warm, moist air flows into an area of low-pressure. Then the air rises and condenses into clouds. Next, more warm air is drawn in over the ocean. It spirals up in a counterclockwise direction. Finally, the clusters of thunderstorms that begin a hurricane form.)

California Standards pp. 53M–53N

R 2.1 Understand text features
R 2.4 Inferences/generalizations
R 2.5 Facts, inferences, opinions
R 3.7 Evaluate author's techniques

W 2.2.a Demonstrate understanding

- Which of the weather instruments shown on page 26 would be most helpful in predicting a hurricane? Explain your answer. (Accept reasonable responses that students can support with evidence from the text.)

- Why did the author choose to begin the book with detailed description of the 1938 storm? (Possible response: In describing how the storm developed and took people by surprise, the author was able to give readers a sense of its power and the devastation hurricanes can cause.)

pages 28–61

- How do the headings help you to predict and remember the type of information presented in each section of the book ? ("Into the Eye of the Storm" tells how scientists have learned to analyze and track hurricanes; "Big Winds and Big Damage" tells of the damage caused by the strong winds of Hurricane Andrew; "More Storms Ahead" explains how scientists make long-range predictions about hurricanes.)

- What words and phrases does the author use to describe the strength of Hurricane Andrew's winds? (*winds gusting to 195 miles per hour, shrieking, growling like a rushing freight train, snatched at shutters, walls bulged in and out, howling*)

- What factors leave the ecology of Everglades National Park in question after Hurricane Andrew? (The hurricane destroyed many of the native plants, and the foreign plants recently brought in have spread quickly. The plant life also affects the ecology of the animal population.)

- What kinds of changes do the diagrams on page 45 illustrate? (Areas that were once swamps, marshes, and flatlands have shrunk considerably, and the east coast of Florida is now heavily populated by humans.)

- Why does the author say that "Today no one who reads a newspaper, listens to radio, or watches television can be taken by surprise when a hurricane strikes"? (With information from hurricane-hunting planes, satellites, and computers, forecasters are able to use all forms of media to warn people of an approaching hurricane.)

▶ Responding

Have students tell whether their predictions were or were not accurate and have them tell how they used the Predict/Infer or Monitor/Clarify strategies as they read. Then have students share their reaction to *Hurricanes: Earth's Mightiest Storms.* Finally, have students summarize the key ideas of the book. Take this opportunity to observe how well students are using strategies and comprehending the book.

Bonus Have students describe an animal that reminds them of a hurricane. Tell them to be prepared to explain the reasons for their comparison.

W 2.2.a

UNIVERSAL ACCESS

Reaching All Students

English Language Learners

Be sure students understand the language the author uses to personify the storm and the floods that accompany it. Discuss the images created by phrases such as *the storm was born, dying out over cool water, water crept up around houses, water swallowed houses, the sea swallowed automobiles, the eye of the storm,* and *Andrew came ashore.*

Eye of the Storm: Chasing Storms with Warren Faidley

Different texts for different purposes

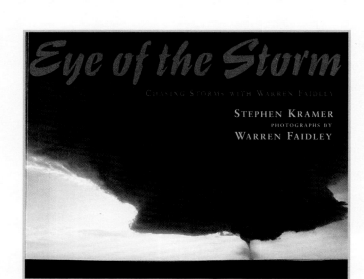

Anthology: Main Selection

Purposes

- strategy focus: question
- comprehension skill: text organization
- vocabulary development
- critical thinking, discussion

Genre: Nonfiction

Nonfiction selection on storm photography

Awards

⭐ **ALA Notable**

⭐ **William Allen White Children's Book Award Nominee**

> **Selection Summary**
> Warren Faidley discusses the challenges involved in photographing tornadoes, lightning, and hurricanes.

Teacher's Edition: Read Aloud

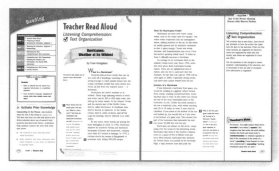

Purposes

- listening comprehension: text organization
- vocabulary development
- critical thinking, discussion

Anthology: Get Set to Read

Purposes

- background building: storms
- developing key vocabulary

Anthology: Content Link

Purposes

- content reading: careers
- skill: how to read a sequence chart
- critical thinking, discussion

Leveled Books and Resources

Use these resources to ensure that students read, outside of class, at least thirty minutes a day. See also Cumulative Listing of Leveled Books.

Reader's Library

Very Easy

White Dragon: Anna Allen in the Face of Danger
by **Maryann Dobeck**

(Also available on blackline masters)

Purposes
- fluency practice in below-level text
- alternate reading for students reading significantly below grade level
- strategy application: question
- comprehension skill application: text organization
- below-level independent reading

Lesson Support
- Lesson Plan, page R4
- Alternate application for Comprehension Skill lesson on text organization, page 81A
- Reteaching for Comprehension Skill: text organization, page R10

Selection Summary Masters

Audiotape

Eye of the Storm: Chasing Storms with Warren Faidley
Audiotape for
Nature's Fury

Eye of the Storm: Chasing Storms with Warren Faidley Teacher's Resource Blackline Masters

Reaching All Students

Inclusion Strategy

R 1.1

Significantly Below-level Readers

Students reading so far below level that they cannot read *Eye of the Storm: Chasing Storms with Warren Faidley* even with the suggested Extra Support should still participate with the class whenever possible.

- Include them in the Teacher Read Aloud (p. 53U) and Preparing to Read (pp. 54A–55C).

- Have them listen to *Eye of the Storm: Chasing Storms with Warren Faidley* on the audiotape for *Nature's Fury* and read the Selection Summary while others read Segment 1.

- Have them read "White Dragon: Anna Allen in the Face of Danger" in the Reader's Library collection for *Nature's Fury* while others read Segment 2 of *Eye of the Storm: Chasing Storms with Warren Faidley.*

- Have all students participate in Wrapping Up Segment 2 (p. 75) and Responding (p. 76).

Theme Paperbacks

Easy

If You Lived at the Time of the Great San Francisco Earthquake
by **Ellen Levine**

Lesson, TE page 53I

On Level

Drylongso
by **Virginia Hamilton**

Lesson, TE page 53K

Challenge

Hurricanes: Earth's Mightiest Storms
by **Patricia Lauber**

Lesson, TE page 53M

Technology

Get Set for Reading CD-ROM
Eye of the Storm: Chasing Storms with Warren Faidley
Provides background building, vocabulary support, and selection summaries in English and Spanish.

Education Place
www.eduplace.com
Log on to Education Place for more activities relating to this selection.

Book Adventure
www.bookadventure.org
This Internet reading incentive program provides thousands of titles for students.

Daily Lesson Plans

Instructional Goals	Day 1	Day 2

Reading

(60–80 minutes)

Strategy Focus: Question

☑ *Comprehension Skill:* Text Organization

Comprehension Skill Review: Sequence of Events; Fact and Opinion

Information and Study Skills: Using Print and Electronic Card Catalogs

Day 1

Teacher Read Aloud, *53U*   R2.1
Preparing to Read *Eye of the Storm*
• Get Set: Background and Vocabulary, *54A*   R1.1, R2.1
• Key Vocabulary, *55A*
  Selection Vocabulary, *Practice Book, 23*
• Strategy/Skill Preview, *55B*
  Selection Map, *Practice Book, 24*
Reading Segment 1, *57–68*   R2.5, W2.2.a
• Supporting Comprehension   R2.3, R2.5
• Strategy Focus, *64*
Wrapping Up Segment 1, *68*   LS1.1, LS2.3.a

Day 2

Reading Segment 2, *69–75*   R2.5, LS2.3.a, W2.2.a
• Supporting Comprehension   R2.3, R2.5
• Strategy Focus, *72*
Wrapping Up Segment 2, *75*   R2.5, LS1.1, LS2.3.a, LS2.3.b, LS2.3.c
Responding
• Comprehension Questions: Think About the Selection, *76*   R3.1, R3.3, W2.2.a
• Comprehension Check, *Practice Book, 25*
Rereading/Revisiting the Text
• Comprehension: Text Organization, *73*

Word Work

(30–40 minutes)

☑ *Spelling:* The / ā /, / ē /, and / ī / Sounds

Decoding Longer Words:

☑ *Structural Analysis:* Syllabication

Phonics: Long Vowels / ā /, / ē /, / ī /

Vocabulary: Dictionary: Alphabetical Order and Guide Words

Day 1

Spelling
• Pretest, *81G*
• Instruction: The / ā /, / ē /, and / ī / Sounds, *81G*
• Take-Home Word List, *Practice Book: Handbook*

Day 2

Decoding Longer Words Instruction
• Structural Analysis: Syllabication, *81E*   LC1.5
• *Practice Book, 28*

Spelling
• *Practice Book, 29*

Writing & Language

(30–40 minutes)

☑ *Grammar:* Conjunctions; Compound Sentences

☑ *Writing:* A Response to a Prompt; Capitalizing and Punctuating Sentences

Listening/Speaking/Viewing: Having a Literature Discussion

☑ = tested skills

Day 1

Daily Language Practice, *81L*
Grammar Instruction
• Conjunctions, *81K*   LC1.1

✏ **Writing**
• Journal Writing, *57*   W2.2.a

Day 2

Daily Language Practice, *81L*
Grammar Instruction
• *Practice Book, 33*

✏ **Writing Instruction**
• A Response to a Prompt, *81M*   W2.1, W2.2, W2.3, W2.4
• *Practice Book, 36*
• Journal Writing, *69*   W2.2.a

California Standards Achieved Each Day

R = Reading
W = Writing
LC = Language Conventions
LS = Listening & Speaking
HSS = History/Social Science
S = Science
M = Math

R 1.1 Read aloud fluently
R 2.1 Understand text features
R 2.3 Discern main ideas
R 2.5 Facts, inferences, opinions
W 2.2.a Demonstrate understanding
LC 1.1 Sentence structure/transition
LS 1.1 Ask new questions
LS 2.3.a Summarize events/details

R 2.5 Facts, inferences, opinions
R 3.1 Analyze literary forms
R 3.3 Determine character traits
W 2.1 Write narratives
W 2.2 Write responses to literature
W 2.3 Write research reports
W 2.4 Write persuasive compositions
LC 1.5 Spell correctly
LS 1.1 Ask new questions
LS 2.3.a Summarize events/details
LS 2.3.b Understand ideas/images
LS 2.3.c Use examples

Leveled Books, pp. 53H–53N
For reading outside of class and homework

Technology

California Lesson Planner CD-ROM
Customize your planning with the Lesson Planner.

Key correlations are provided in this chart.
Additional correlations are provided at point of use.

Day 3

Rereading/Revisiting the Text
- Writer's Craft: Suspense, *61*   R3.7, W2.2.a
- Visual Literacy: Photographs, *63*   R2.1, R3.7, LS2.3.c

Comprehension Skill Instruction
- Text Organization, *81A*
- *Practice Book, 26–27*   R2.1, R2.2

Phonics Instruction
- Long Vowels /ā/, /ē/, /ī/, *81F*

Spelling
- *Practice Book, 30*

Daily Language Practice, *81L*

Grammar Instruction
- Compound Sentences, *81K*   LC1.1

Writing
- Responding: Write a Job Description, *76*

Day 4

Comprehension Skill Instruction
- Reteaching Text Organization with Reader's Library, *R10*   R2.1, R2.2

Reading the Career Link
- "Storm Warning," *78–81*   R1.1, R2.1
- Visual Literacy: Communicating Information, *80*   R2.1

Information and Study Skills Instruction
- Using Print and Electronic Card Catalogs, *81C*

Decoding Longer Words
- Reteaching Structural Analysis: Syllabication, *R16*   LC1.5

Spelling
- Treasure Map Game, *81H*   LC1.5
- *Practice Book, 31*

Vocabulary Skill Instruction
- Dictionary: Alphabetical Order and Guide Words, *81I*
- Activities, *R17*   R1.5, R3.5, LC1.5
- *Practice Book, 32*

Daily Language Practice, *81L*

Grammar
- Reteaching, *R22, R23*   LC1.1
- Compound Sentences, *Practice Book, 34*

Writing
- Capitalizing and Punctuating Sentences, *81N*   LC1.3, LC1.4, W1.6
- *Practice Book, 37*

Listening/Speaking/Viewing
- Having a Literature Discussion, *81O*   R2.3, R2.5, R3.1, LS1.1, LS2.3, LS2.3.b, LS2.3.c

Day 5

Rereading/Revisiting the Text:
Comprehension Review Skill Instruction
- Fact and Opinion, *65*   R2.5
- Sequence of Events, *71*

Rereading for Fluency, *56–75*
Activity Choices
- Responding Activities, *76*   R3.3
- Challenge/Extension Activities, *R11*   R2.4, W2.2.a-c
- Cross-Curricular Activities, *R28–R29*   W1.1.a, LS2.3.a

Spiral Review, *81Q*

Vocabulary Expansion
- Words from Many Languages: Weather Words, *81J*

Spelling
- Posttest, *81H*   LC1.5

Spiral Review, *81R*   LC1.5

Daily Language Practice, *81L*

Grammar
- Avoiding Run-ons, *81L*   W1.6
- *Practice Book, 35*

Writing
- Writing Activities, *R26–R27*   W1.2.a, W2.1.b, W2.3.a, LS1.4
- Sharing Students' Writing: Author's Chair

R 2.1 Understand text features
R 2.2 Use order to analyze text
R 3.7 Evaluate author's techniques
W 2.2.a Demonstrate understanding
LC 1.1 Sentence structure/transition
LS 2.3.c Use examples

R 1.5 Figurative language
R 2.1 Understand text features
R 2.2 Use order to analyze text
R 2.5 Facts, inferences, opinions
R 3.1 Analyze literary forms
R 3.5 Describe literary devices
W 1.6 Edit and revise work
LC 1.1 Sentence structure/transition
LC 1.3 Colons and quotation marks
LC 1.4 Use correct capitalization
LC 1.5 Spell correctly
LS 1.1 Ask new questions
LS 2.3 Respond to literature

R 2.4 Inferences/generalizations
R 2.5 Facts, inferences, opinions
R 3.3 Determine character traits
W 1.1.a Establish a plot
W 1.2.a Establish topic, order
W 1.6 Edit and revise work
W 2.1.b Show events
W 2.2.b Support judgments
W 2.2.c Develop interpretations
W 2.3.a Frame questions
LS 1.4 Select focus
LS 2.3.a Summarize events/details

Reading-Writing Workshop: Description, pp. 52–53G

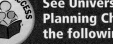

See Universal Access Planning Chart on the following pages.

53R

Universal Access Plans
for Reaching All Learners

Grouping for Instruction

30–45 minutes

	Day 1	**Day 2**
With the Teacher **Extra Support** **Teach**—Use Extra Support Handbook	**Preteach** Syllabication **Preview** Selection, Segment 1 ▪ Extra Support Handbook pp. 24–25	**Preteach** Text Organization **Preview** Selection, Segment 2 ▪ Extra Support Handbook pp. 26–27
Working Independently **On Level** Use Classroom Management Handbook **Challenge** Use Challenge Handbook **English Language Learners** Use Classroom Management Handbook or Challenge Handbook	**Independent Activities** For each group, assign appropriate activities—your own or those in the handbooks listed below. Then get students started on their independent work. ▪ Classroom Management Handbook pp. 8–9 ▪ Challenge Handbook pp. 4–5	See plan for Day 1 **Monitor** Answer questions, if necessary.

30–45 minutes

	Day 1	**Day 2**
With the Teacher **English Language Learners** **Teach**—Use Handbook for English Language Learners	**Preteach** Weather **Preteach** Get Set to Read; Selection, Segment 1 **Preteach** Structural Analysis: Introduction to Syllabication ▪ Handbook for ELL pp. 28–29	**Preteach** Photography **Preteach** Selection, Segment 2 **Reteach** Grammar: Conjunctions ▪ Handbook for ELL pp. 30–31
Working Independently **On Level** Use Classroom Management Handbook **Challenge** Use Challenge Handbook **Extra Support** Use Classroom Management Handbook	**Independent Activities** Students can continue their assigned activities, or you can assign new activities from the handbooks below. ▪ Classroom Management Handbook pp. 8–9 ▪ Challenge Handbook pp. 4–5	See plan for Day 1 **Monitor** Partner Extra Support students, if needed.

Independent Activities

Classroom Management Handbook

- Daily Activities
- Grouping
- Management

Resources for Reaching All Learners

Extra Support Handbook

- Daily Lessons
- Preteaching and Reteaching
- Skill Support

Handbook for English Language Learners

- Daily Lessons
- Language Development
- Skill Support

Challenge Handbook

- Independent Activities
- Instructional Support

Day 3

Reteach Syllabication
Review Selection: Text Organization

■ Extra Support Handbook   pp. 28–29

See plan for Day 1

Check in
Reinforce instruction, if needed.

Preteach Months and Seasons
Preteach Vocabulary/Dictionary: Alphabetical Order/Guidewords

■ Handbook for ELL   pp. 32–33

See plan for Day 1

Check in
Reinforce instruction, if needed.

Day 4

Reteach Conjunctions
Reteach Compound Sentences
Preview Reader's Library: *White Dragon: Anna Allen in the Face of Danger*

■ Extra Support Handbook   pp. 30–31

See plan for Day 1

Check in
Regroup English learners, if needed.

Preteach Compass Directions
Reteach Selection Summary and Review
Reteach Grammar: Compound Sentences

■ Handbook for ELL   pp. 34–35

See plan for Day 1

Monitor
How well are challenge projects progressing?

Day 5

Reteach Text Organization
Revisit Selection and Reader's Library: *White Dragon: Anna Allen in the Face of Danger*

■ Extra Support Handbook   pp. 32–33

See plan for Day 1

Build confidence
Reinforce successful independent work.

Preteach Media
Reteach Writing: Capitalizing and Punctuating Sentences

■ Handbook for ELL   pp. 36–37

See plan for Day 1

Share work
Allow students time to share work.

R 2.1
R 2.2
LS 1.1
LS 2.3

Reading Instruction

DAY 1	• Teacher Read Aloud • Preparing to Read • Reading the Selection, Segment 1
DAY 2	• Reading the Selection, Segment 2 • Responding
DAY 3	• Revisiting the Text • Comprehension Skill Instruction
DAY 4	• Comprehension Skill Reteaching • Reading the Content Link • Information and Study Skills Instruction
DAY 5	• Comprehension Skill Review • Activity Choices

OBJECTIVES

Students

• listen to identify how the author has organized information in a nonfiction selection

• learn academic language: **sequence of events, main idea, details, cause and effect**

► Activate Prior Knowledge

Connecting to the Theme Ask students what the title of this theme is. *(Nature's Fury)* Tell them that next you will read aloud a nonfiction selection about one of nature's most powerful and destructive forces—hurricanes. Help students connect the story with what they know.

■ Ask students to share what they know about hurricanes.

■ Invite students who have witnessed hurricanes firsthand or seen them on television to describe them.

Teacher Read Aloud

Listening Comprehension:
✓ Text Organization

Hurricanes:
Weather at its Wildest

by Fran Hodgkins

This article tells about one of nature's most destructive forces.

1 What details does the author give in the section "What Is a Hurricane?" that help you understand how destructive hurricanes can be? (hurricanes can rip roofs off buildings, wash seaside homes away, and turn streets into rivers; Hurricane Andrew caused more than $15 billion in damage, a cyclone killed 300,000 people in Bangladesh)

R 2.4

What Is a Hurricane?

Hundred-mile-an-hour winds that can rip the roofs off of buildings; towering waves strong enough to wash seaside homes into the ocean; torrential rainfall that turns streets into rivers: all this from one massive storm — a hurricane.

Hurricanes are earth's weather at its wildest. These huge spinning wheels of wind and water can be 300 to 600 miles wide, and they go by many names. In the Atlantic Ocean and the eastern part of the Pacific Ocean, they're called hurricanes. In Southeast Asia, they're known as typhoons. In the Indian Ocean, they're called cyclones, and off the coast of Australia, they're referred to as willy-willys.

By any name, these storms are among the most damaging on earth. In 1992, Hurricane Andrew hit southern Florida and destroyed thousands of homes and businesses, creating more than $15 billion in damage. In 1970, a cyclone struck the nation of Bangladesh in **1** southeast Asia, killing 300,000 people.

California Standards pp. 53U–53V

R 2.1 Understand text features
R 2.2 Use order to analyze text
R 2.4 Inferences/generalization

LS 1.1 Ask new questions
LS 2.3 Respond to literature

How Do Hurricanes Form?

Hurricanes are born over warm ocean water, such as the water near the equator. This warm water evaporates into the atmosphere above, adding moisture to the air. As this moist air spirals upward and its moisture condenses as rain, it gains energy. Clouds and winds increase, and thunderstorms may occur. Once the storm's spiraling winds reach 74 miles an hour, it officially becomes a hurricane.

An average of six hurricanes form in the Atlantic Ocean every year. Since 1953, scientists have given these hurricanes human names. There are six alphabetical lists of names, and one list is used each year (for example, the list that was used in 1996 will be used again in 2002). Especially strong storms may have their names retired from the list.

Journey of a Hurricane

If you followed a hurricane from space, you would be looking at a gigantic wheel formed from clouds, rotating counterclockwise, traveling from east to west. In the center you would see one of the most remarkable parts of the hurricane: its eye. Unlike the storm around it, the eye is relatively calm, with winds reaching only 20 or 30 miles an hour. It may even be cloudless. If you stood at the bottom of the eye and looked up, you would feel as if you were at the bottom of a giant well. The eyewall (the part of the hurricane that surrounds the eye)

2 can tower 50,000 feet into the sky.

Hurricanes are always on the move, swept along over the ocean by the prevailing winds. Hurricanes that form in the southern Atlantic move at a speed of five to fifteen miles per hour. Most Atlantic hurricanes that threaten the United States are pushed by the Bermuda High, a high pressure zone that pulls the

2 What is the first paragraph under the heading "Journey of a Hurricane" mostly about? (a hurricane's eye) How is this paragraph organized, by main idea and details or by sequence? How can you tell? (by main idea and details; most of the sentences give information about what a hurricane's eye is like)

Listening Comprehension: ✓ Text Organization

Tell students that as they listen, they should pay attention to how the author has organized the facts in the selection. Point out that some sections are organized by sequence, others are organized by main idea and details, and others are organized by cause and effect.

Use the questions in the margins to assess students' understanding of the selection, and to determine if they are able to recognize how information is organized.

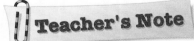

Teacher's Note

Vocabulary You might explain these terms: **torrential** ("very heavy"); **equator** ("the imaginary line that circles the earth halfway between the North and South poles"); **counterclockwise** ("a direction opposite to that of the movement of the hands of a clock"); **prevailing** ("most frequent or common; predominant"); **evacuating** ("sending inhabitants away from an area").

(Teacher Read Aloud, *continued*)

storms away from the coast and back over the ocean. When that happens, the hurricane loses its energy over the cold North Atlantic and dissipates. But a strong, fast-moving hurricane can resist the influence of a high pressure zone, and that's when people on shore find themselves in the path of the storm.

Hurricane Danger

Nearly 50 million people live along the Eastern and Gulf Coasts of the United States. Florida has one of the fastest-growing populations in the country. When a storm threatens, these people can be in serious danger, mostly from the wind. Hurricane winds start at 74 miles an hour, and wind speeds of 200 miles an hour have been recorded. These high winds can tear roofs off houses, uproot trees, and knock down power lines. Loose objects picked up by the winds can smash through windows and walls.

Teacher's Note

Encourage students to use the headings in the selection to help them understand how the information is organized. You might pause after reading each heading and have students predict what the next section of text will be about.

California Standards pp. 53W–53X

W 2.2.a Demonstrate understanding   **LS 2.3.c** Use examples
LS 2.3.a Summarize events/details
LS 2.3.b Understand ideas/images

3 Hurricanes are also dangerous because of the high waves and torrential rainfall they create. The hurricane's "storm surge" can push along a wall of water as it moves across the ocean, finally shoving the water onto the shore, washing out roads, flooding property, and even sweeping buildings off their foundations. At the same time, the hurricane can drench the land with six inches or more of rain, causing even more flooding. A hurricane can cause millions or even billions of dollars worth of damage and disrupt thousands of lives.

Protective Measures

Because of the huge amount of damage and loss of life that hurricanes can cause, scientists are always seeking better ways to track the storms and predict their movements. The National Aeronautics and Space Administration (NASA) has developed a system of satellites to watch hurricanes and figure out their probable **4** paths.

But the most accurate tracking cannot save lives unless people who live in affected areas take the necessary action. That means taking hurricane warnings seriously, and evacuating the area as soon as authorities say it's time to get out.

3 What three things make hurricanes a dangerous threat to people and property? (high winds, high waves, and torrential rains)

LS 2.3.a
LS 2.3.b
LS 2.3.c
W 2.2.a

4 The first paragraph under the heading "Protective Measures" states a cause and an effect. What are they? (*Cause*—Hurricanes cause huge damage and loss of life. *Effect*—Scientists are always looking for better ways to track and predict hurricanes.)

▶ **Discussion**

Summarize After reading, discuss any parts of the selection students did not understand. Then ask them to summarize it by describing the causes and effects of hurricanes.

Listening Comprehension:
✓ **Text Organization** Reread the first paragraph in the section that begins with the heading "How Do Hurricanes Form?" Ask students how the information in this paragraph is organized, by main idea and details or by sequence. (by sequence) Have students work in pairs to create a flow chart showing the sequence of a hurricane's development. Guide students in identifying the sequence words *As* and *Once*.

Personal Response Ask students to evaluate how well the author has explained how hurricanes are formed and the destruction they can cause.

⭐ **Connecting/Comparing** Ask students how they think this selection fits with the other selections in this theme.

R 1.1
R 2.1
LS 2.3

Preparing to Read

▶ Using *Get Set* for Background and Vocabulary

Connecting to the Theme Remind students that this theme is about the power of nature. They have just read about two children who survive a powerful earthquake. They will now read about a person who photographs lightning storms and tornadoes. Use the Get Set to Read on pages 54–55 to introduce photographer Warren Faidley and discuss some of the dangers he faces.

- Ask volunteers to read aloud "Photographing Wild Weather."

- Point out the "storm route" Warren Faidley follows. Have students point out where along the route he might be found in spring and in summer.

- Ask students to explain the meanings of the Key Vocabulary: *sizzling, collide, funnel clouds, tornadoes, lightning,* and *rotate.* Then have them use these words as they share what they know about lightning and tornadoes.

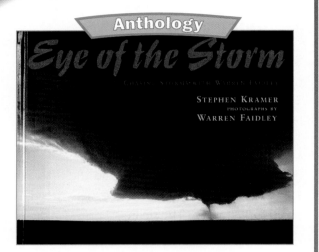

Anthology

Eye of the Storm

STEPHEN KRAMER
PHOTOGRAPHS BY
WARREN FAIDLEY

Get Set for Reading CD-ROM

Eye of the Storm

Provides background building, vocabulary support, and selection summaries in English and Spanish.

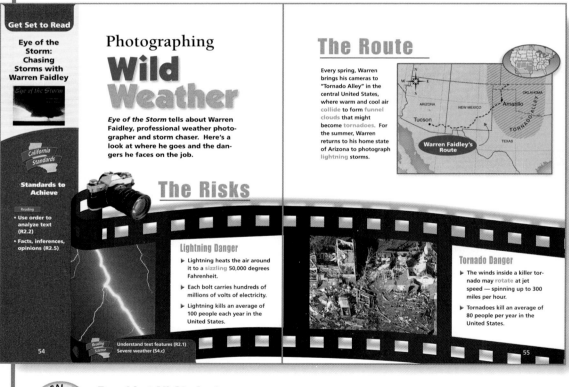

Reaching All Students
English Language Learners

Tell students they will read about a man who takes pictures of storms. Write *tornado* on the board. Point to the map on page 55, and explain that there are many tornadoes in this part of the United States. Ask students to describe the types of storms they have experienced. Use photos and movement to demonstrate the Key Vocabulary.

California Standards pp. 54A–55A

R 1.1 Read aloud fluently
R 2.1 Understand text features
LS 2.3 Respond to literature

Vocabulary

▶ Developing Key Vocabulary

Use **Transparency 1–9** to introduce additional storm-related words from *Eye of the Storm*.

- Model how to figure out the meaning of the word *rotate* from clues in the sentence.

- For each remaining sentence, ask students to use letter sounds and sentence clues to figure out the Key Vocabulary words. Have students explain how they figured out each word.

Remind students that it's helpful to use the Phonics/Decoding Strategy as they read. For students who need more help with decoding, use the lesson below.

Practice/Homework **Practice Book** page 23.

Strategy Review
Phonics/Decoding

Modeling Write this sentence from *Eye of the Storm* on the board, and point to *embankment*.

> He slid a few feet down the rough concrete embankment, using his hands and the soles of his shoe as brakes.

Think Aloud

To figure out this word, I'll look for word parts I know. I see the word bank. That may be a base word. Before it, I see the prefix em-. At the end is the suffix -ment. I can blend these sounds and get ehm BANGK muhnt, but I'm not sure what that means. I know that bank can mean "the edge of a river," but in the sentence, the embankment is concrete. I may need to look this up in the dictionary.

Skill Finder
• Decoding Longer Words, pp. 81E–81F	• Vocabulary Expansion, p. 81J

Eye of the Storm: Chasing Storms with Warren Faidley

Key Concept
the nature of lightning storms and of tornadoes

Key Vocabulary

collide: to bump into another mass with force

funnel cloud: tornado cloud that is wide at the top and narrow where it touches the ground

jagged: having a sharp, pointed edge or outline

lightning: the flash of light in the sky when electricity passes between clouds or between a cloud and the ground

prairies: flat, open grasslands

rotate: to swirl in a circular motion

severe: serious or extreme in nature

sizzling: crackling with intense heat

tornadoes: rotating columns of air accompanied by whirling funnel-shaped downspouts that can cause great destruction

See Vocabulary notes on pages 58, 62, 64, 69, 70, 72, and 74 for additional words to preview.

Practice Book page 23

Eye of the Storm
Key Vocabulary

Name

Stor

Use word

Transparency 1–9

News Flash

Tornado Warning Issued for Texas and Oklahoma

Every spring, warm air from the Gulf of Mexico and cool air from Alaska collide over the Midwest. Powerful weather can brew over the flat prairies when these air masses meet. Today the National Weather Service issued a severe storm warning for northern Texas and Oklahoma. Tornadoes are likely to touch down in this region throughout the weekend. Residents are urged to be on the lookout. These signs show that a tornado may be forming:

- A dense, inky cloud forms over the land.

- Air at the bottom of the cloud begins to rotate. This swirling air is a breeding ground for twisters.

- One or more funnel clouds descend toward the ground like dragon necks.

Tornadoes are often accompanied by sizzling electrical storms. It is not unusual to see jagged bolts of lightning.

R 2.1
R 2.2
R 2.3
LS 1.1

Reading Strategy

▶ Strategy Focus:
Question

Strategy Focus

Warren Faidley's job takes him all over the country, getting close-up shots of dangerous storms. As you read the selection, think of **questions** about his job to discuss with your classmates.

Teacher's Note

Strategy/Skill Connection For a better understanding of *Eye of the Storm,* students can use the

- Question Strategy
- Text Organization Comprehension Skill

Using the headings and graphics to help them form questions will help students gain an understanding of how the text has been organized. This will provide the groundwork for later skill instruction.

As students fill in their *Eye of the Storm* Selection Map (**Practice Book** page 24 and **Transparency 1–10**), they can turn the headings into questions and read each section to find the answer.

Have students turn to page 57 as you read aloud the title of the selection and the author's name. Ask someone to read aloud the Strategy Focus. Invite students to page through the selection, read the headings, and look at the photographs. Also point out the storm-calendar diagram on page 65. Have each student write down a question. Ask them to share the questions they have about storm chasers. Record their responses.

Teacher Modeling Tell students that asking themselves questions that can be answered as they read or after reading can help them understand the selection. Then model the Question Strategy.

Think Aloud

The title, photographs, and headings help me figure out that this selection is all about the dangerous job of chasing and photographing storms. I have these questions about the topic: How, exactly, does Warren chase a storm? What kind of storms does he chase? Maybe I'll find these answers after I read.

Remind students to keep their questions in mind as they read, and to form new questions as they come across new information. Remind them also to use their other reading strategies as they read the selection.

California Standards pp. 55B–55C

R 2.1 Understand text features   LS 1.1 Ask new questions
R 2.2 Use order to analyze text
R 2.3 Discern main ideas

Comprehension Skill

Eye of the Storm: Chasing Storms with Warren Faidley

✓ Comprehension Skill Focus:
Text Organization

Selection Map Explain to students that as they read *Eye of the Storm,* they will focus on the way the author has organized the information. To help them understand the organization of the text, they will fill in a chart as they read. Display **Transparency 1–10,** and demonstrate how to use the graphic organizer.

■ Explain that the headings from the first part of the selection appear in the top half of the chart. Point out the first heading, "Storm Chasing," and have students locate the same heading on page 59 of the Anthology. Then ask a volunteer to read aloud the five paragraphs that follow the heading.

■ Model how to complete the selection map by writing a sentence telling what the first section of text is about.

■ Ask students to complete the first item on **Practice Book** page 24 with the same answer.

■ As students read pages 59–68, have them complete the other items in the top part of the chart. Then point out that the second half of the chart is organized differently because the second part of the selection is organized differently.

Transparency 1–10

Selection Map

Pages 59–68

Page 59   Storm Chasing

Page 60   Warren Faidley: Storm Chaser

Page 64   What Happens to Warren's Photos After He Takes Them?

Page 65   Storm Seasons and Chasing

Page 67   Chasing Tornadoes

Pages 69–75

One Day in the Life of a Storm Chaser

Morning

Afternoon

Evening

Practice Book page 24

Eye of the Storm
Graphic Organizer Selection Map

Name _____

Selection Map

Fill in this selection map.

Pages 59–68

Page 59   Storm Chasing   how Warren chases a lightning storm

Page 60   Warren Faidley: Storm Chaser   how Warren was interested in storms since he was a child

Page 64   What Happens to Warren's Photos After He Takes Them? how Warren created a stock photo agency, where people can go and buy his photos **(1)**

Page 65   Storm Seasons and Chasing   how tornadoes form and how storm chasers follow weather patterns that form tornadoes **(1)**.

Page 67   Chasing Tornadoes   how Warren knows where to go to get the best pictures of tornadoes **(1)**

Pages 69–75

One Day in the Life of a Storm Chaser
Morning   Check the weather, get Shadow Chaser ready for the day, test the equipment, pack supplies **(2)**
Afternoon   Get an update on the weather conditions, change the oil in Shadow Chaser, check maps **(2)**
Evening   Look at the map, call the National Weather Service, head north following the storm, follow the tornadoes from Texas into Oklahoma, shoot the photos **(2)**.

24   Theme 1: **Nature's Fury**
Assessment Tip: Total **15** Points

Graphic Organizer: Selection Map

Page 59 Storm Chasing _This section tells how Warren chases a lightning storm._
Watching the Sky _____

Page 60 Warren Faidley: Storm Chaser _____
Becoming a Storm Chaser _____

Page 64 What Happens to Warren's Photos After He Takes Them?
_____

Page 65 Storm Seasons and Chasing _____

Focus Questions

Have students turn to Responding on page 76. Read the questions aloud and ask them to keep the questions in mind as they read *Eye of the Storm.*

Options for Reading

▶ **Reading in Segments**
Students can read *Eye of the Storm* in two segments (pages 57–68 and 69–75), or read the entire story in one segment.

R 1.1

▶ **Deciding About Support** The high-interest topic of this selection (storm chasers) makes it engaging to read.

■ Despite the selection's length, the many scientific terms, and the lack of a sequential narrative, most students should be able to follow On Level instruction.

■ Students who might have difficulty with scientific terms and the structure of nonfiction will benefit from Extra Support.

■ Significantly below-level readers can listen to the **Audiotape** and read the Selection Summary for *Eye of the Storm,* and then read "White Dragon: Anna Allen in the Face of Danger" in the **Reader's Library**.

▶ **Universal Access** Use the notes at the bottom of the pages.

Meet the Author
Stephen Kramer

Stephen Kramer teaches at an elementary school near Vancouver, Washington. He has written several other books on nature topics, such as *Avalanche, Caves, Tornado,* and *Lightning. Lightning* features the photographs of Warren Faidley.

Meet the Photographer
Warren Faidley

Warren Faidley's dramatic weather photographs appear not only in books, but in movies, videos, calendars, magazines, and museums. Faidley also served as a consultant and cinematographer for the movie *Twister.* He and his cat, Megamouth, live in Tucson, Arizona.

Internet

For more information about Stephen Kramer and Warren Faidley, visit Education Place. **www.eduplace.com/kids**

56

Reaching All Students
Classroom Management

On Level
Reading Cards 5–6

While Reading: Reading Card 1; Selection Map (**Practice Book** p. 24); generate questions

After Reading: Discussion Group (Reading Card 6); Wrapping Up Segment 1 (p. 68) and Segment 2 (p. 75)

Challenge
Reading Cards 5–9

While Reading: Selection Map (**Practice Book** p. 24); Descriptive Language (p. 66, Reading Card 7); Organize Information Visually (p. 71, Reading Card 8); Comparing by Shape (p. 72, Reading Card 9)

After Reading: Discussion Group (Reading Card 6); Wrapping Up Segment 1 (p. 68) and Segment 2 (p. 75)

English Language Learners

Intermediate and Advanced Fluency
Have students read with partners. Ask them to begin by looking at all the headings. Ask them to predict what the selection is about, based on these headings.

For English language learners at other proficiency levels, use the **Handbook for English Language Learners**.

California Standards pp. 56–57

R 1.1   Read aloud fluently
R 2.1   Understand text features
W 2.2.a Demonstrate understanding

Eye of the Storm: Chasing Storms with Warren Faidley

Beginning of Segment 1:
pages 57–68

Selection 2

Eye of the Storm

CHASING STORMS WITH WARREN FAIDLEY

STEPHEN KRAMER

PHOTOGRAPHS BY
WARREN FAIDLEY

Strategy Focus

Warren Faidley's job takes him all over the country, getting close-up shots of dangerous storms. As you read the selection, think of **questions** about his job to discuss with your classmates.

57

Reading Segment 1

pages 57–68

Purpose Setting Have students make predictions about what will happen in the segment. Have them read to confirm or change their predictions as the selection unfolds.

Journal Writing Students can use their journal to record their predictions and to add new ones. They might also record their original questions, any answers they find, and new questions that come to mind as they read.

W 2.2.a

Reinforcing Comprehension and Strategies

- Remind students to use Question and other strategies as they read, and to add to their Selection Map (**Practice Book** page 24).

- Refer to the Strategy Focus notes on pages 64 and 72 to reinforce the Question Strategy.

- Use Supporting Comprehension questions beginning on page 58 to help students develop higher-level understanding of the text.

Extra Support: Previewing the Text

Before each segment, preview the text using the notes below and those on page 69. **While** reading, model strategies (pages 64 and 67). **After** reading, review each segment (pages 68 and 74) before students join the Wrapping Up discussion.

pages 59–60 The author describes Warren Faidley as he photographs an intense lightning storm. Warren has been interested in storms since his childhood. How do you think he became a professional storm chaser?

pages 60–65 Warren took some amazing pictures of lightning. He found a way to make money with his photos by selling his pictures of lightning storms.

pages 65–68 Warren has his own "storm calendar": he photographs tornadoes in spring, thunderstorms in summer, and hurricanes in fall. "Chasing Tornadoes" tells about some of the equipment he uses when he chases tornadoes.

Reading

> ## Supporting Comprehension

R 2.3
R 2.4

1 Based on the details in the section titled "Storm Chasing," what do you think it would be like to photograph a lightning storm up close? (scary and exciting)

2 Why do you think the author included information about how ancient peoples viewed the sky? (to show readers that people have always been fascinated by weather and by stars)

Vocabulary *(page 59)*

saguaros: tall cactuses native to the American Southwest

jagged: having a sharp, pointed edge or outline

lightning: the flash of light in the sky when electricity passes between clouds or between a cloud and the ground

prairies: flat, open grasslands

conditions: the way someone or something is

58

Cross-Curricular Connection

Science Although the pitch of a train whistle seems to get higher as the train approaches and lower as it gets further away, the frequency of the sound waves remains the same. This effect was first described by Austrian physicist Christian Doppler in 1842. Measuring this apparent change in frequency helps astronomers study the movement of stars, meteorologists study storms using the Doppler radar, and police officers catch speeding motorists.

California Standards pp. 58–59

R 2.3 Discern main ideas
R 2.4 Inferences/generalizations
R 3.6 Evaluate patterns/symbols

Storm Chasing

In the evening shadows, a dusty black truck rolls along a dirt road. A rattlesnake feels the vibrations, lifts its head, and crawls off into the rocks. Giant saguaros sprout from the hillsides, arms held high. Somewhere in the distance, a cactus wren calls. But Warren Faidley isn't looking for rattlesnakes, saguaros, or cactus wrens.

He stares through the windshield, eyes glued to a cauliflower-shaped cloud. Behind the cloud, the setting sun turns the sky the color of a ripe peach. Warren has been watching this cloud, and hoping, for almost thirty minutes. The truck heads toward a hill with a clear view of the sky.

Suddenly, a jagged bolt of lightning shoots from the cloud.

"That's it," says Warren.

The truck speeds to the top of the hill and Warren jumps out, arms full of photographic equipment. His fingers fly as he unfolds tripods, mounts his cameras, and points them toward the cloud. Before the road dust has settled, the cameras are clicking.

For twenty minutes, lightning erupts from the cloud. Warren moves back and forth between the cameras — peering through viewfinders, changing film, switching lenses. Tomorrow, when the film is developed, Warren will know whether he had a successful night. In the meantime, he stands and watches, hoping his cameras are capturing the spectacular lights and colors of the evening thunderstorm. **1**

Watching the Sky

From earliest times, people have watched the sky. Astrologers used the positions of the stars to predict the future. Storytellers used rainbows, winds, the sun and moon to weave tales about the past. Farmers, shepherds, and sailors have all watched the clouds, wondering what tomorrow's weather will be like.

The spectacular storms that sometimes appear in the sky have helped to make weather one of the most mysterious of all natural forces. Myths and legends from around the world **2** describe the fear and awe people felt as they watched lightning explode from a cloud or a tornado appear on the horizon, or listened to the howling winds of a hurricane.

For some people, storms have an irresistible call. These storm chasers head for the mountains, prairies, or seacoasts whenever weather conditions are right.

People chase storms for many reasons. Some storm chasers are scientists, who use video cameras, Doppler radar, and other instruments to learn about

59

Reaching All Students

English Language Learners

Intermediate and Advanced Fluency

R 3.6

Point out the words *myths* and *legends* in column two on page 59. Tell students that long ago, people used these stories to help explain things about nature. Ask them if they know a legend or myth from their parents' home country about the sun and moon or the wind and rain. Encourage students to share the story with the class.

Reading

▶ Supporting Comprehension

R 2.3
R 2.4

3 Why do you think the author included the story about Warren riding into the middle of a dust whirlwind? (to show readers that storms have always fascinated Warren)

4 What made Warren want to become a weather photographer? (Taking pictures of lightning in his free time made him dream of turning weather photography into a job.)

5 Why do you think Warren set up his camera near an underpass to photograph the lightning? (probably thought it was safer there; needed a dry place for his camera)

what happens in a tornado or a thunderstorm. Photographers follow storms to try to capture the beauty of wind and sky on film. Still other people chase storms in order to catch a brief glimpse of the awesome power of nature.

Warren Faidley: Storm Chaser

Warren Faidley lives in Tucson, Arizona, with a one-toothed cat named Megamouth. He has been interested in storms for almost as long as he can remember.

Warren still remembers the tremendous thunderstorms he saw as a boy in Tucson. Tucked safely in bed, he watched the lightning and listened to the thunder. After the storms had passed, he fell asleep to the smell of wet creosote bushes outside his window.

Warren also had his first encounter with windstorms when he was a boy. Dust whirlwinds — spinning columns of wind that look like small tornadoes — often formed in the dusty vacant lots of his

60

neighborhood. One day Warren decided to put on safety goggles and a heavy jacket, and ride his bike into the center of a dust whirlwind. He'll never forget the excitement he felt when he rode through the wall of swirling winds:

3

"The inside was still and almost dust free. The light was orange, filtered, I guess, by the wall of dirt that was spinning around me. This rotating wall was filled with all kinds of debris, including tumbleweeds and newspaper pages. Looking up, I could see the very blue sky."

Becoming a Storm Chaser

Warren hadn't always planned to be a storm chaser. He enjoyed studying science in school, and he loved being outside. But he didn't really become interested in taking pictures of the sky until he was working as a photographer for a newspaper.

Warren began by trying to take pictures of lightning from the balcony of his apartment. Although the pictures didn't turn out very well, he soon found himself spending more and more time taking pictures of lightning on summer evenings. Warren read everything he could about weather, and he began to dream about making a living as a weather photographer.

4

The storm that started Warren's career arrived in Tucson long after the end

60 THEME 1: **Nature's Fury**

California Standards pp. 60–61

R 2.3 Discern main ideas
R 2.4 Inferences/generalizations
R 3.7 Evaluate author's techniques

W 2.2.a Demonstrate understanding

of the summer thunderstorm season. On that October afternoon, Warren glanced out the back window of his apartment and saw the sharp edges of the storm cloud. He grabbed his equipment, loaded his car, and drove toward a highway underpass on the east side of town.

When Warren reached the underpass, lightning was flashing just a few miles from it. Snatching up his equipment, he scrambled up the steep bank toward a dry ledge where he could set up his cameras. As he set up his tripods, a huge lightning bolt leaped from a cloud about a mile away, striking the ground next to an air traffic control tower.

But the storm was moving quickly. Suddenly, the air was filled with wind

5

and rain, cutting off the view of any lightning to the east. Warren looked overhead and saw small lightning bolts leaping between the clouds. He knew there was about to be another large bolt — and he was pretty sure that the next big flash would be to the west, on the other side of the underpass.

Warren knew he had to get to the other side of the underpass right away. There wasn't enough room between the ledge and the top of the underpass to walk upright, so he scooted along on his knees. He grabbed hold of overhead rain gutters to keep his balance in the darkness.

Suddenly, Warren stuck his hand into a tangle of thick cobwebs. He quickly pulled his hand back. Then he pointed

61

W 2.2.a
R 3.7

Revisiting the Text

Writer's Craft Lesson
Suspense

OBJECTIVES

Students

- identify a chain of events in the rising action that creates suspense
- record these events in a graphic organizer

Explain to students that writers often build suspense in a story or article by describing a chain of events that move the action forward. The suspense usually ends at the climax, or highest point of tension. Tell students that such a series of events is called *rising action.*

Have students reread pages 60–62. Ask them to identify all the frightening and exciting things Warren goes through before getting his photograph of the lightning bolt. Record students' responses on the board in a diagram like the one below.

Ask students to work in pairs to make a similar diagram of other stories they know about in which the rising action leads to a scary or exciting climax.

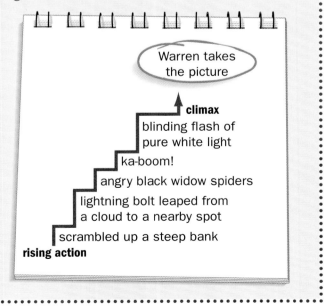

Warren takes the picture

climax
blinding flash of pure white light
ka-boom!
angry black widow spiders
lightning bolt leaped from a cloud to a nearby spot
scrambled up a steep bank
rising action

Reading

▶ Supporting Comprehension

6 How does the author create a sense of excitement and danger as he describes the events leading up to Warren's astonishing photo? (words like *Ka-boom!;* scary events such as the black widows; descriptive language such as *the air was sizzling*)

R 3.7

7 How can you tell that Warren was amazed by his own experience under the underpass? (He stayed under there for a long time, thinking about what had happened.)

R 2.3

8 How do you think Warren felt when he viewed the developed photo of the lightning bolt? (proud and excited; maybe surprised that it came out so well)

Vocabulary *(page 62)*
sizzling: crackling with intense heat

---

his penlight toward the ledge and gutters. The whole walkway was lined with webs, and rainwater washing through cracks in the concrete overhead was driving out hundreds of angry black widow spiders!

6 *Ka-boom!* A huge bolt of lightning flashed overhead. Warren knew the next bolt would strike somewhere on the west side of the underpass, and he knew he had one chance to capture it. Pushing ahead in the darkness, he used the legs of his tripod as a broom, sweeping aside the cobwebs and trying to brush off any spiders that landed on his clothes.

Near the end of the underpass, and clear of the spider webs, he decided to set up his cameras. The air was <u>sizzling</u>, and Warren could feel that something was about to happen. He slid a few feet down the rough concrete embankment, using his hands and the soles of his shoes as brakes. When the cameras were set up, Warren quickly wiped the raindrops off the lenses. Then he moved back up the slope to a safer place to wait.

Seconds later, he heard a loud crackling, and at the same time he saw a blinding flash of pure, white light. It sounded as if the sky were being torn apart. Next came the boom of a thunderclap roaring through the underpass. It had the energy of a bomb blast, and it lifted Warren's body right off the ground.

Warren lost his hold on the slope and began sliding downhill toward his cameras. He knew that he had to close the shutters on them without bumping the tripods — or the film with the lightning would blur and be ruined. Using his hands and feet and the seat of his pants as brakes on the concrete, Warren slid to a stop just above his tripods. Carefully, he reached up and closed the shutters on the cameras. Then he looked down at his palms and saw that they were covered with blood.

7 Warren stayed under the underpass long after the storm had passed, thinking about what had just happened. He knew the lightning strike had been close, because when he closed his eyes he could still see its jagged outline.

The next morning, when Warren had his film developed, he was astonished by what he saw. In the center of one of the rolls was an incredible image of a lightning bolt hitting a light pole in front of some metal storage tanks. The picture had been taken from less than four hundred feet. Warren knew that he was holding the closest good picture ever taken of a lightning bolt hitting an **8** object.

The lightning picture changed Warren's life. It was analyzed and written about by Dr. E. Philip Krider, a lightning scientist at the University of

62

UNIVERSAL ACCESS

Reaching All Students
English Language Learners

Intermediate and Advanced Fluency   LS 2.3

Point out the words *tripod, shutters, developed,* and *rolls* on page 62. Ask what these words have in common. Explain that they relate to cameras and photography. Remind students that many other professions have special vocabulary; ask for examples of other specialized words.

California Standards pp. 62–63

R 2.1 Understand text features
R 2.3 Discern main ideas
R 3.7 Evaluate author's techniques

LS 2.3 Respond to literature
LS 2.3.c Use examples

63

R 2.1
R 3.7
LS 2.3.c

Revisiting the Text

Visual Literacy Lesson
Photographs

OBJECTIVES

Students

- compare a visual image to a written description
- evaluate the use of photographs in nonfiction text

Tell students that selections and articles are illustrated to present a visual explanation of a passage. Some selections include art created by an illustrator, while others use photographs.

Ask students to reread the description of Warren's photograph of the lightning bolt hitting the light pole, and then study the photograph itself. Model for students how to compare the photograph's impact with the impact of the written description.

I read Warren's description of the photograph. Then I look at the photograph and can really appreciate the size of the lightning bolt and understand what made the picture so special. After seeing the illustration, I have a clearer picture of why Warren's photographs are so effective.

You might ask

■ How has the author described the photograph?

■ Which do you think is more powerful, the description of the photo or the photo itself? Why?

■ How would you describe the photograph?

Help students evaluate the purpose of including photographs in this selection. Ask them whether drawings of lightning bolts and tornadoes would be as effective as photographs, and why or why not.

▶ Strategy Focus: Question

Teacher/Student Modeling Ask students what questions they formed about Warren and his work. (Examples: How did he become a storm chaser? What does he do with his photos?)

Then ask students how the article could help them answer their questions. (Example: It explains how Warren's spectacular photograph of a lightning bolt allowed him to start a career as a storm chaser.)

▶ Supporting Comprehension

R 2.3

9 What is the value of a stock photo agency? (It lets people find and use pictures they couldn't take themselves.)

10 What led Warren to photograph tornadoes and hurricanes in addition to lightning? (He realized that people wanted pictures of these kinds of storms, and there was no easy place to get them.)

Vocabulary *(pages 64–65)*

occupation: job a person does to make a living

tornadoes: rotating columns of air accompanied by whirling funnel-shaped downspouts that can cause great destruction

collide: to bump into another mass with force

Arizona. *Life* magazine printed the picture, calling Warren a storm chaser. *National Geographic* called, wanting to film a special program about his work. The *National Enquirer* ran an article about Warren, calling him a "fearless spider-fighting photog." He even got a call from a Japanese game show that wanted to feature him on a TV program in which contestants try to guess a mystery guest's <u>occupation</u>. Warren began making enough money from selling his pictures that he could think about being a full-time storm chaser.

What Happens to Warren's Photos After He Takes Them?

You've probably seen some of Warren's photographs. His pictures of lightning, tornadoes, and hurricanes have appeared in books, magazines, newspapers, advertisements, and scientific films. One of his lightning pictures was even used on stage passes for rock concerts by singer Paul McCartney.

Warren's business is called a stock photo agency. It's like a library of sky and storm photographs. People pay him for the use of his photos.

Suppose, for example, that you are a magazine editor. If you need a lightning

64

Reaching All Students
Extra Support

Strategy Modeling

Phonics/Decoding If students need help reading longer words, model the strategy with the word *occupation*.

I see the familiar ending -tion in this word. I can try dividing the first part of the word between the two cs. The first syllable is ahk. The next part might be either kuh or kyuh. The next part is probably PAY. When I blend the sounds together, ahk kuh PAY shuhn doesn't sound right, but ahk kyuh PAY shuhn does. That word means "a job." It makes sense in the sentence.

 California Standards pp. 64–65

R 2.3	Discern main ideas	LS 1.1 Ask questions
R 2.5	Facts, inferences, opinions	LS 2.3.b Understand ideas/images
W 2.2.a	Demonstrate understanding	

• SELECTION •

**Eye of the Storm: Chasing
Storms with Warren Faidley**

R 2.5
W 2.2.a
LS 1.1
LS 2.3.b

photo for an article, you could go out and try to take a picture of lightning yourself. But you might have to wait a very long time for the right kind of storm, and unless you have lots of practice your lightning photograph probably won't be very good.

An easier way of getting a good lightning photo is to write to Warren. He'll send you samples, and you can select the one you like. Then, after sending Warren a fee, you can use the photo in your magazine.

When Warren began selling his lightning photos, he found that people were also asking for pictures of tornadoes and hurricanes. He didn't have photographs of these kinds of storms, so he read everything he could find about tornadoes and hurricanes —

and he made plans to photograph them as well.

Storm Seasons and Chasing

Storms are caused by certain kinds of weather patterns. The same patterns are found in the same areas year after year. For example, every spring, large areas of cool, dry air and warm, moist air collide over the central United States. If the winds are right, tornado-producing thunderstorms appear. That's why tornadoes in the south central United States are most likely to happen in spring. During July and August, shifting winds push moisture from the south up into the Arizona desert. When the cool, moist air is heated by the hot desert, storm clouds form. That's why Tucson has summer thunderstorms. In the late

| April | May | June | July | August | September | October |

TORNADOES → ← THUNDERSTORMS → HURRICANES →

65

Revisiting the Text
Spiral Review

Comprehension Skill Lesson
Fact and Opinion

OBJECTIVES

Students

- define fact and opinion

- identify facts and opinions in the selection and use them to determine author's point of view

Read aloud the paragraph that begins on page 62 and ends on page 64. Point out that several people thought Warren's lightning bolt photograph was great; this was their opinion. Remind students that an opinion is a statement that tells what someone thinks or how someone feels; an opinion can't be proven.

Provide students with a fact from the selection. Remind them that a fact can be proven. Ask students to identify facts in the first paragraph under "Storm Seasons and Chasing."

Explain that authors of expository nonfiction rarely state their own opinions. However, the author's point of view can sometimes be determined by asking the following:

■ What is the author's purpose for writing?

■ What facts and opinions are given? What information is left out?

Have students work in pairs to discuss what they think the author's opinion might be about Warren Faidley and storm chasing. Ask them to write down statements in the text that support their interpretations.

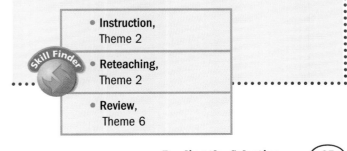

Skill Finder

- **Instruction,**
  Theme 2

- **Reteaching,**
  Theme 2

- **Review,**
  Theme 6

▶ Supporting Comprehension

11 Based on the photograph on page 66, how would you describe the way a tornado looks? (a small spout that shoots downwards from a huge black cloud that is low to the ground)

12 Why does Warren spend so much of the year *on the road?* (so that he can follow the storms, which occur in different places at different times of year)

13 Do you think that Warren's life follows a completely predictable pattern? Why or why not? (probably not, because you can't always tell exactly when storms will hit)

14 What does the author mean by the phrase *a promising storm* on page 67? (a storm that looks as if it will produce tornadoes)

11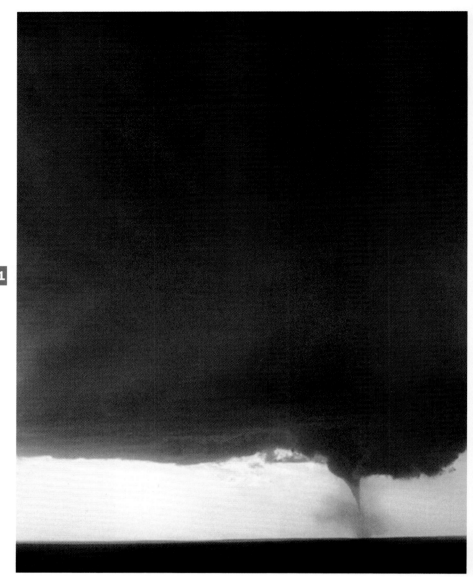

66

Reaching All Students

Challenge

Reading Card 7

W 2.2.a

Descriptive Language

Students can use Reading Card 7 to help them find descriptive words the author uses to describe lightning and tornadoes, and use these descriptive terms as they create their own descriptions.

California Standards pp. 66–67

R 1.1 Read aloud fluently   **LS 1.1** Ask new questions
R 2.3 Discern main ideas
W 2.2.a Demonstrate understanding

summer and early fall, when oceans in the northern Atlantic are warmest, tropical storms form off the west coast of Africa. A few of these turn into the hurricanes that sometimes batter the east and gulf coasts of North America.

12 Because Warren is a storm chaser, his life also follows these weather patterns. Each spring, Warren goes on the road, traveling through parts of the United States likely to be hit by tornadoes. During the summer, he stays near Tucson so he can photograph the thunderstorms that develop over the desert. In the late summer and fall, he keeps an eye on **13** weather activity in the Atlantic Ocean, ready to fly to the east coast if a hurricane appears.

Chasing Tornadoes

One of Warren's favorite tornado photos is a picture he took near Miami, Texas. Most of the sky is filled by the lower end of a huge storm cloud. A tornado hangs from the cloud, kicking up dust from the empty prairie, while the blue and yellow sky seems to go on forever.

In some ways, this wasn't a difficult picture for Warren to take. He's an experienced photographer. But before he could shoot this picture, he had to be in the right place at the right time — and that's what makes photographing tornadoes such hard work.

On a spring day, dozens of thunderstorms may develop over thousands of square miles in Texas, Oklahoma, and Kansas, but usually only a few will produce tornadoes. Since many tornadoes are on the ground only a few minutes, they will disappear before Warren can photograph them unless he is nearby. Other times, he will follow a promising storm, only to have it head off into an **14** area where there are no roads. Tornadoes may be hidden by falling rain, making it impossible to take a picture of them. Still other storms may produce tornadoes at night, when it's too dark for Warren to take pictures and too dangerous for him to be out chasing because he can't see what's happening.

A successful tornado photographer needs patience, a good understanding of

67

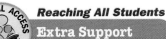

Reaching All Students
Extra Support

Strategy Modeling

LS 1.1

Question If students need help forming questions that can be answered after reading, use this example to model the strategy for them.

I have questions about storm chasing: What do the seasons have to do with chasing storms? What seasons are best for chasing storms? The diagram on page 65 shows seven months and three kinds of storms. I wonder if its purpose is to show when different storm seasons are. I'll read to find the answers.

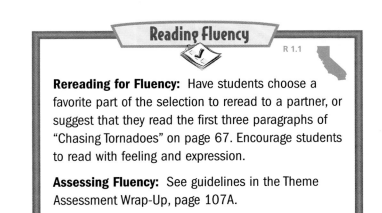

Reading Fluency

R 1.1

Rereading for Fluency: Have students choose a favorite part of the selection to reread to a partner, or suggest that they read the first three paragraphs of "Chasing Tornadoes" on page 67. Encourage students to read with feeling and expression.

Assessing Fluency: See guidelines in the Theme Assessment Wrap-Up, page 107A.

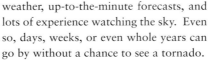

Wrapping Up Segment 1

pages 57–68

First, provide the Extra Support in the box below for students who need it. Then bring all students together.

- **Review Predictions/Purpose** Discuss with students which predictions were accurate and which needed to be revised. Record any changes and new predictions.

- **Model Strategies** Refer students to the Strategies Poster and have them take turns modeling Question and other strategies they used as they read. Provide models if needed (page 67).

LS 1.1
- **Share Group Discussions** Have students share their questions and literature discussions.

LS 2.3.a
- **Summarize** Ask students to use their selection maps to summarize the first segment.

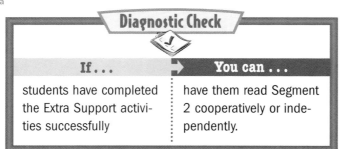

Diagnostic Check ✓

If ...	➤	You can ...
students have completed the Extra Support activities successfully		have them read Segment 2 cooperatively or independently.

weather, up-to-the-minute forecasts, and lots of experience watching the sky. Even so, days, weeks, or even whole years can go by without a chance to see a tornado.

Every spring, Warren makes a trip to an area called Tornado Alley. This area stretches from northern Texas up into Oklahoma, Kansas, and Missouri. Warren and his tornado chase partner, Tom Willett, spend about six weeks tracking down giant storms and searching for tornadoes.

68

Getting ready to go tornado chasing takes lots of time and work. Warren checks all his cameras and buys plenty of film. He makes sure he has up-to-date copies of road maps for all the states he'll be traveling through. He arranges for friends to take care of Megamouth.

Finally, toward the end of April, Warren and Tom stow all their equipment in Shadow Chaser, Warren's black four-wheel-drive vehicle. Warren designed Shadow Chaser to help him find tornadoes and chase them safely. It is packed with electronic equipment, including radios, radio scanners, and a weather center that can take many different kinds of measurements. Shadow Chaser has emergency flashing lights, a long-range cellular phone, and special cabinets for storing equipment. It even has a front-mounted video camera that can make videotapes through the windshield.

As Warren and Tom drive toward Tornado Alley, their hopes are high. They know that they'll cover thousands of miles before returning to Tucson. They know they'll chase storms that never produce tornadoes and they'll probably hear about nearby tornadoes they can't get to in time. But with hard work, careful study of weather data, and a little luck, sometimes they'll have a day like the one they had on May 5, 1993.

End of Segment 1:
pages 57–68

Reaching All Students
Extra Support

Segment 1 Review

Before students join the whole class for Wrapping Up above, they should

- check predictions
- take turns modeling Question and other strategies they used
- add to **Transparency 1–10,** check and revise their Selection Map on **Practice Book** page 24, and use it to summarize

Reaching All Students
On Level   Challenge

Reading Card 6

LS 1.1

Literature Discussion

In mixed-ability groups of five or six, have students discuss the questions they formed while reading. Additionally, suggest some literature discussion prompts (Reading Card 6).

- What personal traits and skills does a storm chaser need? Does Warren Faidley have these? Use examples to support your answer.

- Why do you think people were so amazed by Warren's photo of the lightning bolt hitting the light pole?

California Standards pp. 68–69

W 2.2.a Demonstrate understanding
LS 1.1   Ask new questions
LS 2.3.a Summarize events/details

Eye of the Storm: Chasing Storms with Warren Faidley

Beginning of Segment 2: pages 69–75

Tornado Chase Diary: May 5, 1993

Warren keeps a diary, in which he writes about his storm chases. Here are some of the things that happened on May 5, 1993, a remarkable day.

Amarillo, Texas — Morning

I awaken in a motel in Tornado Alley. As I walk to the window to peek out the drapes, I remember that last night's weather forecast showed that this might be a good chase day. Tom climbs out of bed and turns on The Weather Channel.

Later in the morning, Tom and I get the Shadow Chaser ready for the day. I test the radios, check under the hood, make sure the tires are inflated and the lights and wipers are working. We clean, pack, and return each piece of equipment to its usual place. During a chase, there isn't time to look around for a roll of film or lens for a camera.

Finally, we check out of the motel and head for a nearby restaurant for breakfast. Then we drive into town to fill the gas tank and get a few supplies.

National Weather Service Office — Early Afternoon

We arrive at the Amarillo office of the National Weather Service. Here I get an update on local weather conditions, as well as a chance to see a satellite picture

of the area. I use current weather information to draw a map of where today's thunderstorms are likely to form. The reports are saying that there is a moderate chance of severe weather in our area, and some of the thunderstorms will probably produce tornadoes. Since the storms aren't expected to develop until later in the afternoon, we take some time off and drive to a nearby garage to have the oil changed in Shadow Chaser.

A couple hours later, we're back at the National Weather Service office to make our final chase decisions. It's beginning to look like the area north of town is our best bet. We pull out the highway maps and start looking at possible routes.

As we leave town, I call a friend and fellow chaser who gives weather reports for a local TV station. He confirms that severe storm clouds are building right where we're headed. He also says that a

69

Reading Segment 2
pages 69–75

LS 2.3.a

Purpose Setting Have students summarize the selection so far and predict what will happen during Warren Faidley's tornado chase.

Journal Writing Students can use their journal to record their questions, the answers they find, and additional questions that come to mind as they read.

W 2.2.a

Vocabulary *(page 69)*

severe: serious or extreme in nature

Before reading Segment 2, preview the text using the notes below. **While** reading, model strategies (pages 55A and 55B). **After** reading, review the segment (page 74) before students join the Wrapping Up discussion.

pages 69–72 Warren Faidley kept a tornado chase diary in May of 1993. In one section of the diary, he wrote about what he and his tornado-chasing partner Tom saw and did while chasing tornadoes over the course of one entire day. How does he get ready for a day of tornado chasing? Where and when do they stop as they ride along through northern Texas?

pages 72–75 In the evening Warren drives into Oklahoma to continue the chase. He spots many tornadoes, each with its own shape. It is a record-breaking day for tornado-watching, and Warren gets some spectacular shots. Why was it easy for them to celebrate at the end of the day?

Supporting Comprehension

R 2.3

15 What clues does Warren look for that tell him a tornado might be forming, and how does he go about chasing it? (looks for a large, dark cloud close to the ground with a funnel cloud forming beneath it; watches where the storm goes and follows it)

16 How can tornado chasers and other weather experts help people who are traveling through tornado country? (by telling other drivers what the forecast is and whether it is safe to drive)

17 What does the author mean when he says that chasing a tornado is like playing a game of chess? (A storm moves, and storm chasers must follow the storm's path.)

Vocabulary (page 70)

funnel cloud: tornado cloud that is wide at the top and narrow where it touches the ground

rotate: to swirl in a circular motion

---

news team from his station is already headed there.

Near Panhandle, Texas — Late Afternoon

The sky is hazy, but in the distance we can see the tops of anvil-shaped storm clouds. We stop the truck to pick up the TV report. My forecaster friend is on. He's pointing to an area on his map about fifty miles north of our location. "It looks like we're going to have some severe storms in this area!" he says. We get back into the truck and drive north.

Near Gruver, Texas — Early Evening

The overcast skies clear enough to show a giant thunderstorm just ahead. Then our radio scanner locks onto a message from the TV crew's chase unit. "There's a large funnel cloud coming from this storm," says the message. While the crew describes its location, I look at the map. "They're only eight miles from here," I tell Tom. "Let's go and find it!"

As we approach Gruver, we see the red TV van parked on the side of the road. A cameraman is pointing his camera at a huge, gray-white funnel cloud hanging from the base of a dark cloud. As Tom parks the truck, I use the radio to call in a weather report to the National Weather Service station in Amarillo. The funnel cloud pulls back up into the storm.

We head north, following the storm. As we drive, watching the back of the storm, we can see the clouds darkening and beginning to rotate. The white clouds at the top of the storm take on the shape of a giant mushroom. I'm excited, but I'm worried too. I know that anyone in the path of this storm is in terrible danger.

We follow the storm down the highway. Gradually, it turns and heads back toward the road. We pull over and wait for the storm to cross. While we're waiting, a large semi truck pulls up beside us. The driver opens his window and leans out.

"Hey, are you guys tornado chasers? Is that a tornado forming? Is it safe for me to drive under it?"

"We're not sure if it's going to turn into a tornado, but I'd wait here and let it pass," I answer.

16

We all watch as the swirling mass crosses the highway. A small funnel cloud reaches down from the storm cloud — and then quickly disappears. I reach for the microphone and call Amarillo:

"This is Warren. I'm about eight miles north of Gruver, just west of Highway 207. Tom and I are looking at a large cloud mass that is organizing and rotating."

"Roger, Warren," replies the spotter coordinator. "We're watching the same area on radar. Thanks."

70

Word Study

Radar Students may be interested to know that the word *radar* is an acronym made up of the first letters of the following words: *radio detection and ranging*. A radar set works by emitting radio waves toward an object and then measuring the waves, or echoes, that bounce back.

R 1.2

Reaching All Students

English Language Learners

Intermediate and Advanced Fluency

R 2.1

Draw lines to help teach the compass points *North, South, East,* and *West.* At the end of each line label the points appropriately. On a map, point to your state. Then point to a state north of your state. Continue by pointing to a state *south of, east of,* and *west of.* Help students locate on a map the places mentioned so far in the selection.

California Standards pp. 70–71

R 1.2 Use word origins	**R 2.3** Discern main ideas
R 2.1 Understand text features	**W 2.2.a** Demonstrate understanding
R 2.2 Use order to analyze text	**W 2.2.c** Develop interpretations

R 2.2

Now we begin to worry about losing the storm. There aren't very many roads in this area, and most of them run north–south or east–west. Since most storms don't continue for long in these directions, following a storm is a little like playing a huge game of chess. Tom loads his cameras back into the truck while I check the road map.

We make our way along a tangle of unmarked farm roads a few miles from the Oklahoma border. Since the storm is on our west side, and it's moving northeast, we can safely stay quite close

17

71

Reading Card
8

W 2.2.a
W 2.2.c

Organize Information Visually

Distribute Reading Card 8. Have students use it to help them create a graphic organizer, such as a log book or schedule, that gives an at-a-glance view of the storm chase that occurred on May 5, 1993.

Comprehension Skill Lesson
Sequence of Events

OBJECTIVES

Students identify the sequence of events and words that signal sequence.

Review sequence of events by writing these sentences from page 69 on the board: *I awaken in a motel in Tornado Alley... Later in the morning, Tom and I get the Shadow Chaser ready for the day.* Point out which event happened first and which event happened second. Indicate how the words *later in the morning* signal when the second event happened.

Ask students to name other events from pages 69–70. List them in order on the board. Note words students use to signal sequence. Ask them how the headings on these pages can also help them identify the sequence of events. (They give the times of day when the events happened.)

Next, remind students that sometimes two or more events happen at the same time. Read aloud this sentence from page 69: *As we leave town, I call a friend and fellow chaser who gives weather reports for a local TV station.* Point out that the word *as* signals that two events happen at the same time: *they left town* and *Warren called a friend*. Then have students identify the simultaneous events and signal word in the second complete paragraph on page 70. (While the crew describes the location of the tornado, Warren looks at the map; *while*)

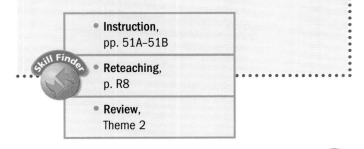

Skill Finder

• **Instruction,**
  pp. 51A–51B

• **Reteaching,**
  p. R8

• **Review,**
  Theme 2

▶ Strategy Focus: Question

Student Modeling Ask students to share some of the questions they formed about this part of the selection. Also ask them to discuss any answers they have found. You might offer these prompts:

- Let's say you want to know what to look for when you're trying to spot a cloud that might produce a tornado. How can the description on page 72 help you answer this question?

- What other questions did you have in mind as you read?

▶ Supporting Comprehension

18 What details does the author include that show that tornadoes have tremendous destructive force? (They suck up soil from fields and rip up fences.)

R 2.3

19 Why is it so difficult for Warren and Tom to photograph "their tornado"? (It keeps moving; the funnel clouds descend but go back up; they can't chase the storm everywhere it goes because the roads sometimes don't go in the same direction as the storm.)

Vocabulary *(page 72)*

updraft: upward-moving current of air

vortices: whirlpools made of rotating air or water; plural of *vortex*

multivortex: having many *vortices* at once

---

to the updraft without getting in the direct path of a tornado.

Near the Oklahoma/Texas Border — Evening

We keep an eye on the swirling clouds as we drive along. Suddenly, from the center of the clouds, a large white funnel appears.

"Look, Tom! Another tornado!" I exclaim. "That thing is less than a mile away!"

I reach for the microphone and call in another report. The funnel cloud begins to stretch. Soon it looks like the trunk of a huge elephant, wiggling over the green fields below. Then it touches down, officially becoming a tornado. When the funnel touches the ground, wispy little vortices appear around the main cloud of wind. As these mini-tornadoes spin, they kick up dust of their

72

own. I grab the microphone and send another message to the spotter coordinator:

"We're about three or four miles south of the Texas/Oklahoma state line," I explain. "And we're looking at a large, multivortex tornado on the ground."

Just inside the Oklahoma state line, the road turns slightly toward the northwest. The tornado begins to cross the road a little ahead of us. We stop to try and get some pictures, but the light isn't good. It's hard to see the tornado clearly against the background of the cloud. The air is hazy, and another storm to the west is blocking the sunlight.

"We've got a great tornado here," I say to Tom, "but the light is terrible." We load our gear back into the truck and roll down a bumpy dirt road, looking for better light, while the tornado swirls along beside us.

As Tom drives, he keeps glancing at the tornado. Suddenly he yells, "Warren! There's another tornado forming!" I peer through the window and see a debris cloud forming, sucking up soil from a field.

18

"Wow," Tom says. "Look what it's doing to that fence!" We watch as it rips a section of barbed-wire fence out of the ground and scatters it across the field. The small area of spinning wind, with no

---

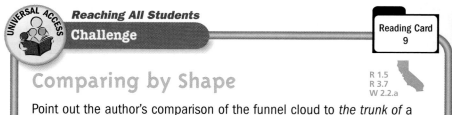
Comparing by Shape

R 1.5
R 3.7
W 2.2.a

Point out the author's comparison of the funnel cloud to *the trunk of a huge elephant, wiggling over the green fields below* on page 72. Reading Card 9 directs students to look through the selection and identify instances in which the author compares tornadoes to the shapes of other objects, and then asks them to sketch what the different tornadoes might look like.

California Standards pp. 72–73

R 1.5 Figurative language
R 2.1 Understand text features
R 2.2 Use order to analyze text

R 3.7 Evaluate author's techniques
W 2.2.a Demonstrate understanding
LS 2.3 Respond to literature

• SELECTION •

Eye of the Storm: Chasing Storms with Warren Faidley

visible funnel cloud above, tears across the fields.

"Slow down, Tom," I say. "I can't see the funnel cloud connected to that thing — and we sure don't want to get hit by it." A few seconds later, the debris cloud disappears.

We follow a maze of unmarked dirt roads until we reach a dead end. As we turn around and drive back toward the highway, we watch as the edges of the storm cloud wrap around the tornado, hiding it from sight. Many sightings of "our" tornado, as well as others in the area, are being reported over the radio. I'm happy to hear that so far the tornadoes haven't hit any populated areas.

19

East of Guymon, Oklahoma — Evening

It's about 7:30 p.m. when we pull back onto the highway. As we head east, we see a long, thin tornado crossing the road a few miles ahead.

"I bet that's our tornado," I tell Tom. "It looks like it's weakening. We've got to shoot it now!" When Tom stops, I jump out the door, set my camera on the hood to steady it, and go through another roll of film. As we watch, the funnel pulls back up into the dark clouds.

West of Hooker, Oklahoma — Evening

Traveling along the highway, we're joined again by the crew from the TV

73

Reaching All Students

English Language Learners

Intermediate and Advanced Fluency

Remind students that on page 73 Warren tells Tom to "*slow down.*" On page 75, the same phrase appears again, this time to describe the tornado's movement. Explain that *slow down* means "to do something more slowly." Tell students that the opposite of *slow down* is *speed up* ("to do something more quickly"). Ask for other examples of two-word phrases that describe action.

LS 2.3
LS 2.3.c

Revisiting the Text

R 2.1
R 2.2

Tested Skill

Comprehension Skill Lesson
Text Organization

OBJECTIVES

Students differentiate nonfiction that is organized by main idea from nonfiction that is organized by sequence of events.

Tell students that giving information in sequence is one way of organizing a nonfiction article. Nonfiction can also be organized by main ideas. Have students look back at the first part of the selection (pages 57–68). Ask them whether this section is organized by sequence or by main ideas, and how they can tell. (ideas; The headings in the first part of the article tell readers what the most important ideas in each section are.)

Ask volunteers to read aloud the headings and subheadings on pages 69–75, in sequence. Record them on the board as they are mentioned. Point out that the author has chosen to write this section of the article in a sequence that begins in the morning, when Tom and Warren get up, and ends in the evening. Ask students how the headings help them understand where Warren went at different times of the day. (Example: Each heading gives a time of day and the name of the place where Warren was at that time.)

Discuss with students the reasons authors might have for using both types of text structure. Have students form pairs and scan their science or social studies textbooks to find examples of both types of text organization to share with the class.

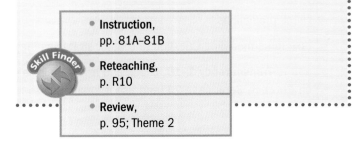

Skill Finder

| • Instruction, pp. 81A–81B |
| • Reteaching, p. R10 |
| • Review, p. 95; Theme 2 |

LS 2.3.c Use examples

Reading

··

▶ Supporting Comprehension

R 2.3
R 2.4

20 Why do you think the author includes so much dialogue in the description of the storm chase? (to make the passage more exciting; to make the people seem real)

21 Why does Warren decide to stop shooting for the day, even though tornadoes are still form-ing? (It's dangerous to try to chase tornadoes at night.)

22 Why do you think Warren and Tom were still shaking their heads that night? (They were in dis-belief; they usually don't see so many tornadoes in one day.)

Vocabulary *(page 75)*
fortunate: lucky

74

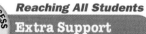

Reaching All Students
Extra Support

Segment 2 Review

Before students join the whole class for Wrapping Up on page 75, they should

• check predictions

• take turns modeling Question and other strategies they used

• add to **Transparency 1–10,** check and revise their Selection Map on **Practice Book** page 24, and use it to summarize

Reaching All Students
On Level / Challenge

Literature Discussion

LS 1.1

In mixed-ability groups of five or six, students can discuss the ques-tions they asked as they read and discuss the Responding questions on page 76 of the Anthology.

California Standards pp. 74–75

R 2.3 Discern main ideas	**LS 2.3.a** Summarize events/details
R 2.4 Inferences/generalizations	**LS 2.3.b** Understand ideas/images
LS 1.1 Ask new questions	**LS 2.3.c** Use examples

Eye of the Storm: Chasing Storms with Warren Faidley

station. Down the road, I see a huge wedge-shaped tornado on the ground.

"Stop!" I yell to Tom. Tom hits the brakes and we stare through the windshield. The tornado looks like it's about seven or eight miles from us, moving away, although the fading light makes it hard to be sure. As we watch, the funnel slows down, and then it disappears. We continue on and I spot another tornado. This one looks like a long stovepipe.

20 "This is incredible," I say to Tom. "We've got two large thunderstorms here, and they're dropping tornadoes everywhere!"

The stovepipe tornado swirls into the clouds before we can get close enough for pictures. As we watch it disappear, I **21** realize that it's getting too dark for any more photos. I know the storms are still active, and I'm worried that the fading light could hide any newly forming tornadoes. Chasing any more tornadoes today would be too dangerous.

Near the Oklahoma/Kansas Border — Evening

As the last of the light disappears, we see two more tornadoes in the distance. One is headed north, rolling into Kansas. As we drive back to Amarillo, we listen to news reports on the radio. "With as many tornadoes as we have had on the ground tonight," says a reporter, "it's a

miracle that none of them have hit a town. We do have at least one report of a farm being destroyed, with no injuries so far. But beyond that, we have been extremely <u>fortunate</u>."

Amarillo, Texas — Night

It's 11:00 p.m. by the time we finally pull back into the motel parking lot. As Tom and I unload Shadow Chaser, we're still shaking our heads about what we've seen. **22** The tornadoes we saw caused some damage, but there have been no reports of any deaths or injuries. That makes it easier to celebrate our seven-tornado day.

End of Segment 2: pages 69–75

Wrapping Up Segment 2

pages 69–75

First, provide Extra Support for students who need it (page 74). Then bring all students together.

- **Review Predictions/Purpose** Ask students whether their predictions turned out to be correct. R 2.4

- **Model Strategies** Draw students' attention to the Strategies Poster. Invite them to take turns modeling the Question Strategy and other strategies they used while reading. If necessary, model the Question Strategy (page 64). LS 1.1

- **Share Group Discussions** Have students share their responses to the questions they formulated while they read the segment. Ask them to use information from the selection to describe the good and bad parts of working as a storm chaser. LS 2.3.a LS 2.3.b LS 2.3.c

- **Summarize** Ask students to use the completed Selection Map (**Practice Book** page 24) to summarize the selection. LS 2.3.a

Comprehension/Critical Thinking

1 How has Warren Faidley turned his interests and skills into a profitable career? (He turned his fascination with storms and his photography skills into a career as a storm chaser and a stock photo agency owner.) **Cause and Effect** R 2.4

2 In what ways do you think Warren Faidley's work as a storm chaser is helpful to people? (His work might help people avoid dangerous storms or learn how to better predict them.) **Making Judgments**

Diagnostic Check

If . . .	You can . . .
students have difficulty summarizing the selection	form small groups and have them retell the information presented in each section.

Responding

► Think About the Selection

Discuss or Write Have students discuss or write their answers. Sample answers are provided; accept reasonable responses that are supported with evidence from the selection.

1 **Drawing Conclusions** He is courageous, he is curious about whirlwinds, and he likes adventure.

R 2.4
R 3.3
W 2.2.a

2 **Making Judgments** No. He stopped taking pictures of tornadoes when it got dark because it wasn't safe. This shows that Warren tries to be safe when chasing tornadoes.

3 **Recognizing Text Organization** The headings helped me understand what each section is about. The calendar helped me understand at what time of year different kinds of storms happen.

R 2.1

4 **Interpreting Figurative Language** He means that the air was filled with the sizzling sound of lightning.

R 3.1

5 **Expressing Opinions** Possible answers: yes, because it would be exciting; no, because it would be scary

6 **Connecting to Personal Experiences** Answers will vary.

7 **Connecting/Comparing** Compare and Contrast *Alike*—Both Warren and Jonathan face danger caused by forces of nature. *Different*—Warren chooses to be in dangerous situations, but Jonathan doesn't; the types of danger they face are different.

R 3.3
W 2.2.a

Responding

Think About the Selection

1. Think about Warren Faidley's decision to ride his bike into a whirlwind. What does this action tell you about about him?

2. Do you think Warren would face any danger in order to get a spectacular storm shot? Use facts from the selection to support your answer.

3. How did the section headings of *Eye of the Storm* help you understand the selection? How did the calendar on page 65 help you understand Warren's job?

4. On page 62, the author writes, "The air was sizzling" before Warren took his famous underpass photograph. What do you think he means?

5. Would you want to accompany Warren on a storm chase? Why or why not? If so, which kind of storm would you want to see up close, and why?

6. Warren's interest in storms led to his career as a weather photographer. What interests do you have that might lead to a career?

7. **Connecting/Comparing** Compare Warren's risk from tornadoes and lightning with Jonathan's risk in *Earthquake Terror*. How are their situations alike and different?

Describing

Write a Job Description

Think about what a storm chaser does. Then write a job description for a storm chaser. Include the character traits and skills a storm chaser should have. Note any special equipment a storm chaser should be able to use.

Tips
- List the job requirements in two categories: traits and skills.
- In the skills category, include special equipment.

Reading | Inferences/generalizations (R2.4)
Writing | Establish topic, order (W1.2.a)

76

Reaching All Students

English Language Learners

Intermediate and Advanced Fluency

Writing Support

Bring the classified section of a local newspaper to class and read aloud some job descriptions. You may also want to provide a model job description for a teacher, for example. Then work with students to list job requirements in two categories: *traits required* and *skills required*. Pairs of students can work together on their job descriptions.

California Standards pp. 76–77

R 2.1 Understand text features
R 2.4 Inferences/generalizations
R 3.1 Analyze literary forms
R 3.3 Determine character traits
W 2.2.a Demonstrate understanding
LS 2.3 Respond to literature

W 2.2.a

Math

Estimate Mileage

Estimate the number of miles Warren Faidley drove from his home to where he began his tornado chase diary for May 5, 1993. Use the map on page 55, a ruler, and this scale — one inch equals 300 miles.

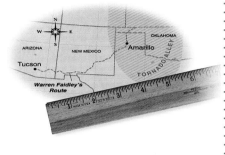

Viewing

Compare Photographs

Choose two photographs from the selection and write a caption that compares and contrasts them. Choose two lightning photographs, two tornado photographs, or one of each kind. Tell about both the details and the mood of each photograph.

Internet

Take an Online Poll

Have you ever seen a lightning strike or a tornado? What kind of storm have you been in? Do you enjoy books about the weather? Take our online poll and let us know. Visit Education Place. **www.eduplace.com/kids**

Math   Use estimation (MMR2.1)

77

Personal Response

Invite volunteers to share their personal responses to *Eye of the Storm*. As an alternative, ask students to write their thoughts and opinions about storm chasing in their journals, or to respond in their own way.

Comprehension Check

Assign **Practice Book** page 25 to assess students' understanding of the selection.

Practice Book page 25

Eye of the Storm
Comprehension Check

Name _____

An Interview with Warren Faidley

The questions below can be used to interview Warren Faidley about his life and work. Write the answer Warren might give to each question.

What is your occupation? I chase tornadoes, hurricanes, and lightning storms and try to photograph them. I sell my pictures through my stock photo agency. **(2 points)**

When did you first become interested in storms? Describe one of your early experiences with storms. I've been interested in storms since I was a boy. One time I rode my bike into the middle of a dust whirlwind. **(2)**

What led you to become a professional storm chaser? I was working for a newspaper. I had a hobby, which was taking photos of lightning from my balcony. During one particular storm, I chased a dark thundercloud and managed to get an astonishing picture of a lightning bolt hitting a pole. I realized I could sell photos of storms, so I started a stock photo agency. **(2)**

How important is it for someone in your line of work to have a good knowledge of weather patterns? Why? It's very important, because weather patterns cause storms, and the same patterns occur in the same places every year. Knowing about storm patterns tells a storm chaser where to go, and when. **(2)**

What advice would you give a young person who wants to become a storm chaser? Possible response: Be patient. Be careful. **(2)**

Theme 1: **Nature's Fury**   25
Assessment Tip: Total **12** Points

Reaching All Students

English Language Learners

Additional Language Development Before assigning the Responding activities on page 77, use these suggestions:

LS 2.3

Beginning/Preproduction Help students create a word web for types of weather. Students can copy the webs and add drawings for the words.

Early Production and Speech Emergence Ask students to describe the types of storms in your area. This can be done orally or in writing.

Intermediate and Advanced Ask: *What is the most frightening storm you have experienced? Describe the storm and what you felt.*

End-of-Selection Assessment

Selection Test Use the test in the **Teacher's Resource Blackline Masters** to assess selection comprehension and vocabulary.

Student Self-Assessment Have students assess their reading with additional questions such as

* What parts of the selection were difficult for me? Why?

* What strategies helped me understand the selection?

* Would I recommend this selection to my friends? Why?

Career Link

pages 78–81

R 1.1
R 2.1
R 2.2

> ## ► Skill: How to Read a Sequence Chart

Read aloud the title of the link and the author's name. Explain that this article is about how a meteorologist gathers the information needed to make a weather forecast.

Point out the sequence chart on page 79 and tell students that the lesson on the left-hand side of page 78 will help them read the chart.

Help students identify the process that is shown on the sequence chart. (the steps in collecting weather data) Ask students to read and discuss the three steps in the process. Have a volunteer point to the arrows that show that this sequence chart is read from top to bottom.

Vocabulary *(pages 78–79)*

meteorologist: scientist who studies the weather

telecast: television broadcast; news report

atmosphere: layer of air that surrounds the earth, where weather systems occur

---

Career Link

Skill: How to Read a Sequence Chart

❶ Read the **title** of the sequence chart. It tells what **process** is being shown.

❷ Read the **steps** in the process by following the **arrows** from top to bottom or left to right.

❸ Look for **order words**, such as *next, then, resulting,* and *now.*

California Standards

Standards to Achieve

Reading
• **Understand text features (R2.1)**
• **Use order to analyze text (R2.2)**

Science
• **Weather forecasts (S4.d)**

STORM WARNING

When TV viewers of 7 News in Boston tune in to Mishelle Michaels's weekend weather forecast, they're seeing the end of a long day of data collection and weather analysis — the complex job of the meteorologist.

Mishelle's New England telecast relies on information collected at thousands of points around the world. These "eyes" and "ears" that scout the weather include radar, satellites, surface observing sites, and weather balloons.

Mishelle Michaels, meteorologist, analyzes computer models to prepare for her evening broadcast.

78

Reaching All Students
Classroom Management

All Students

R 2.1

Reading the Article Involve all students in the activities under How to Read a Sequence Chart, Activating Prior Knowledge, Visual Literacy Lesson, and Comprehension Check. Pair students needing extra support with more proficient partners to read the article. Remind students to get as much information as possible from the photos, charts, and diagrams.

California Standards pp. 78–79

R 1.2 Use word origins
R 2.1 Understand text features
R 2.2 Use order to analyze text

R 2.4 Inferences/generalizations

Collecting the Data

Surface observing sites report the current weather conditions every hour of every day of every year.

Weather balloons take measurements of the atmosphere from ground level to thousands of feet above the earth.

Weather satellites 22,000 miles up take photographs of clouds to show the movement of weather systems.

Through a network of NEXRAD (Next Generation Radar) stations, radar images display the motion and intensity of rain or snow.

The National Weather Service's supercomputer then processes this information, making sixteen billion calculations per second.

The resulting charts and weather images are made available to Mishelle and other meteorologists around the United States to help them create their forecasts.

79

► Activating Prior Knowledge/Background

Ask students what they know about a weather forecaster's job. Invite them to describe different images they have seen on TV weather reports, such as satellite photos and computer-generated weather maps. Tell students that they are going to read an article about how weather forecasters gather the information they need to make predictions about weather.

Purpose Setting Read the title and introduction aloud. Invite students to read the headings in the article, view the photographs and diagrams, and predict what the article will be about. Suggest that students use the Question Strategy as they read.

R 2.4

R 1.2
R 2.2

Vocabulary and Comprehension

Some students may need help reading some of the scientific terms in this article. You might read aloud and explain the boxed vocabulary words before students read.

After reading, work with students to summarize the information on each page. Make sure students understand that all the material on these pages is related to one central topic: gathering information about weather.

Reading

Career Link *continued*
pages 78–81

Revisiting the Text

Visual Literacy Lesson
Communicating Information

R 2.1

OBJECTIVES
◎

Students identify the purposes of a variety of visual formats.

Have students view and describe the images on page 79. (photograph from a satellite; photo of a weather station; computer-generated image of weather patterns) Point out that information can be communicated in many different ways, and that scientists in particular have developed many methods of communicating information in pictures or charts so it is easy to understand.

Ask students to name the different resources Mishelle Michaels uses to gather the information for her forecasts. (computer models, charts showing temperature, radar images) Ask: *Which sources communicate information using pictures? Which sources communicate information using numbers?*

Vocabulary *(pages 80–81)*

analyzes: thinks critically and carefully about information in order to interpret it

atmospheric science: the study of the air that surrounds the earth

(80) THEME 1: **Nature's Fury**

Analyzing the **Weather**

102

Reviewing Conditions

To begin her forecast, Mishelle checks the current conditions — temperatures, winds, and weather patterns — for the city of Boston, its surrounding communities, and much of New England.

Observing Radar Images

Enhanced Doppler radar provides Mishelle with images of thunderstorms moving toward Boston from the west. Next Generation Radar can detect dangerous shifts in wind direction that may result in tornadoes.

Mishelle <u>analyzes</u> hundreds of the charts and images that the National Weather Service provides. But that is only part of the studying and interpreting she has to do before she can create a forecast. The data gathered from the radar and satellites requires the explaining abilities of the meteorologist so that it makes sense to the rest of us.

80

Reaching All Students
English Language Learners

Intermediate and Advanced Fluency

LS 2.3

Tell students that the word *career* means "what a person does; one's profession." Say: *I am a teacher; teaching is my career.* Ask: *What is Warren's career?* (storm chaser) Have students name the careers they think are interesting.

California Standards pp. 80–81

R 2.1 Understand text features	**LS 2.3** Respond to literature
R 2.4 Inferences/generalizations	**LS 2.3.c** Use examples
LS 1.1 Ask new questions	**S 4.d** Use data to predict weather

Hearing from Weather Watchers

Local volunteers of all ages phone Mishelle daily with detailed weather reports from their communities. These observations are often invaluable in helping Mishelle put together the pieces of the forecasting puzzle.

Analyzing Computer Models

By analyzing weather charts and maps created by the National Weather Service from computer models, Mishelle develops a four- to five-day forecast for Greater Boston and New England. She relies on her education and experience to accurately predict how the atmosphere will change.

Career File

Meteorologist

Are you interested in following the weather professionally? You'll need a four-year college degree in Meteorology or Atmospheric Science. It also helps if you enjoy . . .

- Watching clouds and chasing storms (from a safe distance)
- The challenge of problem-solving
- Communicating your knowledge with others

Meanwhile, contact your local television station about becoming a volunteer weather observer.

81

Reaching All Students

Challenge

Science

Have interested students set up an outdoor classroom weather station and keep a log book that shows weather conditions and air temperatures over the course of several days. They can compare their findings with the weather report in the local newspaper. For an additional challenge, ask students to find the average temperature at different times of day and communicate this information in a graph or chart.

► Comprehension Check

R 2.4
LS 1.1
LS 2.3
LS 2.3.c
S 4.d

Comprehension/Critical Thinking Ask students what questions they formulated as they read. Have them share these questions for other students to answer. Then have students answer these questions about the article. Ask them to support their answers with information from the article.

1 Where does a meteorologist get the information needed to prepare a weather forecast? (from charts and images created by the National Weather Service; from current weather conditions in the region; from radar images; from eyewitness accounts of weather volunteers) **Summarizing**

2 Why is it important for a meteorologist to be able to interpret information that is presented in different forms? (because a meteorologist has to interpret graphs, radar pictures, computer images, and satellite photos) **Making Inferences**

3 Do meteorologists rely only on data collected by machines? Explain. (No. They also rely on information from local volunteers, who call and tell them what the weather is like.) **Noting Details**

4 **Connecting/Comparing** How is the work Warren Faidley does similar to the work Mishelle Michaels does? How are the two kinds of work different? (*Alike*—Both study the weather and rely on different sources of information. *Different*—They study the weather for different purposes: Warren studies it so he can get pictures of storms; Mishelle studies it so she can prepare weather forecasts. Also, Warren's job is more dangerous.) **Drawing Conclusions**

R 2.1
R 2.2
W 2.2.a
LS 2.3

Comprehension Skills

✓ Text Organization

Students

- identify different ways in which authors organize text

- distinguish between nonfiction that is organized by main idea and by sequence of events

- use text features such as headings as a guide to the organization of information

- learn academic language: **text organization, main idea, sequence of events**

▶ Teach

Remind students that authors organize information in a variety of ways, to suit different purposes and audiences. Use **Transparency 1–10** and examples from the selection to discuss the following types of text organization:

▪ Text can be organized by main ideas.

▪ Text can be organized according to sequence of events.

Students can refer to the selection for examples of the organizing principles described above, and to **Practice Book** page 24.

Practice Book page 24

Eye of the Storm
Graphic Organizer **Selection Map**

Name

Sele

Transparency 1–10

Fill in thi

Pages

Page 59
Page 60

Page 64

Page 65

Page 67

Pages

Selection Map

Pages 59–68

Page 59   Storm Chasing
Page 60   Warren Faidley: Storm Chaser

Page 64   What Happens to Warren's Photos After He Takes Them?

Page 65   Storm Seasons and Chasing

Page 67   Chasing Tornadoes

Pages 69–75

One Day in the Life of a Storm Chaser
Morning

Afternoon

Evening

24   Theme 1:
Assessment

TRANSPARENCY 1–10
TEACHER'S EDITION PAGES 156C AND 781A

NATURE'S FURY Eye of the Storm
Graphic Organizer Selection Map

Graphic Organizer: Selection Map

Page 67 Chasing Tornadoes _Every spring, Warren goes to Tornado Alley_
to chase tornadoes.

Page 69–75 One Day in the Life of a Storm Chaser

Morning _____

Modeling Remind students that in the first part of *Eye of the Storm,* the author organizes the text by main idea. Point out that this is a good way to organize information about a topic such as storm chasing. Ask a student to identify the main idea in the section under the heading "Chasing Tornadoes" (page 67). Next have a volunteer read the first paragraph on page 69, under the heading "Tornado Chase Diary: May 5, 1993." Model how the author changes the text organization for the second part of the selection, and why.

Think Aloud

The author organized by main idea to give information such as the season for chasing tornadoes. Now he switches to organizing by sequence of events. Why? So that he can show us a typical day in which Warren follows tornadoes, step by step. From this point on, the headings show us the place where Warren is, and the time of day.

California Standards pp. 81A–81B

R 2.1   Understand text features
R 2.2   Use order to analyze text
W 2.2.a Demonstrate understanding

LS 2.3 Respond to literature

► Practice

Have students work in pairs to locate the following examples of text organization in *Eye of the Storm.* Have them record their responses in a chart like the one below. Sample responses are given. Accept all reasonable responses.

Way of Organizing Information	Page	What Is Explained
by main idea	page 65	when tornadoes, hurricanes, and thunderstorms happen
by sequence	page 69	what happened during the morning of May 5, 1993

Have students discuss why they think the author chose to organize the information as he did. Then meet as a class to talk about the examples and reasons.

► Apply

Use **Practice Book** pages 26–27 to diagnose whether students need Reteaching. Students who do not need Reteaching may work on Challenge/Extension activities, page R11. Students who need easier text to apply the skill can use the **Reader's Library** selection, "White Dragon: Anna Allen in the Face of Danger," and its Responding activity.

Skill Finder
- Review, p. 95; Theme 2
- Reteaching, p. R10

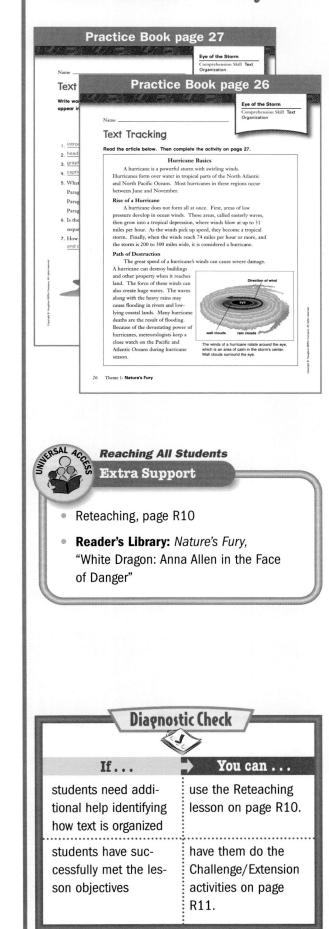

Practice Book page 27

Practice Book page 26

Reaching All Students

Extra Support

- Reteaching, page R10
- **Reader's Library:** *Nature's Fury,* "White Dragon: Anna Allen in the Face of Danger"

Diagnostic Check

If . . .	You can . . .
students need additional help identifying how text is organized	use the Reteaching lesson on page R10.
students have successfully met the lesson objectives	have them do the Challenge/Extension activities on page R11.

Information & Study Skills
Using Print and Electronic Card Catalogs

Transparency 1–11

Electronic Card Catalog

First screen

Your search: A=KRAMER, STEPHEN
                Holdings highlighted for: CENTRAL

LINE
   #   --------Author--------   ----------------Title---------------   Date
   1   Kramer, Stephen P.   Avalanche / by Stephen Kramer; photograph   1992
   2   Kramer, Stephen P.   Caves / by Stephen Kramer; photographs by   1995
   3   Kramer, Stephen P.   Eye of the Storm: chasing storms with War   1997
   4   Kramer, Stephen P.   How to think like a scientist: answering   1987
   5   Kramer, Stephen P.   Theodoric's rainbow / written by Stephen K   1995

Type: the number of a line and press <ENTER> TO SEE MORE INFORMATION.
   N   TO SEE NEXT SCREEN   P   to see the Previous screen
   B   to Backup   ST   to start over

Second screen

CALL NUM: J 502.8 K
AUTHOR: Kramer, Stephen P.
TITLE: How to think like a scientist: answering questions by the scientific method
PUBLISHER: T.Y. Crowell, c1987.
SUBJECTS: Science--Methodology--Juvenile literature.
             Science--Methodology.

LIBRARY HOLDINGS:
             APTOS
             1.   CALL NUMBER: J 502.8 K -- JNONFICTION -- Available
             BOULDER CREEK
             2.   CALL NUMBER: J 502.8 K -- JNONFICTION -- Available

Teach

Card Catalogs Remind students that all the books, videotapes, and other materials in a library are listed in either a card catalog or an electronic catalog, or both. Explain that a card catalog is a cabinet that contains multiple cards for each book in the library. Review these points:

■ The three types of cards in the catalog are title cards, subject cards, and author cards.

■ The cards are filed alphabetically by the first letter of the first word, not including *a, an,* or *the.*

■ A call number, often in the upper left-hand corner, tells the location of the book in the library.

■ Suggestions for related titles may appear at the bottom of a card.

■ All nonfiction books are shelved in numerical order and all fiction books are shelved alphabetically.

Electronic Catalogs Explain that electronic catalogs are organized in much the same way as card catalogs. The first screen tells how to do a simple search. Often the user begins by typing in a letter code that tells the computer whether to search for the book by its author, subject, or title. If there are several books by the same author, books with similar titles, or many books on the same subject, the screen will show a numbered list of choices. The user can type in the number of any selection, press *enter*, and see the same information on the screen as that on the card catalog. The screen will also tell whether the book is available or checked out.

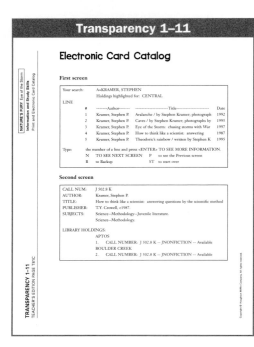

Your search: A=KRAMER, STEPHEN
Holdings highlighted for: CENTRAL

LINE
   #   --------Author--------   ----------------Title---------------   Date
   1   Kramer, Stephen P.   Avalanche / by Stephen Kramer ; photograph   1992
   2   Kramer, Stephen P.   Caves / by Stephen Kramer ; photographs by   1995
   3   Kramer, Stephen P.   Eye of the storm: chasing storms with War   1997
   4   Kramer, Stephen P.   How to think like a scientist: answering   1987
   5   Kramer, Stephen P.   Theodoric's rainbow / written by Stephen K   1995

Type: the number of a line and press <ENTER> TO SEE MORE INFORMATION
   N   TO SEE NEXT SCREEN   P   to see the Previous screen.
   B   to Backup.   ST   to start over.

Modeling Display **Transparency 1–11** and demonstrate how to use an electronic catalog. Have students write their answers to your questions.

> **Think Aloud**
>
> *I want to find out whether the library has any books by Stephen Kramer, the author of* Eye of the Storm: Chasing Storms with Warren Faidley. *I type A=Kramer, Stephen, putting his last name first, and press* enter. *The screen that comes up shows me that the library owns how many of his books?* (five) How to Think Like a Scientist *sounds interesting. Which number is that on the list?* (4) *I type 4 and press* enter. *The screen that comes up next shows me the call number I can use to find the book. What is the call number?* (J502.8K) *It also tells me that book is on the shelves in two branches, and it provides subject headings I can use to find books on similar topics.*

▶ Practice

Have pairs of students select a book from the classroom library. Ask each pair to explain the different ways in which they could search for the book in a public library. Ask them to be specific. Ask:

- Which word or words in the title would you use in your title search?

- How would you type in the author's name in an electronic catalog?

- Under which subject headings would you expect to find this book or similar books?

▶ Apply

Tell students to use a card catalog or electronic catalog to check out a book on extreme weather conditions or one by a favorite author from the school or public library. They can share with the class how they used the catalog and call number to locate the book.

CALL NUM: J 502.8K
TITLE: How to think like a scientist: answering questions by the scientific method

CALL NUM: J 502.8K
SUBJECTS: Science–Methodology–Juvenile literature
Science-- Methodology
AU
TI   CALL NUM: J 502.8K
sci   AUTHOR: Kramer, Stephen P.
PU   TITLE: How to think like a scientist: answering questions by the
      scientific method
LI   PUBLISHER: T.Y. Cowell, c1987.
AP   SUBJECTS: Science–Methodology–Juvenile literature
1.C   Science–Methodology
BO
2.C   LITERARY HOLDINGS:
      APTOS
      1.CALL NUMBER: J 502.8K–JNOFICTION
      BOULDER CREEK
      2.CALL NUMBER: J 502.8K–JNOFICTION

Decoding Longer Words

✓ Structural Analysis: Syllabication

▶ Teach

Write this sentence on the board: *Warren wasn't looking for cactus wrens.* Write V under *a* and *u*. Write C under the second *c* and the *t*. Explain that words with a VCCV syllable pattern break between the consonants. Place a slash between the *c* and *t* and blend the syllables and the suffix: /CAC•tuss/. Tell students the first two syllables are closed and therefore have short vowel sounds.

Write this phrase: *the fury of nature.* Write *V* under *a* and *u* of the word *nature.* Write *C* under *t.* Explain that many words with a VCV pattern divide after the consonant. Tell students that *NAT* is a closed syllable and would have a short vowel sound. Explain, however, that since *NAT yuhr* does not sound familiar, they should try the long vowel sound and divide the word after the first vowel: *NAY chuhr.* Next, write this phrase: keeps a <u>diary</u>. Point out the CVVC pattern in the word *diary.* Explain that in this word, the *i* and *a* each stand for a separate sound, and the word is divided *di/a/ry.*

Teacher Modeling: Write this sentence on the board: *Warren set his camera on the hood.* Point to *camera.* Do not pronounce it. Model how to divide this word with the VCV pattern.

Think Aloud

I see that this word has a VCV pattern, (write V under the first a and e, and write C under the m). I'm not sure if the first vowel is long or short. I'll try the a with a long vowel sound, as in the word came. But /CAYM•uh•ruh /doesn't sound right. I'll try the short vowel sound instead. /CAM•uh•ruh/ sounds right, and it makes sense in the sentence.

▶ Practice

Write these sentences on the board and have students copy the underlined words: *The <u>radio</u> report tells about a <u>spectacular</u> funnel cloud; A <u>tornado</u> appears on the <u>horizon</u>; It was a <u>remarkable</u> day; A cloud mass is <u>organizing</u>.* Tell them to identify and circle the syllabic patterns in each underlined word. Have them work in pairs to decode the words and determine their meanings.

▶ Apply

Have students complete **Practice Book** page 28.

Skill Finder	Strategy Review: Phonics/Decoding, p. 55A	Reteaching, p. R16

California Standards pp. 81E–81F

R 1.2 Use word origins
LC 1.5 Spell correctly

Word Work Instruction	
DAY 1	• Spelling Pretest • Spelling Instruction
DAY 2	• Structural Analysis Instruction • Spelling Practice
DAY 3	• Phonics Instruction • Spelling Practice
DAY 4	• Structural Analysis Reteaching • Vocabulary Skill Instruction • Spelling Game
DAY 5	• Expanding Your Vocabulary • Spelling Test

OBJECTIVES

Students

• read words with two or more syllables

• read words with long vowel sounds

• use the Phonics/Decoding Strategy to decode longer words

Teacher's Note

Make sure students understand that when two or more consonants stand for a single sound, the consonants stay together when the word is divided into syllables. Demonstrate using these examples: *bush/es, hatch/es, wish/ful, path/less.*

Phonics

Spelling Connection

✓ Long Vowels /ā/, /ē/, /ī/

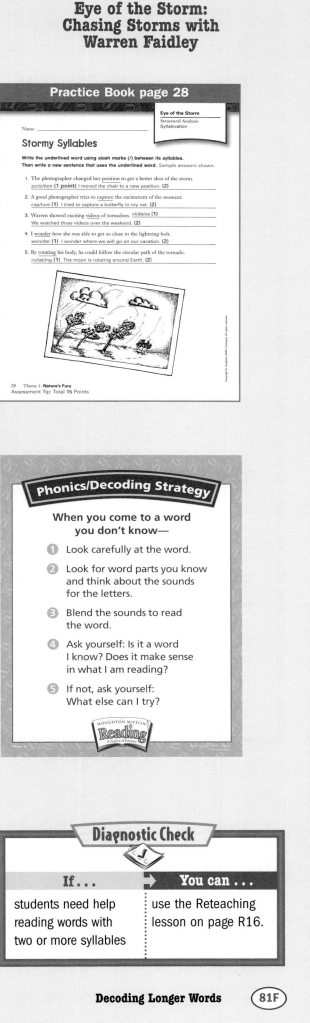

Eye of the Storm
Structural Analysis
Syllabication

Name _____

Stormy Syllables

Write the underlined word using slash marks (/) between its syllables.
Then write a new sentence that uses the underlined word. Sample answers shown.

1. The photographer changed her position to get a better shot of the storm.
   po/si/tion **(1 point)** I moved the chair to a new position. **(2)**

2. A good photographer tries to capture the excitement of the moment.
   cap/ture **(1)** I tried to capture a butterfly in my net. **(2)**

3. Warren showed exciting videos of tornadoes. vi/de/os **(1)**
   We watched three videos over the weekend. **(2)**

4. I wonder how she was able to get so close to the lightning bolt.
   won/der **(1)** I wonder where we will go on our vacation. **(2)**

5. By rotating his body, he could follow the circular path of the tornado.
   ro/tat/ing **(1)** The moon is rotating around Earth. **(2)**

28 Theme 1: **Nature's Fury**
Assessment Tip: Total 15 Points

▶ Teach

Tell students that understanding long vowel sounds can help them use the
Phonics/Decoding Strategy to decode unfamiliar words. Explain that

- the letters *a*-consonant-*e*, *ai*, and *ay* can all stand for the /ā/ sound.

- the letters *ea* and *ee* can stand for the /ē/ sound.

- the letters *i*-consonant-*e*, *igh*, and *i* can stand for the /ī/ sound.

Modeling Write this sentence and model how to decode *hurricane: People
listened to the howling winds of a hurricane.*

Think Aloud

*This word is unfamiliar to me, so I will try to sound it out. I see the pattern a-con-
sonant-e at the end of the word, so the last syllable is probably* kayn. *The first two
syllables are almost like the word* hurry. *When I combine the parts of the word, I
get* HUR ih kayn. *I recognize that word and it makes sense in the sentence.*

▶ Practice

Write these sentences and have students copy the underlined words.

> *In the <u>meantime</u>, he stands and watches; The rotating wall was
> filled with all kinds of debris, including <u>tumbleweeds</u> and
> newspaper pages; "Another tornado!" I <u>exclaimed</u>; There were
> many <u>sightings</u> of our tornado; Warren hadn't always planned
> to be a storm <u>chaser</u>; I reached for the <u>microphone</u>.*

Have pairs of students circle the long vowel sounds in each underlined word,
pronounce the word, and check to see if it makes sense in the sentence. Call on
individuals to model at the board.

▶ Apply

Tell students to decode the following words from *Eye of the Storm* and discuss
their meanings: *lightning, mysterious,* page 59; *tripods,* page 61; *blinding,
astonished,* page 62; *feature,* page 64; *experienced,* page 67.

Phonics/Decoding Strategy

**When you come to a word
you don't know—**

1. Look carefully at the word.

2. Look for word parts you know
   and think about the sounds
   for the letters.

3. Blend the sounds to read
   the word.

4. Ask yourself: Is it a word
   I know? Does it make sense
   in what I am reading?

5. If not, ask yourself:
   What else can I try?

HOUGHTON MIFFLIN
Reading
A Legacy of Literacy

Diagnostic Check

If . . .	➡ You can . . .
students need help reading words with two or more syllables	use the Reteaching lesson on page R16.

Word Work

OBJECTIVES

Students write spelling words with long vowel patterns.

Spelling Words

Basic Words

speech	mild
claim	waist
strike*	sway
stray	beast
fade*	stain
sign*	fleet
leaf	stride
thigh	praise
thief	slight*
height	niece

Review Words	Challenge Words
free*	campaign
twice	describe*
gray*	cease
least*	sacrifice
safe*	plight

*Forms of these words appear in the literature.

Reaching All Students
Extra Support

Basic Word List You may want to use only the left column of Basic Words with students who need extra support.

Spelling
 The /ā/, /ē/, and /ī/ Sounds

Day 1   Teaching the Principle

Pretest Use the Day 5 Test sentences. Say each underlined word, read the sentence, and then repeat the word. Have students write only the underlined word.

Teach Write /ā/, /ē/, /ī/ on the board as column heads. Add the following Basic Words below the corresponding head: /ā/: *fade, claim, stray;* /ē/: *leaf, speech, thief;* /ī/: *strike, thigh, sign, height.* Point to each symbol used as a column head and ask students to identify the sound the symbol stands for. Then say each word in the first column, have students repeat it, and ask them to name its vowel sound. (/ā/) Underline *ade* in *fade, ai* in *claim,* and *ay* in *stray.* Explain that *a*-consonant-*e, ai,* and *ay* are three patterns for spelling the /ā/ sound.

Repeat the procedure for the words in the other two columns. Tell students that the /ē/ sound is often spelled with the patterns *ea* and *ee*, but that it can also be spelled with the *ie* pattern. Explain also that the /ī/ sound is often spelled with the patterns *i*-consonant-*e, igh,* and *i*, but that it is sometimes spelled with the pattern *eigh*.

Next, say each word in the second column of the Basic Word list. Have a student name its vowel sound. Write the word in the correct column and underline the pattern that spells its vowel sound.

Practice/Homework Assign **Practice Book** page 407. Tell students to use this Take-Home Word List to study the words they missed on the Pretest.

Day 2   Reviewing the Principle

Practice/Homework Review the spelling principle and assign **Practice Book** page 29.

Day 3   Vocabulary

Classifying Write the Basic Words on the board. Then dictate each word group below and have students write the Basic Word that completes the group.

flower, stem, (leaf)	*step, walk,* (stride)	*small, little,* (slight)
reward, honor, (praise)	*cousin, uncle,* (niece)	*monster, dragon,*
hit, punch, (strike)	*spot, smudge,* (stain)	(beast)
herd, team, (fleet)		*length, width,* (height)

Day 3 *continued...*

Next, have students use each Basic Word from the board orally in a sentence.

Practice/Homework For spelling practice, assign **Practice Book** page 30.

Day 4 | Treasure Map Game

Have students work in small groups. Each group will make a treasure map game board and twenty-five 3" x 5" word cards, with a Basic or Review Word on one side and its definition on the other. They will also need game markers and a spinner. Students place the cards in a pile, with the definitions facing up. A player picks up the top card, reads the definition aloud, and spells the word that fits it. If the spelling is correct, the player spins the spinner and moves the number of spaces shown. Players take turns until one "finds" the treasure.

Practice/Homework For proofreading and writing practice, assign **Practice Book** page 31.

Day 5 | Spelling Assessment

Test Say each underlined word, read the sentence, and then repeat the word. Have students write only the underlined word.

Basic Words

1. Did you hear the <u>speech</u> about litter?
2. The boys <u>claim</u> that they did not cheat.
3. Do not <u>strike</u> anything with that stick.
4. We found a <u>stray</u> cat.
5. Some colors can <u>fade</u> in the wash.
6. Did you see the name on the <u>sign</u>?
7. This <u>leaf</u> fell from that oak tree.
8. The ball hit my <u>thigh</u>.
9. The police caught the <u>thief.</u>
10. You and I are the same <u>height.</u>
11. The weather is clear and <u>mild</u>.
12. The pants are too big around the <u>waist</u>.
13. The trees <u>sway</u> in the wind.
14. The <u>beast</u> looked like a bear.
15. The ink <u>stain</u> would not wash out.
16. The <u>fleet</u> of ten boats will sail today.
17. That man walks with a long <u>stride</u>.
18. Be sure to <u>praise</u> Mary's good work.
19. The difference between the twins is <u>slight</u>.
20. My sister's daughter is my <u>niece.</u>

Challenge Words

21. Her <u>campaign</u> will begin next week.
22. Can you <u>describe</u> what your house looks like?
23. The sun will come out when the rains <u>cease</u>.
24. It was a <u>sacrifice</u> for Tom to miss the show in order to help his sister.
25. Is there any news about the <u>plight</u> of the people caught in the storm?

Technology LC 1.5

Spelling Spree!™

Students may use the **Spelling Spree!™ CD-ROM** for extra practice with the spelling principles taught in this lesson.

Practice Book page 407

Practice Book page 31

Practice Book page 30

Practice Book page 29

Eye of the Storm
Spelling The /ā/, /ē/, and /ī/ Sounds

Name _____

The /ā/, /ē/, and /ī/ Sounds

When you hear the /ā/ sound, think of the patterns *a*-consonant-*e*, *ai*, and *ay*. When you hear the /ē/ sound, think of the patterns *ea* and *ee*. When you hear the /ī/ sound, think of the patterns i-consonant-*e*, *igh*, and *i*.

/ā/	fade claim stray
/ē/	leaf speech
/ī/	strike thigh sign

► The long vowel sounds in the starred words have different spelling patterns. The /ē/ sound in *thief* and in *niece* is spelled *ie*. The /ī/ sound in *bright* is spelled *igh*.

Write each Spelling Word under its vowel sound.
Order of answers for each category may vary.

/ā/	/ē/	/ī/
claim (1 point)	speech (1)	strike (1)
stray (1)	leaf (1)	sign (1)
fade (1)	thief (1)	thigh (1)
waist (1)	beast (1)	height (1)
sway (1)	fleet (1)	mild (1)
stain (1)	niece (1)	stride (1)
praise (1)		slight (1)

Spelling Words
1. speech
2. claim
3. strike
4. stray
5. fade
6. sign
7. leaf
8. thigh
9. thief*
10. height*
11. mild
12. waist
13. sway
14. beast
15. stain
16. fleet
17. stride
18. praise
19. slight
20. niece*

Theme 1: **Nature's Fury**   29
Assessment Tip: Total 20 Points

••• **Houghton Mifflin Spelling and Vocabulary** •••
Correlated instruction and practice, pp. 18, 24, 91

UNIVERSAL ACCESS

Reaching All Students

Challenge

Challenge Word Practice Have students make word search puzzles, writing the Challenge Words across, down, or diagonally in a grid and filling in other letters to complete the grid. Tell students to trade puzzles and circle the Challenge Words they find.

OBJECTIVES

Students

- use alphabetical order to locate words in a dictionary

- use pairs of guide words to locate the page of specific entry words

- learn academic language: **entry words, guide words**

Practice Book page 32

Eye of the Storm

Name _____

Wor___

Read eac___
words an___
the colun___
and the e___

| trout |
| trust |
| tropical |

| tropical (|
| wayward___ |
| practice (|
| durable (|
| charter (1 |

32   Theme 1:
Assessment

Transparency 1–12

NATURE'S FURY Eye of the Storm
Vocabulary Skill Dictionary: Alphabetical
Order and Guide Words

**Dictionary: Alphabetical
Order and Guide Words**

antiquity / anywhere

anvil (ăn′ vĭl) *n.* A heavy block of iron or steel with a smooth flat top on which metals are shaped by hammering.

picket fence / pie chart
pied / pile
Philippines / phony
phosphate / physical

adrift / adventure: adult, among, account, advance, adverb
frankfurter / freedom: frame, fortune, free, fraud, formal
live / loaf: load, long, lizard, llama, level, lie
top hat / tort: total, torch, talk, tornado, trail

TRANSPARENCY 1–12
TEACHER'S EDITION PAGE T81I

Vocabulary Skills

✓ *Dictionary: Alphabetical Order and Guide Words*

▶ Teach

Display **Transparency 1–12,** covering all but the first two guide words and the sample dictionary entry at the top of the page.

■ Explain to students that the words defined in a dictionary, also known as **entry words,** are arranged in alphabetical order. Point out the entry word *anvil* and its definition.

■ Explain that the words *antiquity* and *anywhere* are called **guide words.** Point out that pairs of guide words at the top of every page of a dictionary indicate the first and last entry on each page. Tell students that looking at guide words is a good way to quickly locate the page on which a particular entry word appears.

---

antiquity / anywhere

anvil A heavy block of iron or steel with a smooth flat top on which metals are shaped by hammering.

Modeling   Uncover the four pairs of guide words on the transparency below the entry for *anvil.* Use them to model how to locate the dictionary page where you would find the entry word *photograph.*

Think Aloud

I know that dictionary entries are in alphabetical order. So the entry word photo-graph *must be on a page with guide words that start with the letters* ph*. I see two sets of these, so I have to look at the next few letters in the word. Now I see that* photograph *would come after* phosphate, *but before* physical. *So it must be on the page with those guide words.*

California Standards pp. 81I–81J

R 1.4 Use roots and affixes

▶ Practice

Display the next section of the transparency with sample guide words and possible entry words. For each pair of entry words, ask students to identify which of the entry words that follow would appear on a page with those guide words. Have students work in pairs to check their work.

▶ Apply

Have students complete **Practice Book** page 32.

Expanding Your Vocabulary
Words from Many Languages: Weather Words

Explain to students that many words used to describe weather phenomena came to English from other languages. For example, the word *typhoon* comes from a Chinese word meaning "great wind," and the word *tornado* comes from a Spanish word meaning "thunderstorm." Have students look in the dictionary or encyclopedia to find the origins of other words for weather phenomena, including *hurricane, monsoon,* and *cyclone.*

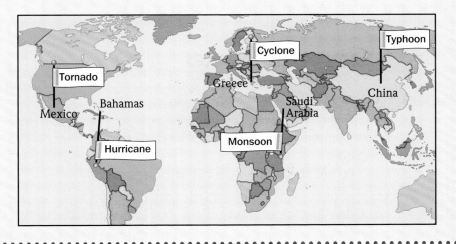

• Challenge/Extension activities, see p. R17

Teacher's Note

Word Histories Explain to students that the Greek root *phot,* meaning "light," forms the base of many English words. Ask students how some of these words and their definitions relate to light.

photograph: an image recorded by a camera and reproduced on a photosensitive surface

photojournalism: journalism making primary use of photographs

photography: the art or occupation of taking and printing photographs

photosensitive: sensitive to light

R 1.4

⋯ **Houghton Mifflin Spelling and Vocabulary** ⋯
Correlated instruction and practice, p. 20

Reaching All Students
UNIVERSAL ACCESS
Extra Support

Vocabulary Support

In order to use guide words effectively, students must be able to alphabetize words to at least the third or fourth letter. Suggest that students work in pairs to practice alphabetizing lists of words with similar spellings.

Writing & Language

Writing and Language Instruction

DAY 1	• Daily Language Practice • Grammar Instruction • Journal Writing
DAY 2	• Daily Language Practice • Writing a Response to a Prompt • Journal Writing • Grammar Practice
DAY 3	• Daily Language Practice • Grammar Instruction • Writing a Job Description
DAY 4	• Daily Language Practice • Listening/Speaking/Viewing • Writing: Improving Your Writing • Grammar Practice
DAY 5	• Daily Language Practice • Grammar: Improving Your Writing

OBJECTIVES

Students

• identify conjunctions

• identify compound sentences

• proofread and correct sentences with grammar and spelling errors

• correct run-on sentences to improve writing

• learn academic language: **conjunction, compound sentence**

Technology

Wacky Web Tales

Students may use the **Wacky Web Tales** floppy disk to create humorous stories and review parts of speech.

Grammar Skills

 **Conjunctions; Compound Sentences**

Day 1   Conjunctions

Display these sentences on **Transparency 1–14.**

> Jill looked at the thermometer and the barometer.
> The weather was not cold yet, but it soon would be.
> Rain was expected that afternoon or evening.

Point out the conjunctions. (*and, but, or*) Go over the following rules with students:

■ A conjunction may be used to join words in a sentence.

■ A conjunction may be used to join sentences.

Have students look again at each sentence on **Transparency 1–14** and write on a separate sheet of paper whether the conjunctions join words or sentences. Then have students look back in *Eye of the Storm* to find sentences with *and, or,* or *but,* and identify what the conjunction in each joins.

Day 2

Practice/Homework Assign **Practice Book** page 33.

Day 3   Compound Sentences

Display these sentences on **Transparency 1–15.**

> *The sky darkened in the west, and a chill wind whistled across the plains.*
> *Jill buttoned up her coat and walked out into the yard.*

Identify the conjunction in each sentence. Point out that the first sentence contains two complete sentences joined by *and.* Explain that it is a compound sentence. Ask students whether the second sentence is a compound sentence. (no)

California Standards pp. 81K–81L

W 1.6 Edit and revise work
LC 1.1 Sentence structure/transition

Day 3 *continued...*

Go over the following rules:

■ If two sentences are related, they can be combined to make one compound sentence.

■ Use a comma (,) and the conjunction *and, but,* or *or* to combine the sentences.

Have students read the remaining sentences on **Transparency 1–15** and tell whether each is a compound sentence. Then have students find additional examples of compound sentences in *Earthquake Terror* or *Eye of the Storm*.

Day 4

Practice/Homework Assign **Practice Book** page 34.

Day 5 Improving Your Writing

Avoiding Run-ons Tell students that a good writer joins short sentences with a comma and a conjunction, rather than letting them run together.

Run-on: Jill usually rode her bike to soccer practice, in this weather she would get a ride with the Carltons.

Run-on: The lights were out at the Carltons' house there was no car in the driveway.

Corrected: Jill usually rode her bike to soccer practice, <u>but</u> in this weather she would get a ride with the Carltons.

Corrected: The lights were out at the Carltons' house<u>, and</u> there was no car in the driveway.

Have students review a piece of their own writing to see if they can improve it by identifying and correcting run-ons.

Practice/Homework Assign **Practice Book** page 35.

Practice Book page 35

Practice Book page 34

Practice Book page 33

Transparency 1–15

Transparency 1–14

Transparency 1–13

Daily Language Practice

Correct two sentences each day.

1. the crowd cheered when the spech was over.

2. The beest walked quickly but it did not run.

3. I will call my neice, or i will write to her.

4. The weather has been maild all winter

5. The theef jumped up but he could not climb the fence.

6. The spill on the rug left a huge stane

7. this backpack has a belt that fits around my wast.

8. Can you read the words on that sine

9. do you see that large flet of boats in the harbor?

10. The hite of the shelf is ten feet but my cat can reach the top.

Daily Language Practice

········· **Houghton Mifflin English** ···········
Correlated instruction and practice, pp. 44–49

Diagnostic Check

If . . .	→	You can . . .
students need extra help identifying conjunctions and compound sentences		use the Reteaching lessons on pages R22 and R23.

W 1.2.a
W 1.2.b
W 1.2.c
W 1.6
W 2.1
W 2.2
W 2.3
W 2.4

OBJECTIVES

Students

- identify the characteristics of a good written response

- write in response to a prompt

- improve their writing by correcting capitalization and punctuation errors

- learn academic language: **writing prompt**

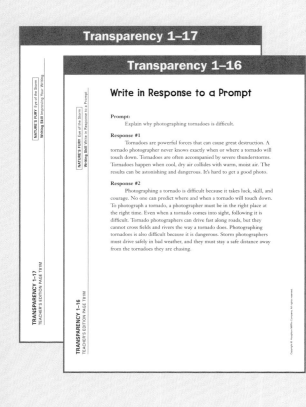

Writing Skills
A Response to a Prompt

▶ Teach

Ask students if they know what a *writing prompt* is. (a direction that asks for a written answer of one or more paragraphs) Tell students that writing prompts are a part of many writing tests, and that there are different kinds of prompts. A prompt might ask them to

- ■ write about an experience

- ■ give a personal opinion about an issue

- ■ explain a process

- ■ persuade readers to do or think something

▶ Practice

Display **Transparency 1–16.** Ask students to restate what the prompt is calling for. (an explanation of why photographing tornadoes is a difficult job) Invite students to read the answers and ask which response answers the prompt most completely. (Response #2) Guide students in explaining why Response #2 is a better response than Response #1. Then discuss with students the guidelines for writing in response to a prompt.

Guidelines for
Writing a Response to a Prompt

- Carefully read the prompt. Identify key words that tell what kind of answer is needed. Think about the meaning of the key words.
- Plan your answer. Jot down main ideas and details. Arrange your ideas in order.
- Begin your answer by restating the prompt.
- Check your answer. Does your response answer the prompt? Edit your response to make sure it does.

Key Word	Meaning
compare	point out similarities
contrast	point out differences
explain	give reasons
describe	give details
summarize	give main points briefly
discuss	consider all aspects of a subject

California Standards pp. 81M–81N

W 1.2.a Establish topic, order
W 1.2.b Use details, transitions
W 1.2.c Conclude with a summary
W 1.6 Edit and revise work

W 2.1 Write narratives
W 2.2 Write responses to literature
W 2.3 Write research reports
W 2.4 Write persuasive compositions

▶ Apply

Have students write a response to one of the following prompts:

- ■ What job do you think is the most difficult or dangerous? Explain why you think it is difficult or dangerous.

- ■ Think about how Warren Faidley customized Shadow Chaser for chasing tornadoes. Describe how you would customize a vehicle for a specific task.

Students can use **Practice Book** page 36 to help them plan and organize their writing.

Improving Your Writing
Capitalizing and Punctuating Sentences

LC 1.3
LC 1.4
W 1.6

Teach Point out to students that when writing in response to a prompt, it's important to use correct capitalization and punctuation.

Practice To model how to find and correct capitalization and punctuation errors in sentences, display **Transparency 1–17.** Ask students to read the sample response. Guide them in identifying the errors in the capitalization and punctuation of the sentences. Then discuss how each error could be fixed so that the sentences are correctly written.

Apply Assign **Practice Book** page 37. Then have students review their responses to the writing prompt and correct capitalization and punctuation as needed.

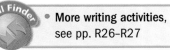

Skill Finder
• More writing activities, see pp. R26–R27

Eye of the Storm: Chasing Storms with Warren Faidley

Technology

The Writer's Resource Library

Students may use this set of reference tools as they work on their own writing.
©Sunburst Technology Corporation, a Houghton Mifflin Company. All Rights Reserved.

Type to Learn™

Students may use **Type to Learn™** to learn proper keyboarding technique.
©Sunburst Technology Corporation, a Houghton Mifflin Company. All Rights Reserved.

Portfolio Opportunity

Save students' responses for samples of their writing development.

Practice Book page 37

Eye of the Storm
Name

Cap
Punc

A fifth-gr
storm ch
wrote the
punctuat
Use thes
and end

Practice Book page 36

Eye of the Storm
Writing Skill: Response to a Prompt

Name

Responding to a Prompt

A **prompt** is a direction that asks for a written answer of one or more paragraphs. Read the following prompts.

Prompt 1
What job do you think is the most difficult or dangerous? Explain why you think it is difficult or dangerous.

Prompt 2
Think about how Warren Faidley customized Shadow Chaser for chasing tornadoes. Describe how you would customize a vehicle for a specific task.

Choose one prompt and use the chart below to help you write a response. First, list key words in the prompt. Then jot down main ideas and details you might include. Finally, number your main ideas, beginning with *1*, from most to least important.

Key Words	Main Ideas	Details
Prompt 1: explain (1 point) Prompt 2: describe	(2)	(2)

Write your response on a separate sheet of paper. Start by restating the prompt. Then write your main ideas and supporting details in order of importance from most to least important, or from least to most important. (5)

36 Theme 1: *Nature's Fury*
Assessment Tip: Total **10** Points

•••••••• **Houghton Mifflin English** ••••••••

Correlated instruction and practice, pp. 180–181, H35–H36

LC 1.3 Colons and quotation marks
LC 1.4 Use correct capitalization

Listening/Speaking/Viewing
Having a Literature Discussion

▶ Teach

Ask students what the purpose is for a discussion of literature. Remind them that in a discussion, two or more people talk together about a topic in order to understand it better. In a literature discussion, people discuss their thoughts and reactions about something they have all read. Ask students to help you start generating a list of guidelines for a group discussion of literature. They will expand the list in small groups. Make sure that the following are mentioned:

- Stay on the subject.

- State facts and ideas clearly and briefly.

- Support ideas by referring to the text.

- Ask thoughtful questions.

- Listen carefully.

- Avoid interrupting others.

- Respect views and interpretations of others, even if you disagree.

Tell students that they will have many opportunities to discuss works of literature. Explain that answering certain questions can be worthwhile in a literature discussion. Have students suggest some questions they might ask. Include some of the following questions as starters:

- What was the author's purpose in writing this selection? How well do you think the author achieved that purpose? Why?

- What passage did you like best? What did you like about it?

- What do you think the author means (in this part/on this page/in this line)?

- Would you like to read another book (on this subject/by this author/about this character)? Why or why not?

Reaching All Students

English Language Learners

Literature Discussion

LS 1.6

English language learners may need additional guidance to help them participate in a literature discussion. Explain that making eye contact shows that a listener is paying attention, and that nodding conveys understanding or agreement. Remind English speakers to allow English language learners enough time to get their thoughts out.

California Standards pp. 810–81P

LS 1.1 Ask new questions
LS 1.6 Verbal and nonverbal cues
LS 2.2 Informative presentations

LS 2.3.a Summarize events/details
LS 2.3.b Understand ideas/images

OBJECTIVES

Students

- generate guidelines for participating in a literature discussion

- identify useful questions and prompts for a discussion of literature

▶ Practice

Have students form small groups and create a poster of guidelines and questions, continuing the lists that you have started with them. Have them organize their posters under two headings: *Rules for a Good Discussion* and *Questions for Discussing Literature.*

▶ Apply

Ask the same groups of students to hold a discussion of *Eye of the Storm: Chasing Storms with Warren Faidley* or of *Earthquake Terror* by Peg Kehret, using their posters to guide them. Encourage students to ask other questions about the selection in addition to those on their poster.

Improving Listening and Speaking Skills
Discussing Literature

LS 1.6

Share with students the following tips for discussing literature in a small group:

- Look at the person who is speaking.

- Use gestures such as nodding your head to show that you understand what's being said.

- If you don't understand something, ask the person to repeat it or restate it another way.

- Compare other people's ideas with your own. Try to keep an open mind.

- If you notice someone in your group who is especially quiet, encourage that person to contribute by asking, for example, "What do you think about that, John?"

Skill Reminder

Encyclopedia

Remind students that encyclopedias contain information on a wide variety of subjects. The information is arranged alphabetically in one volume or many volumes. Some encyclopedias are also in electronic form. Discuss where students can find encyclopedias.

Have students brainstorm subjects that they would like to research. Write their suggestions on the board. Point to one suggestion on the list. Ask students what keywords they would use to find information on that subject in an encyclopedia.

Taught: *Grade 4, Theme 4*

Reviewed: *Grade 4, Theme 6*

California Standards pp. 81Q–81R

R 1.4 Use roots and affixes
W 1.2.a Establish topic, order
LC 1.5 Spell correctly
LS 1.2 Verbal, nonverbal messages

W 1.2.a
LS 1.2

Spiral Review

Comprehension: *Following Directions*

▶ Review

Review what students have learned about following directions.

- Read through each step carefully and be sure you understand all of the directions.
- Gather any necessary materials.
- Follow each step in order and finish each step before going on to the next.
- Look for order words such as *first, next,* and *last.*

Remind students that if they wanted to buy a photograph from Warren Faidley, they would have to follow some directions. Read aloud the section in *Eye of the Storm* that begins on page 64, "What Happens to Warren's Photos After He Takes Them?" Then discuss the steps for buying a photograph from Mr. Faidley as you write them on the board.

1. First, write Mr. Faidley a letter asking for a photograph.
2. Next, choose a photograph from the samples Mr. Faidley sends.
3. Finally, send Mr. Faidley a fee for the photograph.

Discuss with students what might happen if any of these steps were left out.

▶ Apply

Have students work in pairs to create a set of directions for how to walk from their desks to a place or an object in the classroom. For example, have them write directions for how to walk from their desks to the clock. Remind students to use order words. Then have students exchange directions with another pair and try to follow them.

Skill Finder • **Following Directions** Grade 4, Theme 4, p. 449C-D; Grade 5, Theme 3, p. 333A-B

Dictionary and Structural Analysis: Prefixes
re-, dis-, un- and Suffixes *-ness, -ment, -ful, -less, -ion*

▶ Review

Review what students have learned about prefixes and suffixes, listing examples as shown below.

■ A prefix is a word part added to the beginning of a base word. For example, the prefixes *re-, dis-,* and *un-* can be added to the words *name, appear,* and *load* to form the words *rename, disappear,* and *unload.*

■ A suffix is a word part added to the end of a base word. For example, the suffixes *-ness, -ment, -ful, -less,* and *-ion* can be added to the words *happy, require, meaning, relent,* and *act* to form the words *happiness, requirement, meaningful, relentless,* and *action.*

■ Prefixes and suffixes can change the meaning of a word. For example, the word *appear* means "to come into view." The prefix *dis-,* which means "not," changes *appear* to *disappear,* which means "to pass out of sight." The dictionary definition of a prefix or suffix can help students figure out the meaning of a new word.

> Prefixes: re-, dis-, un-. Re + name = rename;
> dis + appear = disappear; un + load = unload
> Suffixes: -ness, -ment, -ful, -less, -ion. Happy +
> ness = happiness, require + ment = require-
> ment, meaning + ful = meaningful, relent +
> less = relentless, act + ion = action

▶ Apply

Have students work in small groups. Assign a prefix or suffix to each group. Ask them to use a dictionary to find the meaning of the prefix or suffix. Then ask each group member to find a word containing that prefix or suffix and identify the base word and its meaning.

- **Structural Analysis: Prefixes *re-, dis-, un-*** Grade 4, Theme 5, p. 555E
- **Structural Analysis: Suffixes *-ness, -ment, -ful, -less, -ion*** Grade 4, Theme 5, p. 555E
- **Dictionary: Prefixes *re-, dis-, un-*** Grade 4, Theme 5, p. 555I

Volcanoes
Different texts for different purposes

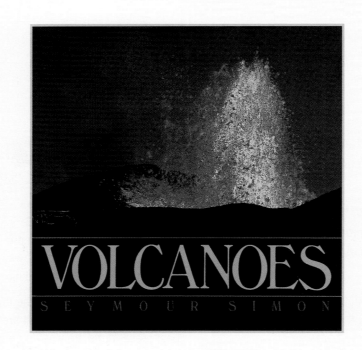

Anthology: **Main Selection**
Purposes

- strategy focus: monitor/clarify
- comprehension skill: categorize and classify
- vocabulary development
- critical thinking, discussion

Genre: Nonfiction
Expository nonfiction selection on volcanoes

Awards
- ★ Garden State Children's Choice Award

Selection Summary
Science writer Seymour Simon explains the characteristics of volcanoes and describes the aftermath of some well-known eruptions.

Teacher's Edition: **Read Aloud**

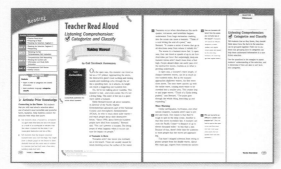

Purposes
- listening comprehension: categorize and classify
- vocabulary development
- critical thinking, discussion

Anthology: **Get Set to Read**

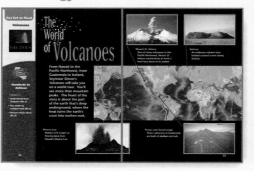

Purposes
- background building: volcanoes
- developing key vocabulary

Anthology: **Content Link**

Purposes
- content reading: folktales
- skill: how to read a folktale
- critical thinking, discussion

California Standards pp. 82A–82B
R 1.1 Read aloud fluently

Leveled Books and Resources

Use these resources to ensure that students read, outside of class, at least thirty minutes a day. See also Cumulative Listing of Leveled Books.

Reader's Library

Very Easy

Floods
by Barbara Brooks Simons

(Also available on blackline masters)

Purposes

- fluency practice in below-level text
- alternate reading for students reading significantly below grade level
- strategy application: clarify/monitor
- comprehension skill application: categorize and classify
- below-level independent reading

Lesson Support

- Lesson Plan, page R6
- Alternate application for Comprehension Skill lesson on categorize and classify, page 105A
- Reteaching for Comprehension Skill: categorize and classify, page R12

Selection Summary Masters

Volcanoes
Teacher's Resource Blackline Masters

Audiotape

Volcanoes
Audiotape for *Nature's Fury*

Theme Paperbacks

Easy

If You Lived at the Time of the Great San Francisco Earthquake
by Ellen Levine

Lesson, TE page 53I

On Level

Drylongso
by Virginia Hamilton

Lesson, TE page 53K

Challenge

Hurricanes: Earth's Mightiest Storms
by Patricia Lauber

Lesson, TE page 53M

Reaching All Students
Inclusion Strategy

Significantly Below-level Readers

R 1.1

Students reading so far below level that they cannot read *Volcanoes* even with the suggested Extra Support should still participate with the class whenever possible.

- Include them in the Teacher Read Aloud (p. 82G) and Preparing to Read (pp. 82K–83C).

- Have them listen to *Volcanoes* on the audiotape for *Nature's Fury* and read the Selection Summary while others read Segment 1 of the selection.

- Have them read "Floods" in the Reader's Library collection for *Nature's Fury* while others read Segment 2 of *Volcanoes*.

- Have all students participate in Wrapping Up Segment 2 (p. 99) and Responding (p. 100).

Technology

Get Set for Reading CD-ROM
Volcanoes
Provides background building, vocabulary support, and selection summaries in English and Spanish.

Education Place
www.eduplace.com
Log on to Education Place for more activities relating to *Volcanoes*.

Book Adventure
www.bookadventure.org
This Internet reading incentive program provides thousands of titles for students to read.

Daily Lesson Plans

Instructional Goals | Day 1 | Day 2

Reading

Strategy Focus: Monitor/Clarify

✓ *Comprehension Skill:* Categorize and Classify

Comprehension Skill Review: Topic, Main Idea, Supporting Details; Text Organization

✓ *Information/Study Skills:* Graphic Aids: Maps, Globes, Charts, Tables, and Graphs

60–80 minutes

Word Work

✓ *Spelling:* The / ō /, / o͞o /, and / yo͞o / Sounds

Decoding Longer Words:

✓ *Structural Analysis:* Word Roots *struct* and *rupt*

Phonics: Long Vowel Sounds / ō /, / o͞o /, and / yo͞o /

✓ *Vocabulary:* Dictionary: Definitions

30–40 minutes

Writing & Language

✓ *Grammar:* Singular and Plural Nouns; More Plural Nouns

✓ *Writing:* A Paragraph of Information; Correcting Sentence Fragments

Listening/Speaking/Viewing: Having Effective Conversations

30–40 minutes

✓ = tested skills

Day 1

Teacher Read Aloud, *82G*
Preparing to Read *Volcanoes*
• Get Set: Background and Vocabulary, *82K*   R 1.1, R 2.1, LS 2.3
• Key Vocabulary, *83A*
  Selection Vocabulary, *Practice Book,* 38
• Strategy/Skill Preview, *83B*
  Category Chart, *Practice Book,* 39
Reading Segment 1, *84–90*   W2.2.a, LS2.3
• Supporting Comprehension   R2.3, R2.4, R3.7
• Strategy Focus, *88*
Wrapping Up Segment 1, *90*   R2.4, LS1.1, LS2.3.a

Spelling
• Pretest, *105G*
• Instruction: The / ō /, / o͞o /, and / yo͞o / Sounds, *105G*
• Take-Home Word List, *Practice Book: Handbook*

Daily Language Practice, *105L*
Grammar Instruction
• Singular and Plural Nouns, *105K*

✏ **Writing**
• Journal Writing, *85*   W2.2.a

Day 2

Reading Segment 2, *91–99*   W2.2.a
• Supporting Comprehension   R2.5, R3.7
• Strategy Focus, *96*
Wrapping Up Segment 2, *99*   LS1.1, LS2.3.a
Responding
• Comprehension Questions: Think About the Selection, *100*   R3.1, R3.6, W2.2.a
• Comprehension Check, *Practice Book,* 40
Rereading/Revisiting the Text
• Comprehension: Categorize/Classify, *97*

Decoding Longer Words Instruction
• Structural Analysis: Word Roots *struct* and *rupt*, *105E*   R1.4
• *Practice Book,* 43
Spelling
• *Practice Book,* 44

Daily Language Practice, *105L*
Grammar Instruction
• *Practice Book,* 48

✏ **Writing Instruction**
• A Paragraph of Information, *105M*   W2.4.a-c
• *Practice Book,* 51
• Journal Writing, *91*

California Standards Achieved Each Day

R = Reading
W = Writing
LC = Language Conventions
LS = Listening & Speaking
HSS = History/Social Science
S = Science
M = Math

R 1.1 Read aloud fluently
R 2.1 Understand text features
R 2.3 Discern main ideas
R 2.4 Inferences/generalizations
R 3.7 Evaluate author's techniques
W 2.2.a Demonstrate understanding
LS 1.1 Ask new questions
LS 2.3 Respond to literature
LS 2.3.a Summarize events/details

R 1.4 Use roots and affixes
R 2.5 Facts, inferences, opinions
R 3.1 Analyze literary forms
R 3.6 Evaluate patterns/symbols
R 3.7 Evaluate author's techniques
W 2.2.a Demonstrate understanding
W 2.4.a State a clear position
W 2.4.b Support position with evidence
W 2.4.c Use organizational pattern
LS 1.1 Ask new questions
LS 2.3.a Summarize events/details

📖 **Leveled Books, pp. 53H–53N**
For reading outside of class and homework

Technology

California Lesson Planner CD-ROM
Customize your planning with the Lesson Planner.

Key correlations are provided in this chart.
Additional correlations are provided at point of use.

Day 3

Comprehension Skill Instruction
* Categorize and Classify, *105A*
* *Practice Book, 41–42*

Phonics Instruction
* Long Vowel Sounds /ō/, /o͞o/, and /yo͞o/, *105F*

Spelling
* *Practice Book, 45*

Daily Language Practice, *105L*
Grammar Instruction
* More Plural Nouns, *105L*

✎ **Writing**
* Explaining: Write a Travel Brochure, *100*
  W1.2

Day 4

Comprehension Skill Instruction
* Reteaching Categorize and Classify with Reader's Library, *R12*

Reading the Folktale Link
* "The Princess and the Warrior," *102–105* R3.6

Information and Study Skills Instruction
* Using Graphic Aids: Maps, Globes, Charts, Tables, and Graphs, *105C*   R2.1, R2.2

Decoding Longer Words
* Reteaching Structural Analysis: Word Roots *struct* and *rupt*, *R18*   R1.4, LC1.5

Spelling
* What's the Question?, *105H*
* *Practice Book, 46*

Vocabulary Skill Instruction
* Dictionary: Definitions, *105I*
* *Practice Book, 47*
* Activities, *R19*

Daily Language Practice, *105L*
Grammar
* Reteaching, *R24, R25*
* *Practice Book, 49*

✎ **Writing**
* Improving Your Writing: Correcting Sentence Fragments, *105N*   W1.6
* *Practice Book, 52*

Listening/Speaking/Viewing
* Having Effective Conversations, *105O*
LS1.1,LS1.2, LS1.1, LS1.2

Day 5

Rereading/Revisiting the Text:
Comprehension Review Skill Instruction
* Topic, Main Idea, and Supporting Details, *89*   R2.3
* Text Organization, *95*   R2.2, R2.3

Rereading for Fluency, *84–99*   LS2.3
Activity Choices
* Responding Activities, *100*   R2.3, R2.4, R3.1, R3.6, LC1.4
* Challenge/Extension Activities, *R13*
* Cross-Curricular Activities, *R28–29*   LS2.3b, W1.1a
Spiral Review, *105Q*   R2.4, W2.3.a

Vocabulary Expansion
* Words from Mythology, *105J*   R1.2
* Activities, *R19*

Spelling
* Posttest, *105H*
Spiral Review, *105R*   R 1.3

Daily Language Practice, *105L*
Grammar
* Exact Nouns, *105L*
* *Practice Book, 50*

✎ **Writing**   W2.1.a, W2.3.a, LS1.4, LS1.5
* Writing Activities, *R26–27*
* Sharing Students' Writing: Author's Chair

W 1.2 Create an exposition

R 1.4 Use roots and affixes
R 2.1 Understand text features
R 2.2 Use order to analyze text
R 3.6 Evaluate patterns/symbols
W 1.6 Edit and revise work
LC 1.5 Spell correctly
LS 1.1 Ask new questions
LS 1.2 Verbal, nonverbal messages

R 1.2 Use word origins
R 1.3 Understand synonyms/antonyms
R 2.3 Discern main ideas
R 2.4 Inferences/generalizations
R 3.1 Analyze literary forms
R 3.6 Evaluate patterns/symbols
W 1.1.a Establish a plot
W 2.1.a Establish plot, setting
W 2.3.a Frame questions
LC 1.4 Use correct capitalization
LS 1.4 Select focus
LS 1.5 Clarify and support ideas
LS 2.3.b Understand ideas/images

✎ **Reading-Writing Workshop: Description, pp. 52–53G**

UNIVERSAL ACCESS

See Universal Access Planning Chart on the following pages.

Universal Access Plans
for Reaching All Learners

Grouping for Instruction

	Day 1	**Day 2**
30–45 minutes		
With the Teacher		
Extra Support **Teach**—Use Extra Support Handbook	**Preteach** Word Roots *struct* and *rupt* **Preview** Selection, Segment 1 ■ Extra Support Handbook pp. 34–35	**Preteach** Categorize and Classify **Preview** Selection, Segment 2 ■ Extra Support Handbook pp. 36–37
Working Independently		
On Level Use Classroom Management Handbook **Challenge** Use Challenge Handbook **English Language Learners** Use Classroom Management Handbook or Challenge Handbook	**Independent Activities** For each group, assign appropriate activities—your own or those in the handbooks listed below. Then get students started on their independent work. ■ Classroom Management Handbook pp. 12–13 ■ Challenge Handbook pp. 6–7	See plan for Day 1 **Monitor** Answer questions, if necessary.
30–45 minutes		
With the Teacher		
English Language Learners **Teach**—Use Handbook for English Language Learners	**Preteach** Describing Volcanoes **Preteach** Get Set to Read; Selection, Segment 1 **Preteach** Structural Analysis: Word Roots *struct* and *rupt* ■ Handbook for ELL pp. 38–39	**Preteach** Land Features **Preteach** Selection, Segment 2 **Reteach** Grammar: Singular and Plural Nouns ■ Handbook for ELL pp. 40–41
Working Independently		
On Level Use Classroom Management Handbook **Challenge** Use Challenge Handbook **Extra Support** Use Classroom Management Handbook	**Independent Activities** Students can continue their assigned activities, or you can assign new activities from the handbooks below. ■ Classroom Management Handbook pp. 12–13 ■ Challenge Handbook pp. 6–7	See plan for Day 1 **Monitor** Partner Extra Support students, if needed.

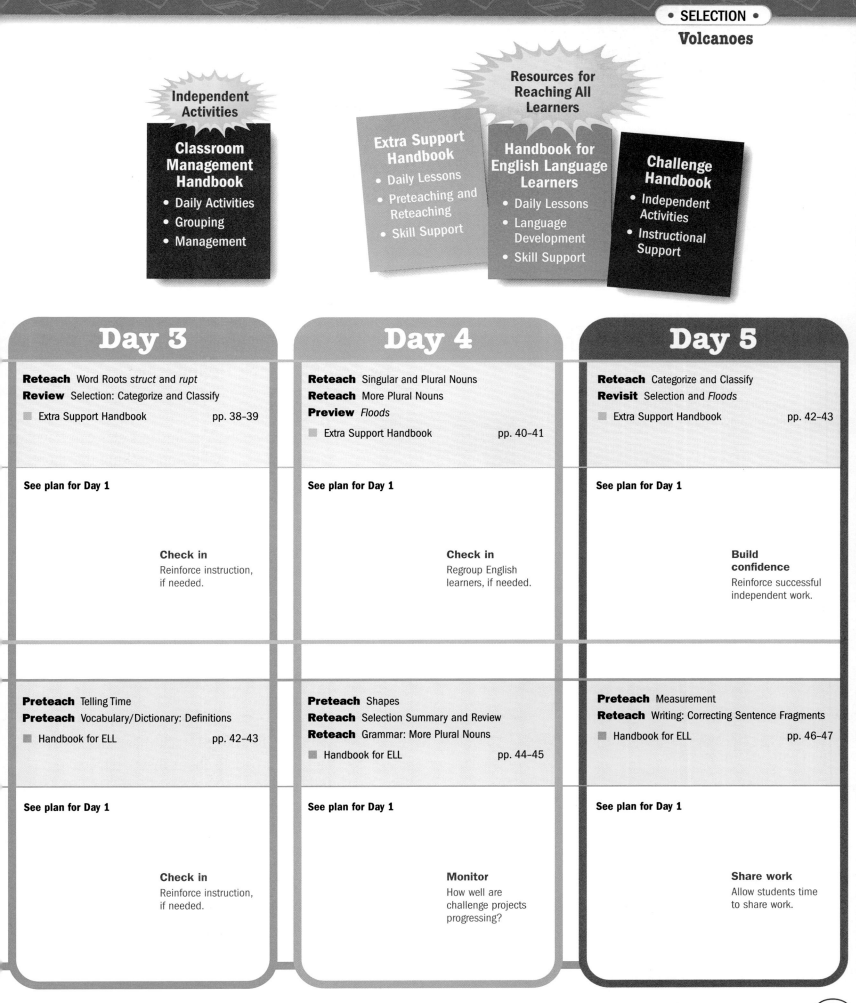

Independent Activities

Classroom Management Handbook
- Daily Activities
- Grouping
- Management

Resources for Reaching All Learners

Extra Support Handbook
- Daily Lessons
- Preteaching and Reteaching
- Skill Support

Handbook for English Language Learners
- Daily Lessons
- Language Development
- Skill Support

Challenge Handbook
- Independent Activities
- Instructional Support

Day 3

Reteach Word Roots *struct* and *rupt*
Review Selection: Categorize and Classify

☐ Extra Support Handbook   pp. 38–39

See plan for Day 1

Check in
Reinforce instruction, if needed.

Preteach Telling Time
Preteach Vocabulary/Dictionary: Definitions

☐ Handbook for ELL   pp. 42–43

See plan for Day 1

Check in
Reinforce instruction, if needed.

Day 4

Reteach Singular and Plural Nouns
Reteach More Plural Nouns
Preview *Floods*

☐ Extra Support Handbook   pp. 40–41

See plan for Day 1

Check in
Regroup English learners, if needed.

Preteach Shapes
Reteach Selection Summary and Review
Reteach Grammar: More Plural Nouns

☐ Handbook for ELL   pp. 44–45

See plan for Day 1

Monitor
How well are challenge projects progressing?

Day 5

Reteach Categorize and Classify
Revisit Selection and *Floods*

☐ Extra Support Handbook   pp. 42–43

See plan for Day 1

Build confidence
Reinforce successful independent work.

Preteach Measurement
Reteach Writing: Correcting Sentence Fragments

☐ Handbook for ELL   pp. 46–47

See plan for Day 1

Share work
Allow students time to share work.

Teacher Read Aloud

Listening Comprehension:
✓ Categorize and Classify

Making Waves!

by Gail Skroback Hennessey

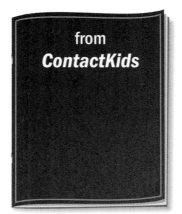

from *ContactKids*

ContactKids *published this article about tsunamis.*

R 2.4

On the open seas, this monster can travel as fast as a 747 jetliner. Approaching the shore, the destructive giant's loud sucking and hissing sounds and rumblings echo through the air like a speeding train. As it attacks, its height can reach a staggering one hundred feet.

No, we're not talking about Godzilla. This monster is real—and even scarier. But it's not a living thing. This killer of the sea is a giant wave called a tsunami.

Eddie Bernard knows all about tsunamis. As director of the Pacific Marine Environmental Laboratory, part of the National Oceanic and Atmospheric Administration (NOAA), he tries to track these killer waves— and teach people about their destructive forces. "Since 1990, about forty-six hundred people have died from tsunamis," Bernard said. "You can't prevent a tsunami. But being aware of what happens when it occurs can ease the impact on people."

A Tsunami Is Born

Tsunamis aren't like waves you normally see at the beach. Those are usually caused by winds blowing across the surface of the water.

Reading Instruction

DAY 1	• Teacher Read Aloud • Preparing to Read • Reading the Selection, Segment 1
DAY 2	• Reading the Selection, Segment 2 • Responding
DAY 3	• Revisiting the Text • Comprehension Skill Instruction
DAY 4	• Comprehension Skill Reteaching • Reading the Content Link • Information and Study Skills Instruction
DAY 5	• Comprehension Skill Review • Activity Choices

OBJECTIVES

Students

• listen in order to categorize and classify information

• learn academic language: **categorize, classify**

▶ Activate Prior Knowledge

Connecting to the Theme Tell students that you will read aloud a selection about one of nature's most incredible and powerful forces, tsunamis. Help students connect the selection with what they know.

■ Ask students what a tsunami is. (A tsunami is a giant wave that forms far out in the ocean as a result of an earthquake or volcanic eruption; when a tsunami hits the shore, it can cause great destruction and loss of life.)

■ Tell students that the largest recorded tsunami wave was 210 feet high. You might draw a simple graph on the board to show students how tall this wave was in relation to a person (six feet tall) and a four-story building (sixty feet tall).

(82G)   THEME 1: **Nature's Fury**

1 Tsunamis occur when disturbances like earthquakes, volcanoes, and landslides happen underwater. Even huge meteorites crashing into the ocean can cause a tsunami. "Think of a rock hitting the end of a pond," says Bernard. "It creates a series of waves that go in all directions away from where it initially hit."

The waves in a tsunami move fast. In open seas, they can travel at speeds of up to six hundred miles per hour. But surprisingly, deep-sea tsunami waves aren't much more than a foot high. People aboard ships can easily pass over the destructive waves, clueless as to what is growing underneath.

In open seas, a tsunami's wave length, or distance between waves, can be as much as one hundred miles. But as the tsunami approaches shallower waters, the first wave slows down. The next wave catches up with the earlier wave, causing more water to be crowded into a smaller area. This creates larger and larger waves. "Think of a Slinky being pushed," says Bernard. "The pulse goes through the whole thing, bunching up and expanding."

Wave Warning

2 Unlike earthquakes, hurricanes, and other natural disasters, tsunamis aren't easy to predict and track. One reason is that they're tough to spot in the deep ocean. Another is that they move incredibly fast. A tsunami can cross the Pacific Ocean—a distance of up to eleven thousand miles—in less than a day. Because of that, there's little time for scientists to warn people that the waves are approaching.

That hasn't stopped scientists from trying to protect people from the deadly waves. About fifty years ago, experts from twenty-six nations

1 How are tsunamis different from the waves you normally see at the beach? (Tsunamis are caused by volcanic eruptions or earthquakes, and regular ocean waves are caused by the wind. Also, tsunamis are much bigger than regular waves.)

2 Why are tsunamis so difficult to predict and prepare for? (They are hard to spot in the open ocean and they move very fast; most suspicious waves that are spotted don't turn into tsunamis.)

Listening Comprehension: ✓ Categorize and Classify

Tell students that as they listen, they should think about how the facts in the selection can be grouped together. Point out to students that grouping facts in categories can help them understand information in a nonfiction selection.

Use the questions in the margins to assess students' understanding of the selection, and to determine if they are able to sort facts into categories.

(Teacher Read Aloud, *continued***)**

banded together to form the Tsunami Warning System (TWS). The group monitors tsunami-prone areas throughout the Pacific Ocean. Sensor instruments placed on the sea floor measure the weight of increased water bunching up—a sign of an approaching tsunami. The measurements are transmitted to a buoy floating on the ocean surface. This relays the information via satellite to a tracking station. If necessary, a warning is issued for the area in the path of the approaching tsunami.

The problem is, many of these tsunamis never occur. In fact, seventy-five percent of all Tsunami Warning Bulletins issued by the TWS's Pacific Tsunami Warning Center in Hawaii since 1948 have been false.

A tsunami's unpredictable nature makes it all the more dangerous—and deadly. Last year, people heard rumbling sounds along the shore of Papua, New Guinea, and went to investigate. Within ten minutes of the roaring thunder (caused by water rushing back over shells, rocks, and semi-dry sand), a forty-foot wave appeared. It took the lives of about three thousand people.

3 Why do you think tsunamis are more likely to hit the coasts of Hawaii, Alaska, Oregon, and California than coastal regions in other parts of the world? (These areas are part of the Pacific ring of fire, an area that experiences a lot of earthquakes and volcanic activity.)

3 ## Tsunami in the U.S.?

According to Bernard, a monster of a tsunami along the shores of Hawaii, Alaska, California, Oregon, or Washington is a real possibility. "Scientists think there is a ten to thirty percent probability of a large earthquake in the next thirty to fifty years along this section of the U.S. coast," he says.

After a tsunami hit Cape Mendocino, California, in 1992, the National Tsunami Hazard Mitigation Program (NTHMP) was formed. The group educates people about the warning signs of tsunamis. It's also working on

California Standards pp. 82I–82J

R **2.5** Facts, inferences, opinions
R **3.4** Understand theme
R **3.7** Evaluate author's techniques

LS **2.3.a** Summarize events/details
LS **2.3.c** Use examples

developing inundation zones (areas scientists feel could be hit hardest during a tsunami) and more accurate warning systems. Signs have been posted up and down the coast, alerting people to tsunami danger areas and routes to take to reach safe areas. Eddie Bernard and other scientists hope groups like the NTHMP can prevent nature's ultimate "wipeout" from doing harm.

4 **Catch a Wave**

All waves are caused by energy. What makes them different are the kinds of energy that produce them:

- **Wind waves** are caused by wind blowing across the surface of the water.
- **Tsunamis** are caused by underwater disturbances like earthquakes and volcanic eruptions.
- **Tidal waves** are caused by the effects of the gravitational attraction of the Earth, moon, and sun.

All three types of waves contain pretty much the same parts:

1. **Crest:** the highest part of the wave
2. **Trough:** the lowest part of the wave
3. **Wave height:** the distance between the crest and trough
4. **Run-up:** the distance between the crest and the surface of the water
5. **Wave length:** the difference between the crests or troughs of two waves

4 How are waves categorized, or grouped? (according to what causes them: wind waves are caused by wind; tidal waves by the gravitational pull of the moon; tsunamis by earthquakes or volcanic eruptions)

▶ **Discussion**

LS 2.3.a
LS 2.3.c

Summarize After reading, discuss any parts of the selection students did not understand. Then ask them to summarize it by describing the work done by the TWS and explaining why their job is so difficult.

Listening Comprehension:
✓ **Fact and Opinion** Ask students to classify two types of tsunami waves according to what causes them. (tsunamis caused by earthquakes and tsunamis caused by volcanic eruptions) Then ask them to think of other ways in which tsunamis might be categorized. (those that hit populated areas and those that hit uninhabited areas; those that were predicted and those that hit without warning)

R 2.5

Personal Response Ask students to evaluate whether the author did a good job of clearly explaining the causes and effects of tsunamis.

R 3.7

⭐ **Connecting/Comparing** Ask students why they think this selection is part of a theme titled "Nature's Fury."

R 3.4

R 1.1
R 2.1
LS 2.3

Preparing to Read

▶ Using *Get Set* for Background and Vocabulary

Connecting to the Theme Remind students that this theme is about nature's power. Ask students to name the forces of nature they have read about so far. (earthquakes, tornadoes, lightning) Explain that the next selection is about volcanoes. Discuss what volcanoes are and ask students to name any volcanoes they have heard of. Then use Get Set to Read on pages 82–83 to introduce Seymour Simon's "world tour" of volcanoes.

■ Have a volunteer read "The World of Volcanoes."

■ Point out the detail map of earth's surface, and have students locate each region on a globe or map of the world.

■ Ask students to explain the meaning of the Key Vocabulary: *lava, crust, molten, crater,* and *cinders*. Then have them use the words as they describe the four volcanoes that are pictured.

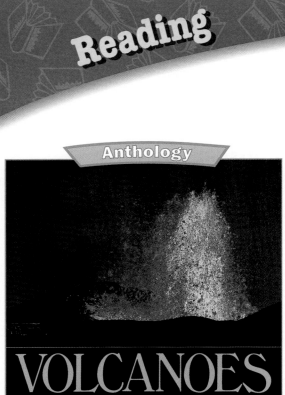

Anthology

VOLCANOES

SEYMOUR SIMON

Technology

Get Set for Reading CD-ROM

Volcanoes

Provides background building, vocabulary support, and selection summaries in English and Spanish.

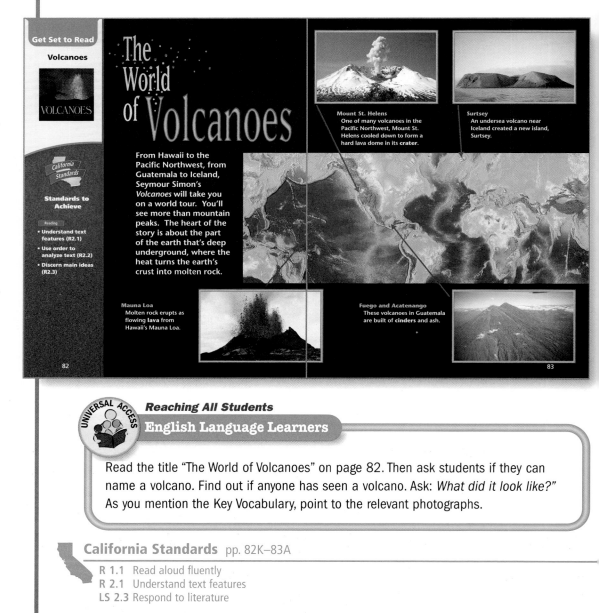

Get Set to Read

Volcanoes

VOLCANOES

California Standards

Standards to Achieve

Reading

• Understand text features (R2.1)

• Use order to analyze text (R2.2)

• Discern main ideas (R2.3)

The World of Volcanoes

From Hawaii to the Pacific Northwest, from Guatemala to Iceland, Seymour Simon's *Volcanoes* will take you on a world tour. You'll see more than mountain peaks. The heart of the story is about the part of the earth that's deep underground, where the heat turns the earth's crust into molten rock.

Mount St. Helens
One of many volcanoes in the Pacific Northwest, Mount St. Helens cooled down to form a hard lava dome in its **crater**.

Surtsey
An undersea volcano near Iceland created a new island, Surtsey.

Mauna Loa
Molten rock erupts as flowing **lava** from Hawaii's Mauna Loa.

Fuego and Acatenango
These volcanoes in Guatemala are built of **cinders** and ash.

82

83

UNIVERSAL ACCESS

Reaching All Students

English Language Learners

Read the title "The World of Volcanoes" on page 82. Then ask students if they can name a volcano. Find out if anyone has seen a volcano. Ask: *What did it look like?"* As you mention the Key Vocabulary, point to the relevant photographs.

California Standards pp. 82K–83A

R 1.1 Read aloud fluently
R 2.1 Understand text features
LS 2.3 Respond to literature

Vocabulary

▶ Developing Key Vocabulary

Use **Transparency 1–18** to introduce additional topic-related words from *Volcanoes.*

■ Model how to figure out the meaning of the word *cinders* from clues in the sentence.

■ Ask students to use what they know about sentence clues, plus the diagram, to figure out Key Vocabulary words. Have students explain how they figured out each word.

Remind students that it's helpful to use the Phonics/Decoding Strategy as they read. For students who need more help with decoding, use the lesson below.

Practice/Homework Practice Book page 38.

UNIVERSAL ACCESS
Strategy Review
Phonics/Decoding

Modeling Write this sentence from *Volcanoes* on the board, and point to *explosion.*

> *Ten years after the <u>explosion</u> that formed Surtsey, another volcano erupted near Iceland.*

Think Aloud

To figure out this word, I'll first look for word parts I know. I see the letters ex- at the beginning of the word. I also see the letters -sion, which come at the end of many nouns. This ending is pronounced zhuhn. I think the middle syllable has the long o sound. I can blend the sounds together to read the whole word: ihk SPLOH zhuhn. This word makes sense in the sentence.

Skill Finder
- Decoding Longer Words, pp. 105E–105F
- Vocabulary Expansion, p. 105J

Preparing to Read

Key Concept
how volcanoes form

Key Vocabulary

cinders: charred bits of rock; ashes

crater: a bowl-shaped depression

crust: the solid outer layer of earth

eruption: a volcanic explosion or large flow of lava

lava: hot melted rock that flows from a volcano

magma: hot melted rock underneath the earth's surface

molten: made liquid by heat

summit: the top of a mountain

See Vocabulary notes on pages 86, 88, 91, 92, 94, and 96 for additional words to preview.

Practice Book page 38

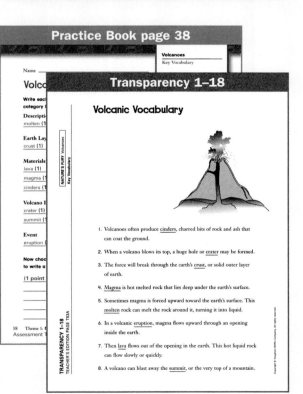

Volcanic Vocabulary

1. Volcanoes often produce <u>cinders</u>, charred bits of rock and ash that can coat the ground.

2. When a volcano blows its top, a huge hole or <u>crater</u> may be formed.

3. The force will break through the earth's <u>crust</u>, or solid outer layer of earth.

4. <u>Magma</u> is hot melted rock that lies deep under the earth's surface.

5. Sometimes magma is forced upward toward the earth's surface. This <u>molten</u> rock can melt the rock around it, turning it into liquid.

6. In a volcanic <u>eruption</u>, magma flows upward through an opening inside the earth.

7. Then <u>lava</u> flows out of the opening in the earth. This hot liquid rock can flow slowly or quickly.

8. A volcano can blast away the <u>summit</u>, or the very top of a mountain.

Reading

Reading Strategy

▶ **Strategy Focus:**
Monitor/Clarify

Strategy Focus

In this selection, Seymour Simon gives you lots of information about volcanoes and how they form. As you read, **monitor** your understanding, and reread or use the photos and the map to **clarify**.

Teacher's Note

Strategy/Skill Connection For a better understanding of *Volcanoes*, students can use the

• Monitor/Clarify Strategy

• Categorize and Classify Comprehension Skill

Monitoring their comprehension and rereading or using photos to clarify can help students understand what causes volcanic eruptions and how scientists classify volcanoes.

As students fill in their *Volcanoes* Category Chart (**Practice Book** page 39 and **Transparency 1–19**), they can use their answers to help them understand what different kinds of volcanoes are like.

Have students turn to page 84 as you read aloud the title of the selection and the author's name. Ask someone to read aloud the Strategy Focus. Invite students to read the first three paragraphs on page 85 and think about how the photograph of the volcano can help them understand why ancient peoples created legends about volcanoes.

Teacher Modeling Review how rereading and using photos can help readers clarify information in text. Then model the strategy.

Think Aloud

The photo shows sparks and fiery lava shooting up from the earth. It seems likely that this spectacular event terrified and fascinated ancient peoples. The photo helps me understand why the Romans believed that Vulcan, the god of fire, worked at a hot forge, striking sparks as he made swords. This was probably their way of explaining what caused the fiery lava that shoots up from volcanoes.

Remind students to monitor their own understanding of the selection as they read, and to try rereading or looking at the photos and graphic aids to help them clarify anything they don't understand. Remind students to use their other reading strategies as they read the selection.

California Standards pp. 83B–83C

R 2.3   Discern main ideas
W2.2.a Demonstrate understanding

Comprehension Skill

✓ Comprehension Skill Focus:
Categorize and Classify

Category Chart Explain to students that as they read *Volcanoes,* they will learn to put the information they read into groups, or categories, such as different kinds of volcanoes. To help them understand what causes volcanoes of various kinds to form, they will fill in a chart as they read. Display **Transparency 1–19,** and demonstrate how to use the graphic organizer.

■ Point out the first heading, "How Volcanoes Form." Have a volunteer read aloud the last two paragraphs on page 85 to find out how volcanoes form. Model how to complete the first box in the Category Chart.

■ Have a volunteer read the second heading in the chart, "Two Types of Volcanic Vents." Then have students read the first paragraph on page 86 to find out what two things a volcano can be. Model completing the second box in the chart.

■ Ask students to complete the first two items on **Practice Book** page 39 with the same answers.

■ As students read the selection, have them work in pairs to monitor their comprehension as they complete the rest of the chart.

Graphic Organizer: Category Chart

How Volcanoes Form
Magma pushes up through vents or cracks in the earth's crust.

Two Types of Volcanic Vents

| a hole in the ground lava flows from | a mountain or hill lava flows from |

Where Volcanoes Form
Most volcanoes form where the plates of the earth come together. Hawaiian volcanoes are in the middle of the Pacific plate.

Types of Volcanoes

| shield volcanoes | cinder cone volcanoes | composite volcanoes | dome volcanoes |
| examples ↓ Mauna Loa Kilauea | examples ↓ Some volcanoes in Guatemala | examples ↓ Mount Shasta Mount Hood | examples ↓ Lassen Peak |

Transparency 1–19

Category Chart

How Volcanoes Form

Two Types of Volcanic Vents

Where Volcanoes Form

Types of Volcanoes

examples | examples | examples | examples

Practice Book page 39

Name _____

Category Chart

Fill in the boxes in each category.

How Volcanoes Form
Magma pushes up through vents or cracks in the earth's crust. **(1 point)**

Two Types of Volcanic Vents

| a hole in the ground that lava flows from **(1)** | a mountain or hill that lava flows from **(1)** |

Where Volcanoes Form
Most volcanoes form where the plates of the earth come together. Hawaiian volcanoes are in the middle of the Pacific plate. **(1)**

Types of Volcanoes

| shield volcanoes **(1)** | cinder cone volcanoes **(1)** | composite volcanoes **(1)** | dome volcanoes **(1)** |
| examples Mauna Loa Kilauea **(1)** | examples some volcanoes in Guatemala **(1)** | examples Mount Shasta Mount Hood **(1)** | examples Lassen Peak **(1)** |

Theme 1: **Nature's Fury**   39
Assessment Tip: Total **12** Points

Focus Questions

Have students turn to Responding on page 100. Read the questions aloud and ask them to keep the questions in mind as they read *Volcanoes.*

Options for Reading

▶ **Reading in Segments** Students can read *Volcanoes* in two segments (pages 84–90 and 91–99), or read the entire selection in one segment.

▶ **Deciding About Support** The high-interest topic of this selection and the vivid photos should make it accessible to most students despite the many scientific terms and the absence of a narrative structure.

- Students who might have difficulty with the structure of nonfiction and with scientific terms will benefit from Extra Support.

- Significantly below-level readers can listen to the **Audiotape** and read the Selection Summary for *Volcanoes,* and then read "Floods" in the **Reader's Library.**

▶ **Universal Access** Use the notes at the bottom of the pages.

VOLCANOES
SEYMOUR SIMON

Strategy Focus

In this selection, Seymour Simon gives you lots of information about volcanoes and how they form. As you read, **monitor** your understanding, and reread or use the photos and the map to **clarify.**

84

Reaching All Students

Classroom Management

On Level
Reading Cards 10–11

While Reading: Reading Card 1; Category Chart (**Practice Book** p. 39); generate questions

After Reading: Discussion Group (Reading Card 11); Wrapping Up Segment 1 (p. 90) and Segment 2 (p. 99)

Challenge
Reading Cards 10–13

While Reading: Category Chart (**Practice Book** p. 39); Make a Time Line (p. 87, Reading Card 12); Comparisons (p. 96, Reading Card 13).

After Reading: Discussion Group (Reading Card 11); Wrapping Up Segment 1 (p. 90) and Segment 2 (p. 99)

English Language Learners

Intermediate and Advanced Fluency
Have students read with partners. Begin by asking them to look at the volcanoes on pages 82–83. Help students describe the differences they see.

R 2.1
LS 2.3

For English language learners at other proficiency levels, use the **Handbook for English Language Learners.**

California Standards pp. 84–85

R 2.1 Understand text features
R 2.4 Inferences/generalizations
W 2.2.a Demonstrate understanding

LS 2.3   Respond to literature

Throughout history, people have told stories about volcanoes. The early Romans believed in Vulcan, their god of fire. They thought that Vulcan worked at a hot forge, striking sparks as he made swords and armor for the other gods. It is from the Roman god Vulcan that we get the word *volcano*.

1

The early Hawaiians told legends of the wanderings of Pele, their goddess of fire. Pele was chased from her homes by her sister Namaka, goddess of the sea. Pele moved constantly from one Hawaiian island to another. Finally, Pele settled in a mountain called Kilauea, on the big island of Hawaii. Even though the islanders tried to please Pele, she burst forth every few years. Kilauea is still an active volcano.

In early times, no one knew how volcanoes formed or why they spouted fire. In modern times, scientists began to study volcanoes. They still don't know all the answers, but they know much about how a volcano works.

Our planet is made up of many layers of rock. The top layers of solid rock are called the crust. Deep beneath the crust, it is so hot that some rock melts. The melted, or molten, rock is called magma.

Volcanoes are formed by cracks or holes that poke through the earth's crust. Magma pushes its way up through the cracks. This is called a volcanic eruption. **2** When magma pours forth on the surface it is called lava. In the above photograph of an eruption, you can see great fountains of boiling lava forming fiery rivers and lakes. As lava cools, it hardens to form rock.

85

Reading Segment 1
pages 84–90

Purpose Setting Ask students what they think they will learn about volcanoes in this selection, based on their preview.

LS 2.3

Journal Writing Students can use their journal to record their predictions, their purpose for reading, and any questions they have about volcanoes.

W 2.2.a

Reinforcing Comprehension and Strategies

- Remind students to use Monitor/Clarify and other strategies as they read, and add to their Category Chart (**Practice Book** page 39).

- Refer to the Strategy Focus notes on pages 88 and 96 to reinforce the Strategy Focus.

- Use Supporting Comprehension questions beginning on page 86 to help students develop higher-level understanding of the text.

Before each segment, preview the text using the notes below and those on page 91. **While** reading, model strategies (pages 86, 89, and 93). **After** reading, review each segment (pages 90 and 98) before students join the Wrapping Up discussion.

R 2.4

pages 85–87 Although modern-day scientists have learned a lot about how volcanoes form and how eruptions occur, they can't predict exactly when volcanoes will erupt. What volcano erupted in the United States in 1980?

pages 88–89 Scientists have learned important facts about the earth's crust that help them understand why volcanoes occur where they do. What type of information is shown in the diagram on page 89?

page 90 The people of the island of Heimaey in Iceland had to evacuate their homes when a volcano erupted there in 1973. When they returned, the island had a new mountain on it. How high do you think this new volcano was?

Reading

▶ Supporting Comprehension

1 Why do you think the author began the selection by writing about Vulcan and Pele? (to show that people have been fascinated by volcanoes for a long time)

R 2.3
R 2.4
R 3.7

2 Describe the sequence of events before, during, and after a volcanic eruption. (Magma pushes up through a crack in the earth's crust; lava flows out; the lava cools and hardens into rock.)

3 What do you think the author means when he says that Mount St. Helens *awakened from its long sleep*? (It seemed like the mountain was sleeping when it was quiet; it seemed like it woke up when it erupted.)

R 2.4
R 3.7

Vocabulary (pages 85–86)

crust: the solid outer layer of earth

molten: made liquid by heat

magma: hot melted rock underneath the earth's surface

eruption: a volcanic explosion or large flow of lava

lava: hot melted rock that flows from a volcano

century: one hundred years

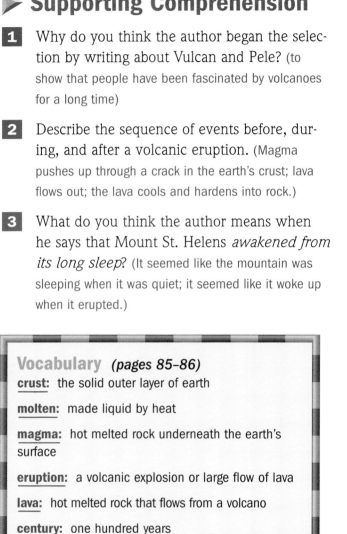

A volcano can be two things: a hole in the ground that lava comes through, or a hill or mountain formed by the lava. Mount Rainier in the state of Washington is a volcano even though it has not erupted since 1882.

Not far from Mount Rainier (top, right) is Mount St. Helens (bottom, left). Native Americans and early settlers in the Northwest had seen Mount St. Helens puff out some ashes, steam, and lava in the mid-1800s. Yet for more than a <u>century</u>, the mountain seemed quiet and peaceful.

3 In March 1980 Mount St. Helens awakened from its long sleep. First there were a few small earthquakes that shook the mountain. Then on March 27 Mount St. Helens began to spout ashes and steam. Each day brought further quakes, until by mid-May more than ten thousand small quakes had been recorded. The mountain began to swell up and crack.

Sunday May 18 dawned bright and clear. The mountain seemed much the same as it had been for the past month. Suddenly, at 8:32 A.M., Mount St. Helens erupted with incredible force. The energy released in the eruption was equal to ten million tons of dynamite.

86

Reaching All Students

Extra Support

Strategy Modeling

Phonics/Decoding If students have difficulty reading the word *dynamite,* model the Phonics/Decoding Strategy.

The first part of this word must be DYE, since the letter y stands for the long i sound when it acts as a vowel. The next part is either nay or nuh. The last part is probably myt. When I first try to blend the parts, I get DYE nay myt. No, that's not right. When I try again, I get DYE nuh myt. That word makes sense in the sentence.

California Standards pp. 86–87

R 2.3 Discern main ideas
R 2.4 Inferences/generalizations
R 3.7 Evaluate author's techniques

87

Reaching All Students
Challenge

Reading Card
12

Make a Time Line

Distribute Reading Card 12 and have students use it to guide them as they create an illustrated time line of Mount St. Helens's recent volcanic history.

Strategy Focus: Monitor/Clarify

Teacher/Student Modeling Ask students if there is anything they read in the selection so far that they do not understand. Then ask them whether rereading or viewing the photos helped them clarify any points.

To guide students in modeling the strategy, you might ask: *If you weren't sure why Mount St. Helens was dedicated as a national monument, how could rereading the first paragraph on page 88 help you clarify?*

Supporting Comprehension

4 Do you think the suddenness of Mount St. Helens's eruption surprised people? Why or why not? (yes, because if they had expected it, everyone would have moved away)

R 2.3
R 2.4

5 What do you think happened to the rest of Mount St. Helens's summit? (Maybe it was blown into small pieces or burned.)

6 Why do you think the author included a diagram on page 89? (to show how the earth's plates go together and where they are)

R 3.7

Vocabulary *(page 88)*
crater: a bowl-shaped depression

The eruption of Mount St. Helens was the most destructive in the history of the United States. Sixty people lost their lives as hot gases, rocks, and ashes covered an area of two hundred thirty square miles. Hundreds of houses and cabins were destroyed, leaving many people homeless. Miles of highways, roads, and railways were badly damaged. The force of the eruption was so great that entire forests were blown down like rows of matchsticks.

4

Compare the way Mount St. Helens looked before and after the eruption. The entire top of the mountain was blown away. In its place is a huge volcanic crater. In 1982 the mountain and the area around it were dedicated as the Mount St. Helens National Volcanic Monument. Visitor centers allow people to view the volcano's astonishing power.

5

88

Reaching All Students
English Language Learners

LS 1.2

Intermediate and Advanced Fluency
Draw a chain on the board or show an example of a bicycle chain or a necklace. Point out that chains are made of many connected links. Then read aloud the phrase *a chain of underwater volcanoes* on page 89. Ask students what they think this phrase means.

California Standards pp. 88–89

R 2.3 Discern main ideas
R 2.4 Inferences/generalizations
R 3.7 Evaluate author's techniques

LS 1.2 Verbal, nonverbal messages
LS 1.5 Clarify and support ideas

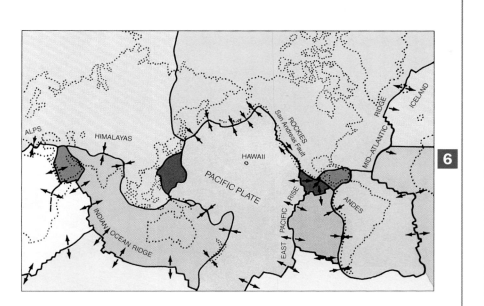

Volcanoes don't just happen anyplace. The earth's crust is broken into huge sections like a giant cracked eggshell. The pieces of the crust are called plates. The United States, Canada, and Mexico and part of the North Atlantic Ocean are all on the North American plate. Almost all the volcanoes in the world erupt in places where two plates meet.

Down the middle of the North Atlantic Ocean, two plates are slowly moving apart. Hot magma pushes up between them. A chain of underwater volcanoes runs along the line where the two plates meet. Some of the underwater volcanoes have grown so high that they stick up from the ocean floor to make islands.

89

Reaching All Students

Extra Support

LS 1.5

Strategy Modeling

Monitor/Clarify If students need help understanding the concept of the earth's plates, model how the diagram can help clear up confusion.

At first I didn't understand the statement that the earth's crust is broken up into huge sections called plates. *The diagram helps me see that the plates are like giant puzzle pieces. Most volcanoes happen along the lines where these pieces meet.*

Revisiting the Text

R 2.3

Spiral Review

Comprehension Skill Lesson
Topic, Main Idea, and Supporting Details

OBJECTIVES

Students determine that the topic of a selection is what it tells about, and that the main idea is what the paragraphs say about the topic.

Tell students that the topic of a selection is the subject most of the paragraphs tell about, and that the main idea is the main point the paragraphs make about a topic. Then ask students to name the topic of this selection. (volcanoes) Point out that identifying topics and main ideas can help them remember what they read.

Remind students that a paragraph or passage can also have a topic and a main idea. Ask a volunteer to read aloud the first paragraph on page 88. Then ask students to find a sentence in the paragraph that states its main idea. (the first one)

Point out that sometimes authors state a main idea in a heading or key sentence; other times readers must figure it out by looking at the supporting details. Then ask pairs of students to reread page 89 and write the topic and main idea in a graphic organizer like the one below.

Topic	the earth's plates
Main Idea	Most volcanoes occur where the plates of the earth meet.

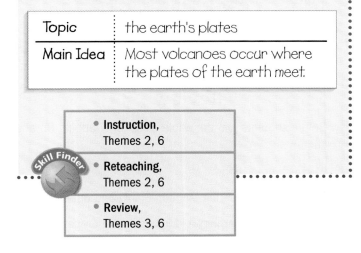

Skill Finder

- **Instruction,** Themes 2, 6
- **Reteaching,** Themes 2, 6
- **Review,** Themes 3, 6

Wrapping Up Segment 1
pages 84–90

First, provide the Extra Support below to students who need it. Then bring all students together.

R 2.4

- **Review Predictions/Purpose** Ask students to share the predictions they made and tell whether their predictions were accurate. Have them record new predictions or additional questions they have about volcanoes.

- **Model Strategies** Refer students to the Strategies Poster and have them take turns modeling Monitor/Clarify and other strategies they used as they read. Provide models if needed (page 89).

LS 1.1

- **Share Group Discussions** Have students share their questions and literature discussions.

LS 2.3.a

- **Summarize** Ask students to use their Category Chart to summarize the first segment of *Volcanoes.*

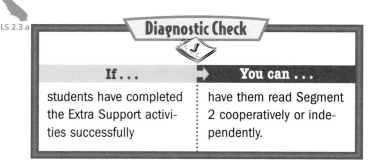

Diagnostic Check

If . . .	You can . . .
students have completed the Extra Support activities successfully	have them read Segment 2 cooperatively or independently.

Iceland is a volcanic island in the North Atlantic. In 1963, an area of the sea near Iceland began to smoke. An undersea volcano was exploding and a new island was being formed. The island was named Surtsey, after the ancient Norse god of fire.

Ten years after the explosion that formed Surtsey, another volcano erupted near Iceland. It was off the south coast of Iceland on the island of Heimaey. Within six hours of the eruption, more than 5,000 people were taken off the island to safety. After two months, hundreds of buildings had burned down and dozens more had been buried in the advancing lava. Then the volcano stopped erupting. After a year's time, the people of Heimaey came back to reclaim their island with its new 735-foot volcano.

90

End of Segment 1:
pages 84–90

Reaching All Students
Extra Support

Segment 1 Review

Before students join the whole class for Wrapping Up above, they should

- check predictions

- take turns modeling Monitor/Clarify and other strategies they used

- add to **Transparency 1–19**, check and revise their Category Chart on **Practice Book** page 39, and use it to summarize

Reaching All Students
On Level **Challenge**

Reading Card 11

LS 1.1

Literature Discussion

In mixed-ability groups of five or six, have students discuss the questions they formed while reading. Additionally, suggest some literature discussion prompts (Reading Card 11).

- On page 85, the author describes two ways in which ancient peoples explained volcanoes. What is another explanation ancient peoples might have had for them?

- What do you think visitors to the Mount St. Helens National Monument might see? How might this view change over time?

California Standards pp. 90–91

R 2.4	Inferences/generalizations	LS 2.3.a Summarize events/details

W 2.2.a Demonstrate understanding
LS 1.1 Ask new questions

Beginning of Segment 2:
pages 91–99

Most volcanoes and earthquakes are along the edges of the large Pacific plate. There are so many that the shoreline of the Pacific Ocean is called the "Ring of Fire." But a few volcanoes are not on the edge of a plate. The volcanoes in the Hawaiian Islands are in the middle of the Pacific plate.

A million years ago, magma pushed up through cracks in the Pacific plate. Over the years, eruption followed eruption. Little by little, thin layers of lava hardened, one atop another. Thousands of eruptions were needed to build mountains high enough to reach from the deep sea bottom and appear as islands.

The largest Hawaiian volcano is Mauna Loa. It is seventy miles long and rises thirty thousand feet from the ocean floor. It is still growing. Every few years, Mauna Loa erupts again.

Hawaiian volcano lava usually bubbles out quietly to form rivers or lakes, or spouts a few hundred feet in the air in a fiery fountain. Hawaiian volcanoes erupt much more gently than did Surtsey or Mount St. Helens. Only rarely does a Hawaiian volcano throw out rock and high clouds of ash.

91

Reading Segment 2
pages 91–99

Purpose Setting Have students preview the second segment of the selection. Ask them to make predictions about additional information they will read about volcanoes.

Journal Writing Students can use their journal to record their questions and their predictions.

W 2.2.a

Vocabulary *(page 90)*

Norse: having to do with the ancient Scandinavians

advancing: moving forward

Reaching All Students

Extra Support: Previewing the Text

Before reading Segment 2, preview the text using the notes below. **While** reading, model strategies (page 93). **After** reading, review the segment (page 98) before students join the Wrapping Up discussion.

pages 91–93 Although most volcanoes are along the edges of one of the earth's plates, the volcanoes of Hawaii are in the middle of the Pacific plate. Which Hawaiian volcano is still erupting?

pages 94–96 Scientists have divided volcanoes into four types, each with its own shape. The shapes are caused by different kinds of volcanic eruptions. Look at the pictures on pages 94, 95, and 96. Which volcano looks like a warrior's shield? Which ones look like they were built up into cone shapes over time?

pages 97–98 These pictures show the results of different volcanoes' eruptions. What do you think the photograph on page 97 shows?

Reading

▶ Supporting Comprehension

7 How is Hawaiian lava different from the lava produced by volcanic eruptions elsewhere? (It can bubble out quietly to form rivers; some of it is thin and flows quickly.)

R 2.5

8 How can scientists tell what kind of eruption occurred by studying cooled lava formations? (The rough, sharp rocks called *aa* tell scientists that the lava flow was thick and slow-moving; the smooth, billowy lava called *pahoehoe* tells them that the lava was thin, hot, and fast-moving.)

9 Why do you think the author included the lava's Hawaiian names? (to show how common lava is in Hawaii)

R 3.7

Vocabulary *(pages 92–93)*

weathered: changed because of being exposed to the weather

billowy: rising in a great wave

Steam clouds billow as a flow of hot lava enters the sea. Hawaii is constantly changing as eruptions add hundreds of acres of new land to the islands. In other parts of the shoreline, old lava flows are quickly weathered by the waves into rocks and black sand.

7 Hawaiian lava is thin and flows quickly. In some lava rivers, speeds as high as thirty-five miles per hour have been measured. In an eruption in 1986, a number of houses were threatened by the quick-moving lava. Fire fighters sprayed water on the lava to slow down its advance.

92

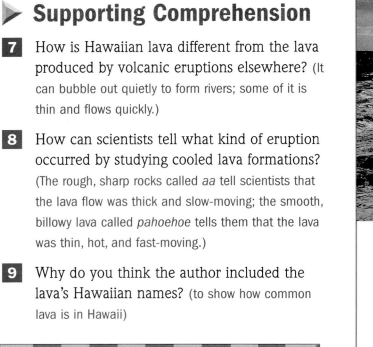

Reaching All Students

English Language Learners

Intermediate and Advanced Fluency   LS 1.2

Draw a line on the board; write the word *line* next to it.
Have students read page 92 and find the word *shoreline.*
Explain that the *shore* is where land and water meet. Point out that where land and water meet a line is created, the *shoreline.*

California Standards pp. 92–93

R 1.1 Read aloud fluently
R 2.1 Understand text features
R 2.5 Facts, inferences, opinions

R 3.7 Evaluate author's techniques
LS 1.2 Verbal, nonverbal messages

When lava cools and hardens, it forms volcanic rocks. The kinds of rocks formed are clues to the kind of eruption. The two main kinds have Hawaiian names. Thick, slow-moving lava called *aa* (AH-ah) hardens into a rough tangle of sharp rocks. Thin, hot, quick-moving lava called *pahoehoe* (pah-HO-ee-ho-ee) forms a smooth, billowy surface.

8

9

Reaching All Students

Extra Support

R 2.1

Strategy Modeling

Monitor/Clarify Ask students to describe what the hot, quick-moving lava called *pahoehoe* might look like. If they have difficulty answering, use this example to model the strategy.

The text says that pahoehoe *forms a smooth, billowy surface. It's hard for me to picture this. The photo shows puffy, black, swirling rock that looks like dry mud. It helps me understand what the flowing lava might look like.*

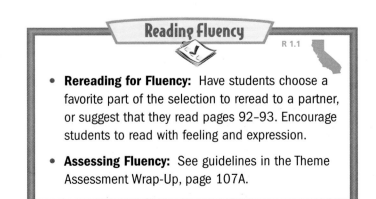

Reading Fluency

R 1.1

- **Rereading for Fluency:** Have students choose a favorite part of the selection to reread to a partner, or suggest that they read pages 92–93. Encourage students to read with feeling and expression.

- **Assessing Fluency:** See guidelines in the Theme Assessment Wrap-Up, page 107A.

▶ Supporting Comprehension

R 2.4
R 2.5

10 Why do you think scientists divide volcanoes into groups? (Maybe it helps them study volcanoes and make predictions about them.)

R 3.7

11 Why do you think the author compares volcanoes to warriors' shields and upside-down ice cream cones? (to give readers familiar objects to compare them to)

R 2.4
R 2.5

12 Based on the information on page 95, what do you think an *active* volcano is? (one that can still erupt but doesn't necessarily erupt for many years)

> **Vocabulary** *(pages 94–95)*
>
> **cinders:** charred bits of rock; ashes
>
> **composite:** made up of different substances or parts

10

11

Earth scientists have divided volcanoes into four groups. Shield volcanoes, such as Mauna Loa and Kilauea, have broad, gentle slopes shaped like an ancient warrior's shield.

Cinder cone volcanoes look like upside-down ice cream cones. They erupt explosively, blowing out burning ashes and <u>cinders</u>. The ashes and cinders build up to form the cone shape. The cinder cone volcano to the near left erupted in Guatemala, Central America, in 1984. The cinder cone volcanoes in the background are still smoking from earlier eruptions.

94

Word Study

Word Roots The word *composite* comes from the Latin roots *com* ("with") and *pos* ("put"). The Latin word *componere* means "put together." Students may be familiar with a number of related words, such as *composition, compose,* and *composer.*

R 1.4

California Standards pp. 94–95

R 1.4 Use roots and affixes
R 2.1 Understand text features
R 2.2 Use order to analyze text

R 2.4 Inferences/generalizations
R 2.5 Facts, inferences, opinions
R 3.7 Evaluate author's techniques

M ost of the volcanoes in the world are <u>composite</u> or strato-volcanoes. Strato-volcanoes are formed by the lava, cinders, and ashes of an eruption. During an eruption, ashes and cinders fall to the ground. The eruption quiets down and lava slowly flows out, covering the layer of ashes and cinders. Further eruptions add more layers of ashes and cinders, followed by more layers of lava. Mount Shasta (above) in California and Mount Hood in Oregon are strato-volcanoes. They are still active even though they have not erupted for many years.

12

95

Reaching All Students
English Language Learners

Intermediate and Advanced Fluency

Two-Word Verbs Have students look at page 95. Point to the two-word verb *flows out*. Ask students what happens when too much water is poured into a glass. Explain that the water spills over or flows out of the top of the glass. Then ask students to look for another two-word verb in the same sentence. (quiets down)

W 2.2.a Demonstrate understanding

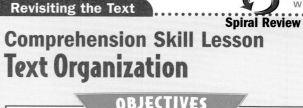

Revisiting the Text

R 2.1
R 2.2
W 2.2.a

Spiral Review

Comprehension Skill Lesson
Text Organization

OBJECTIVES

Students

- conclude that authors organize nonfiction in a certain way

- distinguish nonfiction that is organized by main idea from nonfiction that is organized by sequence of events

Tell students that the facts in a nonfiction selection can be organized by main ideas or sequence of events.

Point out that the information on pages 94–95 is organized by main idea. Ask them what the main idea is. (There are four kinds of volcanoes.) Work with students to create a diagram like the one below. Have them fill it in with appropriate supporting details.

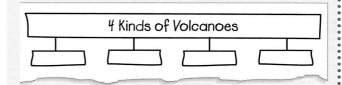

4 Kinds of Volcanoes

Next, ask a volunteer to read aloud the last three paragraphs on page 86 and tell what they are about. (the 1980 eruption of Mount St. Helens) Ask how this passage is organized. (by sequence)

Finally, have pairs of students reread page 90. Ask them to decide how this information is organized (by sequence), and complete a sequence chart together.

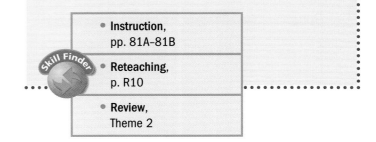

Skill Finder

- **Instruction,**
  pp. 81A–81B

- **Reteaching,**
  p. R10

- **Review,**
  Theme 2

▶ **Strategy Focus:**
Monitor/Clarify

Student Modeling Ask students how they used the Monitor/Clarify Strategy to clear up confusion or clarify points. You might offer prompts such as

- How could rereading page 97 help you understand more clearly how Crater Lake was formed?

- How do the photos on pages 94–96 help you understand the four types of volcanoes?

▶ **Supporting Comprehension**

13 How does the author help readers understand the way a plugged-up dome volcano erupts?
R 3.7
(by comparing it to a bottle of soda water with a cork in it; it helps readers picture the sudden eruption that takes place when the "cork pops")

14 Why do you think Crater Lake is so deep?
R 2.4
(Volcanoes originate below the surface of the earth; when it erupted and blew its top off, the remaining rock fell down into the open vents where magma had flowed up.)

Vocabulary *(pages 96–97)*

summit: the top of a mountain

extinct: no longer active; extinguished

collapsed: fallen inward suddenly

caldera: a crater formed by a collapsed volcano

13 ⊥he fourth kind of volcano is called a dome volcano. Dome volcanoes have thick, slow-moving lava that forms a steep-sided dome shape. After an eruption, the volcano may be plugged with hardened lava. The plug prevents the gases from escaping, like a cork in a bottle of soda water. As the pressure builds up, the volcano blows its top, as Mount St. Helens did. Lassen Peak in California is a dome volcano that erupted violently in 1915. You can see the huge chunks of volcanic rock near the <u>summit</u>.

96

Reaching All Students
Challenge

Reading Card
13

Comparisons

Point out the author's comparison of a dome volcano to a bottle of soda water with a cork in it. Then distribute Reading Card 13. Have students find other examples of colorful comparisons in the selection, and then try to make up their own comparisons.

California Standards pp. 96–97
R 2.4 Inferences/generalizations
R 3.7 Evaluate author's techniques

Around the world there are many very old volcanoes that no longer erupt. These dead volcanoes are called <u>extinct</u>. Crater Lake in Oregon is an extinct volcano. Almost seven thousand years ago, Mount Mazama in Oregon erupted, sending out a thick blanket of ashes that covered the ground for miles around. Then the entire top of the volcano <u>collapsed</u>. A huge crater, called a <u>caldera</u>, formed and was later filled with water. Crater Lake reaches a depth of two thousand feet, the deepest lake in North America.

14

97

Comprehension Skill Lesson
Categorize and Classify

OBJECTIVES

Students

- determine that scientists often categorize information to make it easier to understand
- conclude that readers often categorize and classify information to help them understand what they read
- classify information according to categories

Tell students that organizing information into categories helps readers understand what they read. Explain that

- A *category* is a group of people, animals, things, or ideas that are alike.
- To *classify* means to put items in groups according to their similarities.

Point out to students that the information on pages 94–96 tells how scientists have categorized volcanoes into four types. Work with students to name the four types of volcanoes and describe each one.

Then write the names of these volcanoes on the board: *Lassen Peak, Mount Shasta, Mount Hood, Mauna Loa, Kilauea*. Work with students to classify the volcanoes according to their type. Record their responses in a chart.

shield	cinder cone	composite	dome
Mauna Loa Kilauea		Mount Shasta Mount Hood	Lassen Peak

Skill Finder

- **Instruction,** pp. 105A–105B
- **Reteaching,** p. R12
- **Review,** Theme 2

Reading

Supporting Comprehension

R 2.4
R 3.7

15 How does the author end the selection? (He describes how life returns after a volcano erupts; he tells some of the good things volcanoes do.)

16 Why do you think the author ends the selection in this way? (Maybe he wants people to understand that both good and bad things happen as a result of volcanoes.)

After a volcano erupts, everything is buried under lava or ashes. Plants and animals are nowhere to be found. But in a few short months, life renews itself. Plants grow in the cracks between the rocks. Insects and other animals return. Volcanoes do not just destroy. They bring new mountains, new islands, and new soil to the land. Many good things can come from the fiery explosions of volcanoes.

15

16

98

Reaching All Students
Extra Support

Segment 2 Review

Before students join the whole class for Wrapping Up on page 99, they should

• check predictions

• take turns modeling Monitor/Clarify and other strategies they used

• add to **Transparency 1–19**, check and revise their Category Chart on **Practice Book** page 39, and use it to summarize

Reaching All Students

Literature Discussion

LS 1.1

In mixed-ability groups of five or six, students can discuss their own questions about the selection as well as the Responding questions on page 100 of the Anthology.

California Standards pp. 98–99

R **1.4** Use roots and affixes
R **2.4** Inferences/generalizations
R**3.7** Evaluate author's techniques

LS**1.1** Ask new questions
LS **2.3.a** Summarize events/details

Meet the AUTHOR

Seymour Simon

"Many of the books I write are really in the nature of guidebooks to unknown territories. Each territory has to be discovered again by children venturing into it for the first time."

"I'm always working on several books at the same time. I may be writing a book and researching another book and writing for information about a third book and thinking about plans for still a fourth book."

FACT FILE

- Graduated from the Bronx High School of Science
- President of the Junior Astronomy Club at New York's Museum of Natural History
- Taught science and creative writing in New York City public schools, 1955–1979
- First published work: a magazine article about the moon
- Author of more than two hundred books in thirty years

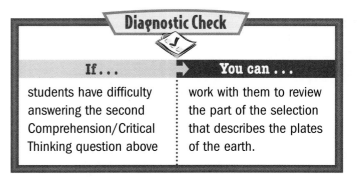

Simon's range of interests shows in his titles, such as: *Our Solar System, The Universe, Tornadoes, Sharks, Gorillas, Out of Sight: Pictures of Hidden Worlds, The Paper Airplane Book,* **and the** *Einstein Anderson, Science Detective* **series.**

Internet

For more information about Seymour Simon, visit Education Place.
www.eduplace.com/kids

End of Segment 2:
pages 91–99

Reaching All Students
English Language Learners

Intermediate and Advanced Fluency   R 1.4

Point out the word *renews* on page 98. Explain that this word begins with the prefix *re-*, which can add the meaning "again" to a base word. Ask students what *renews* means. ("become new again") Then write *read, write, do,* and *make* on the board and have students copy them in their vocabulary notebooks. Ask them to add *re-* to each word and then write the meaning of the new word.

Wrapping Up Segment 2
pages 91–99

First, provide Extra Support for students who need it (page 98). Then bring all students together.

- **Review Predictions/Purpose** Ask students whether the selection contained the information they thought it would contain, and what surprised them about volcanoes. Also ask students if they found the information they wanted to find out about volcanoes.

- **Model Strategies** Draw students' attention to the Strategies Poster. Ask them to take turns modeling the Monitor/Clarify Strategy and other strategies they used while reading.

- **Share Group Discussions** Invite students to share their responses to the questions on Reading Card 11. Encourage them to use selection information to discuss the causes and effects of volcanoes.   LS 1.1

- **Summarize** Ask students to use the completed Category Chart (**Practice Book** page 39) to summarize *Volcanoes.*   LS 2.3.a

Comprehension/Critical Thinking

1 Do you think it is important for scientists to study volcanoes? Why or why not? (yes, so that they can predict when the eruptions will happen)
Making Judgments

2 Based on what you've learned so far, how well do you think scientists can predict when and where volcanoes will happen? (They can predict that new volcanoes will happen where the earth's plates meet; they can't predict exactly when eruptions will happen.) **Drawing Conclusions**

Diagnostic Check

If...	You can ...
students have difficulty answering the second Comprehension/Critical Thinking question above	work with them to review the part of the selection that describes the plates of the earth.

Responding

▶ Think About the Selection

Discuss or Write Have students discuss or write their answers. Sample answers are provided; accept reasonable responses that are supported with evidence from the story.

1 **Making Inferences** People did not know the scientific explanation for volcanoes, so they made up stories to explain them.

R 2.4
R 3.1
R 3.6

2 **Comparing and Contrasting** Volcanoes create new land and beautiful lakes; they destroy homes and property and cause loss of life.

R 2.3

3 **Identifying Cause and Effect** Earthquakes also happen where the plates of the earth meet; before an eruption, the earth probably moves as magma pushes upward.

W 2.2.a

4 **Expressing Personal Opinions** Answers will vary.

5 **Connecting to Personal Experiences** Answers will vary.

6 **Making Judgments** *Worst*—It might be dangerous and scary. *Best*—It would be exciting and awesome to see volcanoes up close.

7 **Connecting/Comparing** Compare and Contrast Volcanoes are caused by forces deep underground, but tornadoes are caused by weather patterns in the atmosphere. Volcanoes happen mostly where the earth's plates meet, but tornadoes happen mostly in the Midwest. Both can give warning signs.

W 2.2.a

Responding

VOLCANOES

Think About the Selection

1 Why do you think people have used folktales to explain volcanoes?

2 Find examples in the selection of both the helpful and harmful things that volcanoes do.

3 Why do you think earthquakes often happen just before volcanoes?

4 Of the different volcanoes mentioned in the selection, which one impressed you the most? Why?

5 Which word best describes a volcano for you: *beautiful, scary, exciting, ugly,* or some other word? Explain why.

6 What do you think would be the best and worst things about studying volcanoes for a living?

7 **Connecting/Comparing** Compare the conditions that cause a volcanic eruption with those that cause a tornado. Think about how, where, and when they happen, and how much warning people have.

Explaining

Write a Travel Brochure

Use information from the selection to create a travel brochure for a tour of the world's volcanoes. Explain where the tour will go and what volcanoes you will see.

Tips

- Fold a sheet of paper into three panels.
- Describe the tour on the inside panels and illustrate the outside panels.
- Check your spelling and capitalize all proper nouns.

100

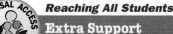

Reading Inferences/generalizations (R2.4)
Writing Write responses to literature (W2.2)

Reaching All Students

UNIVERSAL ACCESS

Extra Support

W 1.2

Writing Support

If possible, bring some examples of travel brochures to class and allow students to examine them. Point out the pictures and captions. Work with students to plan a brochure. Have them work in pairs to write the text for the brochure, as well as to plan the layout, illustrate it, and think of ideas for the illustrations and captions.

California Standards pp. 100–101

R 2.3 Discern main ideas	**R 3.6** Evaluate patterns/symbols
R 2.4 Inferences/generalizations	**W 1.2** Create an exposition
R 3.1 Analyze literary forms	**W 2.2.a** Demonstrate understanding

Science

Create a Poster

Use information from Seymour Simon's *Volcanoes* to make a poster. You might show how magma rises to erupt as lava, or show the four different kinds of volcanoes.

Social Studies

Create a Fact File

With classmates, create a volcano fact file. Using the information in *Volcanoes*, each person chooses a country or state, such as Iceland or Hawaii, and lists the volcanoes for that place, along with a brief description of the volcanoes and a small map.

Bonus: Find information about the volcanoes of a country not mentioned in the selection, such as Italy or Japan. Add a fact file about that place.

Internet

Go on a Web Field Trip

Connect to Education Place and explore a weather center, science museum, and other places to observe nature's fury. **www.eduplace.com/kids**

101

Personal Response

Invite volunteers to share their personal responses to *Volcanoes.* As an alternative, ask students to write in their journals or to respond in their own way.

W 2.2.a

▶ Comprehension Check

Assign **Practice Book** page 40 to assess students' understanding of the selection.

Practice Book page 40

Name _____

Volcanoes
Comprehension Check

Show What You Know!

The following questions ask about volcanoes. Answer each question by writing the letter of the correct answer in the space provided.

B (1) 1. Where does the word *volcano* come from?
A. the Hawaiian name for the goddess of fire, Pele
B. the name for the Roman god of fire, Vulcan
C. the scientific name for mountains that spout fire and ash
D. the name for a race of mythological creatures called Vulcans

A (1) 2. How are volcanoes formed?
A. Hot magma beneath the earth's crust pushes up through cracks or holes.
B. The earth's crust melts and forms rivers of hot lava.
C. Wood and other materials catch fire and cause explosions that melt mountaintops.
D. Glaciers melt, leaving craters through which magma can escape.

B (1) 3. What happened when Mt. St. Helens erupted in 1980?
A. The first of the Hawaiian islands was formed in the Pacific Ocean.
B. Homes, roads, and forests were destroyed, and 60 people were killed.
C. Ash spewed into the air, but no real damage was done.
D. A new volcanic island appeared in the North Atlantic Ocean.

D (1) 4. Where in the earth's crust do most volcanoes erupt?
A. in the weakest parts of the earth's plates, near the center
B. in the Atlantic Ocean
C. wherever mountains or mountain ranges are found
D. in places where two of the earth's plates meet

C (1) 5. How have volcanoes helped to create the Hawaiian Islands?
A. Eruptions destroyed much of the land area, leaving only islands.
B. Eruptions caught the attention of explorers, who settled there.
C. Eruptions built up the islands, and new eruptions add lava to the shoreline.
D. Ash and cinders from thousands of eruptions have mixed with seawater to help form new land.

40 Theme 1: **Nature's Fury**
Assessment Tip: Total 5 Points

Additional Language Development Before assigning the Responding activities above, use these suggestions.

Beginning/Preproduction Ask students to draw different types of volcanoes and to label them using the words they learned in this selection.

Early Production and Speech Emergence Have students work in small groups to describe one type of volcanic eruption. Suggest that students refer to one of the illustrations.

Intermediate and Advanced Have partners talk about the different types of volcanoes. Suggest that they first make a list of characteristics.

End-of-Selection Assessment

Selection Test Use the test in the **Teacher's Resource Blackline Masters** to assess selection comprehension and vocabulary.

Student Self-Assessment Have students assess their reading with additional questions such as

* What parts of the selection were difficult for me? Why?

* What strategies helped me understand the story?

* Would I recommend this story to my friends? Why?

Folktale Link

pages 102–105

▶ Skill: How to Read a Folktale

Read aloud the title of the folktale. Point out that this traditional story is from Mexico, and is a good example of a *pourquoi* (poor KWAH) tale. *Pourquoi* ("why") tales, like many myths, explain the origin of something in nature. Note that a folktale or myth tells a story, while a science book or article gives facts. A folktale or myth also usually features characters who are <u>archetypes,</u> animals or people who represent a certain ideal or type. Invite students, as they read "The Princess and the Warrior," to compare it with the way a science book, such as *Volcanoes,* might explain the same information.

Ask a volunteer to read aloud the three features of a folktale on page 102. After students have read "The Princess and the Warrior," have them give examples of simple characters, quick action, and information about the country.

Vocabulary *(page 103)*

beloved: much loved

brutal: violent and ugly

Folktale Link

Skill: How to Read a Folktale

❶ Notice that the **characters** are simple — good or bad, wise or foolish.

❷ Notice that the **action** moves quickly, in brief episodes.

❸ Look for information about the **country** the folktale comes from.

California Standards

Standards to Achieve

Reading

• Determine character traits (R3.3)

• Evaluate patterns/symbols (R3.6)

THE PRINCESS AND

A Mexican Folktale

Not far from Mexico City, two mountains, only five miles apart, rise more than 17,000 feet into the sky. One is an inactive volcano, Ixtaccihuatl (ees-tah-SEE-wah-tul). Its outline is said to resemble that of a sleeping woman. The other is Popocatépetl (poh-puh-CAT-uh-pet-ul), an active volcano that regularly sends up clouds of smoke and ash. This ancient Mexican folktale tells the story of how the two companion volcanoes came to be.

Many centuries ago, there was an Aztec emperor who had a good and beautiful daughter named Ixtaccihuatl.

One day the emperor received word that his enemies were preparing to attack his lands. He called his brave young warriors to the

102

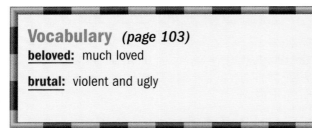

Reaching All Students

Classroom Management

R 3.6
LS 2.3.a

All Students

Reading the Folktale Involve all students in the activities under How to Read a Folktale, Folktale Chart, and Comprehension Check. Pair students needing extra support with more proficient readers as they read the folktale. Suggest that partners pause to summarize events after they read each page.

California Standards pp. 102–103

R 2.4 Inferences/generalizations
R 3.6 Evaluate patterns/symbols
R 3.7 Evaluate author's techniques

W 2.2.a Demonstrate understanding
LS 2.3.a Summarize events/details

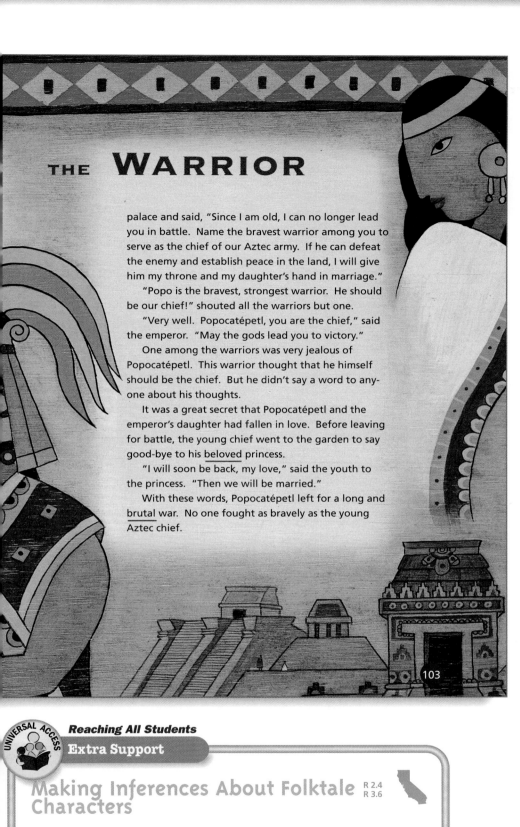

THE WARRIOR

palace and said, "Since I am old, I can no longer lead you in battle. Name the bravest warrior among you to serve as the chief of our Aztec army. If he can defeat the enemy and establish peace in the land, I will give him my throne and my daughter's hand in marriage."

"Popo is the bravest, strongest warrior. He should be our chief!" shouted all the warriors but one.

"Very well. Popocatépetl, you are the chief," said the emperor. "May the gods lead you to victory."

One among the warriors was very jealous of Popocatépetl. This warrior thought that he himself should be the chief. But he didn't say a word to anyone about his thoughts.

It was a great secret that Popocatépetl and the emperor's daughter had fallen in love. Before leaving for battle, the young chief went to the garden to say good-bye to his <u>beloved</u> princess.

"I will soon be back, my love," said the youth to the princess. "Then we will be married."

With these words, Popocatépetl left for a long and <u>brutal</u> war. No one fought as bravely as the young Aztec chief.

103

▶ Folktale Chart

R 2.4
R 3.6
R 3.7
W 2.2.a

Ask students to recall the purpose of and features of folktales. Then draw a chart like the one below on the board.

Ask students to help you fill in the first three items based on the title of this folktale, the introduction, and the How to Read a Folktale lesson on page 102.

- Write the title, "The Princess and the Warrior," on the first line.

- Write the folktale's purpose on the second line. (to explain how something came to be)

- Write what the folktale explains on the third line. (how the companion volcanoes Ixtaccihuatl and Popocatépetl came to be)

- Explain to students that after they have read the folktale, they will complete the remainder of the chart.

Folktale Title: _____

Purpose: _____

What It Explains: _____
_____
_____

How It Explains This: _____
_____
_____

Characters
good   bad

Purpose Setting Suggest to students that they read "The Princess and the Warrior" to find out which characters are good and which are bad. Remind them to use the Evaluate Strategy to help them think about and judge the characters' actions.

Making Inferences About Folktale Characters

R 2.4
R 3.6

Help students interpret the actions of the jealous warrior. Read aloud the third complete paragraph on page 103 and discuss the warrior's refusal to support Popocatépetl as leader. Have students use this behavior to predict what the jealous warrior might do. Make sure students understand that he is the same jealous warrior who returns to the capital ahead of the other warriors after the battle.

Reading

Folktale Link *continued*

pages 104–105

Vocabulary *(pages 104–105)*

claimed: declared with force

transformed: changed

At last the Aztec warriors defeated their enemies and prepared to return to the capital. The jealous warrior was the first to leave. He ran so swiftly that he reached home two days before the others. Immediately he announced that Popocatépetl had been killed and that he himself had been the hero of the final battle. Thus he claimed the right to be the next emperor and the husband of the princess.

The poor princess! She felt she would die of sadness.

The emperor, too, was saddened by Popo's death, for he believed the warrior's story.

The next day at the palace, the people prepared a great celebration to honor the wedding of the princess and the jealous warrior. Suddenly, the princess cried out, "Oh, my poor Popocatépetl!" And she fell dead to the floor.

At that moment, the Aztec warriors entered the palace. Popocatépetl ran to the emperor and announced, "We have returned. Now the princess and I can get married."

There was a great silence. Everyone turned to look at the princess.

At the sight of his beloved, the youth ran to her side and began to cry. He took her in his arms, saying, "My precious, I will be with you until the end of time."

104

Reaching All Students

English Language Learners

Intermediate and Advanced Fluency

R3.1
LS1.1

Remind students that a *pourquoi* tale helps explain the origin of something in nature. Have students read the introduction and find the name of the inactive volcano (Ixtaccihuatl) and the active volcano. (Popcatépetl) Discuss the meaning of *active* and *inactive*. Ask students why they think the two volcanoes are mentioned.

California Standards pp. 104–105

R 1.1 Read aloud fluently	**R 3.1** Analyze literary forms
R 2.3 Discern main ideas	**W 2.2.a** Demonstrate understanding
R 2.4 Inferences/generalizations	**LS 1.1** Ask new questions

Then the brave chief carried her body to the highest mountains. He laid her gently in a bed of beautiful flowers and sat down beside her.

Days passed. Finally, one of the good gods transformed the warrior and the princess into two volcanoes. Ixy remains quiet. But from time to time, Popo trembles and tears of fire flow from his heart. Then all of Mexico knows that Popo is crying for his beloved princess.

105

▶ Comprehension Check

Folktale Chart Complete the folktale chart by having volunteers fill in the remaining items.

W 2.2.a

Comprehension/Critical Thinking Ask students to read aloud parts of the selection that support their answers to these questions.

1 Which characters in this folktale are good? What actions make them so? (the warrior, because he's brave and true; the princess, because she is willing to honor her father's promise even though she doesn't love the jealous warrior) **Making Judgments**

R 1.1
R 2.3
R 2.4

2 Which character or characters are bad? Why? (the jealous warrior, because he lies to the emperor and causes the princess's death) **Making Judgments**

3 According to the folktale, what is happening when Popo "trembles and tears of fire flow from his heart"? (The volcano named after him is erupting.) **Making Inferences**

4 **Connecting/Comparing** Think about the original tellers of "The Princess and the Warrior" and about Seymour Simon, the author of *Volcanoes.* How were their purposes for telling their stories alike? (Both told stories to try to explain how volcanoes originated and to explain why volcanic eruptions occur.) **Compare and Contrast**

R 3.1

Science/Geography

Have students locate the companion volcanoes Ixtaccihuatl and Popocatépetl using an atlas. Also have them look up the volcanoes in an encyclopedia or nonfiction book about volcanoes. Then ask students to write a brief profile of each volcano that includes this information: where the volcano is, its height, how it was formed, what kind of volcano it is.

Skill Finder • Information and Study Skills,
Choosing the Appropriate Reference Source, Theme 2

Reading

OBJECTIVES

Students

- determine that writers often categorize information to make it easier for readers to understand
- categorize and classify information
- organize information by specific criteria
- learn academic language: **categorize, classify**

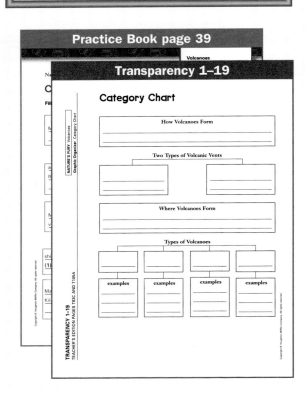

Practice Book page 39

Transparency 1-19

Comprehension Skills
 ## Categorize and Classify

▶ Teach

Display **Transparency 1–19** and use it to review what students have learned so far about categorizing and classifying:

■ A *category* is a group of people, animals, things, or ideas that are alike.

■ To *classify* means to put similar items in groups according to their similarities.

■ Sorting information by categorizing and classifying it helps readers understand and remember what they read. It also helps readers understand the things those categories have in common.

Students can refer to **Practice Book** page 39 to review how they categorized information about volcanoes.

Graphic Organizer: Category Chart

How Volcanoes Form	
Magma pushes up through vents or cracks in the earth's crust.	
Two Types of Volcanic Vents	
a hole in the ground lava flows from	a mountain or hill lava flows from

Modeling Remind students that scientists have classified volcanoes into four different types. Point out that thinking about what the volcanoes in each group have in common can help readers remember how different kinds of volcanoes are alike and different.

Think Aloud

There are four kinds of volcanoes: shield, cinder cone, composite, and dome. Remembering the characteristics of each kind helps me recognize the different kinds of volcanoes described in the selection. For example, knowing that most Hawaiian volcanoes are shield volcanoes, and knowing what shield volcanoes look like, help me identify Mauna Loa as a shield volcano.

California Standards pp. 105A–105B

W 2.2.a Demonstrate understanding

Practice Book page 42

Volcanoes
Comprehension Skill
Categorize and Classify

Name

Class

Follow the

1. Add th
article

| low |
| strat |
| strat |

2. How a
Write

| shee |
| strat |
| altos |
| nimb |
| cirro |

3. How a
Add th

| wate |
| strat |
| altos |
| nimb |
| strat |
| alto |

42   Theme 1:
Assessment

Practice Book page 41

Volcanoes
Comprehension Skill
Categorize and Classify

Name

Classifying Clouds

Read the article. Then complete the activity on page 42.

Clouds

Clouds come in a variety of forms and colors. They occur at different heights. Some are made of water and some of ice. With all these differences, a good way to identify clouds is by their groups.

Clouds are grouped by how high above the earth they are found. Low clouds are usually not more than 6,000 feet above sea level. They include stratus and stratocumulus clouds. A stratus cloud looks like a smooth sheet, while stratocumulus clouds are lumpy. They look like fluffy gray piles of cotton.

Middle clouds form between 6,000 and 20,000 feet. They include altostratus, altocumulus, and nimbostratus clouds. An altostratus cloud forms a white or gray sheet. Altocumulus clouds appear as fluffy piles that may be separated or connected in a lumpy mass. Nimbostratus clouds look like a smooth, gray layer. Rain or snow often falls from them, making them hard to see.

High clouds form above 20,000 feet. Unlike other kinds of clouds, which are made of water droplets, these clouds consist of ice crystals. Cirrus, cirrostratus, and cirrocumulus are types of high clouds. Cirrus clouds are very high in the sky and have a feathery appearance. A cirrostratus cloud is a very thin cloud layer. Cirrocumulus clouds look like millions of bits of fluff high in the sky.

Theme 1: **Nature's Fury**   41

Practice

Have students work individually or in pairs to classify two types of volcanic eruptions according to their similarities. Have students complete a chart like the one below.

Types of Volcanic Eruptions

Gentle Eruptions	Violent Eruptions
What they are like: Lava bubbles out quietly. Lava can move quickly or slowly. Examples: Mauna Loa, Kilauea	What they are like: Lava explodes from the cone. Hot ash bursts out. Examples: Mt. St. Helens, Lassen Peak

Apply

Use **Practice Book** pages 41–42 to diagnose whether students need Reteaching. Students who do not need Reteaching may work on Challenge/Extension activities, page R13. Students who need easier text to apply the skill can use the **Reader's Library** selection, "Floods," and its Responding activity.

Skill Finder

• Review, Theme 2	• Reteaching, p. R12

Diagnostic Check

If . . .	You can . . .
students need extra help classifying information	use the Reteaching lesson on page R12.
students have successfully met the lesson objectives	have them do the Challenge/Extension activities on page R13.

Information & Study Skills

✓ *Using Graphic Aids: Maps, Globes, Charts, Tables, and Graphs*

▶ Teach

Maps and Globes Display a flat map. If available, show how to use these map features: a compass rose, for indicating directions; a map key, for symbolizing land features; and a map scale, for measuring distance. Also explain that

■ **Political maps** show geographical features and political divisions such as countries, states, and cities.

■ **Specialized maps** may focus on such categories as vegetation, population, agricultural products, or rainfall. Discuss what can be learned from the specialized map on page 89 of *Volcanoes.*

Compare a flat map of the world with a globe. Invite volunteers to trace the same route on each.

Charts Tell students that a chart is a type of graphic aid that can be used to compare and contrast the characteristics of two or more things. For example, a chart could be used to compare the characteristics of the four types of volcanoes.

Tables and Graphs Display **Transparency 1–20** and explain how the table and the graph are organized.

Modeling As you model interpreting the information in a table and a graph using the transparency, have students write answers to your questions.

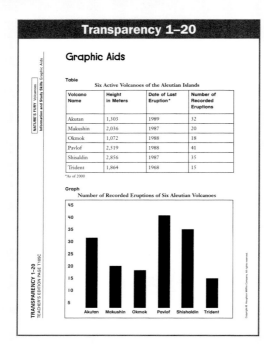

Transparency 1–20

Graphic Aids

Six Active Volcanoes of the Aleutian Islands			
Volcano Name	**Height in Meters**	**Date of Last Eruption***	**Number of Recorded Eruptions**
Akutan	1303	1989	32
Makushin	2036	1987	20
Okmok	1072	1988	18
Pavlof	2519	1988	41
Shishaldin	2856	1987	35
Trident	1864	1968	15

*as of 2000

California Standards pp. 105C–105D

R 2.1 Understand text features
R 2.2 Use order to analyze text

Think Aloud

The caption tells me that the table gives facts about six active volcanoes in the Aleutian Islands. The headings tell me that the columns show each volcano's name, height, the date of its last eruption, and the number of times it has erupted. To find the number of times Okmok has erupted, I find Okmok in the first column and then read across the row until I come to the column titled "Number of Recorded Eruptions." How many times has Okmok erupted? (18)

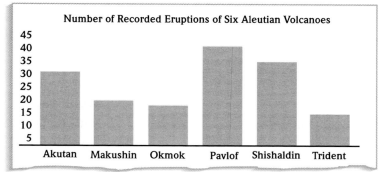

To read the bar graph, I locate the bar above a volcano's name. From the top of the bar I trace across to the number listed on the left to find out roughly how many times that volcano has erupted. Which volcano has erupted the most times? (Pavlof) *Which volcano has erupted the fewest times?* (Trident)

▶ Practice

Have pairs of students demonstrate how to read the graph and table to find answers to these questions:

- Which volcano has had the second highest number of eruptions?

- Which volcano is the tallest? Which is the shortest?

- Which one has erupted most recently?

▶ Apply

Have pairs of students use graphic aids to complete the following project:

- Find the names and locations of five volcanoes on a map or globe. On a blank world map, put a dot and a name to show the location of each volcano.

- Create a table or chart that shows the following information about each volcano: its name, location, and height in meters.

Have partners or groups present their completed graphic aids to the class.

Word Work

Word Work Instruction

DAY 1	• Spelling Pretest • Spelling Instruction
DAY 2	• Structural Analysis Instruction • Spelling Practice
DAY 3	• Phonics Instruction • Spelling Practice
DAY 4	• Structural Analysis Reteaching • Vocabulary Skill Instruction • Spelling Game
DAY 5	• Expanding Your Vocabulary • Spelling Test

OBJECTIVES

Students

- read words with the roots *struct* and *rupt*
- read words with long vowel sounds / ō /, / o͞o /, and / yo͞o /
- use the Phonics/Decoding Strategy to decode longer words
- learn academic language: **word root**

Teacher's Note

You may want to work with students to begin a chart of Greek and Latin roots, their meanings, and example words for each root. Students can refer to this chart when they come across a word that they suspect contains a root. They can add to it as they find words with different roots.

Decoding Longer Words

✓ Structural Analysis: Word Roots struct and rupt

▶ Teach

Write this sentence on the board:

Explain that both underlined words are formed from Latin word roots. A word root is a word part that has meaning but is not a word by itself. The word *eruption* contains the word root *rupt,* which means "break," and the word *destructive* contains the word root *struct,* which means "build." Point out that recognizing word roots can help readers figure out the meanings of words that contain them.

> The eruption of Mount St. Helens was the most destructive in the history of the United States.

Modeling Use the following sentence to model how the Phonics/Decoding Strategy can help to decode longer words with word roots: *The damaged railway lines had to be reconstructed after the blast.*

Think Aloud

I recognize the word root struct *in this word, so I think the word must have to do with building. The word describes something that had to be done to damaged railway lines. Maybe the word means "rebuilt." I try that meaning and it makes sense in the sentence.*

▶ Practice

Write these phrases on the board and have students copy the underlined words: *structures collapsed after the disaster; interrupted regular programming; instructions on where to go; ruptured the earth's surface.* Tell them to circle the word roots in each underlined word. Have them work in pairs to decode the words and figure out their meanings.

▶ Apply

Have students complete **Practice Book** page 43.

Skill Finder	• Strategy Review: Phonics/Decoding, p. 83A	• Reteaching, p. R18

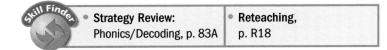

California Standards pp. 105E–105F

R 1.4 Use roots/affixes
LC 1.5 Spell correctly

Phonics

Spelling Connection

Long Vowel Sounds /ō/, /oo/, and /yoo/

Practice Book page 43

▶ Teach

Tell students that understanding long vowel sounds can help them use the Phonics/Decoding Strategy to decode unfamiliar words. Explain that

■ the letters o-consonant-e, oa, ow, and o can stand for the /ō/ sound

■ the letters u-consonant-e, ue, ew, u, ui, ou, and oo can stand for the sound /oo/

■ the letters u-consonant-e, ue, ew, u, and eau can stand for the /yoo/ sound

Modeling Write this sentence and model how to decode *molten*: *The melted, or molten, rock is called magma.*

Think Aloud

I see the vowel o in this word. If I try the short o sound, I get MAHL ten. That doesn't sound right. I know that o can also have long vowel sound. I'll try that: MOHL ten. That sounds like a word I've heard, and it makes sense in the sentence.

▶ Practice

Write these sentences on the board and have students copy the underlined words:

Lava began flowing down the mountainside; There was another episode of rumbling; Scientists are no longer clueless about what happens; The volcano was spewing ash; In a few short months, life renews itself.

Have pairs of students circle the long vowel sounds in each underlined word, pronounce the word, and check to see if it makes sense in the sentence. Call on individuals to model at the board.

▶ Apply

Tell students to decode the following words from *Volcanoes* and discuss their meanings: *explosion*, page 90; *billow*, page 92; *strato-volcanoes, slowly*, page 95; *soda*, page 96.

Phonics/Decoding Strategy

When you come to a word you don't know—

1. Look carefully at the word.

2. Look for word parts you know and think about the sounds for the letters.

3. Blend the sounds to read the word.

4. Ask yourself: Is it a word I know? Does it make sense in what I am reading?

5. If not, ask yourself: What else can I try?

HOUGHTON MIFFLIN
Reading
A Legacy of Literacy

Diagnostic Check

If...	➡ You can...
students need help reading words with word roots *struct* and *rupt*	use the Reteaching lesson on page R18.

Word Work

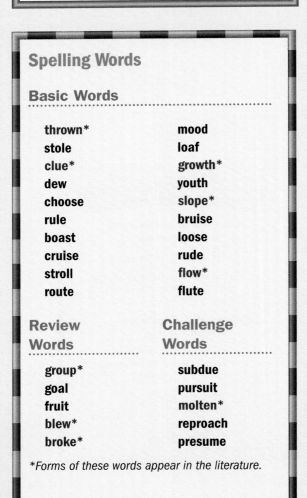

OBJECTIVES

Students write spelling words with long vowel patterns.

Spelling Words

Basic Words

thrown*	mood
stole	loaf
clue*	growth*
dew	youth
choose	slope*
rule	bruise
boast	loose
cruise	rude
stroll	flow*
route	flute

Review Words

group*
goal
fruit
blew*
broke*

Challenge Words

subdue
pursuit
molten*
reproach
presume

Forms of these words appear in the literature.

Reaching All Students

Extra Support

Basic Word List You may want to use only the left column of Basic Words with students who need extra support.

Spelling

✓ The / ō /, / o͞o /, and / yo͞o / Sounds

Day 1 — Teaching the Principle

Pretest Use the Day 5 Test sentences. Say each underlined word, read the sentence, and then repeat the word. Have students write only the underlined word.

Teach Write the first ten Basic Words on the chalkboard, sorting them into these two columns: (column 1) *stole, boast, thrown,* and *stroll;* (column 2) *rule, clue, dew, choose, cruise,* and *route.* Say each word in the first column, have students repeat the words, and then have the class identify the vowel sound they hear in all the words. (/ ō /) Explain that the long *o* sound can be spelled with four patterns: *o*-consonant-*e, oa, ow,* and *o.* Then underline these long *o* patterns in the words: *ole* in *stole, oa* in *boast, ow* in *thrown,* and *o* in *stroll.*

Move to the words in column 2 and repeat the procedure. After students identify the vowel sounds in the words (/ o͞o / or / yo͞o /), underline and discuss the patterns that can stand for these sounds: *u*-consonant-*e, ue, ew, oo, ui,* and *ou.*

Add these symbols to the lists on the board as column heads: (column 1) / ō /; (column 2) / o͞o / or / yo͞o /. Then say each of the last ten Basic Words and ask a student to name its vowel sound. Write the word below the appropriate head.

Practice/Homework Assign **Practice Book** page 409. Tell students to use this Take-Home Word List to study the words they missed on the Pretest.

Day 2 — Reviewing the Principle

Practice/Homework Review the spelling principle and assign **Practice Book** page 44.

Day 3 — Vocabulary

Exact Words Write the following sentence pairs on the board. Select students to tell which underlined word in each pair is more exact, and to explain why.

I can play the <u>flute</u>./I can play an <u>instrument</u>.

They like to <u>talk</u> about their grades./They like to <u>boast</u> about their grades.

We took a <u>walk</u> through the park./We took a <u>stroll</u> through the park.

Rivers <u>flow</u> to the ocean./Rivers <u>go</u> to the ocean.

(The words *flute, boast, stroll,* and *flow* are more exact. Sample explanation: They paint clearer pictures for the reader.)

California Standards pp. 105G–105H

Day 3 continued...

Next, list the Basic Words on the board. Have students use each Basic Word orally in a sentence.

Practice/Homework For spelling practice, assign **Practice Book** page 45.

Day 4   What's the Question?

Tell pairs of students to make a word card for each list word and stack the cards face down. Explain these game rules: Player 1 draws a card and gives a clue for the word on it. The clue must be a statement, such as "It might be black and blue." Player 2 tries to earn a point by asking a question that includes the spelling word and spelling the word correctly (e.g., "What is a *bruise? b-r-u-i-s-e*"). Players take turns, and the one who ends the game with more points wins.

Practice/Homework For proofreading and writing practice, assign **Practice Book** page 46.

Day 5   Spelling Assessment

Test Say each underlined word, read the sentence, and then repeat the word. Have students write only the underlined word.

Basic Words

1. The pitcher has <u>thrown</u> a fastball.
2. Someone <u>stole</u> the book.
3. We need a <u>clue</u> to guess the secret word.
4. The grass is wet with <u>dew.</u>
5. I will <u>choose</u> two books from this list.
6. This class has a <u>rule</u> against shouting.
7. Do not <u>boast</u> about your score.
8. Shall we <u>cruise</u> around the block?
9. Let's <u>stroll</u> through the park.
10. What <u>route</u> do you take to school?
11. I am in a happy <u>mood</u> today.
12. Please buy a <u>loaf</u> of bread.
13. The city's <u>growth</u> has been quick.
14. My mother looked like me in her <u>youth</u>.
15. The seats <u>slope</u> down to the field.
16. I got a <u>bruise</u> when I bumped the table.
17. Tighten the lid so that it is not <u>loose</u>.
18. It is <u>rude</u> to talk back to someone.
19. Which way does the river <u>flow</u>?
20. Jane plays the <u>flute</u> in the band.

Challenge Words

21. Please <u>subdue</u> the crowd.
22. The judge is in <u>pursuit</u> of the truth.
23. Steam rose from the <u>molten</u> lead.
24. Do not <u>reproach</u> them for being late.
25. I <u>presume</u> that you are ready for the test.

Technology

LC 1.5

Spelling Spree!™

Students may use the **Spelling Spree!™ CD-ROM** for extra practice with the spelling principles taught in this lesson.

Practice Book page 409

Practice Book page 46

Practice Book page 45

Practice Book page 44

Volcanoes
Spelling The /ō/, /ōō/, and /yōō/ Sounds

Name _____

The /ō/, /ōō/, and /yōō/ Sounds

When you hear the /ō/ sound, think of the patterns *o-consonant-e*, *oa*, *ow*, and *o*. When you hear the /ōō/ and the /yōō/ sounds, think of the patterns *u-consonant-e*, *ue*, *eu*, *oo*, *ui*, and *ou*. Order of answers for each category may vary.

/ō/   slope, boast, thrown, stroll

/ōō/ or /yōō/   rule, clue, dew, choose, cruise, route

Write each Spelling Word under its vowel sound.

/ō/ Sound

thrown (1° point)	loaf (1)
stole (1)	growth (1)
boast (1)	slope (1)
stroll (1)	flow (1)

/ōō/ or /yōō/ Sounds

clue (1)	mood (1)
dew (1)	youth (1)
choose (1)	bruise (1)
rule (1)	loose (1)
cruise (1)	rude (1)
route (1)	flute (1)

Spelling Words
1. thrown
2. stole
3. clue
4. dew
5. choose
6. rule
7. boast
8. cruise
9. stroll
10. route
11. mood
12. loaf
13. growth
14. youth
15. slope
16. bruise
17. loose
18. rude
19. flow
20. flute

44   Theme 1: **Nature's Fury**
Assessment Tip: Total 20 Points

Houghton Mifflin Spelling and Vocabulary

Correlated instruction and practice, pp. 24, 28, 30, 130, 178

UNIVERSAL ACCESS

Reaching All Students
Challenge

Challenge Word Practice Have students make rebus puzzles, using both small drawings and word parts, for the Challenge Words. Then ask them to trade papers and solve their partner's puzzles.

Vocabulary Skills

✓ Dictionary: Definitions

▶ Teach

Display **Transparency 1–21**, covering all but the dictionary entry for *destructive*.

Dictionary: Definitions

destructive (dĭ **strŭk´** tĭv) *adj.* Causing destruction; ruinous.
The destructive storm knocked down several homes.

eruption (ĭ **rŭp´** shən) *n.* The act of forcing out or releasing violently.
With the eruption of the geyser, steam shot out of the ground.

Explain that next to each entry word in the dictionary is at least one definition, or statement that explains the word's meaning. Point out the italicized sentence that follows the definition of *destructive*. Explain that sample sentences such as this one are often provided after a definition to give an example of the word's meaning in context.

Modeling Display the dictionary entry for *eruption* and model how to figure out its meaning.

> **Think Aloud**
>
> *After the word, I see the definition "The act of forcing out or releasing violently." I'm having a little trouble understanding what that means. Maybe the sample sentence can help. It says, "With the eruption of the geyser, steam shot out of the ground." I know that a geyser is an underground spring from which water boils up. That helps me understand what an eruption is.*

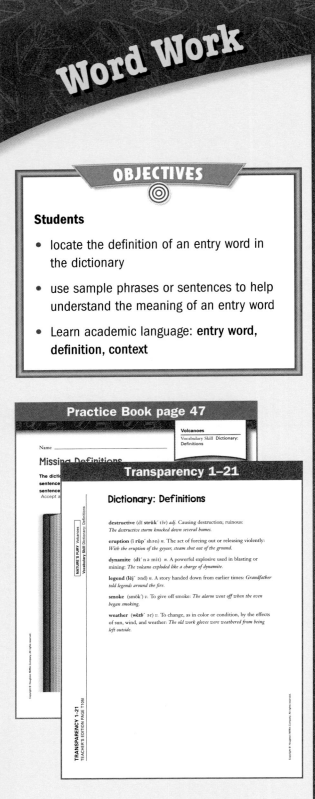

OBJECTIVES

Students

- locate the definition of an entry word in the dictionary
- use sample phrases or sentences to help understand the meaning of an entry word
- Learn academic language: **entry word, definition, context**

Practice Book page 47

Transparency 1–21

California Standards pp. 105I–105J

R 1.2 Use word origins

R 1.2

▶ Practice

Write the following sentences on the board: *The early Hawaiians told legends about Pele, their goddess of fire. The energy released in the eruption was equal to ten million tons of dynamite. The volcano was still smoking from earlier eruptions. The old lava flows are quickly weathered by waves into rocks and black sand.*

Display the definitions on the rest of **Transparency 1–21**. Have students work in pairs to use the dictionary to figure out the meaning of each underlined word. When they have finished, ask them to discuss how the sample sentences below helped them figure out each word's meaning.

▶ Apply

Have students complete **Practice Book** page 47.

R 1.2

Expanding Your Vocabulary
Words from Mythology

Remind students that the word *volcano* comes from the name of the Roman god of fire, *Vulcan*. Then explain that many other words in English have their origins in Roman or Greek mythology, the stories the ancient Greeks and Romans told about their ancestors and heroes. For example, point out that the

Mercury	⟶	mercurial
Jove	⟶	jovial
Tantalus	⟶	tantalize
Siren	⟶	siren
Pan	⟶	panic
Titan	⟶	titanic

word *atlas*, a book of world maps, has its origins in the name *Atlas*, a giant of Roman mythology who was forced to carry the world on his shoulders. Have students look in the dictionary or encyclopedia to find the Roman or Greek mythological characters whose names provide the origin of these words: *mercurial, jovial, tantalize, siren, panic, titanic.*

Skill Finder
• Challenge/Extension activities, p. R19

📎 Teacher's Note

Spelling-Meaning Connection Point out that keeping in mind the *t* at the end of the word *extinct* can help students remember how to spell the word *extinction*, in which the sound of the *t* changes from *t* to *sh*. Have students write the words *distinct* and *distinction*, underlining the letter in *distinct* that can help them spell the /sh/ sound in *distinction*.

Houghton Mifflin Spelling and Vocabulary
Correlated instruction and practice, p. 26

UNIVERSAL ACCESS
Reaching All Students
English Language Learners

Vocabulary Support

Pair students with English-proficient partners to read the definitions and sample phrases or sentences. Suggest that students try to rephrase the definitions in their own words to see if they understand the word.

Writing and Language Instruction

DAY 1	• Daily Language Practice • Grammar Instruction • Journal Writing
DAY 2	• Daily Language Practice • Writing a Paragraph of Information • Journal Writing • Grammar Practice
DAY 3	• Daily Language Practice • Grammar Instruction • Writing a Travel Brochure
DAY 4	• Daily Language Practice • Listening/Speaking/Viewing • Writing: Improving Your Writing • Grammar Practice
DAY 5	• Daily Language Practice • Grammar: Improving Your Writing

OBJECTIVES

Students

- identify singular nouns

- identify plural nouns

- determine the plural forms of nouns with regular and irregular plurals

- proofread and correct sentences with grammar and spelling errors

- replace general nouns with specific nouns to improve writing

- learn academic language: **singular nouns, plural nouns, exact nouns**

Technology

Wacky Web Tales

Students may use the **Wacky Web Tales** floppy disk to create humorous stories and review parts of speech.

Grammar Skills

 Singular and Plural Nouns; More Plural Nouns

Day 1   Singular and Plural Nouns

Display these sentences on **Transparency 1–23.**

> The forest stretched between two deep valleys.
>
> Slim birches grew beside an eddy in the stream.
>
> The hiker had an impulse to make a sketch of the ferns and mosses.
>
> A bear was eating wild blackberries while a bluejay scolded him.

Point out the singular nouns (*forest, eddy, stream, hiker, impulse, sketch, bear, bluejay*) and plural nouns. (*valleys, birches, ferns, mosses, blackberries*) Go over the following rules with students:

- A noun names a person, a place, a thing, or an idea.

- To form the plural of most nouns, add *-s* or *-es.*

- To form the plural of a noun ending with *x, s, ch, sh,* or *ss,* add *-es.*

- To form the plural of a noun ending with a consonant + *y,* change the *y* to *i* and add *-es.*

- To form the plural of a noun ending in a vowel + *y,* add *-s.*

Have students look again at **Transparency 1–23** to find plural nouns to illustrate each rule. Next, tell them to write, on a separate sheet of paper, the plurals of the singular nouns in those sentences. Have them tell which rule each plural illustrates. Then have students suggest additional plural nouns for the examples.

Day 2

Practice/Homework Assign **Practice Book** page 48.

Day 3 · More Plural Nouns

Write this sentence on the board:

> *All the children had their own guidebooks.*

Have students identify the plural nouns. (children, guidebooks) Ask which noun does not end in *-s* or *-es.* (children) Go over these rules with students:

- In some nouns that end in *f* or *fe,* the *f* changes to a *v* before *-s* or *-es* is added.

- In nouns that end in *o,* the plural may be formed by adding either *-s* or *-es.*

- Some nouns have plural forms that do not end in *-s* or *-es.*

- Some nouns have the same singular and plural form.

Have students identify the plural nouns in the rest of the sentences on **Transparency 1–24,** and tell which rule each noun illustrates. Then tell students to think of and list other plural nouns that follow each rule.

Day 4

Practice/Homework Assign **Practice Book** page 49.

Day 5 · Improving Your Writing

Exact Nouns Tell students that a good writer uses specific singular or plural nouns rather than general ones in a description or an explanation. Model replacing general nouns with exact ones, using the following example:

We saw a lot of animals on our trip to British Columbia.

Improved: We saw several moose, a herd of buffalo, three bighorn sheep, and a pack of wolves on our trip to British Columbia.

Have students review a piece of their own writing to see if they can improve it by replacing general nouns with exact nouns.

Practice/Homework Assign **Practice Book** page 50.

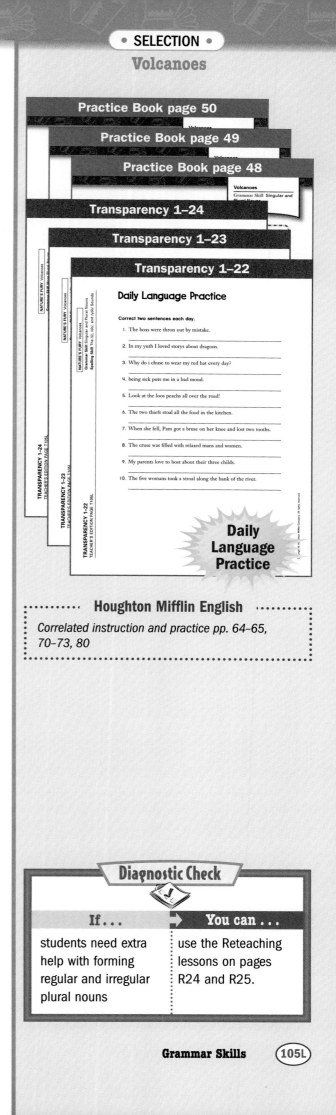

Practice Book page 50
Practice Book page 49
Practice Book page 48
Transparency 1–24
Transparency 1–23
Transparency 1–22

Daily Language Practice

Correct two sentences each day.

1. The boxs were thron out by mistake.
2. In my yuth I loved storys about dragons.
3. Why do i chuse to wear my red hat every day?
4. being sick puts me in a bad moud.
5. Look at the loos peachs all over the road!
6. The two thiefs stoal all the food in the kitchen.
7. When she fell, Pam got a bruse on her knee and lost two tooths.
8. The cruse was filled with relaxed mans and women.
9. My parents love to bost about their three childs.
10. The five womans took a stroal along the bank of the river.

Daily Language Practice

········· **Houghton Mifflin English** ·········
Correlated instruction and practice pp. 64–65, 70–73, 80

Diagnostic Check

If . . .	You can . . .
students need extra help with forming regular and irregular plural nouns	use the Reteaching lessons on pages R24 and R25.

W 1.2.a
W 2.2.a

OBJECTIVES

Students

- identify the characteristics of a good paragraph of information
- write a paragraph of information
- improve their writing by correcting sentence fragments
- learn academic language: **topic, topic sentence, supporting details**

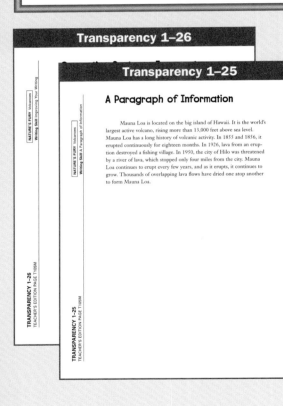

Transparency 1–26

Transparency 1–25

A Paragraph of Information

Mauna Loa is located on the big island of Hawaii. It is the world's largest active volcano, rising more than 13,000 feet above sea level. Mauna Loa has a long history of volcanic activity. In 1855 and 1856, it erupted continuously for eighteen months. In 1926, lava from an eruption destroyed a fishing village. In 1950, the city of Hilo was threatened by a river of lava, which stopped only four miles from the city. Mauna Loa continues to erupt every few years, and as it erupts, it continues to grow. Thousands of overlapping lava flows have dried one atop another to form Mauna Loa.

Writing Skills
A Paragraph of Information

▶ Teach

Remind students that they have learned many facts about volcanoes and volcanic eruptions. Tell them that a good way to share some of the facts they learned is to write a paragraph of information.

▶ Practice

Display **Transparency 1–25.** Have students read the paragraph of information. Ask the following questions:

■ What is the topic of the paragraph? (Mauna Loa)

■ What sentence states the topic? (the first one)

■ What information do the remaining sentences give about Mauna Loa? (information about its size, its past eruptions, and its make-up)

Topic	Mauna Loa
Topic Sentence	Mauna Loa is located on the big island of Hawaii.
Supporting Details	size, past eruptions, make-up of mountain

Discuss with students the guidelines for writing a paragraph of information.

Guidelines for
Writing a Paragraph of Information

- Select an interesting **topic** that you know something about.
- Include a topic sentence that tells what the whole paragraph is about. The **topic sentence** is usually the first sentence in the paragraph.
- Include several **supporting sentences** that give more information about the topic. Make sure your sentences are in a logical order.
- Make sure all your sentences give information about the topic. Include facts only—don't include your opinions.
- Remember to indent the first sentence of the paragraph.

California Standards pp. 105M–105N

W 1.2.a Establish topic, order
W 2.2.a Demonstrate understanding

W 1.6 Edit and revise work
LC 1.1 Sentence structure/transition

▶ Apply

Have students write their own paragraphs of information. They might write about one of the volcanoes described in *Volcanoes*, or about a certain type of volcano. Remind students to include a topic sentence and to check their facts to make sure they are accurate. You might collect students' paragraphs into a volcano fact book. Students can use **Practice Book** page 51 to help plan and organize their paragraphs.

W 1.6
LC 1.1

Improving Your Writing
✓ Correcting Sentence Fragments

Teach Tell students that it is important to check the paragraphs they write to make sure that each sentence is complete. Remind them that every sentence needs a subject that tells who or what the sentence is about, and a predicate that tells what the subject did or what the subject is like.

Practice To model how to correct sentence fragments, display **Transparency 1–26.** Call on volunteers to underline each sentence fragment and tell whether it is missing a subject, a predicate, or both. Then guide students in rewriting each fragment as a complete sentence by adding the missing elements.

Apply Assign **Practice Book** page 52. Then have students review their paragraphs of information and make sure that each sentence is complete.

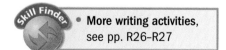
• More writing activities, see pp. R26–R27

 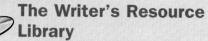
The Writer's Resource Library

Students may use this set of reference tools as they work on their own writing. *©Sunburst Technology Corporation, a Houghton Mifflin Company. All Rights Reserved.*

Type to Learn™

Students may use **Type to Learn™** to learn proper keyboarding technique. *©Sunburst Technology Corporation, a Houghton Mifflin Company. All Rights Reserved.*

Portfolio Opportunity

Save students' paragraphs of information for samples of their writing development.

Practice Book page 52

Name ____
Volcanoes
Writing Skill Improving

Corr
Frag

A senten
subject o
fragment
a subject
on the li

1. Many
   Many

2. Clou
   Clou

3. Burie
   Quick

4. The
   The

5. Are s
   Hund

52   Theme 1:
Assessment

Practice Book page 51

Name ____
Volcanoes
Writing Skill Paragraph of Information

Writing a Paragraph of Information

Read the following paragraph of information from page 87 of Volcanoes.

> Volcanoes are formed by cracks or holes that poke through the earth's crust. Magma pushes its way up through the cracks. This is called a volcanic eruption. When magma pours onto the surface it is called lava. . . . As lava cools, it hardens to form rock.

Now get ready to write your own paragraph of information about volcanoes. Use the following graphic organizer to help you organize your paragraph. (5 points)

Topic

Topic Sentence

Supporting Sentences

Now, write your paragraph of information on a separate sheet of paper. Arrange your supporting sentences in a logical order, and make sure all of the sentences contain facts about the topic. (5 points)

Theme 1: Nature's Fury   51
Assessment Tip: Total **10** Points

·········· **Houghton Mifflin English** ··········
Correlated instruction and practice, pp. 32–33, 357–360

Students

- generate guidelines for holding a conversation
- hold a conversation with a partner about a topic of mutual interest
- use active listening strategies

Conversation Do's	Conversation Don't's

Listening/Speaking/Viewing
Having Effective Conversations

▶ Teach

Discuss with students some characteristics of a good conversation. Ask them to help you begin generating a list of guidelines for participating in a conversation. Include some of the following to get started:

- Take turns speaking.
- Speak and listen respectfully.
- Ask each other's opinion about the topic, and listen carefully to the answer.
- Ask questions if you don't understand something the person has said.
- Remember that it's all right to disagree.
- If the conversation stalls, try asking a question.

▶ Practice

Have each student jot down one or two additional tips not yet on the list. Then ask volunteers to contribute their ideas as you work with students to complete a class list of conversation tips. You might organize the list under two categories: *Conversation Dos* and *Conversation Don'ts*. Post the tips where all students can see them.

UNIVERSAL ACCESS

Reaching All Students

English Language Learners

Conversations

Have pairs of English speakers model conversations as English language learners watch from a slight distance and take notes. As an alternative, you can videotape and later play the tape. Ask students to look for answers to the following: *How close do the two people sit or stand? What do they do with their hands? What do they do with their eyes? What else do you notice?* Then ask students to compare these conversations with ones they have seen between two people from their own culture.

California Standards pp. 105O–105P

LS 1.6 Verbal and nonverbal cues

▶ Apply

Have students form pairs and use the conversation tips to conduct a conversation. You might have them choose a topic for their conversation from the following prompts:

- What is your favorite way of spending a summer day?

- Who is your favorite celebrity or sports star? What do you like about him or her?

- What kind of work would you like to do when you're an adult?

- What TV shows are best and worst, in your opinion? Why?

- Where would you like to live if you could live anywhere in the world?

LS 1.6

Improving Conversations
Using Tone and Body Language

Explain to students that tone, expression, and body language play important parts in making a conversation satisfying for participants. Help them generate these additional guidelines:

- Give full attention to the person you are talking with.

- Make eye contact.

- Show you understand the other person by nodding your head or responding in some other way.

- Ask questions if you don't understand something the person has said.

- If you disagree with the other person, give your opinions and reasons calmly and respectfully.

Predicting Outcomes

Remind students to combine what they know about a character with their personal knowledge to make reasonable predictions about what the character might do. Ask students to predict what would have happened in the folktale *The Princess and the Warrior* if the princess had not died. (Answers will vary.) Ask students to support their prediction with details from the story.

Taught: *Grade 4, Theme 4*
Reviewed: *Grade 4, Theme 6*

California Standards p. 105Q

R 2.4   Inferences/generalizations
W 2.3.a Frame questions
W 2.3.b Establish focused topic
W 2.3.c Develop topic
LS 2.3   Respond to literature

Spiral Review

W 2.3.a
W 2.3.b
W 2.3.c

Information & Study Skills: *Collecting Data and Outlining*

▷ Review

Review what students have learned about collecting data and outlining.

- Collecting data may mean gathering information firsthand rather than relying on printed materials.

- It's important to choose the right research method. Methods include interviews, which provide personal information about a subject; polls, which provide opinions about a subject; and questionnaires or surveys, which provide personal responses from a group about a subject.

- Outlines help you organize, record, and remember important information.

- Topics in an outline can be just a few words instead of a full sentence.

As a class, write an outline on "What Students Like for Lunch."

Title of Paper: What Students Like for Lunch
Main Topic : Eating Lunch at School
   A. Subtopic: Cafeteria Lunches
      1. Pizza
      2. Sloppy Joes
   B. Subtopic: Lunches From Home
      1. Peanut butter and jelly sandwich
      2. Tuna sandwich

Remind students that a report on "What Students Like for Lunch" would require some firsthand data. To gather that data, they might interview fifth graders, take a poll of cafeteria workers, or take a survey of all students.

▷ Apply

Have partners interview each other about what they like to do after school. Have one student record the information and then organize it in an outline, using the above model. Ask partners to read their outlines to the class.

Skill Finder
- **Collecting Data** Grade 4, Theme 5, p. 607C-D
- **Outlining** Grade 4, Theme 6, p. 653C-D; Grade 5, Theme 4, p. 388-391

Vocabulary: *Homophones and Analogies*

▶ Review

Remind students that homophones are words that are pronounced the same way but have different meanings and spellings. Write the following homophones on the board and discuss their different meanings and spellings: *through, threw; heard, herd; would, wood.*

Review that analogies compare one pair of words to another pair. The words in the second pair should be related in the same way as the words in the first pair. Write the following analogies on the board and discuss the relationship between the word pairs: Apple is to fruit as red is to color; Ground is to walk as water is to swim.

Homophones:
through   threw
heard   herd
would   wood
Analogies:
Apple is to fruit as red is to color. Ground is to walk as water is to swim.

▶ Apply

Group students in pairs and give each pair two index cards. Have partners write a "What Am I?" riddle on one index card. The riddle should contain clues for a pair of homophones. For example: *I am a large body of water. I am a word that means "look."* They should write the answers *(sea, see)* on the back of the card. Have partners write an analogy on the other index card. Ask them to omit one word from the analogy. For example, *Skiing is to winter as surfing is to* summer . Ask pairs to exchange cards and solve the riddle and analogy.

Skill Reminder

Adjectives and Comparing with Adjectives
Remind students that adjectives describe nouns and can tell what kind or how many of something. *A, an,* and *the* are types of adjectives called articles. To compare two subjects, *-er* is added to most adjectives. To compare three or more subjects, *-est* is added.

Have students choose three items on their desks or in the classroom and use adjectives to compare them. For example, *My math book is thicker than my social studies book. The dictionary is the thickest book in the classroom.* Have students share their sentences with the class.

Taught: Grade 4, Theme 4
Reviewed: Grade 4, Theme 6

California Standards p. 105R
R 1.3 Understand synonyms/antonyms

Skill Finder
• **Homophones** Grade 4, Theme 5, pp. 581I-581J; Grade 5, Theme 2, p. 207I
• **Analogies** Grade 4, Theme 6, pp. 685I-685J; Grade 5, Theme 5, p. 491I

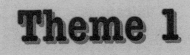

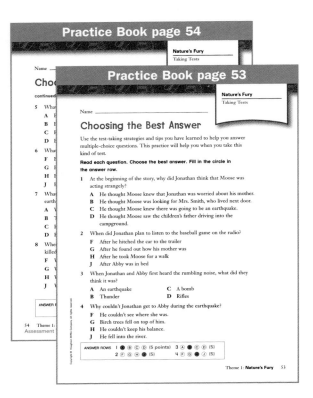

Practice Book page 54

Practice Book page 53

Theme Assessment Wrap-Up

▶ Preparing for Testing

Remind students that they can use test-taking strategies to help them do well on important tests.

Choosing the Best Answer Tell students that today they will learn strategies for answering multiple-choice questions. Have them read Taking Tests on Anthology pages 106–107.

Discuss the tips and the model student think aloud on Anthology pages 106–107 with students. Mention these points:

- Tell students, in this kind of test, to review all the answer choices to sort out the correct answers from answers that seem possible but are incorrect and to clarify how the answer choices differ.

- Often standardized tests ask students to mark their answers at the bottom of the test page or on a separate answer sheet. It is important that students carefully check that they are marking the answer choice in the corresponding answer row.

More Practice The **Practice Book,** pages 53–54, contains additional multiple-choice comprehension questions for more practice.

▶ Assessing Student Progress

Formal Assessment The **Integrated Theme Test** and the **Theme Skills Test** are formal group assessments used to evaluate student performance on theme objectives. The **Theme Skills Test** may be used as a pretest or may be administered following the theme.

The **Integrated Theme Test** assesses students' progress as readers and writers in a format that reflects instruction. Authentic literary passages test reading skills in context.

The **Theme Skills Test** assesses students' mastery of specific reading and language art skills taught in the theme. Individual skill subtests can be administered separately.

■ Integrated test of reading and writing skills: Comprehension strategies and skills, word skills, spelling, grammar, and writing

■ Tests discrete skills: Comprehension skills, word skills, spelling, grammar, writing, and information and study skills

Spelling Review/Assessment

Review with students the Spelling Words and, if appropriate, the Challenge Words from the spelling lessons on pages 51G–H, 81G–H, and 105G–H. Have volunteers summarize each spelling principle and explain how the words in each lesson illustrate the principle.

Practice Book

Practice Book pp. 55–57
Take-Home Word Lists: Practice Book Handbook

5-Day Spelling Plan

See p. 51G

Pretest/Test

1. During the storm she <u>slept</u> soundly in her <u>bunk</u>.
2. They will <u>split</u> and <u>crush</u> the shell of the coconut.
3. She feared that a <u>beast</u> might <u>dwell</u> there.
4. He is <u>fond</u> of early morning when the stars <u>fade</u>.
5. In his <u>youth</u>, Mr. Tan took a <u>cruise</u> abroad.
6. The boy's <u>mood</u> changed with the <u>flute</u> music.
7. A footprint in the <u>dew</u> was their only <u>clue</u>.
8. His injured <u>thigh</u> hurt as he climbed the <u>slope</u>.
9. The masts <u>sway</u> as the <u>fleet</u> reaches rough water.
10. His <u>boast</u> was that he never <u>stole</u> from the poor.
11. The hero was <u>thrown</u> into the <u>swift</u> river.
12. The fine performance got only <u>mild</u> <u>praise</u>.
13. One of the <u>staff</u> members heard about the <u>strike</u>.
14. Their <u>grasp</u> of the conflict was <u>slight</u>.
15. He took a <u>stroll</u> and decided to <u>claim</u> the treasure.

Challenge Words

16. The farmers' <u>campaign</u> to <u>subdue</u> the insects won.
17. We <u>rested</u> in a rustic cabin at the end of our <u>trek</u>.
18. Lee was <u>frantic</u> as he tried to <u>describe</u> the scene.
19. We watched the <u>molten</u> lava <u>cease</u> flowing.
20. No one will <u>reproach</u> their <u>pursuit</u> of the answer.

Reaching All Students
Challenge

Challenge Words Practice Have students use the Challenge Words from the Take-Home Word List to write a safety manual for their families.

Theme 1

Oral Reading Fluency

Early Grade 5	106–132 words per min.
Mid-Grade 5	118–143 words per min.
Late Grade 5	128–151 words per min.

For some students in Grade 5, you may want to check the oral fluency rate twice during the year. Students can check their own fluency by timing themselves reading easier text. The rates above are approximate.

Decoding and comprehension should be considered together in evaluating students' reading development. For information on how to select appropriate text, administer fluency checks, and interpret results, see the **Teacher's Assessment Handbook.**

For more information on assessing fluency, also see the Back to School section of this **Teacher's Edition.**

Assessing Fluency Oral reading fluency is a useful measure of a student's development of rapid automatic word recognition. Students who are reading on level in Grade 5 should be able to read, accurately and with expression, in appropriate level text at the approximate rates shown in the table to the left. In this theme, an appropriate selection for most students is *Earthquake Terror.*

Using Multiple Measures Student progress is best evaluated through multiple measures, which can be collected in a portfolio. The portfolio provides a record of student progress over time and can be useful in conferencing with the student, parents, or other educators. In addition to some tests, portfolios might include

- Observation Checklist for this theme
- Descriptive writing from the Reading-Writing Workshop
- Other writing, projects, or artwork
- One or more items selected by the student

Using Assessment for Planning Instruction You can use the results of theme assessments to evaluate individual students' needs and to modify instruction during the next theme. For more detail, see the test manuals or the **Teacher's Assessment Handbook.**

Customizing Instruction

Student Performance Shows:	Modifications to Consider:
Difficulty with Decoding or Word Skills	**Emphasis:** Word skills, phonics, reading for fluency; check for phonemic awareness **Resources:** Teacher's Edition: *Phonics Review, Structural Analysis Reteaching lessons;* Phonics Screening Test; Lexia Quick Phonics Assessment CD-ROM; Lexia Phonics CD-ROM: Intermediate Intervention
Difficulty with Oral Fluency	**Emphasis:** Reading and rereading of independent level text; vocabulary development **Resources:** Teacher's Edition: *Leveled Books for Fluency;* Reader's Library; Theme Paperbacks; Literature Resources; Book Adventure Website
Difficulty with Comprehension	**Emphasis:** Oral comprehension; strategy development; story comprehension; vocabulary development **Resources:** Teacher's Edition: *Extra Support notes, Comprehension Reteaching lessons;* Get Set for Reading CD-ROM
Overall High Performance	**Emphasis:** Independent reading and writing; vocabulary development; critical thinking **Resources:** Teacher's Edition: *Think About the Selection questions, Challenge notes;* Theme Paperbacks; Literature Resources; Book Adventure Website; Education Place Website; Challenge Handbook

Reading

1.0 Word Analysis, Fluency, and Systematic Vocabulary Development

R1.1 Read aloud narrative and expository text fluently and accurately and with appropriate pacing, intonation, and expression.

R1.2 Use word origins to determine the meaning of unknown words.

R1.4 Know abstract, derived roots and affixes from Greek and Latin and use this knowledge to analyze the meaning of complex words (e.g., *controversial*).

R1.5 Understand and explain the figurative and metaphorical use of words in context.

2.0 Reading Comprehension

R2.1 Understand how text features (e.g., format, graphics, sequence, diagrams, illustrations, charts, maps) make information accessible and usable.

R2.2 Analyze text that is organized in sequential or chronological order.

R2.3 Discern main ideas and concepts presented in texts, identifying and assessing evidence that supports those ideas.

R2.4 Draw inferences, conclusions, or generalizations about text and support them with textual evidence and prior knowledge.

3.0 Literary Response and Analysis

R3.5 Describe the function and effect of common literary devices (e.g., imagery, metaphor, symbolism).

Writing

1.0 Writing Strategies

W1.2 Create multiple-paragraph expository compositions:

W1.2a. Establish a topic, important ideas, or events in sequence or chronological order.

W1.2b. Provide details and transitional expressions that link one paragraph to another in a clear line of thought.

W1.2c. Offer a concluding paragraph that summarizes important ideas and details.

W1.5 Use a thesaurus to identify alternative word choices and meanings.

2.0 Writing Applications

W2.1 Write narratives:

W2.1a. Establish a plot, point of view, setting, and conflict.

W2.1b. Show, rather than tell, the events of the story.

W2.2 Write responses to literature:

W2.2a. Demonstrate an understanding of a literary work.

W2.2b. Support judgments through references to the text and to prior knowledge.

W2.2c. Develop interpretations that exhibit careful reading and understanding.

W2.4 Write persuasive letters or compositions:

W2.4a. State a clear position in support of a proposal.

W2.4b. Support a position with relevant evidence.

W2.4c. Follow a simple organizational pattern.

continued

English Language Conventions

use prepositional phrases, appositives, and indent clauses; use transitions and conjunctions to con-

prefixes, contractions, and syllable constructions cor-

1.0 Listening and Speaking Strategies

LS1.1 Ask questions that seek information not already discussed.

LS1.4 Select a focus, organizational structure, and point of view for an oral presentation.

LS1.5 Clarify and support spoken ideas with evidence and examples.

2.0 Speaking Applications

LS2.1 Deliver narrative presentations:

LS2.1b. Show, rather than tell, the listener what happens.

LS2.3 Deliver oral responses to literature:

LS2.3a. Summarize significant events and details.

LS2.3c. Use examples or textual evidence from the work to support conclusions.

History/Social Science

HSS5.8 6 Relate how and when California, Texas, Oregon, and other western lands became part of the United States, including the significance of the Texas War for Independence and the Mexican-American War.

Theme Resources
Resources *for* Nature's Fury

Contents

Riding Out the Storm
by Kathryn Snyder

Selection Summary

In *Riding Out the Storm*, young Raylee finds herself trapped in her home with her dog during a hurricane. Through misunderstandings, she has not been picked up by family members and taken to a nearby shelter. She must ride out the storm on her own. Raylee and Chomper endure power outages, shrieking wind, and flooding. They end up in the attic where, much later, they are finally rescued.

Key Vocabulary

shelter: a place that provides protection

splattered: splashed forcefully, as heavy rain in a storm

fixed: placed or fastened securely

rescue: to save from danger

Riding Out the Storm

Readers Library for Earthquake Terror

▶ Preparing to Read

Building Background Ask students what they know about hurricanes. After volunteers offer answers, make sure students understand that hurricanes are tropical ocean storms that can hit land with powerful winds and heavy rains, causing damage and even death.

Developing Key Vocabulary Make sure students understand the meanings of the Key Vocabulary words listed at the left. Remind them to use the Phonics/Decoding Strategy when they come to a word they don't know. For students who need more help with decoding, use the review on the next page.

▶ Strategy/Skill Focus

Refer students to the Strategy Poster. Review when and how to use the Predict/Infer Strategy.

R 2.2

Sequence of Events Remind students also to pay attention to the sequence of events. Explain that when they make predictions about what will happen next in a story, they are thinking in advance about the sequence of events. Help them revise their predictions as they track the sequence of events in this story.

On the board, write the sentences below, which provide a key story event.

> *There was no sign of the dog. Raylee walked through the house. Then, glancing out the kitchen window, she saw Chomper by the fence.*

Point out the use of the signal word *then* to students, and discuss how it sets in motion a key story event: Raylee's leaving the house to rescue her dog.

▶ Previewing the Text

R 2.1
R 2.4

Walk students through the pages of *Riding Out the Storm* and discuss the illustrations, using words from the story as often as possible. As you leaf through the book, read aloud the chapter titles ("Where's Aunt Luelle?," "Storm Power," etc.) Ask students to predict what they expect to read about in each chapter.

California Standards pp. R2–R3

R 1.1 Read aloud fluently	**R 2.4** Inferences/generalizations
R 2.1 Understand text features	**LS 1.1** Ask new questions
R 2.2 Use order to analyze text	**LS 2.3.a** Summarize events/details
R 2.3 Discern main ideas	

▶ Supporting the Reading

Have students read silently or with a partner. If needed, use these prompts: R 2.3 R 2.4

pages 4–8

- *Why does Raylee need to get to a shelter? What is about to happen?*

- *What is Momma's plan to get her daughter to the shelter?*

- *Why isn't Raylee able to go to the shelter with Aunt Luelle?*

pages 9–18

- *As the storm hits, what happens to Raylee's electricity? to the phone?*

- *What is Aunt Luelle's experience with "riding out" a storm?*

- *Why do Raylee and Chomper run to hide in the bathroom? in the attic?*

pages 19–24

- *What is a hurricane's "eye"? When it passes over, is the storm done?*

- *Why does Raylee decide to stay in the attic and not swim away?*

- *How does Raylee feel waiting in the attic? when she gets rescued?*

▶ Responding

After students have finished reading *Riding Out the Storm*, begin a discussion of R 1.1 LS 1.1 LS 2.3.a
the story by helping students answer the three comprehension questions on page 25. Then have students use the sequence chart on page 25 to summarize the story. Have students continue with similar charts for the remaining sections of the story.

Sample Answers Questions 1) a hurricane 2) making do until the storm is over 3) speaks to Chomper, changes into dry clothes, turns on the TV **Chart** "Where's Aunt Luelle?" (3) runs outside to get Chomper (4) returns to see Aunt Luelle driving off.

UNIVERSAL ACCESS
Reaching All Students
English Language Learners

R 2.4

Building Background Some students may come from countries where hurricanes or other big storms are common. Ask them to contribute to the discussion.

Key Vocabulary Make sure students understand what an *attic* and a *helicopter* are, and the less familiar meanings of *froze* and *dead* that are used in the story, and with the idiom *making do*.

UNIVERSAL ACCESS
Strategy Review
Phonics/Decoding

Model using the Phonics/Decoding Strategy. Write this sentence on the board and point to the word *hurricane*.

> But the storm watch of last night had become a <u>hurricane</u> warning in the past two hours.

Think Aloud

To figure out this word, I'll look for parts I know. I see /c-a-n/, which spells "can." But then I see there's also an /e/ at the end, which signals that the first vowel is long, so it's "cane." The word begins with a /h/ sound followed by /u-r-r-i/, which reminds me of the word "hurry." So if I blend the parts together, I get /hurry-cane/ or "hurri-cane." That's a bad storm. It fits with the sentence from the story.

Diagnostic Check

If . . .	You can . . .
students need help with decoding	use the lesson above to review the Phonics/Decoding Strategy.
students have difficulty understanding the sequence of the story	use the Reteaching lesson on page R8.

White Dragon: Anna Allen in the Face of Danger

by Maryann Dobeck

Selection Summary

White Dragon tells the story of Anna Allen, who was working at a California ski resort in March, 1982, when an avalanche ("white dragon") struck the lodge she was in. She found herself trapped in a cave-like space, where she fought cold and hunger for five days, until searchers finally dug her out. Having lost part of a leg, intrepid Anna learned to walk and ski again.

Key Vocabulary

ski resort: a place to go skiing that includes trails, lifts, and a central lodge

survived: lived through

artificial: not natural, made by humans

disabled: not fully functioning; having a mental or physical problem

---

White Dragon: Anna Allen in the Face of Danger

Reader's Library for Eye of the Storm

▶ Preparing to Read

Building Background Invite students to share what they know about snow skiing and the dangers people face on snow-covered mountain slopes. Be sure avalanches are included and that students realize a major avalanche can destroy everything in its path.

Developing Key Vocabulary Make sure students understand the meanings of the Key Vocabulary words listed at the left. Remind them to use the Phonics/Decoding Strategy when they come to a word they don't know. For students who need more help with decoding, use the review on the next page.

▶ Strategy/Skill Focus

Refer students to the Strategy Poster. Review when and how to use the Question Strategy.

R 2.1
R 2.2
Text Organization Remind students that paying attention to how a text is organized can help them understand and remember the selection better. Suggest that students pause before reading each set of pages in *White Dragon* to ask themselves questions about the text, such as, "What should I read first on these pages?"

On the board, write the first three section headings from the selection:

> *"Mountains of Snow," "Blasting the Slopes," "Buried Alive"*

Point out that the selection has been divided into parts. The headings tell you what each part is about. Model using the headings to identify the topic for each section and turning it into a question: "Mountains of Snow" is probably about snow-covered mounains. How will mountains of snow be important to Anna Allen?

▶ Previewing the Text

R 2.1
R 2.2
Walk students through the pages of *White Dragon*, pointing out the various text features: photographs and art, captions, headings, text. Ask students to come up with questions about what they expect to read under each heading.

California Standards pp. R4–R5

R 2.1 Understand text features   LS 2.3.a Summarize events/details
R 2.2 Use order to analyze text
R 2.3 Discern main ideas

▶ Supporting the Reading

Have students read silently or with a partner. If needed, use these prompts:

pages 26–34

- *Where did Anna work? Why did she go to her locker that day in March?*
- *Why was it dangerous to ski on the main road that day?*
- *What disaster had apparently hit Anna while she was at her locker?*

pages 35–40

- *Why did searchers wait to search the part of the lodge where Anna was?*
- *Who found Anna first? Why was this search later called off?*
- *What did Anna do while the searchers were working?*

pages 41–46

- *Tell how Anna was finally rescued.*
- *What happened to Anna as a result of the accident?*
- *What has Anna done since her accident? How would you describe her?*

▶ Responding

When students finish *White Dragon*, begin a discussion of the story by reviewing the answers to the questions on page 47. Then have students use the text's organization to summarize the story by filling in the chart on page 47.

Sample Answers Questions 1) She skied into a dangerous area. 2) In deep snow, like that covering Anna, sounds easily travel down, but not up. 3) They give you a hint of what each part of the story is about. **Chart** (2) Why Anna shouldn't have skied to the lodge. (3) What the avalanche does to Anna. (4) The first search. (5) Anna is first discovered. (6) What Anna does to survive. (7) Anna's rescue. (8) Anna's recovery. (9) What a *white dragon* is.

UNIVERSAL ACCESS

Reaching All Students

English Language Learners

Building Background Students from warm climates may be unfamiliar with snow and the dangers of cold. Display snow scenes; discuss snow activities (sports, games, shoveling) and dangers (frostbite, hypothermia).

Key Vocabulary Help students with the expressions *(mountain) chain, a booming business,* and *pass out (as in "lose consciousness")*.

UNIVERSAL ACCESS

Strategy Review
Phonics/Decoding

Model using the Phonics/Decoding Strategy. Write this sentence on the board and point to the word *avalanche*.

> He knew that the heavy snow might slide down the slope and become an <u>avalanche</u>.

Think Aloud

Looking at this word from left to right, I see a consonant between two vowels. I'll try breaking after the second vowel, giving the first vowel a short sound and the second vowel a long sound: /â vuh/. The letters /l-a-n-c-h/ remind me of the word "ranch." Is that final /e/ a long /e/? Let's see... /A vuh lanch ee/. That doesn't sound right. I see a description of a big snow slide. This word must be "avalanche."

R 2.2
R 2.3
LS 2.3.a

Diagnostic Check

If . . .	▶ You can . . .
students need help with decoding	use the lesson above to review the Phonics/Decoding Strategy.
students have difficulty understanding the text structure of the selection	use the Reteaching lesson on page R10.

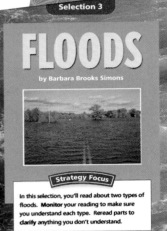

Floods
by Barbara Brooks Simons

Selection Summary

Floods focuses on the causes and damage resulting from river floods and ocean floods. It covers famous floods, including the 1993 flooding along the Mississippi, the 1889 Johnstown flood, flooding caused by Hurricane Agnes in 1972, and the tsunami (tidal wave) that hit Hawaii in 1975. After discussing flood prevention, the author charts 10 floods in U.S. history.

Key Vocabulary

downstream: in the direction that the river current is moving

break: to split apart from force or pressure

rose: got higher (as in water level rising)

whip up: stir up

Floods

Reader's Library for Volcanoes

▶ Preparing to Read

R 2.3

Building Background Invite students to share experiences with flooding, major and minor. Be sure students understand that a serious flood can devastate an area. Use a map to locate the following locales mentioned in the selection: Mississippi River; Hawaii; Johnstown (southwest central Pennsylvania), Caribbean; Gulf of Mexico; and Florida.

Developing Key Vocabulary Make sure students understand the meanings of the Key Vocabulary words listed at the left. Remind them to use the Phonics/Decoding Strategy when they come to a word they don't know. For students who need more help with decoding, use the review on the next page.

▶ Strategy/Skill Focus

Refer students to the Strategy Poster. Review when and how to use the Monitor/Clarify Strategy.

Categorize and Classify Remind students that ideas and things can often be classified by grouping them in categories. As students read *Floods*, suggest they monitor their understanding of the important ideas presented by trying to classify them. This will also help them better remember the information in the article.

On the board use this sentence to demonstrate that categories aren't fixed:

> *Rivers and oceans give people food, such as fish and water birds.*

Point to *fish* and *water birds*. Explain that these creatures might be classified as water animals in an article about animals, but in this article, they are classified as food. Categories vary, depending on the author's purpose.

▶ Previewing the Text

Walk students through *Floods,* drawing attention to the title, reading the introduction, and pointing out the various photographs and captions. Encourage students to use this information to predict what they will learn from reading this article.

California Standards pp. R6–R7

R 2.1 Understand text features
R 2.3 Discern main ideas
R 2.4 Inferences/generalizations

▶ Supporting the Reading

R 2.3
R 2.4

Have students read silently or with a partner. If needed, use these prompts:

pages 48-54

- *How is living near rivers or oceans a good thing?*

- *What is one danger? How is this dangerous?*

- *Which kind of floods are more common? What can cause such floods?*

pages 55-61

- *Name the largest U.S. river. How do people try to keep it from flooding?*

- *What helped cause the flood of 1993 that hit the Midwest?*

- *Why did the Johnstown Flood catch people by surprise? What happened?*

pages 62–68

- *How do hurricanes cause ocean flooding?*

- *What is a tsunami? What U.S. state is hardest hit by tsunamis?*

- *Name some things people can do to try to stop floods.*

▶ Responding

R 2.1

After students finish *Floods*, discuss the selection by reviewing the answers to the questions on page 69. Then use the diagrams to discuss the damage floods do, to compare and contrast floods, and to brainstorm categories to classify floods.

Sample Answers Questions 1) River. 2) knock down trees, carry away homes, wreck towns, drown people and animals 3) ocean and river. **Diagram** (Ocean Floods) not as common; (tsunamis) cause flooding in the Pacific. (River Floods) most common; can happen at any time; caused by heavy rains, melting snow, or ice; dams or levees can break

UNIVERSAL ACCESS

Reaching All Students

English Language Learners

Background Building Students still learning American weights and measures may need help with these terms: *tons, miles, square miles, feet high,* and *mph.*

Developing Vocabulary Point out that *hurricane* comes from a Caribbean Indian word and that *tsunami* is a Japanese word.

UNIVERSAL ACCESS **Strategy Review**

Phonics/Decoding

Model how to use the Phonics/Decoding Strategy. Write this sentence from *Floods* on the board and point to the name *Mississippi.*

> The <u>Mississippi</u> is the largest river in the United States.

💭 Think Aloud

To figure out this word, I'll look for parts I know. I see the word part "miss" at the beginning. Then I see /is/ and /sip/. /Miss-is-sip/ . . . I'll blend the sounds together and add a long /e/ at the end: /Mississippi/. I know that word. It's the name of a state, and it's also the name of the largest river in the United States, as the sentence says.

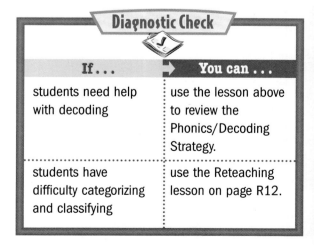

Diagnostic Check	
If . . .	**You can . . .**
students need help with decoding	use the lesson above to review the Phonics/Decoding Strategy.
students have difficulty categorizing and classifying	use the Reteaching lesson on page R12.

Comprehension Skills: Sequence of Events

Reteaching R 2.2 W 2.2.a

OBJECTIVES

Students
- identify order of events
- identify time-order clue words
- place events in sequence on a time line

Teach

Ask volunteers to name three things they did before class this morning, in the order in which they did them. Jot down time words that students use, such as *first, next, then, before,* and *after.* Tell students that they have just described a sequence of events—the order in which events happened.

Point out that the story *Earthquake Terror* describes a sequence of exciting events. Draw a time line on a long sheet of paper and display it. Tell students that the left side of the time line is the beginning of the story and the right side is the end.

On the left side of the time line, tack an index card that says, "Jonathan and Abby are left alone in the woods." On the right side, tack a card that says, "The earthquake ends, and the children are safe." Show students three index cards with the following story events written on them:

Then the rumbling noise comes closer.
First, Jonathan hears a rumbling noise in the distance.
Finally, Jonathan feels a jolt and stumbles.

Think aloud as you ask students to help you put these story events in order on the time line.

Think Aloud

I see words Then, First, and Finally that will help me know the order. The sentence that begins with the word First must tell the first thing that happened after Jonathan and Abby were left alone. I'll put it next to the first card on the left side of the time line. Which event should I put next on the time line? Which one should I put last?

Practice

Have students work with a partner to copy the time line with the events you have ordered so far. Then have them add the following events:

As Jonathan tries to rescue Abby, a giant tree crashes beside him.
When the earthquake begins, Abby falls and screams.
Finally, Jonathan reaches Abby and drags her to safety.

Afterward, have students compare their time lines in a class discussion and point out word clues.

Apply

Have students keep track of sequence of events, with an eye to identifying and using order clue words, such as *first, next, then, before,* and *after,* in the **Reader's Library** selection *Riding Out the Storm* by Katheryn Snyder. Ask students to complete the questions and activity on the Responding Page.

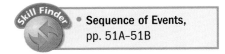

Skill Finder
- Sequence of Events, pp. 51A–51B

Diagnostic Check

If . . .	You can . . .
students need more practice with sequence of events	suggest that they put events in order in other stories they read.

California Standards pp. R8–R9

R 2.2 Use order to analyze text	W 2.2.a Demonstrate understanding
W 1.2.a Establish topic, order	LS 2.1 Make narrative presentations
W 2.1.b Show events	LS 2.1.b Show what happens

Comprehension Skills: Sequence of Events
Challenge/Extension

Listening/Speaking
Sharing Personal Narratives

W 1.2.a
LS 2.1

Partner Activity Have pairs of students take turns describing what they did last weekend. As one partner speaks, the other should listen carefully to the sequence of events being described. The listener should then try to list the events in order, using time-order words such as *first, next, after, later, on Saturday morning, on Sunday afternoon.*

Challenge
Science
Explaining a Process

LS 2.1.b

Small Group Activity Invite a small group of students interested in science to explain a sequence of events that occurs in nature. For example, they might explain the water cycle, day and night, the seasons, or the growth of a seed. Have them draw a picture of each step in the process, and write a caption for each one, using time-order words.

First, the seed sprouts in the soil.

Next, the seedling grows.

Finally, the plant has a stem and leaves.

Writing
Writing a Comic Strip

W 2.1.b

Partner Activity Have pairs of students work together to summarize the sequence of events in a newspaper comic strip. Have them write one sentence for each frame of the strip. Encourage them to use time-order words such as *first, then, after,* and *finally.*

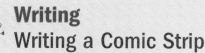

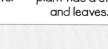

Reader's Library

Comprehension Skills: Text Organization

UNIVERSAL ACCESS

Reteaching
R 2.1
R 2.2
R 2.3

Students

- use headings and visual features to predict the focus of information in a selection or section of text

- use headings to recognize important information in a particular section

Teach

Tell students that reading a long nonfiction article is like taking a long car trip. Readers need to know where they are in the article and where the author is taking them next, or they can get "lost."

Point out to students that writers of nonfiction often include features such as headings, photographs, and charts to help readers understand the information in an organized way. Add that the headings are like road signs on a highway. They let us know what kinds of information we can expect to find as we read.

Think aloud as you ask students to help you make predictions about the article, based on its headings.

Think Aloud

I know this article is about a man named Warren Faidley, a man who chases storms. The title tells me that. I wonder what I'm going to find out about him. I can look at the headings in this article to get an idea of what it's about.

On page 59 I see two headings. I'll probably learn how Faidley chases storms in the first section and what he or others learn from watching the sky in the second section.

On page 60 I see two headings. The first one mentions Warren Faidley, so it probably gives some background about him. The second one is "Becoming a Storm Chaser." What do you think this section will be about?

Discuss the headings in the rest of the article. Encourage students to make their own predictions about the article, based on the headings.

Practice

Separate students into three groups. Assign each group one of the following sections of the article to read and discuss the text and visual features: pages 56–59; pages 60–63; pages 64–67.

Have all the groups gather together to discuss what they learned. Write each heading on the board, and ask group members to tell the most important information in the section they read.

Apply

Have students keep track of text organization, with an eye to identifying features authors use, in the **Reader's Library** selection *White Dragon: Anna Allen in the Face of Danger* by Maryann Dobeck. Ask students to complete the questions and activity on the Responding Page.

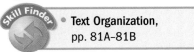

Skill Finder • Text Organization, pp. 81A–81B

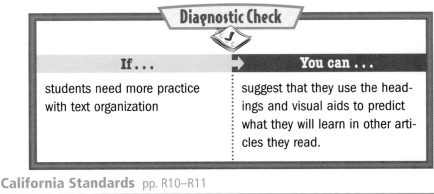

Diagnostic Check

If . . .	You can . . .
students need more practice with text organization	suggest that they use the headings and visual aids to predict what they will learn in other articles they read.

California Standards pp. R10–R11

R 2.1 Understand text features
R 2.2 Use order to analyze text
R 2.3 Discern main ideas

W 2.2.a Demonstrate understanding
W 2.2.b Support judgments
W 2.2.c Develop interpretations

Comprehension Skills: Text Organization
Challenge/Extension

Viewing
Interpreting a Graphic Aid

R 2.1

Partner Activity Have students work in pairs to ask each other questions about the information presented in the graphic aid on page 65. Each student should choose a month on the calendar and ask the partner which type or types of storms are most likely to occur in that month.

December						
			1	2	3	4
5	6	7	8	9	10	11
12	13	14	15	16	17	18
19	20	21	22	23	24	25
26	27	28	29	30	31	

Science
Previewing a Textbook Chapter

R 2.1

Partner Activity Have pairs of students work together to preview a chapter in their science textbook that they have not yet read. Have them take turns choosing a heading from the chapter and predicting what kinds of information they might learn in that section of the text. In each section, have them also discuss the purpose of any other text features, such as highlighted words, and visual aids, such as charts and diagrams.

Challenge
Writing
Writing a Study Guide

W 2.2.a
W 2.2.b
W 2.2.c

Small Group Activity Have students meet in small groups to create a study guide for a chapter the class is currently reading in science or social studies. The study guide should briefly summarize the most important ideas in the chapter and should use text structures such as headings, highlighted terms, and visual aids to help other students remember the key ideas in the chapter. Have students share their study guide with the rest of the class.

Reader's Library

Comprehension Skills: Categorize and Classify

Reteaching

OBJECTIVES

Students

- sort items into groups
- name categories for groups of items

Teach

Invite students to suggest items that we often group together in our everyday lives in order to organize them. Students might suggest forks, knives, food items, and so on. Discuss the ways in which the items in each group are alike.

Display index cards with the names or pictures of six animals: robin, dog, cat, blue jay, squirrel, cardinal. Ask students to suggest ways to sort, or group, the cards into two stacks.

If students need help with this sorting activity, use a Think Aloud to model the process.

Think Aloud

Let's see. Do I see any animals with something in common? Well, a robin is a bird. It has feathers and wings. Are there any other birds here? Yes, there are. A bluejay and a cardinal are birds too. I'll put the robin, the blue jay, and the cardinal in the same stack. I'll call it the bird stack.

Discuss the remaining three cards and whether or not they are a group. (Yes, a dog, a cat, and a squirrel all have fur.) Explain that sorting similar things into groups is called classifying.

Ask students what name they might give to the other stack. (furry animals or mammals) Explain that giving a name to all the items in a group is called categorizing.

Tell students that a good way to organize the information in what they read is to classify and categorize facts. Add that this helps readers to remember important information and be able compare the facts.

Practice

Point out to students that *Volcanoes* gives facts about four different groups of volcanoes. Put the following chart on the board, with the headings only. Have students copy it.

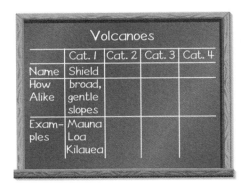

Volcanoes				
	Cat. 1	Cat. 2	Cat. 3	Cat. 4
Name	Shield			
How Alike	broad, gentle slopes			
Examples	Mauna Loa Kilauea			

1. Read the first paragraph on page 94 aloud. Ask students what information should be added to the chart for Category 1. Fill in the information on your chart and have students do the same.
2. Repeat the procedure after reading aloud the second paragraph on page 94.
3. Have students work in pairs to read pages 95–96 and fill in the chart for Categories 3 and 4.

Let students compare their charts.

Apply

Have students keep track of categorizing and classifying, with an eye to sorting into groups, in the **Reader's Library** selection *Floods* by Barbara Brooks Simons. Ask students to complete the questions and activity on the Responding Page.

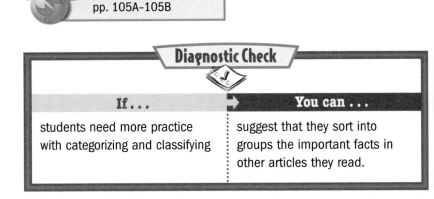

Skill Finder • **Categorize and Classify** pp. 105A–105B

Diagnostic Check

If . . .	You can . . .
students need more practice with categorizing and classifying	suggest that they sort into groups the important facts in other articles they read.

Comprehension Skills: Categorize and Classify
Challenge/Extension

Listening/Speaking/Viewing
Play a Map Game

Small Group Activity Divide the class into teams, and display a map of the United States. Read aloud different categories of states, and have students name as many states as possible that fit the category. Possible categories include states bordering the Pacific, states bordering the Atlantic, states starting with the letter *C* or the letter *A,* states east of the Mississippi, and states north of New York.

Health
Make a Poster

Small Group Activity Have students work in groups to make posters that classify and categorize foods that make a healthy diet. First, have students cut out pictures of nutritious foods. Then have them sort the pictures into groups based on similarities and give each group a name. Finally, they can glue their pictures onto poster board and print the name of each category.

Challenge
Writing
Write a Personal Essay

Individual Activity Have students list their ten favorite movies and classify the movies into two or more categories. Then ask them to write an essay explaining how the movies in each category are similar and why they enjoy that category of movie.

Structural Analysis Skills: Base Words

Reteaching

R 1.2
LC 1.5

OBJECTIVES

Students identify base words.

Theme Resources

Word Work

Teach

Ask students if they have ever taken something apart to find out how it works (for example, a toy, a motor, a kitchen appliance). Tell them that a good way to figure out the meaning of long words is to take them apart.

Explain that the first step in taking a word apart is to look for a shorter word you already know inside the longer word. This shorter word is called the *base word.* Other word parts can be added to the beginning or the end of a base word.

On the board write the following sentence from the selection: *In his mind, Jonathan could see his father unhitching the small camping trailer.*

Think Aloud

If I didn't know the word unhitching, *I could take it apart to figure out its meaning. First, I'd look for a shorter word within it that I already know. Oh, I see the word* hitch. *I know that* hitch *means "to hook one thing up to another thing." I can take the word apart this way:* un hitch ing

Tell students that if they also know the meanings of the word parts added to the beginning and the end of *hitch,* they can figure out what *unhitching* means. Point out that *un-* can mean "the opposite of." So *unhitching* means "taking apart two things that used to be hooked together."

Practice

Write the following words from the story on the board: *rewrapped, unbearably, comforting, connecting.* Have students copy the words and underline the base word in each.

Apply

Take eight index cards, and write one of the following words on each one: *rewrapped, unbearably, comforting, connecting, unwrapping, bearable, disconnected, uncomfortable.* Have students work in pairs to sort the cards according to their base words. Any cards that have the same base word should be put into the same pile.

Skill Finder
● Base Words, pp. 51E–51F

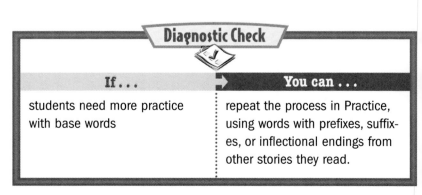

Diagnostic Check

If . . .	You can . . .
students need more practice with base words	repeat the process in Practice, using words with prefixes, suffixes, or inflectional endings from other stories they read.

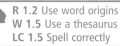 **California Standards** pp. R14–R15

R 1.2 Use word origins
W 1.5 Use a thesaurus
LC 1.5 Spell correctly

Vocabulary Activities

Challenge
Using a Thesaurus

W 1.5

Write the following passage from page 33 of the story on the board, with underlined words as shown:

As he <u>yelled</u>, Jonathan felt a <u>jolt</u>. He <u>stumbled</u> forward, <u>thrusting</u> an arm out to brace himself against a tree. Another loud noise <u>exploded</u> as Jonathan <u>lurched</u> sideways.

Have students locate the underlined words in a thesaurus. Then ask them to rewrite the passage, replacing each underlined word with a synonym. Have students read their passages aloud and compare their word choices.

Vocabulary Expansion

Review the following specific words for *go* from the story: *meandered, lunged, buckled, swayed.* Invite students to look up the definitions and then act out the verbs for their classmates to identify.

Encourage students to continue the activity by listing as many other specific words for *go* as they can find in the story. After stu-dents share and compare their lists, they can check the definitions and take turns acting out the verbs.

Theme Resources

Word Work

Structural Analysis Skills: Syllabication

UNIVERSAL ACCESS

Reteaching

R 1.1
R 1.2
LC 1.5

Teach

Remind students that sometimes they can recognize a shorter word inside a long word they are trying to figure out. Some long words, however, do not contain shorter words. Point out that a good way to decode a long word is to break it into syllables. A syllable is a word part with just one vowel sound.

To make sure students understand syllables, pronounce these words: *school, kitchen, president, gymnasium.* Have students tell how many vowels sounds they hear in each word and then how many syllables each has.

Write the following sentence from page 59 on the board: *The spectacular storms that sometimes appear in the sky have helped to make weather one of the most mysterious of all natural forces.*

Underline the word *spectacular*, and use a Think Aloud to model the process of syllabication.

Think Aloud

I see that the first vowel in this word is e. The letters spec *form a syllable with one vowel sound. I know that when a vowel is followed by a consonant, the vowel sound is short. I'll pronounce that syllable / spec /.*

Where is the next vowel sound in the word? Oh, there's the vowel a between the consonants t and c. The letters tac *form another syllable with a short vowel sound. I'll pronounce this / tak /.*

What's left now? There's the letter u. A vowel can be a syllable all by itself. Then there are the letters lar. *I'll try making u and* lar *into separate syllables.*

Write *spec / tac / u / lar* on the board. Have students pronounce the syllables and then the whole word.

Practice

Have pairs of students break these words from the article into syllables: *mysterious, tornado, horizon, hurricane.* Discuss with students how they decoded the words.

Apply

Have the same pairs read aloud pages 60–61. Ask them to jot down words they do not know and to try to decode them by breaking them into syllables.

Skill Finder
- Syllabication, pp. 81E–81F

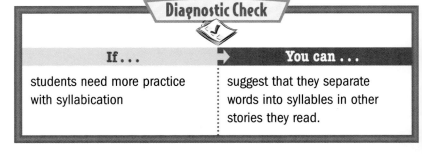

Diagnostic Check

If...	You can...
students need more practice with syllabication	suggest that they separate words into syllables in other stories they read.

California Standards pp. R16–R17

R 1.1 Read aloud fluently
R 1.2 Use word origins
R 1.5 Figurative language

R 3.5 Describe literary devices
LC 1.5 Spell correctly

R16   THEME 1: **Nature's Fury**

Nature's Fury

Vocabulary Activities

Challenge
Alphabetical Order/Guide Words

LC 1.5

Have students use alphabetical order and guide words to look up in a dictionary the words they separated into syllables in Practice and Apply of the syllabication lesson: *mysterious, tornado, horizon, hurricane, irresistible, conditions* (and other words that students have noted on their own). When students find each entry word, have them compare the syllables shown for each word with the syllable divisions students made for decoding the words.

ice · idea

ice (īs) *n.* **1.** Water frozen solid. **2.** A frozen water. **3.** Something r

Challenge
Vocabulary Expansion

R 1.5
R 3.5

Small Group Activity Review the paragraph of the story with the students. Point to the images of food used to make these comparisons: *a cauliflower-shaped cloud, the sky the color of a ripe peach.*

Encourage students to offer similar comparisons to create their own descriptions. To spark ideas, ask *What other shapes might a cloud have? What color might the rising sun have?*

Structural Analysis Skills: Roots: *struct-* and *-rupt*

Reteaching

OBJECTIVES
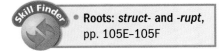

Students

- identify the roots *struct-* and *-rupt* in words
- use the roots *struct-* and *-rupt* as an aid to decoding and word meaning

Teach

Write the following list of words on the board: *erupt, interrupt, disrupted, eruption, rupture.* Ask students if they can see anything alike in all of the words. Underline the root *-rupt* in each word.

Tell students that the word part *-rupt* is called a root. Explain that recognizing this root in unfamiliar words can help students decode new words. Also point out that most words with this root have a similar meaning. They are related, like members of the same family.

Use a Think Aloud to model the process of figuring out the meaning of the root *-rupt.*

Think Aloud

Let's see. When a volcano erupts, it explodes. Erupt means "to explode" or "to break out." When you interrupt someone, you "break into" their conversation. If someone disrupts the class, he or she disturbs, or breaks the flow of, the lesson. It looks like all these words have something to do with breaking things. I think the root -rupt means "to break."

Now use a process similar to that above to discuss the root *struct-* with the following list of words: *construct, structure, destructive, construction.*

Lead students to recognize that the words all have something to do with building or with taking apart something that has been built. Help students recognize that the root *struct-* means "to build, arrange, or put together."

Practice

Have pairs of students work together to read pages 85–88 and look for words containing the roots *-rupt* and *struct-*. Have them copy the sentences in which the words appear. Then have students share their sentences with the class and discuss the meanings of the words in context.

Apply

Have students write a paragraph in which they include four words with the root *-rupt* or four words with the root *struct-*. Have students underline the root in each word. Invite students to read their paragraphs aloud in small groups.

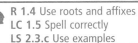
Roots: *struct-* and *-rupt*, pp. 105E–105F

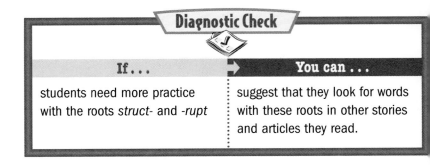

Diagnostic Check

If...	You can...
students need more practice with the roots *struct-* and *-rupt*	suggest that they look for words with these roots in other stories and articles they read.

California Standards pp. R18–R19

R 1.4 Use roots and affixes
LC 1.5 Spell correctly
LS 2.3.c Use examples

Theme Resources

Word Work

Nature's Fury

Vocabulary Activities

Challenge
Definitions

Have students look up the definitions of the following words in a dictionary and then use the words in sentences: *destructible, indestructible, constructive, disruptive, interruption, interrupter.* Students might enjoy making two cartoon books called "Meet the *struct-* Family" and "Meet the *-rupt* Family." Each page in the books should include a word, its definition, and a cartoon illustrating its meaning.

LS 2.3.c

Vocabulary Expansion

Begin a word web with the word *volcano* in the center. Then have students look through the selection to find terms associated with a volcano, such as *magma, lava,* and *gases.* Record responses on the word web.

Engage students in a discussion about the four types of volcanoes, referring them to pages 94–96 of the story. Record responses in a bubble on the word web four-kinds.

Finally, encourage volunteers to tell how each term in the word web adds to their understanding of volcanoes.

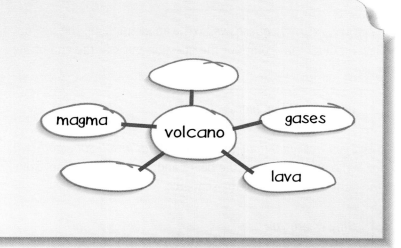

Grammar Skills: Kinds of Sentences

 Reteaching

Teach

Tell students that there are four kinds of sentences and that the author of *Earthquake Terror* uses all four kinds in the story.

Read aloud the passage on page 35 that begins "That was school." Continue reading to the end of the page. Ask students to listen to how your voice changes as you read each sentence. After you read, ask: *Did you hear any sentence that simply states, or tells, what is happening?* Write an example on the board and label it Statement. Point out that a statement ends with a period.

> *He struggled to his feet again.*

Ask: *Did you hear any questions?* Write an example on the board and label it Question. Point out the question mark at the end of the sentence.

> *Where could he hide?*

Ask: *Did you hear Jonathan give a command, or tell somebody what to do?* Write an example on the board and label it Command. Point out the period at the end of the sentence.

> *Stay where you are.*

Ask: *Did you hear Jonathan say something with strong feeling?* Write an example on the board and label it Exclamation. Point out the exclamation point at the end of the sentence.

> *I'm coming!*

Practice

In small groups, have students write each sentence type and its punctuation on an index card. As one student reads page 38 aloud, sentence by sentence, have the other students hold up the appropriate card to identify the kind of sentence.

Apply

Have students work in pairs to read the rest of the story and find more examples of each kind of sentence. Have them write at least two examples of each kind of sentence on a four-column chart labeled Statement, Question, Command, and Exclamation.

Skill Finder • Kinds of Sentences, p. 51K

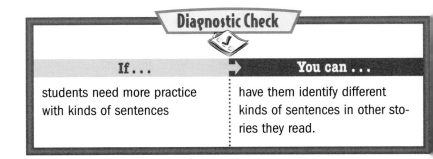

Diagnostic Check	
If . . .	**You can . . .**
students need more practice with kinds of sentences	have them identify different kinds of sentences in other stories they read.

Writing & Language | Theme Resources

Grammar Skills: Subjects and Predicates

 Reteaching

Teach

Remind students that a sentence is a group of words that expresses a complete thought. Explain that every sentence has two parts: a subject and a predicate. Then write the following sentence on the board:

> *Jonathan looked in all directions.*

Ask: *Who or what is the sentence about?* Tell students that *Jonathan* is the subject of the sentence. The subject is the sentence part that tells who or what the sentence is about. Ask: *What did Jonathan do?* Tell students that *looked* is the predicate. The predicate is the sentence part that tells what the subject does or is.

Point out that a subject and a predicate can have more than one word. Insert the word *Young* before *Jonathan* in the sentence on the board. Underline the sentence as shown below.

> *Young Jonathan looked in all directions.*

Clarify that *Jonathan* by itself is the simple subject, and *Young Jonathan* is called the complete subject. A complete subject has one main word as well as others. Point out that *looked* is the simple predicate; *looked in all directions* is the complete predicate.

Make a two-column chart on the board. Label one column Subject and the other Predicate. Write *Young Jonathan* in the Subject column and *looked in all directions* in the Predicate column.

Now write this sentence on the board:

> *Moose is Jonathan's dog.*

Ask: *Who or what is the sentence about?* Write *Moose* in the Subject column of the chart. Ask: *What words tell what Moose does or is?* Write *is Jonathan's dog* in the Predicate column.

Practice

Have students copy the chart on a sheet of paper. Then write these sentences on the board:

> *A huge tree crashes near Jonathan.*
> *Abby is very scared.*
> *Jonathan takes Abby to a safe place.*
> *The earthquake is finally over.*

Have students write the complete subjects and predicates on their charts in the correct columns.

Apply

Have students work in pairs to write four sentences about the story. Have them add the subjects and predicates to the chart.

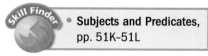

Skill Finder
- Subjects and Predicates, pp. 51K–51L

Diagnostic Check

If...	You can ...
students need more practice with subjects and predicates	suggest that they identify subjects and predicates in other stories they read.

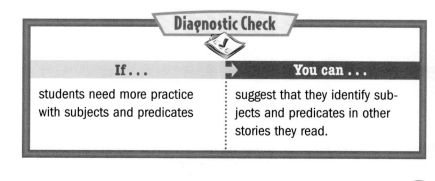

Grammar Reteaching (R21)

Grammar Skills: Conjunctions

Reteaching

LC 1.1

OBJECTIVES

Students

- use the conjunctions *and* and *or* to combine sentences
- identify sentences that contain the conjunction *and* or *or*

Teach

Write the following two sentences on the board:

> *Warren Faidley photographs tornadoes.*
> *Warren Faidley photographs lightning.*

Ask students if they can think of a way to express both of these ideas in one sentence.

Use a Think Aloud to model a way to combine the ideas.

Think Aloud

The beginnings of both sentences are exactly the same. If Warren Faidley photographs two different things, I could name both things in the same sentence. What would I put in between the two words to show that he photographs both things? I know. I'll put the conjunction and. *I know that I can use the conjunction* and *or* or *to combine sentences.*

Write the following sentence on the board. Underline the words *tornadoes* and *lightning,* and circle the conjunction *and.*

> *Warren Faidley photographs* <u>tornadoes</u> (and) <u>lightning</u>.

Now write these two sentences on the board:

> *A thunderstorm might occur in August.*
> *A hurricane might occur in August.*

Point out that the ends of the two sentences are the same, but the beginnings are different. Ask students to suggest a way to express both of these ideas in one sentence. If necessary, tell students that they can combine the sentences by using the conjunction *or.* Write the sentence on the board: *A* <u>thunderstorm</u> *or a* <u>hurricane</u> *might occur in August.*

Practice

Have pairs of students read page 59 together and look for sentences that include the conjunction *and* or the conjunction *or.* Ask students to copy the sentences, circle the conjunction in each one, and underline the words that are joined by the conjunction. Bring students together to share and compare their sentences.

Apply

Have students work in pairs to write three original sentences about thunderstorms, tornadoes, and hurricanes.

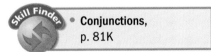

Skill Finder
- Conjunctions, p. 81K

Diagnostic Check

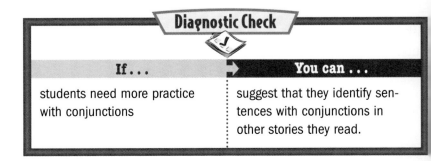

If . . .	You can . . .
students need more practice with conjunctions	suggest that they identify sentences with conjunctions in other stories they read.

California Standards pp. R22–R23

LC 1.1 Sentence structure/transition

Writing & Language   **Theme Resources**

Grammar Skills: Compound Sentences

 Reteaching

LC 1.1

OBJECTIVES

Students

- form a compound sentence using a conjunction
- separate ideas in a compound sentence by using a comma

Teach

Remind students that they have already learned how to join words in a sentence by using a conjunction. Now they will learn how to join two complete thoughts by using a conjunction.

Write the following sentences on the board:

> The air is hazy.
> Another storm to the west is blocking the sunlight.

Use the following Think Aloud to model the process of forming a compound sentence.

Think Aloud

I can use a conjunction to join two whole sentences together.

Combine the two sentences into a compound sentence. Mark the sentence as shown below.

> The air is hazy (and) another storm to the west is blocking the sunlight.

Now I have a sentence that joins two complete thoughts. This kind of sentence is called a compound sentence. I need to add a comma to show where the first thought ends and the second one begins. I'll add it now.

Write these two sentences and continue the Think Aloud:

> Warren tries to photograph a huge tornado.
> The light isn't good enough for a picture.

I can't use the conjunction and to join these sentences because the ideas are different. I can use the conjunction but to show a contrast between the first thought and the second thought.

Write the compound sentence on the board. Circle the conjunction, underline the two complete thoughts, and add a comma.

Practice

On the board, write these compound sentences from the selection:

> We've got two large thunderstorms here and they're dropping tornadoes everywhere.
> The sky is hazy but in the distance we can see the tops of anvil-shaped storm clouds.

Have students copy the sentences and repeat the procedure you used above to mark the two thoughts, the conjunction, and to add the comma.

Apply

Have students form a compound sentence using these sentences:

> Warren Faidley takes amazing pictures.
> His work appears in many magazines.

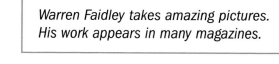 • Compound Sentences, pp. 81K–81L

Diagnostic Check

If...	You can...
students need more practice with compound sentences	suggest that they identify compound sentences in other stories they read.

Grammar Skills: Singular and Plural Nouns

Reteaching

Teach

Write these two sentences on the board:

> *A highway, a road, and a railway were destroyed.*
> *Highways, roads, and railways were destroyed.*

Ask students what is different about the nouns in the two sentences. Then ask how the two sentences differ in meaning.

If students need help, use a Think Aloud to model the process.

Think Aloud

Well, first I'll look at the beginnings of the two sentences. The first one begins with the words A highway; *the second one begins with the word* Highways. Highway *and* highways *are almost the same, except* highways *has an* s *at the end of it. It means more than one highway.*

Underline the *s* in *highways*. Continue in this way until students have found all the differences between the nouns.

Tell students that the nouns *highway, road,* and *railway* are singular. They each name one thing. The nouns *highways, roads,* and *railways* are plural. They each name more than one thing. To form the plural of most nouns, we simply add the letter *s.*

Now display these two sentences:

> *A hot ash came out of the volcano.*
> *Hot ashes came out of the volcano.*

Ask students to find the difference between these two sentences. If necessary, model the process, and underline the words *ash* and *ashes.*

Point out that *ash* is singular and *ashes* is plural. Tell students that the plural of *ash* is formed by adding *es,* instead of *s.* Then give them this rule: Add *es* to form the plural of singular nouns ending in *s, ss, x, ch,* or *sh.*

Practice

Write the following sentences on the board. Have students find the nouns and tell whether they are singular or plural.

> *The early Hawaiians told legends about two goddesses named Pele and Namaka.*
> *Pele was the goddess of fire, and Namaka was the goddess of the sea.*

Apply

Have students rewrite each sentence, changing each noun from its singular form to its plural form.

> *Hot gas, rock, and ash destroyed the home.*
> *The eruption blew down the tree and formed the crater.*

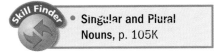

Skill Finder • Singular and Plural Nouns, p. 105K

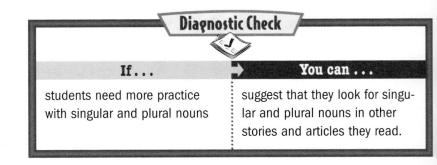

Diagnostic Check

If . . .	You can . . .
students need more practice with singular and plural nouns	suggest that they look for singular and plural nouns in other stories and articles they read.

Writing & Language   Theme Resources

Grammar Skills: More Plural Nouns

Reteaching

OBJECTIVES

Students

- identify plurals of nouns ending in *o* or *y*
- form plurals of nouns ending in *o* or *y*

Teach

Write these two sentences on the board:

> The volcano destroyed many homes.
> The volcanoes destroyed many homes.

Ask students to find the difference between the two sentences. If necessary, model the process as you did for the sentences on the previous page.

Tell students that many singular nouns ending in *o* add *-es* to form the plural, especially if a consonant comes before the *o*. Give them the following additional examples:

Singular	Plural
tornado	tornado<u>es</u>
potato	potato<u>es</u>
tomato	tomato<u>es</u>

Write these two sentences on the board, and help students identify the difference in them:

> The Hawaiians told a story about the goddess Pele.
> The Hawaiians told stories about the goddess Pele.

Tell students that when a singular noun ends in *y* preceded by a consonant, they must change the *y* to *i* and then add *-es* to form the plural. Give them the following additional examples:

Singular	Plural
party	part<u>ies</u>
puppy	pupp<u>ies</u>
baby	bab<u>ies</u>

Practice

Have students help you find the nouns in the following sentence and then rewrite the sentence, making each noun plural.

> The tornado and the volcano destroyed the country.

Apply

Have students copy the following list of singular nouns and then write the plural form of each one.

Singular	Plural
hero	
memory	
echo	
dictionary	

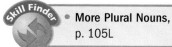
Skill Finder • More Plural Nouns, p. 105L

Diagnostic Check

If . . .	You can . . .
students need more practice with more plural nouns	suggest that they look for nouns ending in o or y in other stories they read, and then write the plural form of those nouns.

Nature's Fury
Writing Activities

Your Story

Have students write a personal narrative about a time when they experienced an example of nature's fury. Suggest that they describe a flood, lightning storm, fire, blizzard, or tornado they have experienced and tell how their family or community coped with the natural disaster.

Write a Folktale

Using *The Princess and the Warrior* as a model, have students write their own *pourquoi* tale, an imaginative story about how earthquakes, volcanoes, lightning, or tornadoes came to be.

Challenge
Script for a Radio Play

Have a group of students adapt either *Earthquake Terror,* the Tornado Chase diary from *Eye of the Storm,* or *The Princess and the Warrior* as a radio play. Explain that they can use some of the existing dialogue in the selection for their script. In addition, suggest that they use a narrator to provide background information to the audience. Encourage students to find ways to create sound effects of an earthquake, tornado, or volcano to build suspense. Have students tape their drama and play the tape for the class.

California Standards pp. R26–R27

W 1.2.a Establish topic, order
W 1.2.b Use details, transitions
W 1.2.c Conclude with a summary
W 2.1.a Establish plot, setting

W 2.1.b Show events
W 2.2 Write responses to literature
W 2.2.a Demonstrate understanding
W 2.3.a Frame questions

Theme Resources

Writing & Language

Nature's Fury

Writing Activities

W 2.3.a
W 2.3.b
W 2.3.c

Write a Report

Have students write factual reports about earthquakes, tornadoes, volcanoes, or some other example of nature's fury. Suggest that they begin by brainstorming a list of questions about the natural disaster that they would like to find answers to. Then have them research the answers in encyclopedias, library books, or web sites. When students write their reports, have them include text organization features such as headings, boldface type, color, and graphic aids to help readers understand the information.

W 2.2
LS 1.4
LS 1.5

List for a Disaster

On the chalkboard, with the help of students, write a list of potential disasters that your community might face. Lead a discussion of the impact such disasters could have on daily life. Then have each student write a list of supplies that people should have on hand to be prepared for such disasters. Afterward, have students compare their lists and explain why they included each item.

1. candles
2. radio with batteries
3. bottled water
4.

W 1.2.a
W 1.2.b
W 1.2.c

Challenge
Write a Comparison-Contrast Essay

Have students compare and contrast the effects of two recent natural disasters that have been reported in the news. Students can compare the amounts and kinds of damage caused by the disasters, how prepared each community was for the disaster, and the progress each community has made in recovering from the disaster.

Portfolio Opportunity

Save responses to activities on these two pages for writing samples.

W 2.3.b Establish focused topic
W 2.3.c Develop topic
LS 1.4   Select focus
LS 1.5   Clarify and support ideas

Cross-Curricular Activities

Science
Make a Barometer

Students can predict stormy weather by making a simple bottle barometer. All they need is a small plastic soda bottle, a bowl, and an index card.

1. Pour a thin layer of water into the bowl.
2. Tape the index card to the side of the bottle.
3. Fill the bottle 3/4 full of water.
4. Holding your thumb over the top of the bottle, place it upside down in the bowl. Air pressure will keep the water in the bottle.
5. Mark the water level on the index card.

6. Have students record the changes in the water level each day. A falling water level indicates low air pressure and the approach of stormy weather.

Social Studies/Speaking and Listening
Interview a Disaster Relief Worker

LS 1.1

Invite a representative from your local office of the American Red Cross to visit your classroom. Before the visit, give students some background about the work that the Red Cross does in providing disaster relief. Then ask students to prepare a list of questions they would like to ask the speaker. After the visit, have students discuss what they have learned.

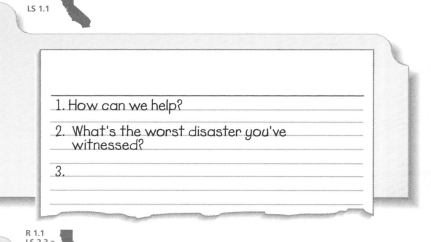

1. How can we help?
2. What's the worst disaster you've witnessed?
3.

Literature/Speaking
Tell Folktales About Nature's Fury

R 1.1
LS 2.3.a
LS 2.3.b
LS 2.3.c

Have students read a *pourquoi* folktale about nature's fury, learn the story, and then tell it to a class of first-graders. Two good anthologies on this theme, available in many libraries, are *Tales of Thunder and Lightning* by Harry Devlin and *Earthmaker Tales* by Gretchen Will Mayo.

California Standards pp. R28–R29

R 1.1 Read aloud fluently	**W 2.2.a** Demonstrate understanding
W 1.1.a Establish a plot	**LS 1.1** Ask new questions
W 1.1.b Describe setting	**LS 2.3.a** Summarize events/details
W 1.1.c Present ending	**LS 2.3.b** Understand ideas/images

Nature's Fury

Cross-Curricular Activities

Challenge
Geography
Make a Natural Disaster Map

W 2.2.a

Have students make a special map of the United States that shows where different types of natural disasters are most likely to happen. First, have students research where disasters such as tornadoes, hurricanes, earthquakes, and floods occur most often. Then suggest that they create a color code or a system of symbols to indicate each type of disaster. Have them place the symbols where they belong on the map.

Viewing/Language Arts
Write a Review of a Video

W 1.1.a
W 1.1.b
W 1.1.c

Have students watch a fiction or nonfiction video about natural disasters and then write a review of the video. Students may review nonfiction videos such as Natural Geographic's *Nature's Fury* or *Born of Fire*, evaluating them on their interest level and how well they explain the causes and effects of natural disasters.

As an alternative, students may review fictional films such as *Twister* or *Earthquake*, evaluating them for their accuracy, realism, and special effects.

Music
Perform a Folk Song

Students with musical talent can learn and perform a folk song about nature's fury. One possibility is "Wasn't That a Mighty Storm" by Tom Rush, which commemorates the devastating hurricane that hit Galveston, Texas, in 1900. The song can be heard on Nanci Griffith's CD *Other Voices, Too*. Other possibilities include Woody Guthrie's "Dust Bowl Blues" and "The Great Dust Storm," recorded by various artists.

LS 2.3.c Use examples

Technology Resources

American Melody
P. O. Box 270
Guilford, CT 06437
800-220-5557

Audio Bookshelf
174 Prescott Hill Road
Northport, ME 04849
800-234-1713

Baker & Taylor
100 Business Court Drive
Pittsburgh, PA 15205
800-775-2600

BDD Audio
1540 Broadway
New York, NY 10036
800-223-6834

Big Kids Productions
1606 Dywer Ave.
Austin, TX 78704
800-477-7811
www.bigkidsvideo.com

Blackboard Entertainment
2647 International
Boulevard
Suite 853
Oakland, CA 94601
800-968-2261
www.blackboardkids.com

Books on Tape
P.O. Box 7900
Newport Beach, CA 92658
800-626-3333

Filmic Archives
The Cinema Center
Botsford, CT 06404
800-366-1920
www.filmicarchives.com

Great White Dog Picture Company
10 Toon Lane
Lee, NH 03824
800-397-7641
www.greatwhitedog.com

HarperAudio
10 E. 53rd St.
New York, NY 10022
800-242-7737

Houghton Mifflin Company
222 Berkeley St.
Boston, MA 02116
800-225-3362

Informed Democracy
P.O. Box 67
Santa Cruz, CA 95063
831-426-3921

JEF Films
143 Hickory Hill Circle
Osterville, MA 02655
508-428-7198

Kimbo Educational
P. O. Box 477
Long Branch, NJ 07740
900-631-2187

The Learning Company (dist. for Broderbund)
1 Athenaeum St.
Cambridge, MA 02142
800-716-8506
www.learningcompanyschool.com

Library Video Co.
P. O. Box 580
Wynnewood, PA 19096
800-843-3620

Listening Library
One Park Avenue
Old Greenwich, CT 06870
800-243-4504

Live Oak Media
P. O. Box 652
Pine Plains, NY 12567
800-788-1121
liveoak@taconic.net

Media Basics
Lighthouse Square
PO Box 449
Guilford, CT 06437
800-542-2505
www.mediabasicsvideo.com

Microsoft Corp.
One Microsoft Way
Redmond, WA 98052
800-426-9400
www.microsoft.com

National Geographic Society
1145 17th Street N. W.
Washington, D. C. 20036
800-368-2728
www.nationalgeographic.com

New Kid Home Video
1364 Palisades Beach Road
Santa Monica, CA 90401
310-451-5164

Puffin Books
345 Hudson Street
New York, NY 10014
212-366-2000

Rainbow Educational Media
4540 Preslyn Drive
Raleigh, NC 27616
800-331-4047

Random House Home Video
201 E. 50th St.
New York, NY 10022
212-940-7620

Recorded Books
270 Skipjack Road
Prince Frederick, MD 20678
800-638-1304
www.recordedbooks.com

Sony Wonder
Dist. by Professional Media
Service
19122 S. Vermont Ave.
Gardena, CA 90248
800-223-7672

Spoken Arts
8 Lawn Avenue
P. O. Box 100
New Rochelle, NY 10802
800-326-4090

SRA Media
220 E. Danieldale Rd.
DeSoto, TX 75115
800-843-8855

Sunburst Communications
101 Castleton St.
P. O. Box 100
Pleasantville, NY 10570
800-321-7511
www.sunburst.com

SVE & Churchill Media
6677 North Northwest
Highway
Chicago, IL 60631
800-829-1900

Tom Snyder Productions
80 Coolidge Hill Road
Watertown, MA 02472
800-342-0236
www.tomsnyder.com

Troll Communications
100 Corporate Drive
Mahwah, NJ 07430
800-526-5289

Weston Woods
12 Oakwood Avenue
Norwalk, CT 06850-1318
800-243-5020
www.scholastic.com

　THEME 1: **Nature's Fury**

Lesson Planning Support

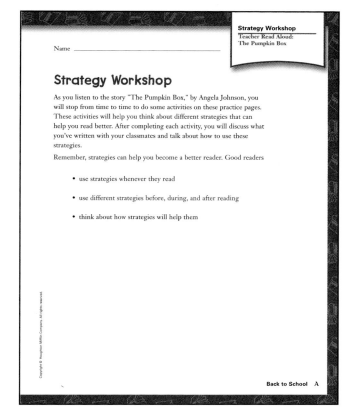

Name _____

Strategy Workshop

As you listen to the story "The Pumpkin Box," by Angela Johnson, you will stop from time to time to do some activities on these practice pages. These activities will help you think about different strategies that can help you read better. After completing each activity, you will discuss what you've written with your classmates and talk about how to use these strategies.

Remember, strategies can help you become a better reader. Good readers

- use strategies whenever they read

- use different strategies before, during, and after reading

- think about how strategies will help them

Back to School   A

Teacher's Book, page BTS 2

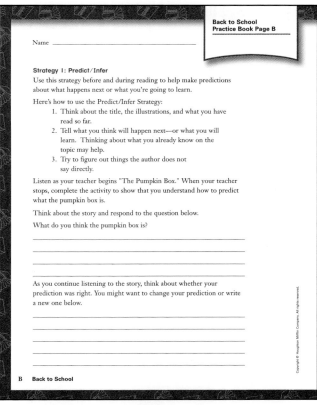

Reading Strategies Guide

Use these strategies. Be a better reader!

Predict/Infer
- Think about the title, the illustrations, and what you have read so far.
- Tell what you think will happen next or what you will learn.
- Try to figure out things that the author does not say directly.

Question
- Ask questions that can be answered as you read or after you finish reading.

Monitor/Clarify
- Ask yourself if what you are reading makes sense or if you are learning what you want to learn.
- If you don't understand something, reread, read ahead, or use the illustrations.

Summarize
- Think about the main ideas or the important parts of the story.
- Tell in your own words the important things you have read.

Evaluate
- Ask yourself: How do I feel about what I read? Do I agree or disagree with it? Am I learning what I wanted to know? How good a job has the author done?

TRANSPARENCY BTS-A1
TEACHER'S EDITION PAGE BTS2

Teacher's Book, page BTS 2

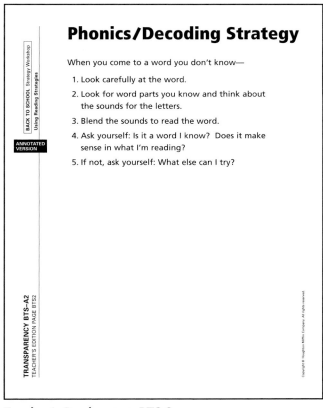

Phonics/Decoding Strategy

When you come to a word you don't know—

1. Look carefully at the word.

2. Look for word parts you know and think about the sounds for the letters.

3. Blend the sounds to read the word.

4. Ask yourself: Is it a word I know? Does it make sense in what I'm reading?

5. If not, ask yourself: What else can I try?

TRANSPARENCY BTS-A2
TEACHER'S EDITION PAGE BTS2

Teacher's Book, page BTS 2

Name _____

Strategy 1: Predict/Infer
Use this strategy before and during reading to help make predictions about what happens next or what you're going to learn.

Here's how to use the Predict/Infer Strategy:
1. Think about the title, the illustrations, and what you have read so far.
2. Tell what you think will happen next—or what you will learn. Thinking about what you already know on the topic may help.
3. Try to figure out things the author does not say directly.

Listen as your teacher begins "The Pumpkin Box." When your teacher stops, complete the activity to show that you understand how to predict what the pumpkin box is.

Think about the story and respond to the question below.

What do you think the pumpkin box is?

_____
_____
_____

As you continue listening to the story, think about whether your prediction was right. You might want to change your prediction or write a new one below.

_____
_____
_____
_____

B   Back to School

Teacher's Book, page BTS 3

Lesson Planning Support *(Continued)*

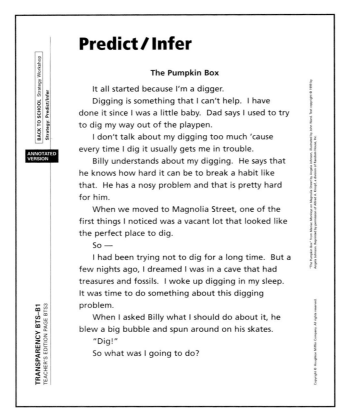

Predict / Infer

The Pumpkin Box

It all started because I'm a digger.

Digging is something that I can't help. I have done it since I was a little baby. Dad says I used to try to dig my way out of the playpen.

I don't talk about my digging too much 'cause every time I dig it usually gets me in trouble.

Billy understands about my digging. He says that he knows how hard it can be to break a habit like that. He has a nosy problem and that is pretty hard for him.

When we moved to Magnolia Street, one of the first things I noticed was a vacant lot that looked like the perfect place to dig.

So —

I had been trying not to dig for a long time. But a few nights ago, I dreamed I was in a cave that had treasures and fossils. I woke up digging in my sleep. It was time to do something about this digging problem.

When I asked Billy what I should do about it, he blew a big bubble and spun around on his skates.

"Dig!"

So what was I going to do?

Teacher's Book, page BTS 3

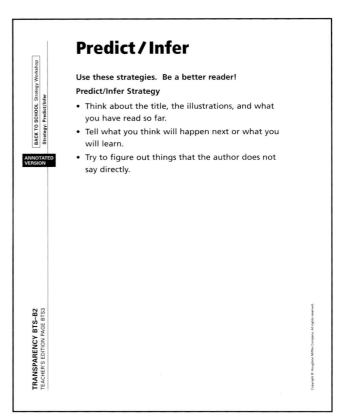

Predict / Infer

Use these strategies. Be a better reader!

Predict/Infer Strategy

- Think about the title, the illustrations, and what you have read so far.
- Tell what you think will happen next or what you will learn.
- Try to figure out things that the author does not say directly.

Teacher's Book, page BTS 3

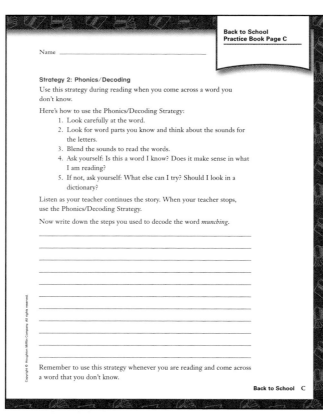

Back to School
Practice Book Page C

Name _____

Strategy 2: Phonics/Decoding

Use this strategy during reading when you come across a word you don't know.

Here's how to use the Phonics/Decoding Strategy:

1. Look carefully at the word.
2. Look for word parts you know and think about the sounds for the letters.
3. Blend the sounds to read the words.
4. Ask yourself: Is this a word I know? Does it make sense in what I am reading?
5. If not, ask yourself: What else can I try? Should I look in a dictionary?

Listen as your teacher continues the story. When your teacher stops, use the Phonics/Decoding Strategy.

Now write down the steps you used to decode the word *munching*.

_____
_____
_____
_____
_____
_____
_____
_____

Remember to use this strategy whenever you are reading and come across a word that you don't know.

Back to School   C

Teacher's Book, page BTS 4

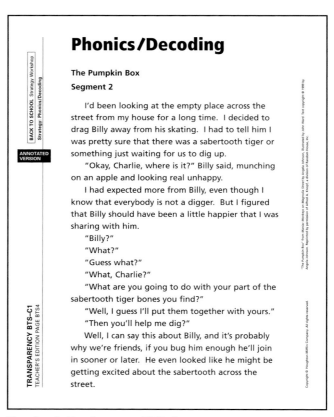

Phonics/Decoding

The Pumpkin Box
Segment 2

I'd been looking at the empty place across the street from my house for a long time. I decided to drag Billy away from his skating. I had to tell him I was pretty sure that there was a sabertooth tiger or something just waiting for us to dig up.

"Okay, Charlie, where is it?" Billy said, munching on an apple and looking real unhappy.

I had expected more from Billy, even though I know that everybody is not a digger. But I figured that Billy should have been a little happier that I was sharing with him.

"Billy?"

"What?"

"Guess what?"

"What, Charlie?"

"What are you going to do with your part of the sabertooth tiger bones you find?"

"Well, I guess I'll put them together with yours."

"Then you'll help me dig?"

Well, I can say this about Billy, and it's probably why we're friends, if you bug him enough he'll join in sooner or later. He even looked like he might be getting excited about the sabertooth across the street.

Teacher's Book, page BTS 4

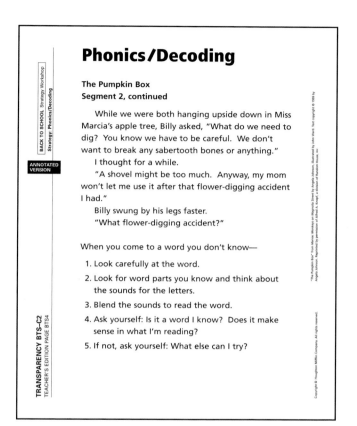

Phonics/Decoding

The Pumpkin Box
Segment 2, continued

While we were both hanging upside down in Miss Marcia's apple tree, Billy asked, "What do we need to dig? You know we have to be careful. We don't want to break any sabertooth bones or anything."

I thought for a while.

"A shovel might be too much. Anyway, my mom won't let me use it after that flower-digging accident I had."

Billy swung by his legs faster.

"What flower-digging accident?"

When you come to a word you don't know—

1. Look carefully at the word.
2. Look for word parts you know and think about the sounds for the letters.
3. Blend the sounds to read the word.
4. Ask yourself: Is it a word I know? Does it make sense in what I'm reading?
5. If not, ask yourself: What else can I try?

Teacher's Book, page BTS 4

Back to School
Practice Book Page D

Name _____

Strategy 3: Monitor/Clarify
Use this strategy during reading whenever you're confused about what you are reading.

Here's how to use the Monitor/Clarify Strategy:
- Ask yourself if what you're reading makes sense—or if you are learning what you need to learn.
- If you don't understand something, reread, use the illustrations, or read ahead to see if that helps.

Listen as your teacher continues the story. When your teacher stops, complete the activity to show that you understand how to figure out how the pumpkin box got underground.

Think about the pumpkin box and respond below.

1. Describe the pumpkin box.
   _____
   _____

2. Can you tell from listening to the story how the pumpkin box got there? Why or why not?
   _____
   _____
   _____

3. How can you find out why the pumpkin box was buried in the ground?
   _____
   _____
   _____

D   Back to School

Teacher's Book, page BTS 6

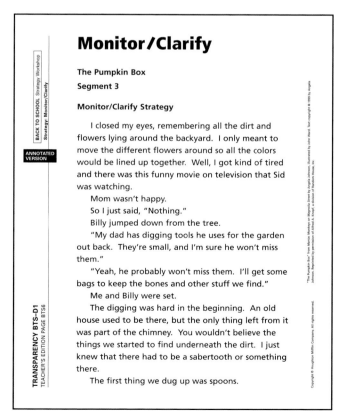

Monitor/Clarify

The Pumpkin Box
Segment 3

Monitor/Clarify Strategy

I closed my eyes, remembering all the dirt and flowers lying around the backyard. I only meant to move the different flowers around so all the colors would be lined up together. Well, I got kind of tired and there was this funny movie on television that Sid was watching.

Mom wasn't happy.

So I just said, "Nothing."

Billy jumped down from the tree.

"My dad has digging tools he uses for the garden out back. They're small, and I'm sure he won't miss them."

"Yeah, he probably won't miss them. I'll get some bags to keep the bones and other stuff we find."

Me and Billy were set.

The digging was hard in the beginning. An old house used to be there, but the only thing left from it was part of the chimney. You wouldn't believe the things we started to find underneath the dirt. I just knew that there had to be a sabertooth or something there.

The first thing we dug up was spoons.

Teacher's Book, page BTS 6

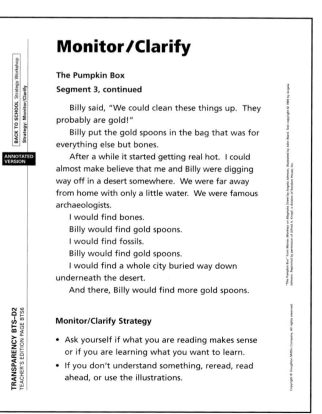

Monitor/Clarify

The Pumpkin Box
Segment 3, continued

Billy said, "We could clean these things up. They probably are gold!"

Billy put the gold spoons in the bag that was for everything else but bones.

After a while it started getting real hot. I could almost make believe that me and Billy were digging way off in a desert somewhere. We were far away from home with only a little water. We were famous archaeologists.

I would find bones.

Billy would find gold spoons.

I would find fossils.

Billy would find gold spoons.

I would find a whole city buried way down underneath the desert.

And there, Billy would find more gold spoons.

Monitor/Clarify Strategy

- Ask yourself if what you are reading makes sense or if you are learning what you want to learn.
- If you don't understand something, reread, read ahead, or use the illustrations.

Teacher's Book, page BTS 6

Back to School
Practice Book Page E

Name ______________________

Strategy 4: Question

Use this strategy during and after reading to ask questions about important ideas in the story.

Here's how to use the Question Strategy:

- Ask yourself questions about important ideas in the story.
- Ask yourself if you can answer these questions.
- If you can't answer the questions, reread and look for answers in the text. Thinking about what you already know and what you've read in the story may help you.

Listen as your teacher continues the story. Then complete the activity to show that you understand how to ask yourself questions about important ideas in the story.

Think about the story and respond below.

Write a question you might ask yourself at this point in the story.

____

____

____

____

____

____

____

____

____

____

If you can't answer your question now, think about it while you listen to the rest of the story.

Back to School E

Teacher's Book, page BTS 8

BACK TO SCHOOL Strategy Workshop
Strategy: Question

ANNOTATED VERSION

Question

The Pumpkin Box

Segment 4

Me and Billy didn't even talk to each other while we dug. We were too busy finding all kinds of treasures.

Billy found a cracked mirror.

I found a scrub brush.

Billy found a bottle with a metal top on it, and I found an old can.

The non-bone bag was filling up, and I noticed that Billy was smiling. Sometimes you just have to bring out the digger in some people.

Just as I was starting to get a little worried 'cause we hadn't run into any bones yet, I hit something with the little hand shovel I had. I took a while to dig it up 'cause I didn't want to wreck any of it.

I'd found something better than a sabertooth.

It was a pumpkin box.

It was metal and square, and somebody had pasted paper pumpkins all over it.

Billy said, "Can we open it?"

"I don't know."

"Try."

So I did. I just wiggled the lock a little and it opened right up.

TRANSPARENCY BTS–E1
TEACHER'S EDITION PAGE BTS8

"The Pumpkin Box" from Maniac Monkeys on Magnolia Street by Angela Johnson, illustrated by John Ward. Text copyright © 1999 by Angela Johnson. Reprinted by permission of Alfred A. Knopf, a division of Random House, Inc.

Teacher's Book, page BTS 8

BACK TO SCHOOL Strategy Workshop
Strategy: Question

ANNOTATED VERSION

The Pumpkin Box

Segment 4, continued

And the things inside. I knew then that to be a digger was probably to be one of the most exciting things in the world.

Me and Billy sat side by side and stared at the pumpkin box. Most of the pumpkins had fallen off, but there were a couple left. Inside, there was magic.

Billy looked at me and smiled.

I looked at him and smiled.

Question Strategy

- Ask questions that can be answered as you read or after you finish reading.

TRANSPARENCY BTS–E2
TEACHER'S EDITION PAGE BTS8

"The Pumpkin Box" from Maniac Monkeys on Magnolia Street by Angela Johnson, illustrated by John Ward. Text copyright © 1999 by Angela Johnson. Reprinted by permission of Alfred A. Knopf, a division of Random House, Inc.

Teacher's Book, page BTS 8

Back to School
Practice Book Page F

Name ______________________

Strategy 5: Evaluate

Use this strategy during and after reading to help you form an opinion about what you read.

Here's how to use the Evaluate Strategy:

- Tell whether or not you think this story is entertaining and why.
- Is the writing clear and easy to understand?
- This is a realistic fiction story. Did the author make the characters believable and interesting?

Listen as your teacher continues the story. When your teacher stops, complete the activity to show that you are thinking of how you feel about what you are reading and why you feel that way.

Think about the story and respond below.

1. Tell whether or not you think this story is entertaining and why.

____

____

____

____

2. Is the writing clear and easy to understand?

____

____

____

____

3. This is a realistic fiction story. Did the author make the characters interesting and believable?

____

____

____

____

F Back to School

Teacher's Book, page BTS 10

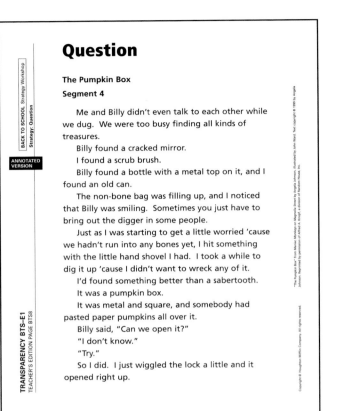

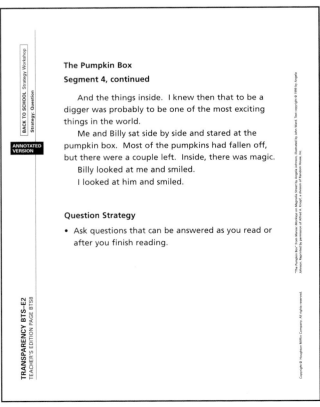

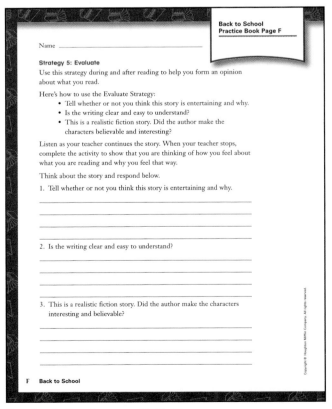

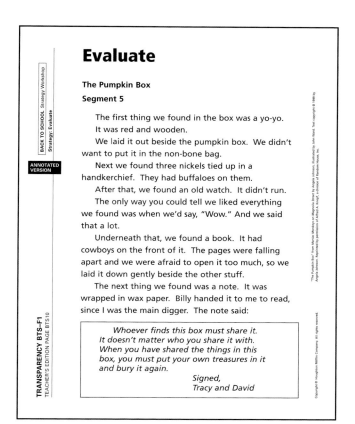

Evaluate

The Pumpkin Box

Segment 5

The first thing we found in the box was a yo-yo. It was red and wooden.

We laid it out beside the pumpkin box. We didn't want to put it in the non-bone bag.

Next we found three nickels tied up in a handkerchief. They had buffaloes on them.

After that, we found an old watch. It didn't run.

The only way you could tell we liked everything we found was when we'd say, "Wow." And we said that a lot.

Underneath that, we found a book. It had cowboys on the front of it. The pages were falling apart and we were afraid to open it too much, so we laid it down gently beside the other stuff.

The next thing we found was a note. It was wrapped in wax paper. Billy handed it to me to read, since I was the main digger. The note said:

> *Whoever finds this box must share it.*
> *It doesn't matter who you share it with.*
> *When you have shared the things in this*
> *box, you must put your own treasures in it*
> *and bury it again.*
> Signed,
> *Tracy and David*

Teacher's Book, page BTS 10

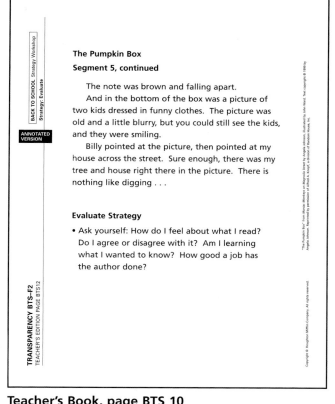

The Pumpkin Box

Segment 5, continued

The note was brown and falling apart.

And in the bottom of the box was a picture of two kids dressed in funny clothes. The picture was old and a little blurry, but you could still see the kids, and they were smiling.

Billy pointed at the picture, then pointed at my house across the street. Sure enough, there was my tree and house right there in the picture. There is nothing like digging . . .

Evaluate Strategy

• Ask yourself: How do I feel about what I read? Do I agree or disagree with it? Am I learning what I wanted to know? How good a job has the author done?

Teacher's Book, page BTS 10

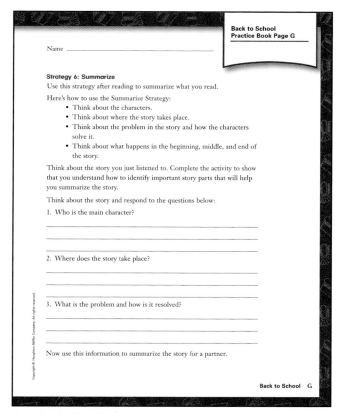

Name _____

Strategy 6: Summarize

Use this strategy after reading to summarize what you read.

Here's how to use the Summarize Strategy:
• Think about the characters.
• Think about where the story takes place.
• Think about the problem in the story and how the characters solve it.
• Think about what happens in the beginning, middle, and end of the story.

Think about the story you just listened to. Complete the activity to show that you understand how to identify important story parts that will help you summarize the story.

Think about the story and respond to the questions below:

1. Who is the main character?

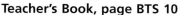
_____
_____

2. Where does the story take place?
_____
_____

3. What is the problem and how is it resolved?
_____
_____
_____

Now use this information to summarize the story for a partner.

Teacher's Book, page BTS 12

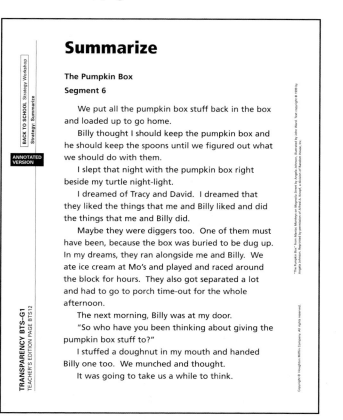

Summarize

The Pumpkin Box

Segment 6

We put all the pumpkin box stuff back in the box and loaded up to go home.

Billy thought I should keep the pumpkin box and he should keep the spoons until we figured out what we should do with them.

I slept that night with the pumpkin box right beside my turtle night-light.

I dreamed of Tracy and David. I dreamed that they liked the things that me and Billy liked and did the things that me and Billy did.

Maybe they were diggers too. One of them must have been, because the box was buried to be dug up. In my dreams, they ran alongside me and Billy. We ate ice cream at Mo's and played and raced around the block for hours. They also got separated a lot and had to go to porch time-out for the whole afternoon.

The next morning, Billy was at my door.

"So who have you been thinking about giving the pumpkin box stuff to?"

I stuffed a doughnut in my mouth and handed Billy one too. We munched and thought.

It was going to take us a while to think.

Teacher's Book, page BTS 12

Theme Resources

Lesson Planning Support

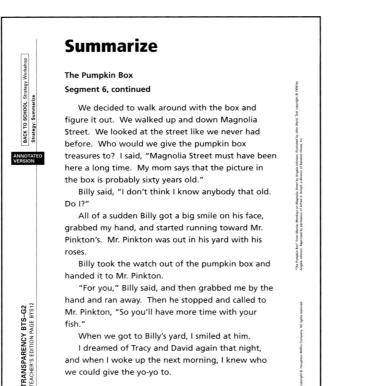

Summarize

The Pumpkin Box
Segment 6, continued

We decided to walk around with the box and figure it out. We walked up and down Magnolia Street. We looked at the street like we never had before. Who would we give the pumpkin box treasures to? I said, "Magnolia Street must have been here a long time. My mom says that the picture in the box is probably sixty years old."

Billy said, "I don't think I know anybody that old. Do I?"

All of a sudden Billy got a big smile on his face, grabbed my hand, and started running toward Mr. Pinkton's. Mr. Pinkton was out in his yard with his roses.

Billy took the watch out of the pumpkin box and handed it to Mr. Pinkton.

"For you," Billy said, and then grabbed me by the hand and ran away. Then he stopped and called to Mr. Pinkton, "So you'll have more time with your fish."

When we got to Billy's yard, I smiled at him.

I dreamed of Tracy and David again that night, and when I woke up the next morning, I knew who we could give the yo-yo to.

ANNOTATED VERSION

BACK TO SCHOOL Strategy Workshop
Strategy: Summarize

TRANSPARENCY BTS-G2
TEACHER'S EDITION PAGE BTS12

"The Pumpkin Box" from *Maniac Monkeys on Magnolia Street* by Angela Johnson. Illustrated by John Ward. Text copyright © 1999 by Angela Johnson. Reprinted by permission of Alfred A. Knopf, a division of Random House, Inc.

Copyright © Houghton Mifflin Company. All rights reserved.

Teacher's Book, page BTS 12

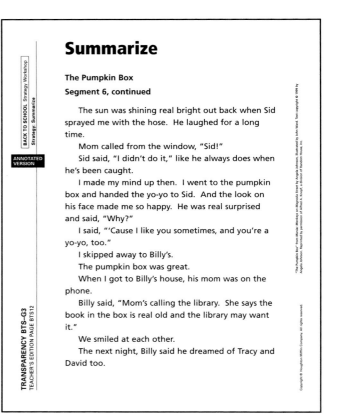

Summarize

The Pumpkin Box
Segment 6, continued

The sun was shining real bright out back when Sid sprayed me with the hose. He laughed for a long time.

Mom called from the window, "Sid!"

Sid said, "I didn't do it," like he always does when he's been caught.

I made my mind up then. I went to the pumpkin box and handed the yo-yo to Sid. And the look on his face made me so happy. He was real surprised and said, "Why?"

I said, "'Cause I like you sometimes, and you're a yo-yo, too."

I skipped away to Billy's.

The pumpkin box was great.

When I got to Billy's house, his mom was on the phone.

Billy said, "Mom's calling the library. She says the book in the box is real old and the library may want it."

We smiled at each other.

The next night, Billy said he dreamed of Tracy and David too.

ANNOTATED VERSION

BACK TO SCHOOL Strategy Workshop
Strategy: Summarize

TRANSPARENCY BTS-G3
TEACHER'S EDITION PAGE BTS12

"The Pumpkin Box" from *Maniac Monkeys on Magnolia Street* by Angela Johnson. Illustrated by John Ward. Text copyright © 1999 by Angela Johnson. Reprinted by permission of Alfred A. Knopf, a division of Random House, Inc.

Copyright © Houghton Mifflin Company. All rights reserved.

Teacher's Book, page BTS 12

Summarize

The Pumpkin Box
Segment 6, continued

While Billy skated behind me, I rode my bike to Mo's. I walked up to the counter and handed Mo the nickels. The whole store smelled like cookies and French fries.

Mo looked confused when I said, "For you."

Mo said, "I used to collect these when I was your age."

He wiped his eyes, smiled, and said, "Thanks, kid."

Being a digger must be the best thing you could ever be in this world. You can find things that nobody ever thought could be found again.

Being a digger helps people remember gone things.

Me and Billy have decided to keep the picture of Tracy and David. He will keep it for a week, then I will have it for a week. We will always think about them running and playing on Magnolia Street like us.

We were swinging from the tree in my front yard, wondering what to put back into the pumpkin box.

Billy said, "Why do you think they put what they put in the pumpkin box, Charlie?"

"I don't know. Maybe it was stuff that they found. But it was probably stuff that made them happy."

ANNOTATED VERSION

BACK TO SCHOOL Strategy Workshop
Strategy: Summarize

TRANSPARENCY BTS-G4
TEACHER'S EDITION PAGE BTS12

"The Pumpkin Box" from *Maniac Monkeys on Magnolia Street* by Angela Johnson. Illustrated by John Ward. Text copyright © 1999 by Angela Johnson. Reprinted by permission of Alfred A. Knopf, a division of Random House, Inc.

Copyright © Houghton Mifflin Company. All rights reserved.

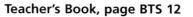
Teacher's Book, page BTS 12

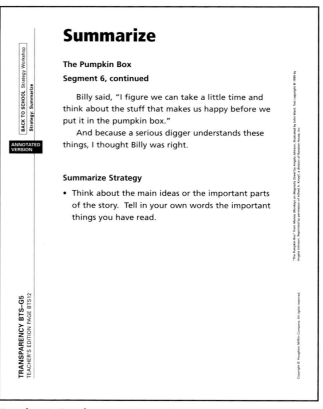

Summarize

The Pumpkin Box
Segment 6, continued

Billy said, "I figure we can take a little time and think about the stuff that makes us happy before we put it in the pumpkin box."

And because a serious digger understands these things, I thought Billy was right.

Summarize Strategy
• Think about the main ideas or the important parts of the story. Tell in your own words the important things you have read.

ANNOTATED VERSION

BACK TO SCHOOL Strategy Workshop
Strategy: Summarize

TRANSPARENCY BTS-G5
TEACHER'S EDITION PAGE BTS12

"The Pumpkin Box" from *Maniac Monkeys on Magnolia Street* by Angela Johnson. Illustrated by John Ward. Text copyright © 1999 by Angela Johnson. Reprinted by permission of Alfred A. Knopf, a division of Random House, Inc.

Copyright © Houghton Mifflin Company. All rights reserved.

Teacher's Book, page BTS 12

Worksheet 1 (top left)

Launching the Theme
Selection Connections

Name _____

Nature's Fury

After reading each selection, complete the chart below and on the next page to show what you discovered. **Sample answers shown.**

	What is the setting or settings for the action or descriptions in the selection?	What dangers do people face in the selection?
Earthquake Terror	Magpie Island, in California **(2.5 Points)**	Jonathan and Abby are stranded on Magpie Island when an earthquake strikes, toppling trees all around them. **(2.5)**
Eye of the Storm	Tucson, Arizona and Tornado Alley (Amarillo, Texas and towns in Texas, Oklahoma and Kansas) **(2.5)**	Warren Faidley faces danger from lightning bolts and spiders while photographing from an underpass. He and Tom Willett face danger from tornadoes forming around them in Tornado Alley. **(2.5)**
Volcanoes	Hawaii, Washington state, Iceland, Guatemala, California, Oregon **(2.5)**	People face danger from the eruption of Mount St. Helens; people on the island of Heimaey, Iceland, face danger from a volcano; people in Hawaii face danger to their houses from quick-moving lava. **(2.5)**

Theme 1: **Nature's Fury**   1

Assessment Tip: Total **10** points per selection and **2** points for the final question

Teacher's Book, page 21A

Worksheet 2 (top right)

Launching the Theme
Selection Connections

Name _____

Nature's Fury

After reading each selection, complete the chart to show what you discovered. **Sample answers shown.**

	What warnings or events happen before nature's fury occurs in the selection?	What did you learn about an example of nature's fury in the selection?
Earthquake Terror	Moose, the dog, is nervous, barking and shaking. The air is still and there is a deep rumbling sound. **(2.5)**	Most earthquakes occur along the shores of the Pacific Ocean, many of them on the San Andreas fault. **(2.5)**
Eye of the Storm	Cool, moist air meets hot desert air to cause thunderstorms in Arizona. Cool, dry air collides with warm, moist air to cause tornadoes. **(2.5)**	Tornadoes form from funnel clouds. When a funnel cloud touches the ground, it becomes a tornado. **(2.5)**
Volcanoes	Before volcanoes erupt, magma pushes up through cracks in the earth's crust. Before Mount St. Helens erupted, there were thousands of small earthquakes. **(2.5)**	There are different kinds of volcanoes: shield, strato-volcanoes, cinder cone, and dome volcanoes. **(2.5)**

What advice would you give others about the different kinds of nature's fury featured in this theme?

Student answers should reflect an understanding of the dangers and

settings of the different kinds of nature's fury in the theme. **(2)**

2   Theme 1: **Nature's Fury**

Assessment Tip: Total **10** Points per selection and **2** points for the final question

Teacher's Book, page 21A

Worksheet 3 (bottom left)

Earthquake Terror
Key Vocabulary

Name _____

A Scientist's Report

Use the words in the box to complete the scientist's report on the Magpie Island earthquake.

Vocabulary

shuddered
debris
undulating
fault
jolt

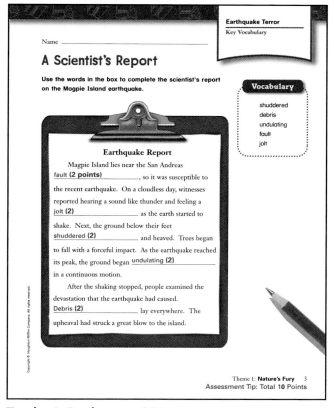

Earthquake Report

Magpie Island lies near the San Andreas fault **(2 points)** _____, so it was susceptible to the recent earthquake. On a cloudless day, witnesses reported hearing a sound like thunder and feeling a jolt **(2)** _____ as the earth started to shake. Next, the ground below their feet shuddered **(2)** _____ and heaved. Trees began to fall with a forceful impact. As the earthquake reached its peak, the ground began undulating **(2)** _____ in a continuous motion.

After the shaking stopped, people examined the devastation that the earthquake had caused. Debris **(2)** _____ lay everywhere. The upheaval had struck a great blow to the island.

Theme 1: **Nature's Fury**   3
Assessment Tip: Total **10** Points

Teacher's Book, page 27A

Worksheet 4 (bottom right)

Earthquake Words

Interviewer:	Today I am happy to welcome Isaac Ramstein, an expert on earthquakes. Mr. Ramstein, help readers of the *California Daily* understand why earthquakes leave so much <u>debris</u> in their wake.
Mr. Ramstein:	Earthquakes cause a tremendous amount of <u>devastation</u> because of the great <u>upheaval</u> of the ground itself.
Interviewer:	Tell us what it feels like to be in an earthquake.
Mr. Ramstein:	First, you may sense that the ground has <u>shuddered</u> ever so slightly beneath your feet. Next, you may feel a powerful <u>jolt</u> that can knock you down with a terrific <u>impact</u> if the quake is forceful enough. As the quake builds, the ground can feel like it is <u>undulating</u> up and down.
Interviewer:	Why is California so <u>susceptible</u> to earthquakes?
Mr. Ramstein:	A major <u>fault</u> runs through California, so when the crust of the earth shifts, it often shifts along that crack. Residents of the state should take precautions so they are not caught unprepared.
Interviewer:	We appreciate your talking with us today, Mr. Ramstein. I'm sure our readers will take your suggestion to heart.

Teacher's Book, page 27A

Lesson Planning Support (Continued)

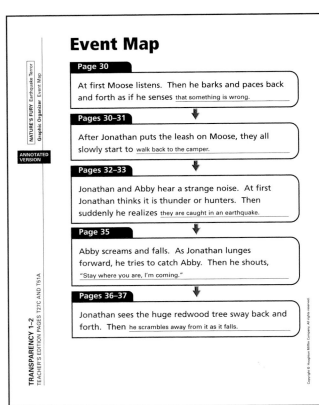

Event Map

Page 30

At first Moose listens. Then he barks and paces back and forth as if he senses that something is wrong.

Pages 30–31

After Jonathan puts the leash on Moose, they all slowly start to walk back to the camper.

Pages 32–33

Jonathan and Abby hear a strange noise. At first Jonathan thinks it is thunder or hunters. Then suddenly he realizes they are caught in an earthquake.

Page 35

Abby screams and falls. As Jonathan lunges forward, he tries to catch Abby. Then he shouts, "Stay where you are, I'm coming."

Pages 36–37

Jonathan sees the huge redwood tree sway back and forth. Then he scrambles away from it as it falls.

Teacher's Book, pages 27C and 51A

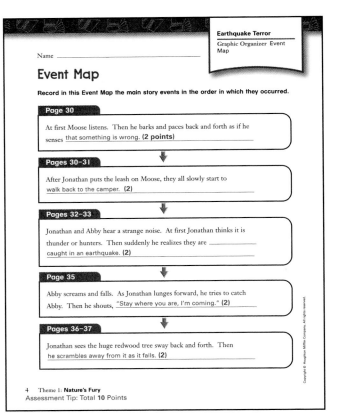

Name _____

Earthquake Terror
Graphic Organizer Event Map

Event Map

Record in this Event Map the main story events in the order in which they occurred.

Page 30

At first Moose listens. Then he barks and paces back and forth as if he senses that something is wrong. **(2 points)**

Pages 30–31

After Jonathan puts the leash on Moose, they all slowly start to walk back to the camper. **(2)**

Pages 32–33

Jonathan and Abby hear a strange noise. At first Jonathan thinks it is thunder or hunters. Then suddenly he realizes they are _____ caught in an earthquake. **(2)**

Page 35

Abby screams and falls. As Jonathan lunges forward, he tries to catch Abby. Then he shouts, "Stay where you are, I'm coming." **(2)**

Pages 36–37

Jonathan sees the huge redwood tree sway back and forth. Then he scrambles away from it as it falls. **(2)**

4   Theme 1: **Nature's Fury**
Assessment Tip: Total **10** Points

Teacher's Book, pages 27C and 51A

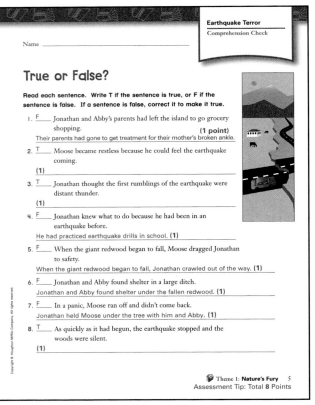

Name _____

Earthquake Terror
Comprehension Check

True or False?

Read each sentence. Write T if the sentence is true, or F if the sentence is false. If a sentence is false, correct it to make it true.

1. __F__ Jonathan and Abby's parents had left the island to go grocery shopping. **(1 point)**
   Their parents had gone to get treatment for their mother's broken ankle.

2. __T__ Moose became restless because he could feel the earthquake coming.
   (1)

3. __T__ Jonathan thought the first rumblings of the earthquake were distant thunder.
   (1)

4. __F__ Jonathan knew what to do because he had been in an earthquake before.
   He had practiced earthquake drills in school. **(1)**

5. __F__ When the giant redwood began to fall, Moose dragged Jonathan to safety.
   When the giant redwood began to fall, Jonathan crawled out of the way. **(1)**

6. __F__ Jonathan and Abby found shelter in a large ditch.
   Jonathan and Abby found shelter under the fallen redwood. **(1)**

7. __F__ In a panic, Moose ran off and didn't come back.
   Jonathan held Moose under the tree with him and Abby. **(1)**

8. __T__ As quickly as it had begun, the earthquake stopped and the woods were silent.
   (1)

Theme 1: **Nature's Fury**   5
Assessment Tip: Total **8** Points

Teacher's Book, page 47

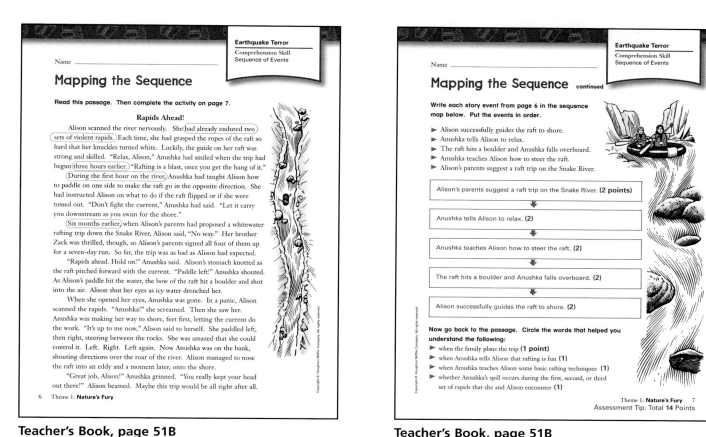

Earthquake Terror

Comprehension Skill
Sequence of Events

Name _____

Mapping the Sequence

Read this passage. Then complete the activity on page 7.

Rapids Ahead!

Alison scanned the river nervously. She had already endured two sets of violent rapids. Each time, she had grasped the ropes of the raft so hard that her knuckles turned white. Luckily, the guide on her raft was strong and skilled. "Relax, Alison," Anushka had smiled when the trip had begun three hours earlier. "Rafting is a blast, once you get the hang of it."

During the first hour on the river, Anushka had taught Alison how to paddle on one side to make the raft go in the opposite direction. She had instructed Alison on what to do if the raft flipped or if they were tossed out. "Don't fight the current," Anushka had said. "Let it carry you downstream as you swim for the shore."

Six months earlier, when Alison's parents had proposed a whitewater rafting trip down the Snake River, Alison said, "No way." Her brother Zack was thrilled, though, so Alison's parents signed all four of them up for a seven-day run. So far, the trip was as bad as Alison had expected.

"Rapids ahead. Hold on!" Anushka said. Alison's stomach knotted as the raft pitched forward with the current. "Paddle left!" Anushka shouted. As Alison's paddle hit the water, the bow of the raft hit a boulder and shot into the air. Alison shut her eyes as icy water drenched her.

When she opened her eyes, Anushka was gone. In a panic, Alison scanned the rapids. "Anushka!" she screamed. Then she saw her. Anushka was making her way to shore, feet first, letting the current do the work. "It's up to me now," Alison said to herself. She paddled left, then right, steering between the rocks. She was amazed that she could control it. Left. Right. Left again. Now Anushka was on the bank, shouting directions over the roar of the river. Alison managed to nose the raft into an eddy and a moment later, onto the shore.

"Great job, Alison!" Anushka grinned. "You really kept your head out there!" Alison beamed. Maybe this trip would be all right after all.

6   Theme 1: **Nature's Fury**

Teacher's Book, page 51B

Earthquake Terror

Comprehension Skill
Sequence of Events

Name _____

Mapping the Sequence *continued*

Write each story event from page 6 in the sequence map below. Put the events in order.

► Alison successfully guides the raft to shore.
► Anushka tells Alison to relax.
► The raft hits a boulder and Anushka falls overboard.
► Anushka teaches Alison how to steer the raft.
► Alison's parents suggest a raft trip on the Snake River.

Alison's parents suggest a raft trip on the Snake River. **(2 points)**

↓

Anushka tells Alison to relax. **(2)**

↓

Anushka teaches Alison how to steer the raft. **(2)**

↓

The raft hits a boulder and Anushka falls overboard. **(2)**

↓

Alison successfully guides the raft to shore. **(2)**

Now go back to the passage. Circle the words that helped you understand the following:

► when the family plans the trip **(1 point)**
► when Anushka tells Alison that rafting is fun **(1)**
► when Anushka teaches Alison some basic rafting techniques **(1)**
► whether Anushka's spill occurs during the first, second, or third set of rapids that she and Alison encounter **(1)**

Theme 1: **Nature's Fury**   7
Assessment Tip: Total **14** Points

Teacher's Book, page 51B

Earthquake Terror

Structural Analysis
Base Words

Name _____

Getting to Base

Read the sentences. For each underlined word, identify the base word. Write the base word and the ending.

Example: shake + -ing

1. Magpie Island was a popular place for hiking. hike + -ing **(1 point)**

2. Jonathan was nervous about staying in such an isolated place.
   isolate + -ed **(1)**

3. He thought it would be safer to go back to their trailer.
   safe + -er **(1)**

4. Jonathan and Abby followed the trail past blackberry bushes.
   bush + -es **(1)**

5. Neither of them had the slightest idea how the day would end.
   slight + -est **(1)**

6. Moose cocked his head and began sniffing the ground.
   sniff + -ing **(1)**

7. At first the earthquake was a thunderous noise in the distance.
   thunder + -ous **(1)**

8. Trees swayed all around Jonathan and Abby.
   sway + -ed **(1)**

9. The ground began rising and falling like ocean waves.
   wave + -s **(1)**

10. Abby cried for Jonathan to come help her. cry + -ed **(1)**

8   Theme 1: **Nature's Fury**
Assessment Tip: Total **10** Points

Teacher's Book, page 51F

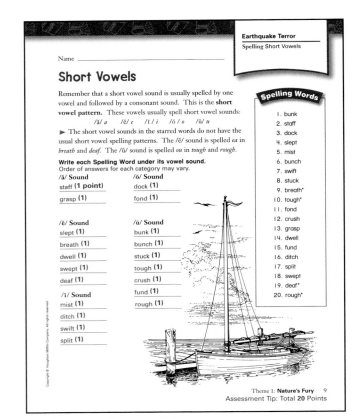

Short Vowels

Earthquake Terror
Spelling Short Vowels

Name _____

Remember that a short vowel sound is usually spelled by one vowel and followed by a consonant sound. This is the **short vowel pattern.** These vowels usually spell short vowel sounds:
/ă/ a   /ĕ/ e   /ĭ/ i   /ŏ/ o   /ŭ/ u

► The short vowel sounds in the starred words do not have the usual short vowel spelling patterns. The /ĕ/ sound is spelled *ea* in *breath* and *deaf*. The /ŭ/ sound is spelled *ou* in *tough* and *rough*.

Write each Spelling Word under its vowel sound.
Order of answers for each category may vary.

/ă/ Sound
staff (**1 point**)
grasp (**1**)

/ŏ/ Sound
dock (**1**)
fond (**1**)

/ĕ/ Sound
slept (**1**)
breath (**1**)
dwell (**1**)
swept (**1**)
deaf (**1**)

/ŭ/ Sound
bunk (**1**)
bunch (**1**)
stuck (**1**)
tough (**1**)
crush (**1**)
fund (**1**)
rough (**1**)

/ĭ/ Sound
mist (**1**)
ditch (**1**)
swift (**1**)
split (**1**)

Spelling Words
1. bunk
2. staff
3. dock
4. slept
5. mist
6. bunch
7. swift
8. stuck
9. breath*
10. tough*
11. fond
12. crush
13. grasp
14. dwell
15. fund
16. ditch
17. split
18. swept
19. deaf*
20. rough*

Theme 1: **Nature's Fury**   9
Assessment Tip: Total **20** Points

Teacher's Book, page 51H

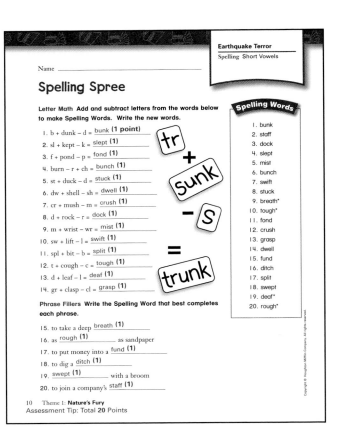

Spelling Spree

Earthquake Terror
Spelling Short Vowels

Name _____

Letter Math Add and subtract letters from the words below to make Spelling Words. Write the new words.

1. b + dunk – d = bunk (**1 point**)
2. sl + kept – k = slept (**1**)
3. f + pond – p = fond (**1**)
4. burn – r + ch = bunch (**1**)
5. st + duck – d = stuck (**1**)
6. dw + shell – sh = dwell (**1**)
7. cr + mush – m = crush (**1**)
8. d + rock – r = dock (**1**)
9. m + wrist – wr = mist (**1**)
10. sw + lift – l = swift (**1**)
11. spl + bit – b = split (**1**)
12. t + cough – c = tough (**1**)
13. d + leaf – l = deaf (**1**)
14. gr + clasp – cl = grasp (**1**)

Phrase Fillers Write the Spelling Word that best completes each phrase.

15. to take a deep breath (**1**)
16. as rough (**1**) as sandpaper
17. to put money into a fund (**1**)
18. to dig a ditch (**1**)
19. swept (**1**) with a broom
20. to join a company's staff (**1**)

Spelling Words
1. bunk
2. staff
3. dock
4. slept
5. mist
6. bunch
7. swift
8. stuck
9. breath*
10. tough*
11. fond
12. crush
13. grasp
14. dwell
15. fund
16. ditch
17. split
18. swept
19. deaf*
20. rough*

10   Theme 1: **Nature's Fury**
Assessment Tip: Total **20** Points

Teacher's Book, page 51H

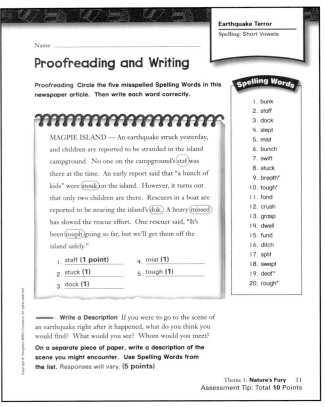

Proofreading and Writing

Earthquake Terror
Spelling Short Vowels

Name _____

Proofreading Circle the five misspelled Spelling Words in this newspaper article. Then write each word correctly.

MAGPIE ISLAND — An earthquake struck yesterday, and children are reported to be stranded in the island campground. No one on the campground's staf was there at the time. An early report said that "a bunch of kids" were stouk on the island. However, it turns out that only two children are there. Rescuers in a boat are reported to be nearing the island's dok. A heavy missed has slowed the rescue effort. One rescuer said, "It's been touph going so far, but we'll get them off the island safely."

1. staff (**1 point**)   4. mist (**1**)
2. stuck (**1**)   5. tough (**1**)
3. dock (**1**)

Spelling Words
1. bunk
2. staff
3. dock
4. slept
5. mist
6. bunch
7. swift
8. stuck
9. breath*
10. tough*
11. fond
12. crush
13. grasp
14. dwell
15. fund
16. ditch
17. split
18. swept
19. deaf*
20. rough*

Write a Description If you were to go to the scene of an earthquake right after it happened, what do you think you would find? What would you see? Whom would you meet?

On a separate piece of paper, write a description of the scene you might encounter. Use Spelling Words from the list. Responses will vary. (**5 points**)

Theme 1: **Nature's Fury**   11
Assessment Tip: Total **10** Points

Teacher's Book, page 51H

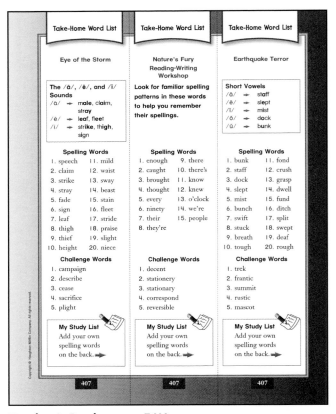

Take-Home Word List   **Take-Home Word List**   **Take-Home Word List**

Eye of the Storm

The /ā/, /ē/, and /ī/ Sounds
/ā/ → male, claim, stray
/ē/ → leaf, fleet
/ī/ → strike, thigh, sign

Spelling Words
1. speech   11. mild
2. claim   12. waist
3. strike   13. sway
4. stray   14. beast
5. fade   15. stain
6. sign   16. fleet
7. leaf   17. stride
8. thigh   18. praise
9. thief   19. slight
10. height   20. niece

Challenge Words
1. campaign
2. describe
3. cease
4. sacrifice
5. plight

My Study List
Add your own spelling words on the back. ➡

Nature's Fury
Reading-Writing Workshop

Look for familiar spelling patterns in these words to help you remember their spellings.

Spelling Words
1. enough   9. there
2. caught   10. there's
3. brought   11. know
4. thought   12. knew
5. every   13. o'clock
6. ninety   14. we're
7. their   15. people
8. they're

Challenge Words
1. decent
2. stationery
3. stationary
4. correspond
5. reversible

My Study List
Add your own spelling words on the back. ➡

Earthquake Terror

Short Vowels
/ă/ → staff
/ĕ/ → slept
/ĭ/ → mist
/ŏ/ → dock
/ŭ/ → bunk

Spelling Words
1. bunk   11. fond
2. staff   12. crush
3. dock   13. grasp
4. slept   14. dwell
5. mist   15. fund
6. bunch   16. ditch
7. swift   17. split
8. stuck   18. swept
9. breath   19. deaf
10. tough   20. rough

Challenge Words
1. trek
2. frantic
3. summit
4. rustic
5. mascot

My Study List
Add your own spelling words on the back. ➡

407   407   407

Teacher's Book, page 51H

Using a Thesaurus

Thesaurus Index

Main entry words are shown in dark print. For example, *information* is a main entry.

Antonyms are shown in regular print. For example, *decrease* is an antonym.

Subentries are shown in italic dark print. For example, *deny* is a subentry.

D

data **information** *n.*
decline *v.*

decrease **grow** *v.*
dedicated **earnest** *adj.*
defeat **surrender** *v.*
deny **decline** *v.*
desire **wish** *v.*
determine **think** *v.*
devastation *n.*
dim **bright** *adj.*

Thesaurus Entry

devastation *n.* The state of being destroyed; ruin; destruction. *It took years to repair the devastation caused by the earthquake.*

destruction The act or process of destroying. *The fires in California caused the destruction of several campsites.*

havoc The state of being destroyed. *The tropical storm caused havoc across the islands.*

ruin Total destruction or collapse. *The rainy season could easily ruin the harvest this year.*

wreck To cause the destruction of in a collision. *The demolition team can wreck that old building in a few hours.*
antonyms: create, produce

Teacher's Book, page 51I

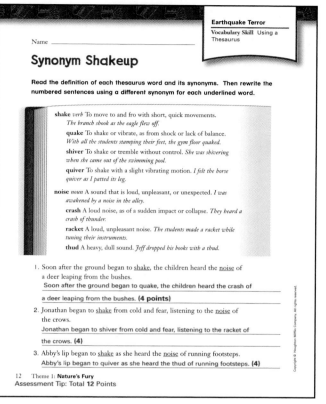

Name _____

Synonym Shakeup

Read the definition of each thesaurus word and its synonyms. Then rewrite the numbered sentences using a different synonym for each underlined word.

shake *verb* To move to and fro with short, quick movements. *The branch shook as the eagle flew off.*
  quake To shake or vibrate, as from shock or lack of balance. *With all the students stamping their feet, the gym floor quaked.*
  shiver To shake or tremble without control. *She was shivering when she came out of the swimming pool.*
  quiver To shake with a slight vibrating motion. *I felt the horse quiver as I patted its leg.*

noise *noun* A sound that is loud, unpleasant, or unexpected. *I was awakened by a noise in the alley.*
  crash A loud noise, as of a sudden impact or collapse. *They heard a crash of thunder.*
  racket A loud, unpleasant noise. *The students made a racket while tuning their instruments.*
  thud A heavy, dull sound. *Jeff dropped his books with a thud.*

1. Soon after the ground began to <u>shake</u>, the children heard the <u>noise</u> of a deer leaping from the bushes.
   Soon after the ground began to quake, the children heard the crash of a deer leaping from the bushes. **(4 points)**

2. Jonathan began to <u>shake</u> from cold and fear, listening to the <u>noise</u> of the crows.
   Jonathan began to shiver from cold and fear, listening to the racket of the crows. **(4)**

3. Abby's lip began to <u>shake</u> as she heard the <u>noise</u> of running footsteps.
   Abby's lip began to quiver as she heard the thud of running footsteps. **(4)**

12 Theme 1: **Nature's Fury**
Assessment Tip: Total **12** Points

Teacher's Book, page 51I

Daily Language Practice

Correct two sentences each day.

1. Did you tie the boat to the doct
   Did you tie the boat to the dock?

2. take a deep breeth before you begin.
   Take a deep breath before you begin.

3. The mayor will set up a fuhnd for the flood victims!
   The mayor will set up a fund for the flood victims.

4. watch out for that dich!
   Watch out for that ditch!

5. The two boys sleept until noon?
   The two boys slept until noon.

6. Who swepped the leaves under the fence.
   Who swept the leaves under the fence?

7. Be careful not to cresh your fingers in the car door?
   Be careful not to crush your fingers in the car door. (or door!)

8. Justin and amanda shared a buhch of bananas.
   Justin and Amanda shared a bunch of bananas.

9. Did the staf tell you when your puppy could come home
   Did the staff tell you when your puppy could come home?

10. is she fonde of chocolate chip cookies?
    Is she fond of chocolate chip cookies?

Teacher's Book, page 51L

Kinds of Sentences

An earthquake can be very dangerous.
Have you ever felt the ground move?
Stay calm during an earthquake.
What a scary feeling that must be!

1. Do you know what to do during an earthquake?
   interrogative sentence

2. What can you do to prepare ahead of time?
   interrogative sentence

3. Try to find shelter as quickly as possible.
   imperative sentence

4. What a roaring sound the earth can make!
   exclamatory sentence

5. An earthquake can stop as suddenly as it can start.
   declarative sentence

6. How silent it is right after an earthquake!
   exclamatory sentence

Teacher's Book, page 51L

Subjects and Predicates

NATURE'S FURY Earthquake Terror
Grammar Skill Subjects and Predicates

ANNOTATED VERSION

TRANSPARENCY 1–6
TEACHER'S EDITION PAGE T51L

The tornado caused a great deal of damage.

1. Many tornadoes happen during the months of April, May, and June.
2. Thunderstorms do not always produce tornadoes.
3. Certain weather conditions cause these storms.
4. Sometimes, several tornadoes will develop from a thunderstorm.
5. Tornadoes can destroy very heavy objects in their path.
6. A funnel-shaped cloud is the characteristic shape of a tornado.

1. complete subject: Many tornadoes/simple subject: tornadoes/complete predicate: happen during the months of April, May, and June/simple predicate: happen
2. complete subject: Thunderstorms/simple subject: Thunderstorms/complete predicate: do not always produce tornadoes/simple predicate: do produce
3. complete subject: Certain weather conditions/simple subject: conditions/complete predicate: cause these storms/simple predicate: cause
4. complete subject: Sometimes, several tornadoes/simple subject: tornadoes/complete predicate: will develop from a thunderstorm/simple predicate: will develop
5. complete subject: Tornadoes/simple subject: Tornadoes/complete predicate: can destroy very heavy objects in their path/simple predicate: can destroy
6. complete subject: A funnel-shaped cloud/simple subject: cloud/complete predicate: is the characteristic shape of a tornado/simple predicate: is

Teacher's Book, page 51L

Earthquake Terror
Grammar Skill Kinds of Sentences

Name _____

Sensing Danger

Kinds of Sentences There are four kinds of sentences:

1. A declarative sentence tells something and ends with a period.
   Earthquakes occur along fault lines in the earth.
2. An interrogative sentence asks a question and ends with a question mark.
   Can earthquakes be predicted?
3. An imperative sentence gives a request or an order and usually ends with a period.
   Protect your head in an earthquake.
4. An exclamatory sentence expresses strong feeling and ends with an exclamation mark.
   How frightening an earthquake is!

Add the correct punctuation mark to each sentence below. Then write what kind of sentence each one is.

1. Why is the dog barking? **(1 point)**
   interrogative sentence **(1)**
2. Put him on his leash. **(1)**
   imperative sentence **(1)**
3. Some animals can sense a coming earthquake. **(1)**
   declarative sentence **(1)**
4. How frightened I am! **(1)**
   exclamatory sentence **(1)**
5. The earth has stopped shaking at last. **(1)**
   declarative sentence **(1)**

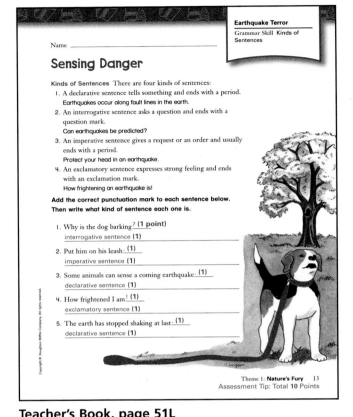

Theme 1: **Nature's Fury** 13
Assessment Tip: Total **10** Points

Teacher's Book, page 51L

Earthquake Terror
Grammar Skill Subjects and Predicates

Name _____

On Vacation

Subjects and Predicates Every sentence has a subject. It tells whom or what the sentence is about. The complete subject includes all the words in the subject, and the simple subject is the main word or words in the complete subject.

Every sentence has a predicate too. It tells what the subject is or does. The complete predicate includes all the words in the predicate, and the simple predicate is the main word or words in the complete predicate.

Draw a slash mark (/) between the complete subject and the complete predicate in the sentences below. Then circle the simple subject and underline the simple predicate. (3 points each sentence)

1. The whole family/travels in our new camper.
2. Everybody/helps to pitch the tent under a tree.
3. They/will use a compass on their hike.
4. A good fire/is difficult to build.
5. The smell of cooking/is delicious to the hungry campers.

14 Theme 1: **Nature's Fury**
Assessment Tip: Total **15** Points

Teacher's Book, page 51L

Earthquake Terror
Grammar Skill Compound Subjects and Compound Predicates

Name _____

Sentence Combining

A **compound subject** is made up of two or more simple subjects that have the same predicate. Use a connecting word such as *and* or *or* to join the simple subjects.
   Jonathan yelled. **Abby** yelled.   **Jonathan and Abby** yelled.
Combine two simple subjects into one compound subject, as shown above, to make your writing clearer and less choppy.
   A **compound predicate** is made up of two or more simple predicates that have the same subject. Use a connecting word such as *and* or *or* to join the simple predicates.
   Moose **barked**. Moose **howled**.   Moose **barked and howled**.
Combine simple predicates into compound predicates, as shown above, to make your writing smoother.

Suppose Jonathan wrote a draft of a letter to his aunt about his vacation. Revise his letter by combining sentences. Each new sentence will have either a compound subject or a compound predicate. Only Jonathan's first sentence will remain the same.

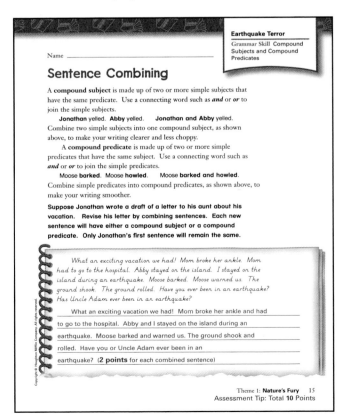

What an exciting vacation we had! Mom broke her ankle. Mom had to go to the hospital. Abby stayed on the island. I stayed on the island during an earthquake. Moose barked. Moose warned us. The ground shook. The ground rolled. Have you ever been in an earthquake? Has Uncle Adam ever been in an earthquake?

What an exciting vacation we had! Mom broke her ankle and had to go to the hospital. Abby and I stayed on the island during an earthquake. Moose barked and warned us. The ground shook and rolled. Have you or Uncle Adam ever been in an earthquake? **(2 points for each combined sentence)**

Theme 1: **Nature's Fury** 15
Assessment Tip: Total **10** Points

Teacher's Book, page 51L

A News Article

The Dog Days of Summer

When Roberto Garrigues and Robin Foster became firefighters, little did they know what creative thinking skills they would be called upon to use. For on October 11, a small puppy managed to fall into a storm drain on Main Street. How the puppy got into the drainpipe is not clear. It was even less clear how to get it out. But Roberto and Robin were assigned to solve the problem, and solve it they did.

The pipe was too small for either firefighter to crawl into. Likewise, the puppy wouldn't come when it was called, so the firefighters could not lift a storm grate and grab the puppy from above as it approached. Finally, Robin had an idea. "I realized that if we cut a puppy-sized hole in the side of the pipe," she said, "the dog would probably come out on its own." The clever solution worked. With the added incentive of a bowl of puppy food near the hole, the hungry puppy eventually poked its head out, and the firefighters grabbed it.

Within an hour, the puppy was reunited with its grateful owner. "I didn't even know Tornado was missing," said owner Jerry Emerson of his aptly named pup, who had just caused a whirlwind of trouble. "Somehow Tornado must have slipped out when I was carrying in my groceries. I'm certainly glad he had a dog license, so he could be quickly returned. And I'll be forever grateful to the firefighters for their ingenious rescue."

Teacher's Book, page 51M

Adding Details

An Earthshaking Experience

Passage 1

Two hikers on Magpie Island felt the ground swell and retreat beneath their feet. The devastating quake harmed or trapped many on the island, but Jonathan managed to pull his sister Abby to safety.

Passage 2

Two hikers, <u>Jonathan and Abby Palmer</u>, on Magpie Island <u>for a camping trip</u>, felt the ground swell and retreat beneath their feet <u>during yesterday's quake</u>. The devastating quake harmed or trapped many on the island, but Jonathan, <u>crawling on hands and knees</u>, managed to pull his sister Abby to safety <u>beneath a fallen redwood tree</u>.

Teacher's Book, page 51M

Name _____

Writing a News Article

Jonathan and Abby Palmer experience firsthand an unforgettable event — the terror of an earthquake. Imagine you are a reporter for the *Daily Gazette*. Use the chart below to gather details for a news article about an interesting or unusual event at your school, in your neighborhood, or in your town. Answer these questions: What happened? Who was involved? When, where, and why did this event occur? How did it happen?

Who? (2 points)
What? (2)
When? (2)
Where? (2)
Why? (2)
How? (2)

Now use the details you gathered to write your news article on a separate sheet of paper. Include a headline and a beginning that will capture your reader's attention. Present facts in order of importance, from most to least important. Try to use quotations from eyewitnesses to bring this news event to life. (3)

16   Theme 1: **Nature's Fury**
Assessment Tip: Total **15** Points

Teacher's Book, page 51N

Name _____

Adding Details

A good reporter uses details to explain what happened and to bring an event to life. Read the following news article that might have been written about the earthquake. Then rewrite it on the lines below, adding details from the list to improve the article.

(1 point per detail)

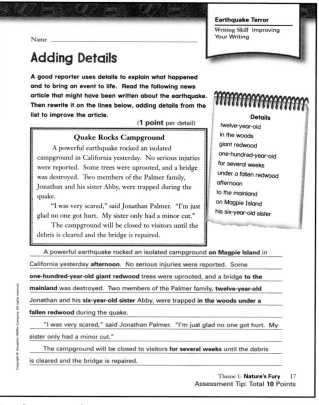

> **Quake Rocks Campground**
>
> A powerful earthquake rocked an isolated campground in California yesterday. No serious injuries were reported. Some trees were uprooted, and a bridge was destroyed. Two members of the Palmer family, Jonathan and his sister Abby, were trapped during the quake.
>
> "I was very scared," said Jonathan Palmer. "I'm just glad no one got hurt. My sister only had a minor cut."
>
> The campground will be closed to visitors until the debris is cleared and the bridge is repaired.

Details
twelve-year-old
in the woods
giant redwood
one-hundred-year-old
for several weeks
under a fallen redwood
afternoon
to the mainland
on Magpie Island
his six-year-old sister

A powerful earthquake rocked an isolated campground **on Magpie Island** in California yesterday **afternoon**. No serious injuries were reported. Some **one-hundred-year-old giant redwood** trees were uprooted, and a bridge **to the mainland** was destroyed. Two members of the Palmer family, **twelve-year-old** Jonathan and his **six-year-old sister** Abby, were trapped **in the woods under a fallen redwood** during the quake.

"I was very scared," said Jonathan Palmer. "I'm just glad no one got hurt. My sister only had a minor cut."

The campground will be closed to visitors **for several weeks** until the debris is cleared and the bridge is repaired.

Theme 1: **Nature's Fury**   17
Assessment Tip: Total **10** Points

Teacher's Book, page 51N

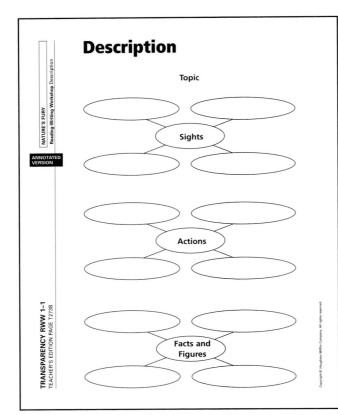

Teacher's Book, page 53B

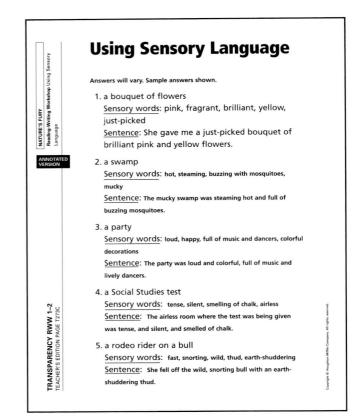

Teacher's Book, page 53C

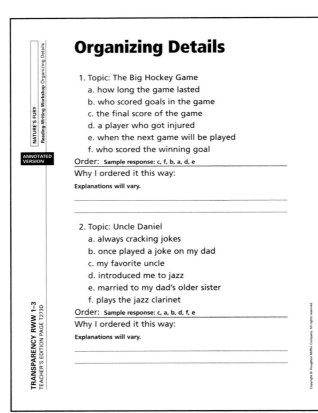

Teacher's Book, page 53D

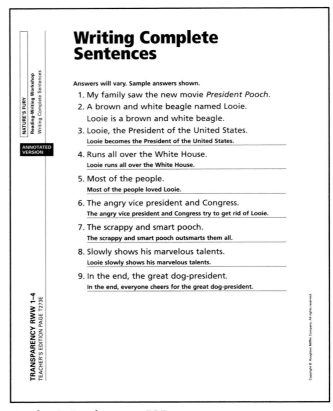

Teacher's Book, page 53E

Revising Your Description

Name _____

Reread your description. What do you need to make it better? Use this page to help you decide. Put a checkmark in the box for each sentence that describes what you have written.

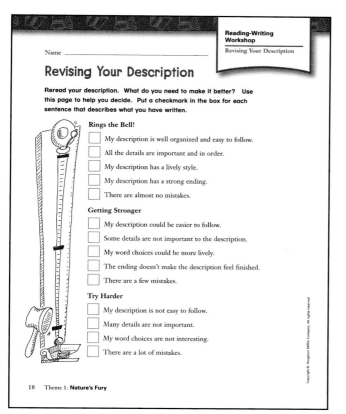

Rings the Bell!

☐ My description is well organized and easy to follow.

☐ All the details are important and in order.

☐ My description has a lively style.

☐ My description has a strong ending.

☐ There are almost no mistakes.

Getting Stronger

☐ My description could be easier to follow.

☐ Some details are not important to the description.

☐ My word choices could be more lively.

☐ The ending doesn't make the description feel finished.

☐ There are a few mistakes.

Try Harder

☐ My description is not easy to follow.

☐ Many details are not important.

☐ My word choices are not interesting.

☐ There are a lot of mistakes.

18   Theme 1: **Nature's Fury**

Teacher's Book, page 53E

Writing Complete Sentences

Name _____

Make each incomplete sentence complete. Change words or add extra words if you need to. Answers will vary. Sample answers given.

1. Being a photographer
   Being a photographer can be exciting. **(1 point)**

2. Photographing nature
   Photographing nature can be dangerous. **(1)**

3. Lightning flashing in the sky
   You can take pictures of lightning flashing in the sky. **(1)**

4. Chasing storms
   You could travel the world while chasing storms. **(1)**

5. Tornadoes in the distance
   You could take pictures of tornadoes in the distance. **(1)**

6. The black funnel is impressive, even far away.
   Complete. **(1)**

7. Planes in storms
   Planes can get tossed about in storms. **(1)**

8. A bumpy ride
   Turbulence can create a bumpy ride for passengers. **(1)**

9. Dangerous to be out in some storms
   It's dangerous to be out in some storms. **(1)**

10. Don't stand under a tree when there's lightning.
    Complete. **(1)**

Theme 1: **Nature's Fury**   19
Assessment Tip: Total **10** Points

Teacher's Book, page 53E

Spelling Words

Name _____

Words Often Misspelled Look for familiar spelling patterns to help you remember how to spell the Spelling Words on this page. Think carefully about the parts that you find hard to spell in each word.

Write the missing letters and apostrophes in the Spelling Words below.

1. en o u g h (1 point)
2. c a u g h t (1)
3. br o u g h t (1)
4. th o u g h t (1)
5. ev e ry (1)
6. nin e ty (1)
7. th e i r (1)
8. th e y ' re (1)
9. th e r e (1)
10. th e r e ' s (1)
11. k n ow (1)
12. k n ew (1)
13. o ' c lock (1)
14. w e ' r e (1)
15. p e o ple (1)

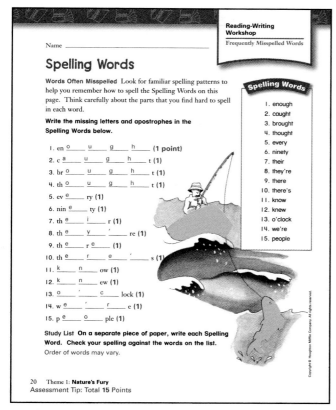

Study List On a separate piece of paper, write each Spelling Word. Check your spelling against the words on the list.
Order of words may vary.

Spelling Words

1. enough
2. caught
3. brought
4. thought
5. every
6. ninety
7. their
8. they're
9. there
10. there's
11. know
12. knew
13. o'clock
14. we're
15. people

20   Theme 1: **Nature's Fury**
Assessment Tip: Total **15** Points

Teacher's Book, page 53F

Spelling Spree

Name _____

Word Clues Write the Spelling Word that best fits each clue.

1. the sum of eighty-nine and one
2. a contraction for describing what other people are doing
3. to be aware of a fact
4. a time-telling word
5. as much as is needed
6. a word for other people's belongings
7. took along
8. a contraction for "there is"

1. ninety **(1 point)**   5. enough **(1)**
2. they're **(1)**   6. their **(1)**
3. know **(1)**   7. brought **(1)**
4. o'clock **(1)**   8. there's **(1)**

Word Addition Write a Spelling Word by adding the beginning of the first word to the end of the second word.

then

fair

their

9. caution + fight   9. caught **(1)**
10. we'll + more   10. we're **(1)**
11. knight + flew   11. knew **(1)**
12. peony + steeple   12. people **(1)**
13. even + wary   13. every **(1)**
14. them + cure   14. there **(1)**
15. think + bought   15. thought **(1)**

Spelling Words

1. enough
2. caught
3. brought
4. thought
5. every
6. ninety
7. their
8. they're
9. there
10. there's
11. know
12. knew
13. o'clock
14. we're
15. people

Theme 1: **Nature's Fury**   21
Assessment Tip: Total **15** Points

Teacher's Book, page 53F

Lesson Planning Support *(Continued)*

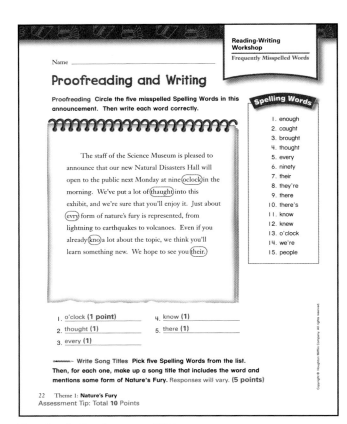

Teacher's Book, page 53F

Proofreading and Writing

Name _____

Proofreading Circle the five misspelled Spelling Words in this announcement. Then write each word correctly.

The staff of the Science Museum is pleased to announce that our new Natural Disasters Hall will open to the public next Monday at nine (oclock) in the morning. We've put a lot of (thaught) into this exhibit, and we're sure that you'll enjoy it. Just about (evry) form of nature's fury is represented, from lightning to earthquakes to volcanoes. Even if you already (kno) a lot about the topic, we think you'll learn something new. We hope to see you (their.)

Spelling Words
1. enough
2. caught
3. brought
4. thought
5. every
6. ninety
7. their
8. they're
9. there
10. there's
11. know
12. knew
13. o'clock
14. we're
15. people

1. o'clock **(1 point)**
2. thought **(1)**
3. every **(1)**
4. know **(1)**
5. there **(1)**

Write Song Titles Pick five Spelling Words from the list. Then, for each one, make up a song title that includes the word and mentions some form of Nature's Fury. Responses will vary. **(5 points)**

22   Theme 1: **Nature's Fury**
Assessment Tip: Total **10** Points

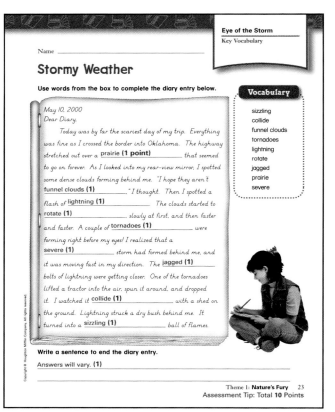

Teacher's Book, page 53F

Take-Home Word List | **Take-Home Word List** | **Take-Home Word List**

Eye of the Storm | **Nature's Fury Reading-Writing Workshop** | **Earthquake Terror**

The /ā/, /ē/, and /ī/ Sounds
/ā/ → male, claim, stray
/ē/ → leaf, fleet
/ī/ → strike, thigh, sign

Look for familiar spelling patterns in these words to help you remember their spellings.

Short Vowels
/ŏ/ → staff
/ĕ/ → slept
/ĭ/ → mist
/ŏ/ → dock
/ŭ/ → bunk

Spelling Words
1. speech
2. claim
3. strike
4. stray
5. fade
6. sign
7. leaf
8. thigh
9. thief
10. height
11. mild
12. waist
13. sway
14. beast
15. stain
16. fleet
17. stride
18. praise
19. slight
20. niece

Spelling Words
1. enough
2. caught
3. brought
4. thought
5. every
6. ninety
7. their
8. they're
9. there
10. there's
11. know
12. knew
13. o'clock
14. we're
15. people

Spelling Words
1. bunk
2. staff
3. dock
4. slept
5. mist
6. bunch
7. swift
8. stuck
9. breath
10. tough
11. fond
12. crush
13. grasp
14. dwell
15. fund
16. ditch
17. split
18. swept
19. deaf
20. rough

Challenge Words
1. campaign
2. describe
3. cease
4. sacrifice
5. plight

Challenge Words
1. decent
2. stationery
3. stationary
4. correspond
5. reversible

Challenge Words
1. trek
2. frantic
3. summit
4. rustic
5. mascot

My Study List Add your own spelling words on the back.

My Study List Add your own spelling words on the back.

My Study List Add your own spelling words on the back.

407 | 407 | 407

News Flash

Tornado Warning Issued for Texas and Oklahoma

Every spring, warm air from the Gulf of Mexico and cool air from Alaska <u>collide</u> over the Midwest. Powerful weather can brew over the flat <u>prairies</u> when these air masses meet. Today the National Weather Service issued a <u>severe</u> storm warning for northern Texas and Oklahoma. <u>Tornadoes</u> are likely to touch down in this region throughout the weekend. Residents are urged to be on the lookout. These signs show that a tornado may be forming:

- A dense, inky cloud forms over the land.

- Air at the bottom of the cloud begins to <u>rotate</u>. This swirling air is a breeding ground for twisters.

- One or more <u>funnel clouds</u> descend toward the ground like dragon necks.

Tornadoes are often accompanied by <u>sizzling</u> electrical storms. It is not unusual to see <u>jagged</u> bolts of <u>lightning</u>.

Teacher's Book, page 55A

Name _____

Stormy Weather

Use words from the box to complete the diary entry below.

May 10, 2000
Dear Diary,

Today was by far the scariest day of my trip. Everything was fine as I crossed the border into Oklahoma. The highway stretched out over a prairie **(1 point)** *that seemed to go on forever. As I looked into my rear-view mirror, I spotted some dense clouds forming behind me. "I hope they aren't* funnel clouds **(1)** *," I thought. Then I spotted a flash of* lightning **(1)** *. The clouds started to* rotate **(1)** *, slowly at first, and then faster and faster. A couple of* tornadoes **(1)** *were forming right before my eyes! I realized that a* severe **(1)** *storm had formed behind me, and it was moving fast in my direction. The* jagged **(1)** *bolts of lightning were getting closer. One of the tornadoes lifted a tractor into the air, spun it around, and dropped it. I watched it* collide **(1)** *with a shed on the ground. Lightning struck a dry bush behind me. It turned into a* sizzling **(1)** *ball of flames.*

Vocabulary
sizzling
collide
funnel clouds
tornadoes
lightning
rotate
jagged
prairie
severe

Write a sentence to end the diary entry.
Answers will vary. **(1)**

Theme 1: **Nature's Fury**   23
Assessment Tip: Total **10** Points

Teacher's Book, page 55A

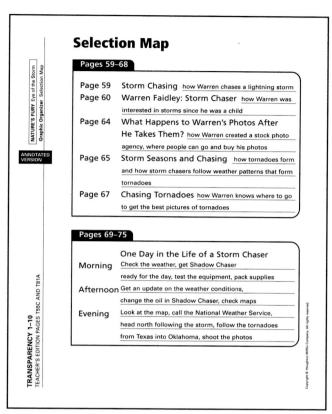

Selection Map

Pages 59–68

Page 59 Storm Chasing how Warren chases a lightning storm

Page 60 Warren Faidley: Storm Chaser how Warren was interested in storms since he was a child

Page 64 What Happens to Warren's Photos After He Takes Them? how Warren created a stock photo agency, where people can go and buy his photos

Page 65 Storm Seasons and Chasing how tornadoes form and how storm chasers follow weather patterns that form tornadoes

Page 67 Chasing Tornadoes how Warren knows where to go to get the best pictures of tornadoes

Pages 69–75

One Day in the Life of a Storm Chaser

Morning Check the weather, get Shadow Chaser ready for the day, test the equipment, pack supplies

Afternoon Get an update on the weather conditions, change the oil in Shadow Chaser, check maps

Evening Look at the map, call the National Weather Service, head north following the storm, follow the tornadoes from Texas into Oklahoma, shoot the photos

Teacher's Book, pages 55C and 81A

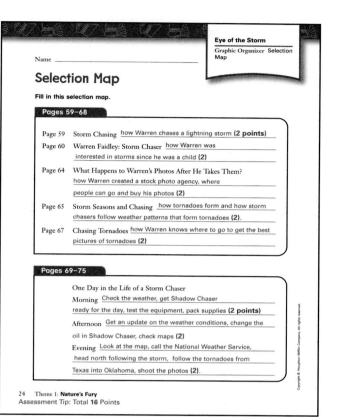

Name _____

Selection Map

Fill in this selection map.

Pages 59–68

Page 59 Storm Chasing how Warren chases a lightning storm **(2 points)**

Page 60 Warren Faidley: Storm Chaser how Warren was interested in storms since he was a child **(2)**

Page 64 What Happens to Warren's Photos After He Takes Them? how Warren created a stock photo agency, where people can go and buy his photos **(2)**

Page 65 Storm Seasons and Chasing how tornadoes form and how storm chasers follow weather patterns that form tornadoes **(2)**

Page 67 Chasing Tornadoes how Warren knows where to go to get the best pictures of tornadoes **(2)**

Pages 69–75

One Day in the Life of a Storm Chaser

Morning Check the weather, get Shadow Chaser ready for the day, test the equipment, pack supplies **(2 points)**

Afternoon Get an update on the weather conditions, change the oil in Shadow Chaser, check maps **(2)**

Evening Look at the map, call the National Weather Service, head north following the storm, follow the tornadoes from Texas into Oklahoma, shoot the photos **(2)**.

24 Theme 1: **Nature's Fury**
Assessment Tip: Total **16** Points

Teacher's Book, pages 55C and 81A

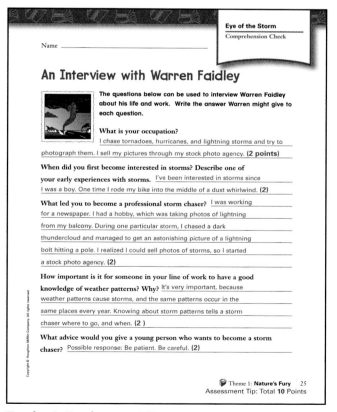

Name _____

An Interview with Warren Faidley

The questions below can be used to interview Warren Faidley about his life and work. Write the answer Warren might give to each question.

What is your occupation? I chase tornadoes, hurricanes, and lightning storms and try to photograph them. I sell my pictures through my stock photo agency. **(2 points)**

When did you first become interested in storms? Describe one of your early experiences with storms. I've been interested in storms since I was a boy. One time I rode my bike into the middle of a dust whirlwind. **(2)**

What led you to become a professional storm chaser? I was working for a newspaper. I had a hobby, which was taking photos of lightning from my balcony. During one particular storm, I chased a dark thundercloud and managed to get an astonishing picture of a lightning bolt hitting a pole. I realized I could sell photos of storms, so I started a stock photo agency. **(2)**

How important is it for someone in your line of work to have a good knowledge of weather patterns? Why? It's very important, because weather patterns cause storms, and the same patterns occur in the same places every year. Knowing about storm patterns tells a storm chaser where to go, and when. **(2)**

What advice would you give a young person who wants to become a storm chaser? Possible response: Be patient. Be careful. **(2)**

Theme 1: **Nature's Fury** 25
Assessment Tip: Total **10** Points

Teacher's Book, page 77

Lesson Planning Support *(Continued)*

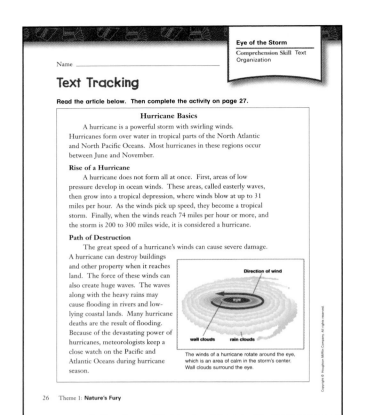

Teacher's Book, page 81B

Eye of the Storm

Comprehension Skill Text Organization

Name _____

Text Tracking

Read the article below. Then complete the activity on page 27.

Hurricane Basics

A hurricane is a powerful storm with swirling winds. Hurricanes form over water in tropical parts of the North Atlantic and North Pacific Oceans. Most hurricanes in these regions occur between June and November.

Rise of a Hurricane

A hurricane does not form all at once. First, areas of low pressure develop in ocean winds. These areas, called easterly waves, then grow into a tropical depression, where winds blow at up to 31 miles per hour. As the winds pick up speed, they become a tropical storm. Finally, when the winds reach 74 miles per hour or more, and the storm is 200 to 300 miles wide, it is considered a hurricane.

Path of Destruction

The great speed of a hurricane's winds can cause severe damage. A hurricane can destroy buildings and other property when it reaches land. The force of these winds can also create huge waves. The waves along with the heavy rains may cause flooding in rivers and low-lying coastal lands. Many hurricane deaths are the result of flooding. Because of the devastating power of hurricanes, meteorologists keep a close watch on the Pacific and Atlantic Oceans during hurricane season.

The winds of a hurricane rotate around the eye, which is an area of calm in the storm's center. Wall clouds surround the eye.

26   Theme 1: **Nature's Fury**

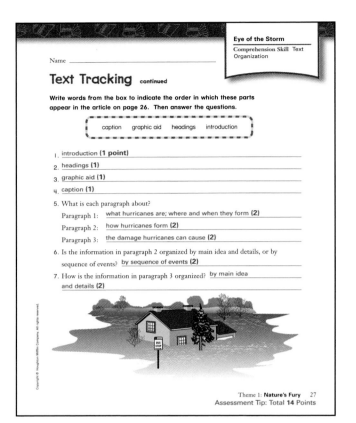

Teacher's Book, page 81B

Eye of the Storm

Comprehension Skill Text Organization

Name _____

Text Tracking *continued*

Write words from the box to indicate the order in which these parts appear in the article on page 26. Then answer the questions.

> caption   graphic aid   headings   introduction

1. introduction **(1 point)**
2. headings **(1)**
3. graphic aid **(1)**
4. caption **(1)**
5. What is each paragraph about?

   Paragraph 1: what hurricanes are; where and when they form **(2)**

   Paragraph 2: how hurricanes form **(2)**

   Paragraph 3: the damage hurricanes can cause **(2)**

6. Is the information in paragraph 2 organized by main idea and details, or by sequence of events? by sequence of events **(2)**
7. How is the information in paragraph 3 organized? by main idea and details **(2)**

Theme 1: **Nature's Fury**   27
Assessment Tip: Total **14** Points

Teacher's Book, page 81C

Electronic Card Catalog

First screen

Your search:	A=KRAMER, STEPHEN		
	Holdings highlighted for: CENTRAL		
LINE			
#	------Author------	------Title------	Date
1	Kramer, Stephen P.	Avalanche / by Stephen Kramer; photograph	1992
2	Kramer, Stephen P.	Caves / by Stephen Kramer; photographs by	1995
3	Kramer, Stephen P.	Eye of the Storm: chasing storms with War	1997
4	Kramer, Stephen P.	How to think like a scientist: answering	1987
5	Kramer, Stephen P.	Theodoric's rainbow / written by Stephen K	1995

Type: the number of a line and press <ENTER> TO SEE MORE INFORMATION.
        N   TO SEE NEXT SCREEN   P   to see the Previous screen
        B   to Backup   ST to start over

Second screen

CALL NUM:	J 502.8 K
AUTHOR:	Kramer, Stephen P.
TITLE:	How to think like a scientist: answering questions by the scientific method
PUBLISHER:	T.Y. Crowell, c1987.
SUBJECTS:	Science--Methodology--Juvenile literature.
	Science--Methodology.
LIBRARY HOLDINGS:	
	APTOS
	1. CALL NUMBER: J 502.8 K -- JNONFICTION -- Available
	BOULDER CREEK
	2. CALL NUMBER: J 502.8 K -- JNONFICTION -- Available

Teacher's Book, page 81F

Eye of the Storm

Structural Analysis Syllabication

Name _____

Stormy Syllables

Write the underlined word using slash marks (/) between its syllables. Then write a new sentence that uses the underlined word. Sample answers shown.

1. The photographer changed her position to get a better shot of the storm.
   po/si/tion **(1 point)** I moved the chair to a new position. **(2)**

2. A good photographer tries to capture the excitement of the moment.
   cap/ture **(1)** I tried to capture a butterfly in my net. **(2)**

3. Warren showed exciting videos of tornadoes. vi/de/os **(1)**
   We watched three videos over the weekend. **(2)**

4. I wonder how she was able to get so close to the lightning bolt.
   won/der **(1)** I wonder where we will go on our vacation. **(2)**

5. By rotating his body, he could follow the circular path of the tornado.
   ro/tat/ing **(1)** The moon is rotating around Earth. **(2)**

28   Theme 1: **Nature's Fury**
Assessment Tip: Total **15** Points

Worksheet 1 (top-left)

Name _____

The /ā/, /ē/, and /ī/ Sounds

When you hear the /ā/ sound, think of the patterns *a*-consonant-*e*, *ai*, and *ay*. When you hear the /ē/ sound, think of the patterns *ea* and *ee*. When you hear the /ī/ sound, think of the patterns i-consonant-*e*, *igh*, and *i*.

/ā/	fade	claim	stray
/ē/	leaf	speech	
/ī/	strike	thigh	sign

► The long vowel sounds in the starred words have different spelling patterns. The /ē/ sound in *thief* and in *niece* is spelled *ie*. The /ī/ sound in *height* is spelled *eigh*.

Write each Spelling Word under its vowel sound.
Order of answers for each category may vary.

/ā/	/ē/	/ī/
claim (**1 point**)	speech (1)	strike (1)
stray (1)	leaf (1)	sign (1)
fade (1)	thief (1)	thigh (1)
waist (1)	beast (1)	height (1)
sway (1)	fleet (1)	mild (1)
stain (1)	niece (1)	stride (1)
praise (1)		slight (1)

Spelling Words
1. speech
2. claim
3. strike
4. stray
5. fade
6. sign
7. leaf
8. thigh
9. thief*
10. height*
11. mild
12. waist
13. sway
14. beast
15. stain
16. fleet
17. stride
18. praise
19. slight
20. niece*

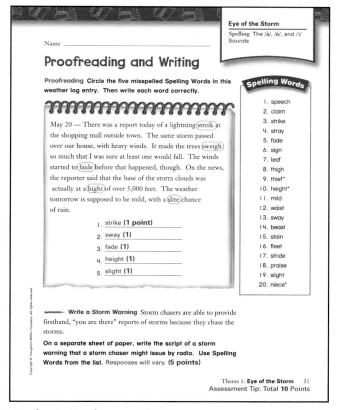

Theme 1: **Nature's Fury**   29
Assessment Tip: Total **20** Points

Teacher's Book, page 81H

Worksheet 2 (top-right)

Name _____

Spelling Spree

Find a Rhyme For each sentence write a Spelling Word that rhymes with the underlined word and makes sense in the sentence.

1. On what <u>day</u> did you last see the stray (**1 point**) cat?
2. It looks like the stain (1) got washed out by the <u>rain</u>.
3. She liked to stride (1) down the beach at low <u>tide</u>.
4. They swam out to meet the fleet (1) of ships.
5. How <u>high</u> on the thigh (1) did the ball hit you?
6. His niece (1) asked for another <u>piece</u> of pie.
7. The police <u>chief</u> took credit for catching the thief (1).
8. The young <u>child</u> liked mild (1) food better than spicy food.

Crack the Code Some Spelling Words have been written in the code below. Use the code to figure out each word. Then write the word correctly. (**1 point** each)

CODE:	R	V	L	O	C	A	D	X	P	T	Y	Q	J	N	E	I	M
LETTER:	a	b	c	e	f	g	h	i	l	m	n	p	r	s	t	w	y

9. LPRXT   claim
10. IRXNE   waist
11. VORNE   beast
12. NQOOLD   speech
13. NXAY   sign
14. DOXADE   height
15. NPXADE   slight
16. NIRM   sway
17. QJRXNO   praise
18. PORC   leaf

Spelling Words
1. speech
2. claim
3. strike
4. stray
5. fade
6. sign
7. leaf
8. thigh
9. thief*
10. height*
11. mild
12. waist
13. sway
14. beast
15. stain
16. fleet
17. stride
18. praise
19. slight
20. niece*

30   Theme 1: **Nature's Fury**
Assessment Tip: Total **18** Points

Teacher's Book, page 81H

Worksheet 3 (bottom-left)

Name _____

Proofreading and Writing

Proofreading Circle the five misspelled Spelling Words in this weather log entry. Then write each word correctly.

May 20 — There was a report today of a lightning (streik) at the shopping mall outside town. The same storm passed over our house, with heavy winds. It made the trees (sweigh) so much that I was sure at least one would fall. The winds started to (faide) before that happened, though. On the news, the reporter said that the base of the storm clouds was actually at a (hight) of over 5,000 feet. The weather tomorrow is supposed to be mild, with a (slite) chance of rain.

1. strike (**1 point**)
2. sway (1)
3. fade (1)
4. height (1)
5. slight (1)

Spelling Words
1. speech
2. claim
3. strike
4. stray
5. fade
6. sign
7. leaf
8. thigh
9. thief*
10. height*
11. mild
12. waist
13. sway
14. beast
15. stain
16. fleet
17. stride
18. praise
19. slight
20. niece*

Write a Storm Warning Storm chasers are able to provide firsthand, "you are there" reports of storms because they chase the storms.

On a separate sheet of paper, write the script of a storm warning that a storm chaser might issue by radio. Use Spelling Words from the list. Responses will vary. (**5 points**)

Theme 1: **Eye of the Storm**   31
Assessment Tip: Total **10** Points

Teacher's Book, page 81H

Worksheet 4 (bottom-right)

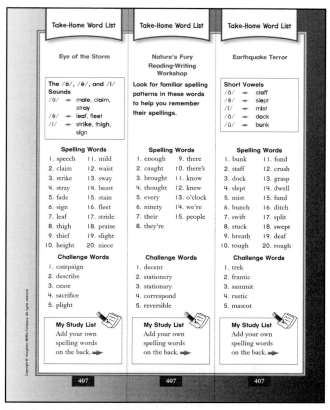

Take-Home Word List

Eye of the Storm

The /ā/, /ē/, and /ī/ Sounds

/ā/	→	male, claim, stray
/ē/	→	leaf, fleet
/ī/	→	strike, thigh, sign

Spelling Words
1. speech   11. mild
2. claim   12. waist
3. strike   13. sway
4. stray   14. beast
5. fade   15. stain
6. sign   16. fleet
7. leaf   17. stride
8. thigh   18. praise
9. thief   19. slight
10. height   20. niece

Challenge Words
1. campaign
2. describe
3. cease
4. sacrifice
5. plight

My Study List
Add your own spelling words on the back. ➡

Take-Home Word List

Nature's Fury
Reading-Writing Workshop

Look for familiar spelling patterns in these words to help you remember their spellings.

Spelling Words
1. enough   9. there
2. caught   10. there's
3. brought   11. know
4. thought   12. knew
5. every   13. o'clock
6. ninety   14. we're
7. their   15. people
8. they're

Challenge Words
1. decent
2. stationery
3. stationary
4. correspond
5. reversible

My Study List
Add your own spelling words on the back. ➡

Take-Home Word List

Earthquake Terror

Short Vowels

/ă/	→	staff
/ĕ/	→	slept
/ĭ/	→	mist
/ŏ/	→	dock
/ŭ/	→	bunk

Spelling Words
1. bunk   11. fond
2. staff   12. crush
3. dock   13. grasp
4. slept   14. dwell
5. mist   15. fund
6. bunch   16. ditch
7. swift   17. split
8. stuck   18. swept
9. breath   19. deaf
10. tough   20. rough

Challenge Words
1. trek
2. frantic
3. summit
4. rustic
5. mascot

My Study List
Add your own spelling words on the back. ➡

407   407   407

Teacher's Book, page 81H

Teacher's Book, page 81I

Eye of the Storm

Vocabulary Skill Dictionary:
Alphabetical Order
and Guide Words

Name _____

Words in Their Places

Read each set of words, and decide which two could be the guide
words and which one the entry word on a dictionary page. Then in
the columns below, write the guide words under the correct heading,
and the entry word beside them.

trout	weather	prance	durable	chase
trust	wayward	practice	dust	charter
tropical	weave	prairie	dusky	chatterbox

Guide Words		Entry Word
tropical **(1)**	trust **(1)**	trout **(1)**
wayward **(1)**	weave **(1)**	weather **(1)**
practice **(1)**	prance **(1)**	prairie **(1)**
durable **(1)**	dust **(1)**	dusky **(1)**
charter **(1)**	chatterbox **(1)**	chase **(1)**

32   Theme 1: **Nature's Fury**
Assessment Tip: Total **15** Points

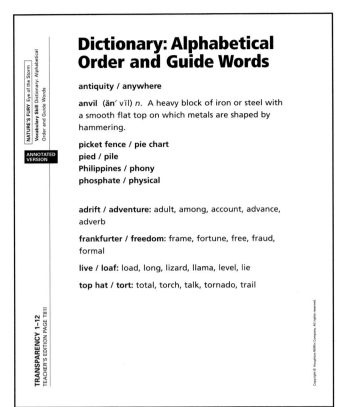

NATURE'S FURY Eye of the Storm
Vocabulary Skill Dictionary: Alphabetical
Order and Guide Words

**ANNOTATED
VERSION**

Dictionary: Alphabetical Order and Guide Words

antiquity / anywhere

anvil (ăn′ vĭl) *n.* A heavy block of iron or steel with
a smooth flat top on which metals are shaped by
hammering.

picket fence / pie chart
pied / pile
Philippines / phony
phosphate / physical

adrift / adventure: adult, among, account, advance,
adverb

frankfurter / freedom: frame, fortune, free, fraud,
formal

live / loaf: load, long, lizard, llama, level, lie

top hat / tort: total, torch, talk, tornado, trail

TRANSPARENCY 1–12
TEACHER'S EDITION PAGE T81I

Teacher's Book, page 81I

Eye of the Storm

Grammar Skill Conjunctions

Name _____

It's a Twister!

Conjunctions The words *and, or,* and *but* are **conjunctions.** A
conjunction may be used to join words in a sentence or to join
sentences. Use *and* to add information. Use *or* to give a choice.
Use *but* to show contrast.

■ Clouds **and** wind signal a coming storm.
This conjunction joins words.
■ I saw lightning, **and** I heard thunder.
This conjunction joins sentences.

Write the conjunction *and, or,* or *but* to best complete each sentence.
Then decide whether each conjunction you wrote joins words or joins
sentences. Write W after a sentence in which words are joined.
Write S after a sentence in which sentences are joined.

1. Kansas ___and___ Oklahoma have many tornadoes. _W_ **(2 points)**
2. Warren Faidley chases tornadoes _or/and_ thunderstorms. _W_ **(2)**
3. Warren has special equipment, ___and___ he has a special vehicle
to carry it. _S_ **(2)**
4. I have never seen a tornado, ___but___ I have seen lightning many
times. _S_ **(2)**
5. Go into a cellar ___or___ another low place if you see a funnel
cloud. _W_ **(2)**

Theme 1: **Nature's Fury**   33
Assessment Tip: Total **10** Points

Teacher's Book, page 81L

Eye of the Storm

Grammar Skill
Compound Sentences

Name _____

In Focus

Compound Sentences A **compound sentence** is made by joining two
closely related simple sentences with a comma and a conjunction.
I like to read.   } I like to read, but you like to write.
You like to write.

Draw a line from each simple sentence in column A to the most
closely related sentence in column B. Read all the choices before
you decide. Answers may vary. (**1 point** for each line.)

A	B
1. Zoe takes photos for the school paper	Zoe took pictures of the musicians.
2. Should Zoe use color film	Tom writes stories for the paper.
3. Color photos are nice	the photos in our newspaper are black and white.
4. Tom wrote about the school concert	should she use black and white film?

Now, write the sentences above and join them by using
conjunctions instead of lines. Don't forget to put a comma
before each conjunction!

1. Zoe takes photos for the school paper, and Tom writes
stories for the paper. **(1)**
2. Should Zoe use color film, or should she use black and
white film? **(1)**
3. Color photos are nice, but the photos in our newspaper
are black and white. **(1)**
4. Tom wrote about the school concert, and Zoe took
pictures of the musicians. **(1)**

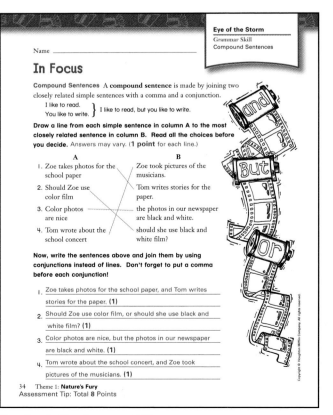

34   Theme 1: **Nature's Fury**
Assessment Tip: Total **8** Points

Teacher's Book, page 81L

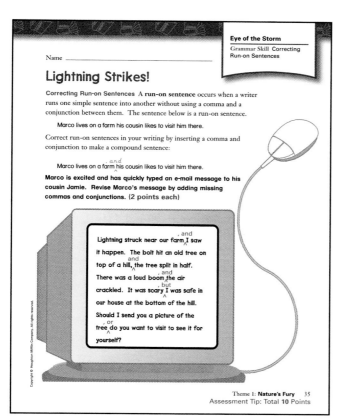

Lightning Strikes!

Name _____

Eye of the Storm
Grammar Skill Correcting
Run-on Sentences

Correcting Run-on Sentences A **run-on sentence** occurs when a writer runs one simple sentence into another without using a comma and a conjunction between them. The sentence below is a run-on sentence.

> Marco lives on a farm his cousin likes to visit him there.

Correct run-on sentences in your writing by inserting a comma and conjunction to make a compound sentence:

> Marco lives on a farm‚ and his cousin likes to visit him there.

Marco is excited and has quickly typed an e-mail message to his cousin Jamie. Revise Marco's message by adding missing commas and conjunctions. (2 points each)

> Lightning struck near our farm‚ and I saw
> it happen. The bolt hit an old tree on
> top of a hill‚ and the tree split in half.
> There was a loud boom‚ and the air
> crackled. It was scary‚ but I was safe in
> our house at the bottom of the hill.
> Should I send you a picture of the
> tree‚ or do you want to visit to see it for
> yourself?

Theme 1: **Nature's Fury**   35
Assessment Tip: Total **10** Points

Teacher's Book, page 81L

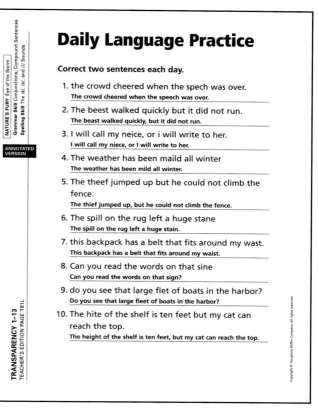

Daily Language Practice

Correct two sentences each day.

1. the crowd cheered when the spech was over.
   The crowd cheered when the speech was over.

2. The beest walked quickly but it did not run.
   The beast walked quickly, but it did not run.

3. I will call my neice, or i will write to her.
   I will call my niece, or I will write to her.

4. The weather has been maild all winter
   The weather has been mild all winter.

5. The theef jumped up but he could not climb the fence.
   The thief jumped up, but he could not climb the fence.

6. The spill on the rug left a huge stane
   The spill on the rug left a huge stain.

7. this backpack has a belt that fits around my wast.
   This backpack has a belt that fits around my waist.

8. Can you read the words on that sine
   Can you read the words on that sign?

9. do you see that large flet of boats in the harbor?
   Do you see that large fleet of boats in the harbor?

10. The hite of the shelf is ten feet but my cat can reach the top.
    The height of the shelf is ten feet, but my cat can reach the top.

Teacher's Book, page 81L

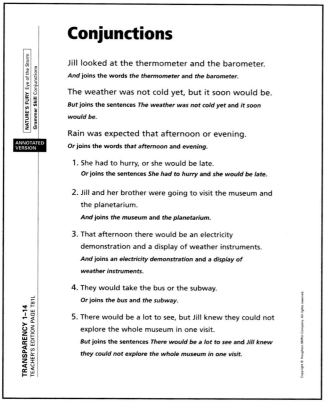

Conjunctions

Jill looked at the thermometer and the barometer.
And joins the words the thermometer and the barometer.

The weather was not cold yet, but it soon would be.
But joins the sentences The weather was not cold yet and it soon would be.

Rain was expected that afternoon or evening.
Or joins the words that afternoon and evening.

1. She had to hurry, or she would be late.
   Or joins the sentences She had to hurry and she would be late.

2. Jill and her brother were going to visit the museum and the planetarium.
   And joins the museum and the planetarium.

3. That afternoon there would be an electricity demonstration and a display of weather instruments.
   And joins an electricity demonstration and a display of weather instruments.

4. They would take the bus or the subway.
   Or joins the bus and the subway.

5. There would be a lot to see, but Jill knew they could not explore the whole museum in one visit.
   But joins the sentences There would be a lot to see and Jill knew they could not explore the whole museum in one visit.

Teacher's Book, page 81L

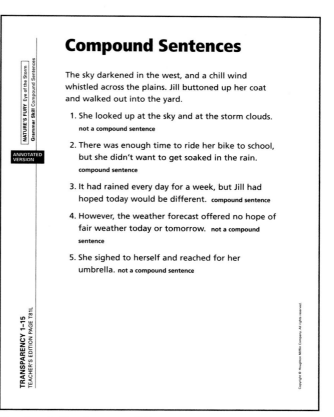

Compound Sentences

The sky darkened in the west, and a chill wind whistled across the plains. Jill buttoned up her coat and walked out into the yard.

1. She looked up at the sky and at the storm clouds.
   not a compound sentence

2. There was enough time to ride her bike to school, but she didn't want to get soaked in the rain.
   compound sentence

3. It had rained every day for a week, but Jill had hoped today would be different.   compound sentence

4. However, the weather forecast offered no hope of fair weather today or tomorrow.   not a compound sentence

5. She sighed to herself and reached for her umbrella.   not a compound sentence

Teacher's Book, page 81L

Lesson Planning Support *(Continued)*

Theme Resources

Lesson Planning Support

Write in Response to a Prompt

NATURE'S FURY *Eye of the Storm*
Writing Skill Write in Response to a Prompt

ANNOTATED VERSION

Prompt:

Explain why photographing tornadoes is difficult.

Response #1

Tornadoes are powerful forces that can cause great destruction. A tornado photographer never knows exactly when or where a tornado will touch down. Tornadoes are often accompanied by severe thunderstorms. Tornadoes happen when cool, dry air collides with warm, moist air. The results can be astonishing and dangerous. It's hard to get a good photo.

Response #2

Photographing a tornado is difficult because it takes luck, skill, and courage. No one can predict where and when a tornado will touch down. To photograph a tornado, a photographer must be in the right place at the right time. Even when a tornado comes into sight, following it is difficult. Tornado photographers can drive fast along roads, but they cannot cross fields and rivers the way a tornado does. Photographing tornadoes is also difficult because it is dangerous. Storm photographers must drive safely in bad weather, and they must stay a safe distance away from the tornadoes they are chasing.

TRANSPARENCY 1-16
TEACHER'S EDITION PAGE T81M

Copyright © Houghton Mifflin Company. All rights reserved.

Teacher's Book, page 81M

Capitalizing and Punctuating Sentences

NATURE'S FURY *Eye of the Storm*
Writing Skill Improving Your Writing

ANNOTATED VERSION

I think firefighters are true heroes. they rush inside burning buildings and they can never be sure what dangers they will meet? these dangers include exposure to poisonous fumes, collapsing floors, and extreme heat. Firefighters risk becoming trapped by flames, and they may also suffer smoke inhalation. in addition to courage, fighting fires requires great strength. Have you ever thought about how strong a person must be to carry a victim down a ladder or to break down a door? Firefighting is certainly one of the most dangerous and challenging jobs of all

I think firefighters are true heroes. They rush inside burning buildings, and they can never be sure what dangers they will meet. These dangers include exposure to poisonous fumes, collapsing floors, and extreme heat. Firefighters risk becoming trapped by flames, and they may also suffer smoke inhalation. In addition to courage, fighting fires requires great strength. Have you ever thought about how strong a person must be to carry a victim down a ladder or to break down a door? Firefighting is certainly one of the most dangerous and challenging jobs of all!

TRANSPARENCY 1-17
TEACHER'S EDITION PAGE T81M

Copyright © Houghton Mifflin Company. All rights reserved.

Teacher's Book, page 81M

Eye of the Storm

Writing Skill Response to a Prompt

Name _____

Responding to a Prompt

A **prompt** is a direction that asks for a written answer of one or more paragraphs. Read the following prompts.

Prompt 1
What job do you think is the most difficult or dangerous? Explain why you think it is difficult or dangerous.

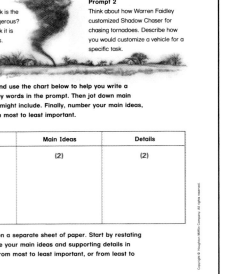

Prompt 2
Think about how Warren Faidley customized Shadow Chaser for chasing tornadoes. Describe how you would customize a vehicle for a specific task.

Choose one prompt and use the chart below to help you write a response. First, list key words in the prompt. Then jot down main ideas and details you might include. Finally, number your main ideas, beginning with 1, from most to least important.

Key Words	Main Ideas	Details
Prompt 1: explain **(1 point)** Prompt 2: describe	**(2)**	**(2)**

Write your response on a separate sheet of paper. Start by restating the prompt. Then write your main ideas and supporting details in order of importance from most to least important, or from least to most important. (5)

36   Theme 1: **Nature's Fury**
Assessment Tip: Total **10** Points

Copyright © Houghton Mifflin Company. All rights reserved.

Teacher's Book, page 81N

Eye of the Storm

Writing Skill Improving Your Writing

Name _____

Capitalizing and Punctuating Sentences

A fifth-grade class was given this writing prompt: **Warren Faidley is a storm chaser. Summarize what he does for a living.** One fifth grader wrote the response below but forgot to check for capitalization and punctuation errors.

Use these proofreading marks to add the necessary capital letters and end punctuation. (1 point each)

- ⊙ Add a period.
- ≡ Make a capital letter.
- ∧! Add an exclamation point.
- ∧? Add a question mark.

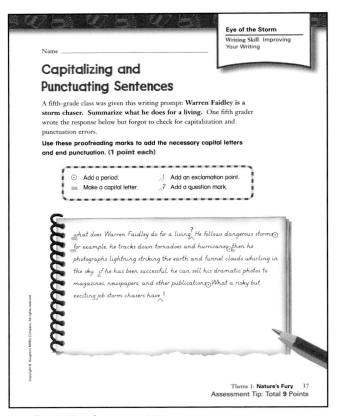

what does Warren Faidley do for a living? He follows dangerous storms. for example, he tracks down tornadoes and hurricanes. then he photographs lightning striking the earth and funnel clouds whirling in the sky. if he has been successful, he can sell his dramatic photos to magazines, newspapers, and other publications. What a risky but exciting job storm chasers have!

Theme 1: **Nature's Fury**   37
Assessment Tip: Total **9** Points

Copyright © Houghton Mifflin Company. All rights reserved.

Teacher's Book, page 81N

R52   THEME 1: **Nature's Fury**

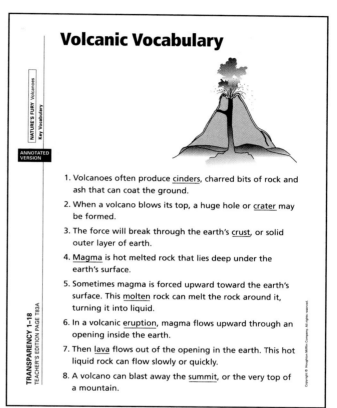

Teacher's Book, page 83A

Teacher's Book, page 83A

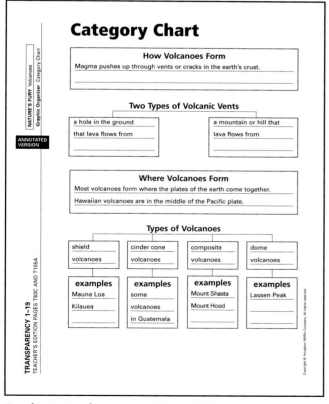

Teacher's Book, pages 83C and 105A

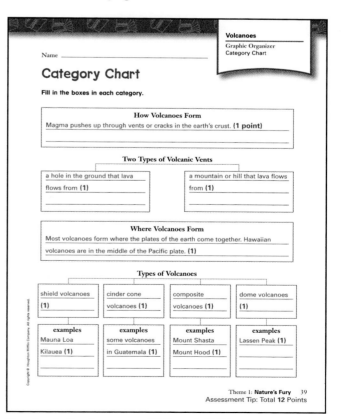

Teacher's Book, pages 83C and 105A

Teacher's Book, page 101

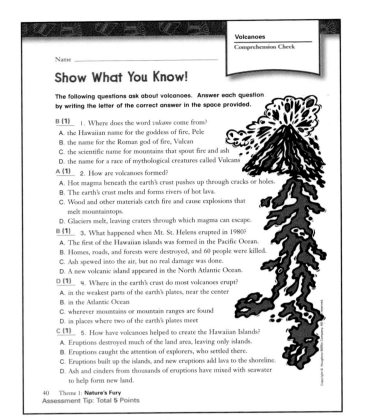

Volcanoes
Comprehension Check

Name _____

Show What You Know!

The following questions ask about volcanoes. Answer each question by writing the letter of the correct answer in the space provided.

B (1) 1. Where does the word *volcano* come from?
A. the Hawaiian name for the goddess of fire, Pele
B. the name for the Roman god of fire, Vulcan
C. the scientific name for mountains that spout fire and ash
D. the name for a race of mythological creatures called Vulcans

A (1) 2. How are volcanoes formed?
A. Hot magma beneath the earth's crust pushes up through cracks or holes.
B. The earth's crust melts and forms rivers of hot lava.
C. Wood and other materials catch fire and cause explosions that melt mountaintops.
D. Glaciers melt, leaving craters through which magma can escape.

B (1) 3. What happened when Mt. St. Helens erupted in 1980?
A. The first of the Hawaiian islands was formed in the Pacific Ocean.
B. Homes, roads, and forests were destroyed, and 60 people were killed.
C. Ash spewed into the air, but no real damage was done.
D. A new volcanic island appeared in the North Atlantic Ocean.

D (1) 4. Where in the earth's crust do most volcanoes erupt?
A. in the weakest parts of the earth's plates, near the center
B. in the Atlantic Ocean
C. wherever mountains or mountain ranges are found
D. in places where two of the earth's plates meet

C (1) 5. How have volcanoes helped to create the Hawaiian Islands?
A. Eruptions destroyed much of the land area, leaving only islands.
B. Eruptions caught the attention of explorers, who settled there.
C. Eruptions built up the islands, and new eruptions add lava to the shoreline.
D. Ash and cinders from thousands of eruptions have mixed with seawater to help form new land.

40   Theme 1: **Nature's Fury**
Assessment Tip: Total **5** Points

Teacher's Book, page 101

Teacher's Book, page 105B

Volcanoes
Comprehension Skill
Categorize and Classify

Name _____

Classifying Clouds

Read the article. Then complete the activity on page 42.

Clouds

Clouds come in a variety of forms and colors. They occur at different heights. Some are made of water and some of ice. With all these differences, a good way to identify clouds is by their groups.

Clouds are grouped by how high above the earth they are found. Low clouds are usually not more than 6,000 feet above sea level. They include stratus and stratocumulus clouds. A stratus cloud looks like a smooth sheet, while stratocumulus clouds are lumpy. They look like fluffy gray piles of cotton.

Middle clouds form between 6,000 and 20,000 feet. They include altostratus, altocumulus, and nimbostratus clouds. An altostratus cloud forms a white or gray sheet. Altocumulus clouds appear as fluffy piles that may be separated or connected in a lumpy mass. Nimbostratus clouds look like a smooth, gray layer. Rain or snow often falls from them, making them hard to see.

High clouds form above 20,000 feet. Unlike other kinds of clouds, which are made of water droplets, these clouds consist of ice crystals. Cirrus, cirrostratus, and cirrocumulus are types of high clouds. Cirrus clouds are very high in the sky and have a feathery appearance. A cirrostratus cloud is a very thin cloud layer. Cirrocumulus clouds look like millions of bits of fluff high in the sky.

Theme 1: **Nature's Fury**   41

Teacher's Book, page 105B

Teacher's Book, page 105B (continued)

Volcanoes
Comprehension Skill
Categorize and Classify

Name _____

Classifying Clouds   continued

Follow the directions or answer the questions based on the article.

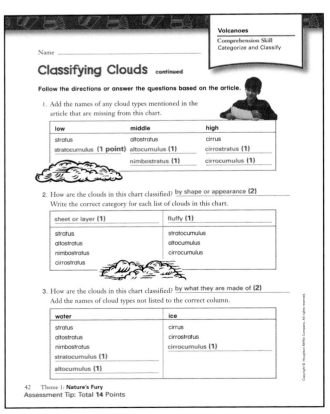

1. Add the names of any cloud types mentioned in the article that are missing from this chart.

low	middle	high
stratus	altostratus	cirrus
stratocumulus **(1 point)**	altocumulus **(1)**	cirrostratus **(1)**
	nimbostratus **(1)**	cirrocumulus **(1)**

2. How are the clouds in this chart classified? by shape or appearance **(2)**
Write the correct category for each list of clouds in this chart.

sheet or layer **(1)**	fluffy **(1)**
stratus	stratocumulus
altostratus	altocumulus
nimbostratus	cirrocumulus
cirrostratus	

3. How are the clouds in this chart classified? by what they are made of **(2)**
Add the names of cloud types not listed to the correct column.

water	ice
stratus	cirrus
altostratus	cirrostratus
nimbostratus	cirrocumulus **(1)**
stratocumulus **(1)**	
altocumulus **(1)**	

42   Theme 1: **Nature's Fury**
Assessment Tip: Total **14** Points

Teacher's Book, page 105B

Teacher's Book, page 105C

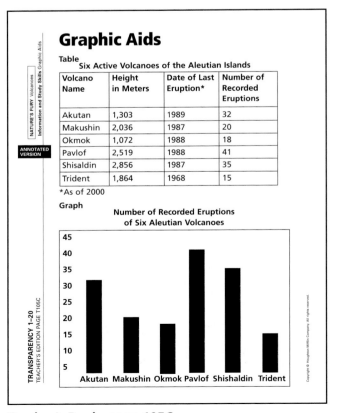

NATURE'S FURY Volcanoes
Information and Study Skills Graphic Aids

ANNOTATED VERSION

Graphic Aids

Table
Six Active Volcanoes of the Aleutian Islands

Volcano Name	Height in Meters	Date of Last Eruption*	Number of Recorded Eruptions
Akutan	1,303	1989	32
Makushin	2,036	1987	20
Okmok	1,072	1988	18
Pavlof	2,519	1988	41
Shisaldin	2,856	1987	35
Trident	1,864	1968	15

*As of 2000

Graph

Number of Recorded Eruptions of Six Aleutian Volcanoes

(bar graph with values: Akutan ~32, Makushin ~20, Okmok ~18, Pavlof ~41, Shishaldin ~35, Trident ~15; y-axis from 5 to 45)

TRANSPARENCY 1–20
TEACHER'S EDITION PAGE T105C

Teacher's Book, page 105C

Worksheet 1 (Teacher's Book, page 105F)

Name _____

Volcanoes

Structural Analysis Word
Roots *-struct* and *-rupt*

Construct a Word

Read each sentence. Then, using two or three columns in the chart, build a word containing the root *-struct* or *-rupt* that completes the sentence. Write the word on the line.

de	rupt	ive
dis	struct	or
con		ion
e		ure
inter		
in		

1. Sam's swimming <u>instructor **(1 point)**</u>
   taught him how to do the backstroke.

2. I watched the <u>eruption **(1)**</u> of the
   volcano from my window.

3. We helped our cousin <u>construct **(1)**</u> a tree house
   in the backyard.

4. The hurricane left a path of <u>destruction **(1)**</u>
   along the coast.

5. Please don't <u>interrupt **(1)**</u> me when
   I'm talking!

6. The noise in the hall was very <u>disruptive **(1)**</u>
   during our rehearsal.

7. The leak was caused by a <u>rupture **(1)**</u>
   in the pipeline.

8. The children sat on top of the climbing
   <u>structure **(1)**</u> in the playground.

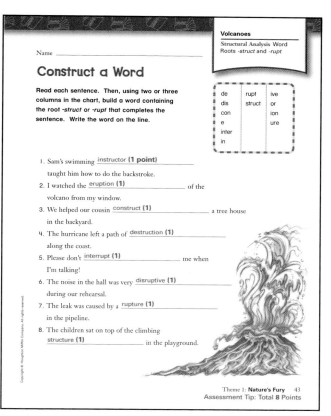

Theme 1: **Nature's Fury** 43
Assessment Tip: Total **8** Points

Teacher's Book, page 105F

Worksheet 2 (Teacher's Book, page 105H)

Name _____

Volcanoes

Spelling The /ō/, /ōō/, and
/yōō/ Sounds

The /ō/, /ōō/, and /yōō/ Sounds

When you hear the /ō/ sound, think of the patterns
o-consonant-e, oa, ow, and *o*. When you hear the /ōō/ and the
/yōō/ sounds, think of the patterns *u-consonant-e, ue, ew, oo,
ui,* and *ou*. Order of answers for each category may vary.

/ō/ slope, boast, thrown, stroll
/ōō/ or /yōō/ rule, clue, dew, choose, cruise, route

Write each Spelling Word under its vowel sound.

/ō/ Sound

thrown **(1 point)**	loaf **(1)**
stole **(1)**	growth **(1)**
boast **(1)**	slope **(1)**
stroll **(1)**	flow **(1)**

/ōō/ or /yōō/ Sounds

clue **(1)**	mood **(1)**
dew **(1)**	youth **(1)**
choose **(1)**	bruise **(1)**
rule **(1)**	loose **(1)**
cruise **(1)**	rude **(1)**
route **(1)**	flute **(1)**

Spelling Words

1. thrown
2. stole
3. clue
4. dew
5. choose
6. rule
7. boast
8. cruise
9. stroll
10. route
11. mood
12. loaf
13. growth
14. youth
15. slope
16. bruise
17. loose
18. rude
19. flow
20. flute

44 Theme 1: **Nature's Fury**
Assessment Tip: Total **20** Points

Teacher's Book, page 105H

Worksheet 3 (Teacher's Book, page 105H)

Name _____

Volcanoes

Spelling The /ō/, /ōō/, and
/yōō/ Sounds

Spelling Spree

Letter Swap Write a Spelling Word by changing the underlined letter to a different letter.

1. st<u>a</u>le <u>stole **(1 point)**</u>
2. l<u>ou</u>se <u>loose **(1)**</u>
3. cl<u>u</u>b <u>clue **(1)**</u>
4. lo<u>a</u>d <u>loaf **(1)**</u>
5. r<u>o</u>le <u>rule **(1)**</u>
6. to<u>a</u>st <u>boast **(1)**</u>
7. mo<u>o</u>n <u>mood **(1)**</u>
8. d<u>e</u>n <u>dew **(1)**</u>

Word Switch Write a Spelling Word to replace each underlined definition in the sentences. Write your words on the lines.

9. My parents are taking a <u>sea voyage for pleasure</u> on that ship.
10. Which item did you <u>pick out</u> from the catalog?
11. Many people are active in sports in their <u>time of life before adulthood.</u>
12. You can use a ruler to measure the <u>increase in size</u> of the plant.
13. I play the <u>woodwind instrument shaped like a tube</u> in the band.
14. A clerk should never be <u>lacking in courtesy</u> to a shopper.
15. Would you care to <u>walk slowly</u> down the beach with me?

9. <u>cruise **(1)**</u>
10. <u>choose **(1)**</u>
11. <u>youth **(1)**</u>
12. <u>growth **(1)**</u>
13. <u>flute **(1)**</u>
14. <u>rude **(1)**</u>
15. <u>stroll **(1)**</u>

Spelling Words

1. thrown
2. stole
3. clue
4. dew
5. choose
6. rule
7. boast
8. cruise
9. stroll
10. route
11. mood
12. loaf
13. growth
14. youth
15. slope
16. bruise
17. loose
18. rude
19. flow
20. flute

fⱷlow

Theme 1: **Nature's Fury** 45
Assessment Tip: Total **15** Points

Teacher's Book, page 105H

Worksheet 4 (Teacher's Book, page 105H)

Name _____

Volcanoes

Spelling The /ō/, /ōō/, and
/yōō/ Sounds

Proofreading and Writing

Proofreading Circle the five misspelled Spelling Words in this paragraph from a personal narrative. Then write each word correctly.

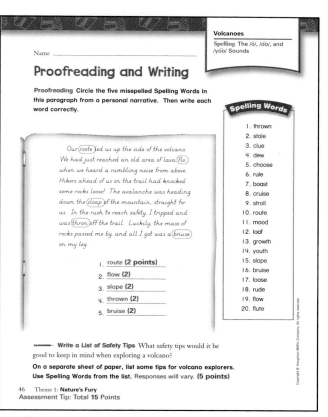

Our *roote* led us up the side of the volcano. We had just reached an old area of lava *flo* when we heard a rumbling noise from above. Hikers ahead of us on the trail had knocked some rocks loose! The avalanche was heading down the *sloap* of the mountain, straight for us. In the rush to reach safety, I tripped and was *thron* off the trail. Luckily, the mass of rocks passed me by, and all I got was a *briuse* on my leg.

1. <u>route **(2 points)**</u>
2. <u>flow **(2)**</u>
3. <u>slope **(2)**</u>
4. <u>thrown **(2)**</u>
5. <u>bruise **(2)**</u>

Spelling Words

1. thrown
2. stole
3. clue
4. dew
5. choose
6. rule
7. boast
8. cruise
9. stroll
10. route
11. mood
12. loaf
13. growth
14. youth
15. slope
16. bruise
17. loose
18. rude
19. flow
20. flute

Write a List of Safety Tips What safety tips would it be good to keep in mind when exploring a volcano?

On a separate sheet of paper, list some tips for volcano explorers. Use Spelling Words from the list. Responses will vary. **(5 points)**

46 Theme 1: **Nature's Fury**
Assessment Tip: Total **15** Points

Teacher's Book, page 105H

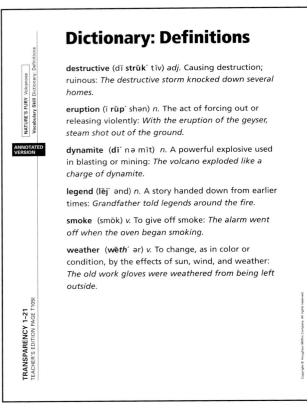

Teacher's Book, page 105H

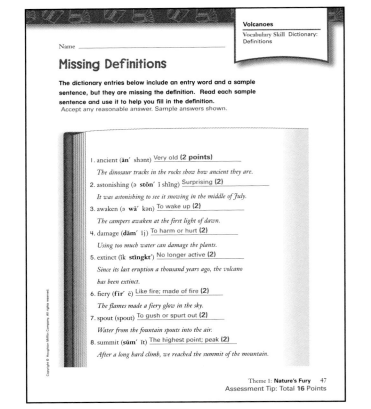

Teacher's Book, page 105I

Teacher's Book, page 105I

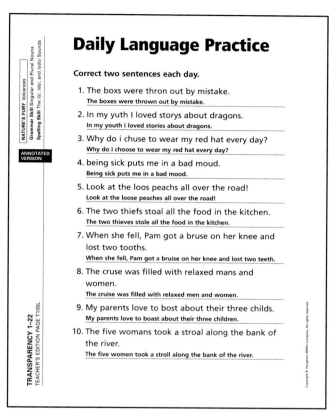

Daily Language Practice

Correct two sentences each day.

1. The boxs were thron out by mistake.
   The boxes were thrown out by mistake.

2. In my yuth I loved storys about dragons.
   In my youth I loved stories about dragons.

3. Why do i chuse to wear my red hat every day?
   Why do I choose to wear my red hat every day?

4. being sick puts me in a bad moud.
   Being sick puts me in a bad mood.

5. Look at the loos peachs all over the road!
   Look at the loose peaches all over the road!

6. The two thiefs stoal all the food in the kitchen.
   The two thieves stole all the food in the kitchen.

7. When she fell, Pam got a bruse on her knee and lost two tooths.
   When she fell, Pam got a bruise on her knee and lost two teeth.

8. The cruse was filled with relaxed mans and women.
   The cruise was filled with relaxed men and women.

9. My parents love to bost about their three childs.
   My parents love to boast about their three children.

10. The five womans took a stroal along the bank of the river.
    The five women took a stroll along the bank of the river.

NATURE'S FURY Volcanoes
Grammar Skill Singular and Plural Nouns
Spelling Skill The /ŏ/, /ōō/, and /yōō/ Sounds

ANNOTATED VERSION

TRANSPARENCY 1–22
TEACHER'S EDITION PAGE T105L

Teacher's Book, page 105L

Lesson Planning Support

Singular and Plural Nouns

The forest stretched between two deep valleys.
singular noun forest/plural noun valleys

Slim birches grew beside an eddy in the stream.
singular nouns eddy, stream/plural noun birches

The hiker had an impulse to make a sketch of the ferns and mosses.
singular nouns hiker, impulse, sketch/plural nouns ferns, mosses

A bear was eating wild blackberries while a bluejay scolded him.
singular nouns bear, bluejay/plural noun blackberries

- A noun names a person, place, thing, or idea.
  plural nouns valleys, birches, ferns, mosses, blackberries

- To form the plural of most nouns, add -s or -es.
  plural nouns valleys, birches, ferns, mosses; singular nouns to plural forests, streams, hikers, impulses, bears, bluejays

- To form the plural of a noun ending with x, s, ch, sh, or ss, add -es.
  plural nouns birches, mosses; singular noun to plural sketches

- To form the plural of a noun ending with a consonant + y, change the y to i and add -es.
  eddies, blackberries; singular noun to plural eddies

- To form the plural of a noun ending with a vowel + y, add -s.
  valleys; singular noun to plural bluejays

Additional plural nouns will vary.

NATURE'S FURY Volcanoes
Grammar Skill Singular and Plural Nouns

ANNOTATED VERSION

TRANSPARENCY 1–23
TEACHER'S EDITION PAGE T105L

Teacher's Book, page 105L

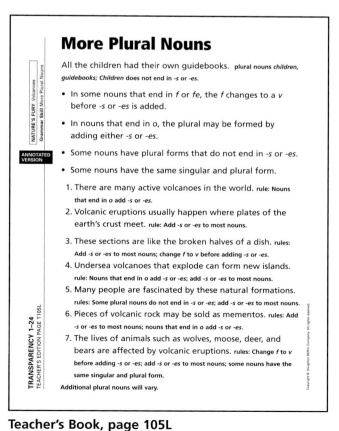

More Plural Nouns

All the children had their own guidebooks. *plural nouns children, guidebooks; Children does not end in -s or -es.*

- In some nouns that end in f or fe, the f changes to a v before -s or -es is added.

- In nouns that end in o, the plural may be formed by adding either -s or -es.

- Some nouns have plural forms that do not end in -s or -es.

- Some nouns have the same singular and plural form.

1. There are many active volcanoes in the world. *rule: Nouns that end in o add -s or -es.*

2. Volcanic eruptions usually happen where plates of the earth's crust meet. *rule: Add -s or -es to most nouns.*

3. These sections are like the broken halves of a dish. *rules: Add -s or -es to most nouns; change f to v before adding -s or -es.*

4. Undersea volcanoes that explode can form new islands. *rule: Nouns that end in o add -s or -es; add -s or -es to most nouns.*

5. Many people are fascinated by these natural formations. *rules: Some plural nouns do not end in -s or -es; add -s or -es to most nouns.*

6. Pieces of volcanic rock may be sold as mementos. *rules: Add -s or -es to most nouns; nouns that end in o add -s or -es.*

7. The lives of animals such as wolves, moose, deer, and bears are affected by volcanic eruptions. *rules: Change f to v before adding -s or -es; add -s or -es to most nouns; some nouns have the same singular and plural form.*

Additional plural nouns will vary.

NATURE'S FURY Volcanoes
Grammar Skill More Plural Nouns

ANNOTATED VERSION

TRANSPARENCY 1–24
TEACHER'S EDITION PAGE T105L

Teacher's Book, page 105L

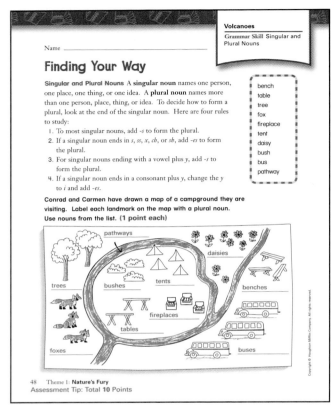

Volcanoes

Grammar Skill Singular and Plural Nouns

Name _____

Finding Your Way

Singular and Plural Nouns A **singular noun** names one person, one place, one thing, or one idea. A **plural noun** names more than one person, place, thing, or idea. To decide how to form a plural, look at the end of the singular noun. Here are four rules to study:

1. To most singular nouns, add -*s* to form the plural.
2. If a singular noun ends in *s, ss, x, ch,* or *sh,* add -*es* to form the plural.
3. For singular nouns ending with a vowel plus *y,* add -*s* to form the plural.
4. If a singular noun ends in a consonant plus *y,* change the *y* to *i* and add -*es.*

bench
table
tree
fox
fireplace
tent
daisy
bush
bus
pathway

Conrad and Carmen have drawn a map of a campground they are visiting. Label each landmark on the map with a plural noun. Use nouns from the list. (1 point each)

48   Theme 1: **Nature's Fury**
Assessment Tip: Total **10** Points

Teacher's Book, page 105L

Volcanoes

Grammar Skill More Plural Nouns

Name _____

Science Fair

More Plural Nouns Here are a few more rules for forming plurals:

1. To form the plural of some nouns ending in *f* or *fe,* change the *f* to *v* and add -*es.* For others ending in *f,* simply add -*s.*
2. To form the plural of nouns ending with a vowel plus *o,* add -*s.*
3. To form the plural of nouns ending with a consonant plus *o,* add -*s* or -*es.*
4. Some nouns have special plural forms.
5. Some nouns are the same in the singular and the plural.

For the science fair, Jody made a model of the volcano Mount Saint Helens and wrote a report about it. Jody isn't sure how to form the plural of some words in her report. She made a list of these words.

Write the plural next to each word on Jody's list. Check your dictionary if you are unsure of a plural.

leaf	leaves **(1 point)**
child	children **(1)**
volcano	volcanoes **(1)**
man	men **(1)**
ash	ashes **(1)**
home	homes **(1)**
deer	deer **(1)**
woman	women **(1)**
plant	plants **(1)**
mouse	mice **(1)**

Theme 1: **Nature's Fury**   49
Assessment Tip: Total **10** Points

Teacher's Book, page 105L

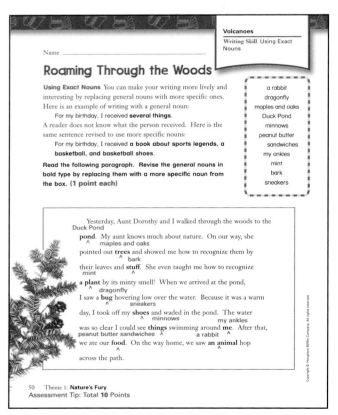

Volcanoes

Writing Skill Using Exact Nouns

Name _____

Roaming Through the Woods

Using Exact Nouns You can make your writing more lively and interesting by replacing general nouns with more specific ones. Here is an example of writing with a general noun:

For my birthday, I received **several things.**

A reader does not know what the person received. Here is the same sentence revised to use more specific nouns:

For my birthday, I received **a book about sports legends, a basketball, and basketball shoes.**

Read the following paragraph. Revise the general nouns in bold type by replacing them with a more specific noun from the box. (1 point each)

a rabbit
dragonfly
maples and oaks
Duck Pond
minnows
peanut butter
sandwiches
my ankles
mint
bark
sneakers

Yesterday, Aunt Dorothy and I walked through the woods to the
Duck Pond
pond. My aunt knows much about nature. On our way, she
         ^   maples and oaks
pointed out **trees** and showed me how to recognize them by
                                          ^ bark
their leaves and **stuff.** She even taught me how to recognize
                  mint
a plant by its minty smell! When we arrived at the pond,
        ^ dragonfly
I saw a **bug** hovering low over the water. Because it was a warm
                ^ sneakers
day, I took off my **shoes** and waded in the pond. The water
                   ^ minnows   my ankles
was so clear I could see **things** swimming around **me.** After that,
peanut butter sandwiches ^   a rabbit
we ate our **food.** On the way home, we saw **an animal** hop
                                             ^
across the path.

50   Theme 1: **Nature's Fury**
Assessment Tip: Total **10** Points

Teacher's Book, page 105L

A Paragraph of Information

Mauna Loa is located on the big island of Hawaii. It is the world's largest active volcano, rising more than 13,000 feet above sea level. Mauna Loa has a long history of volcanic activity. In 1855 and 1856, it erupted continuously for eighteen months. In 1926, lava from an eruption destroyed a fishing village. In 1950, the city of Hilo was threatened by a river of lava, which stopped only four miles from the city. Mauna Loa continues to erupt every few years, and as it erupts, it continues to grow. Thousands of overlapping lava flows have dried one atop another to form Mauna Loa.

Teacher's Book, page 105M

Correcting Sentence Fragments

Italy's Mount Vesuvius. One of the world's most famous volcanoes. Its best-known eruption occurred on August 24, A.D. 79. On that day, a violent explosion of rocks, ash, and lava. A river of lava swiftly buried the cities that lay beneath. In the centuries that followed, many destructive eruptions occurred. People around the world, fascinated by Vesuvius. In the early part of the twentieth century, thousands of visitors came to Vesuvius each year for a firsthand look at flowing lava. A cable railway. Took visitors down into the cone. There they could view a red stream of glowing lava. The cable railway was destroyed in 1944 by an eruption. Vesuvius has been frequently studied by scientists. Because it erupts often and is easy to reach. In fact, Vesuvius is the most carefully studied volcano in the world.

Answers will vary. Sample answers shown.

Italy's Mount Vesuvius is one of the world's most famous volcanoes. Its best-known eruption occurred on August 24, A.D. 79. On that day, a violent explosion of rocks, ash, and lava spewed from the volcano. A river of lava swiftly buried the cities that lay beneath. In the centuries that followed, many destructive eruptions occurred. People around the world were fascinated by Vesuvius. In the early part of the twentieth century, thousands of visitors came to Vesuvius each year for a firsthand look at flowing lava. A cable railway took visitors down into the cone. There they could view a red stream of glowing lava. The cable railway was destroyed in 1944 by an eruption. Vesuvius has been frequently studied by scientists because it erupts often and is easy to reach. In fact, Vesuvius is the most carefully studied volcano in the world.

Teacher's Book, page 105M

Volcanoes

Writing Skill Paragraph of Information

Name _____

Writing a Paragraph of Information

Read the following paragraph of information from page 87 of *Volcanoes.*

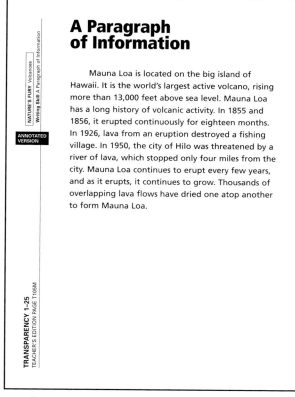

Volcanoes are formed by cracks or holes that poke through the earth's crust. Magma pushes its way up through the cracks. This is called a volcanic eruption. When magma pours onto the surface it is called lava.... As lava cools, it hardens to form rock.

Now get ready to write your own paragraph of information about volcanoes. Use the following graphic organizer to help you organize your paragraph. (5 points)

Topic

Topic Sentence

Supporting Sentences

Now, write your paragraph of information on a separate sheet of paper. Arrange your supporting sentences in a logical order, and make sure all of the sentences contain facts about the topic. (5 points)

Theme 1: **Nature's Fury**   51
Assessment Tip: Total **10** Points

Teacher's Book, page 105N

Volcanoes

Writing Skill Improving Your Writing

Name _____

Correcting Sentence Fragments

A sentence fragment is a group of words that is missing either a subject or a predicate. The following groups of words are sentence fragments. Turn them into complete sentences by adding either a subject or a predicate. Write the complete sentence on the lines. Responses will vary.

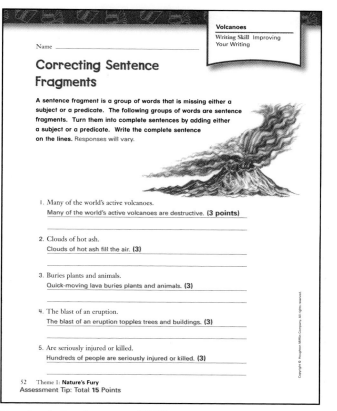

1. Many of the world's active volcanoes.
   Many of the world's active volcanoes are destructive. **(3 points)**

2. Clouds of hot ash.
   Clouds of hot ash fill the air. **(3)**

3. Buries plants and animals.
   Quick-moving lava buries plants and animals. **(3)**

4. The blast of an eruption.
   The blast of an eruption topples trees and buildings. **(3)**

5. Are seriously injured or killed.
   Hundreds of people are seriously injured or killed. **(3)**

52   Theme 1: **Nature's Fury**
Assessment Tip: Total **15** Points

Teacher's Book, page 105N

Worksheet 1 (top left)

Nature's Fury
Taking Tests

Name _____

Choosing the Best Answer

Use the test-taking strategies and tips you have learned to help you answer multiple-choice questions. This practice will help you when you take this kind of test.

Read each question. Choose the best answer. Fill in the circle in the answer row.

1 At the beginning of the story, why did Jonathan think that Moose was acting strangely?
   A He thought Moose knew that Jonathan was worried about his mother.
   B He thought Moose was looking for Mrs. Smith, who lived next door.
   C He thought Moose knew there was going to be an earthquake.
   D He thought Moose saw the children's father driving into the campground.

2 When did Jonathan plan to listen to the baseball game on the radio?
   F After he hitched the car to the trailer.
   G After he found out how his mother was
   H After he took Moose for a walk
   J After Abby was in bed

3 When Jonathan and Abby first heard the rumbling noise, what did they think it was?
   A An earthquake   C A bomb
   B Thunder   D Rifles

4 Why couldn't Jonathan get to Abby during the earthquake?
   F He couldn't see where she was.
   G Birch trees fell on top of him.
   H He couldn't keep his balance.
   J He fell into the river.

ANSWER ROWS 1 ● Ⓑ Ⓒ Ⓓ (5 points)   3 Ⓐ ● Ⓒ Ⓓ (5)
             2 Ⓕ Ⓖ Ⓗ ● (5)   4 Ⓕ Ⓖ ● Ⓙ (5)

Theme 1: **Nature's Fury**   53

Teacher's Book, page 106

Worksheet 2 (top right)

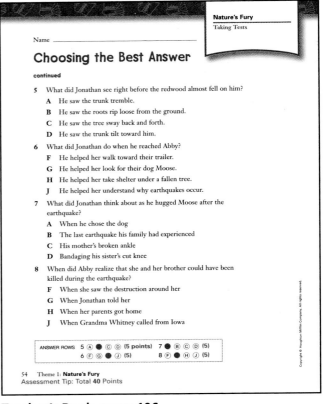

Nature's Fury
Taking Tests

Name _____

Choosing the Best Answer

continued

5 What did Jonathan see right before the redwood almost fell on him?
   A He saw the trunk tremble.
   B He saw the roots rip loose from the ground.
   C He saw the tree sway back and forth.
   D He saw the trunk tilt toward him.

6 What did Jonathan do when he reached Abby?
   F He helped her walk toward their trailer.
   G He helped her look for their dog Moose.
   H He helped her take shelter under a fallen tree.
   J He helped her understand why earthquakes occur.

7 What did Jonathan think about as he hugged Moose after the earthquake?
   A When he chose the dog
   B The last earthquake his family had experienced
   C His mother's broken ankle
   D Bandaging his sister's cut knee

8 When did Abby realize that she and her brother could have been killed during the earthquake?
   F When she saw the destruction around her
   G When Jonathan told her
   H When her parents got home
   J When Grandma Whitney called from Iowa

ANSWER ROWS 5 Ⓐ ● Ⓒ Ⓓ (5 points)   7 Ⓐ ● Ⓒ Ⓓ (5)
             6 Ⓕ Ⓖ ● Ⓙ (5)   8 Ⓕ ● Ⓗ Ⓙ (5)

54   Theme 1: **Nature's Fury**
Assessment Tip: Total **40** Points

Teacher's Book, page 106

Worksheet 3 (bottom left)

Nature's Fury:
Theme 1 Wrap-Up

Spelling Review

Name _____

Spelling Review

Write Spelling Words from the list on this page to answer the questions.
Order of answers in each category may vary.

1–9. Which nine words have a short vowel sound?

1. fond **(1 point)**   6. bunk **(1)**
2. swift **(1)**   7. dwell **(1)**
3. slept **(1)**   8. split **(1)**
4. staff **(1)**   9. crush **(1)**
5. grasp **(1)**

10–19. Which ten words have the /ā/, /ē/, or /ī/ sound?

10. beast **(1)**   15. strike **(1)**
11. fleet **(1)**   16. slight **(1)**
12. thigh **(1)**   17. claim **(1)**
13. fade **(1)**   18. sway **(1)**
14. praise **(1)**   19. mild **(1)**

20–30. Which eleven words have the /ō/, /yōō/, or /ōō/ sound?

20. flute **(1)**   26. stroll **(1)**
21. dew **(1)**   27. cruise **(1)**
22. clue **(1)**   28. mood **(1)**
23. slope **(1)**   29. youth **(1)**
24. boast **(1)**   30. thrown **(1)**
25. stole **(1)**

Spelling Words
1. fond
2. swift
3. beast
4. slept
5. fleet
6. staff
7. flute
8. grasp
9. thigh
10. dew
11. bunk
12. fade
13. dwell
14. strike
15. praise
16. slight
17. split
18. claim
19. sway
20. mild
21. clue
22. slope
23. boast
24. stole
25. stroll
26. cruise
27. mood
28. crush
29. youth
30. thrown

Theme 1: **Nature's Fury**   55
Assessment Tip: Total **30** Points

Teacher's Book, page 107

Worksheet 4 (bottom right)

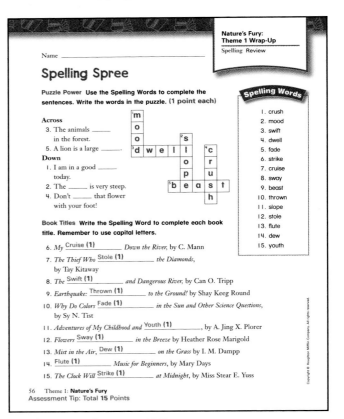

Nature's Fury:
Theme 1 Wrap-Up

Spelling Review

Name _____

Spelling Spree

Puzzle Power Use the Spelling Words to complete the sentences. Write the words in the puzzle. (1 point each)

Across
3. The animals _____ in the forest.
5. A lion is a large _____.

Down
1. I am in a good _____ today.
2. The _____ is very steep.
4. Don't _____ that flower with your foot!

Crossword puzzle answers:
- m o o (down 1)
- d w e l l (across 3)
- s (down 2)
- c r u (down 4)
- b e a s t (across 5)
- h

Book Titles Write the Spelling Word to complete each book title. Remember to use capital letters.

6. *My* Cruise **(1)** *Down the River,* by C. Mann
7. *The Thief Who* Stole **(1)** *the Diamonds,* by Tay Kitaway
8. *The* Swift **(1)** *and Dangerous River,* by Can O. Tripp
9. *Earthquake:* Thrown **(1)** *to the Ground!* by Shay Keeg Round
10. *Why Do Colors* Fade **(1)** *in the Sun and Other Science Questions,* by Sy N. Tist
11. *Adventures of My Childhood and* Youth **(1)** *,* by A. Jing X. Plorer
12. *Flowers* Sway **(1)** *in the Breeze* by Heather Rose Marigold
13. *Mist in the Air,* Dew **(1)** *on the Grass* by I. M. Dampp
14. Flute **(1)** *Music for Beginners,* by Mary Days
15. *The Clock Will* Strike **(1)** *at Midnight,* by Miss Stear E. Yuss

Spelling Words
1. crush
2. mood
3. swift
4. dwell
5. fade
6. strike
7. cruise
8. sway
9. beast
10. thrown
11. slope
12. stole
13. flute
14. dew
15. youth

56   Theme 1: **Nature's Fury**
Assessment Tip: Total **15** Points

Teacher's Book, page 107

THEME 1: **Nature's Fury**

Teacher's Book, page 107 (top left)

Name _____

Nature's Fury:
Theme 1 Wrap-Up
Spelling Review

Proofreading and Writing

Proofreading Circle the six misspelled Spelling Words in this newspaper article. Then write each word correctly.

At 11:30 last night, a (milde) earthquake gently rocked the city. Little damage was reported, and some people (sleept) right through it. This morning Helen and Joe Dalton (boste) that they were not afraid. There was only (slite) damage downtown. With (prayse) for his workers, the mayor said, "My (staf) responded quickly to all questions."

Spelling Words

1. slept
2. praise
3. fond
4. clue
5. staff
6. thigh
7. stroll
8. slight
9. claim
10. fleet
11. mild
12. grasp
13. split
14. bunk
15. boast

1. mild **(1 point)**   4. slight **(1)**
2. slept **(1)**   5. praise **(1)**
3. boast **(1)**   6. staff **(1)**

In the News A reporter takes notes after an earthquake. Complete his ideas by writing Spelling Words in the blanks.

- No one is fond **(1)** of surprises like this.
- Scientists have no clue **(1)** about why this quake occurred at night.
- It is a strange time to stroll **(1)** through town!
- I'd rather be in my bunk **(1)** sleeping.
- A man has cuts on his thigh **(1)** and ankle.
- A large fleet **(1)** of fire trucks roars by.
- Large crevice in ground. Oak street is split **(1)** in two!
- It's hard to fully grasp **(1)** the power of a quake.
- Some people claim **(1)** that animals can predict earthquakes.

Write a Safety Plan On a separate sheet of paper, write about what you should do in an earthquake. Use the Spelling Review Words. Responses will vary. **(5 points)**

Theme 1: **Nature's Fury**   57
Assessment Tip: Total **20** Points

Teacher's Book, page 107

Teacher's Book, page 107 (top right)

Take-Home Word List	Take-Home Word List	Take-Home Word List
Michelle Kwan: Heart of a Champion	**Nature's Fury Spelling Review**	**Volcanoes**
Compound Words wheel + chair = wheelchair up + to + date = up-to-date first + aid = first aid	**Spelling Words**	**The /ō/, /o͞o/, and /yo͞o/ Sounds** /ō/ → stole, boast, thrown, stroll /o͞o/ or → rule, clue, /yo͞o/ dew, mood, cruise, route

Nature's Fury Spelling Review – Spelling Words

1. slept   16. boast
2. split   17. flute
3. staff   18. sway
4. fade   19. cruise
5. praise   20. mild
6. slope   21. grasp
7. claim   22. swift
8. stroll   23. bunk
9. mood   24. slight
10. beast   25. thrown
11. crush   26. stole
12. fond   27. fleet
13. dwell   28. dew
14. strike   29. youth
15. clue   30. thigh

See the back for **Challenge Words.**

Michelle Kwan – Spelling Words

1. basketball   12. daytime
2. wheelchair   13. whoever
3. cheerleader   14. test tube
4. newscast   15. turnpike
5. weekend   16. shipyard
6. everybody   17. homemade
7. up-to-date   18. household
8. grandparent   19. salesperson
9. first aid   20. brother-in-law
10. wildlife
11. highway

Challenge Words

1. extraordinary
2. self-assured
3. quick-witted
4. limelight
5. junior high school

Volcanoes – Spelling Words

1. thrown   11. mood
2. stole   12. loaf
3. clue   13. growth
4. dew   14. youth
5. choose   15. slope
6. rule   16. loose
7. boast   17. rude
8. cruise   18. rule
9. stroll   19. flow
10. route   20. flute

Challenge Words

1. subdue
2. pursuit
3. molten
4. reproach
5. presume

My Study List Add your own spelling words on the back. (×3)

409   409   409

Teacher's Book, page 107

Teacher's Book, page F109 (bottom left)

Name _____

Focus On Tall Tales
Genre Connection

You'll Never Believe Who I Just Met

Think about characters you might find in a tall tale. Describe five tall tale characters by completing each sentence with an exaggeration.

Sample answers shown.

1. This character is so tall that he has to duck whenever the space shuttle goes by. **(2 points)**

2. This character is so loud that when she clears her throat it causes an avalanche. **(2)**

3. This character is so old that he used to play hide-and-go-seek with the dinosaurs when he was a little boy. **(2)**

4. This character is so fast that she can run to the store, buy a quart of milk, and be back with the change before her father has finished writing *milk* on the shopping list. **(2)**

5. This character is so strong that when he loses something, he really *does* turn the house upside down to find it. **(2)**

Focus on Tall Tales   59
Assessment Tip: Total **10** Points

Teacher's Book, page F109

Teacher's Book, page F109 (bottom right)

Name _____

Focus On Tall Tales
Genre Connection

That Could Never Happen!

Each of the four selections in *Focus on Tall Tales* contains at least one exaggerated event. Write the event after each story title.

Sample answers shown.

Paul Bunyan, the Mightiest Logger of Them All
Paul Bunyan chops down ten pine trees with one swing of his axe.

(2 points)

John Henry Races the Steam Drill
John Henry swings his hammer so hard and fast that it catches fire. **(2)**

Sally Ann Thunder Ann Whirlwind
Sally talks the grizzly bear into dancing with her, and at the same time he churns her butter. **(2)**

February
McBroom saws chunks of the frozen wind during the winter and thaws them out during the summer. **(2)**

60   **Focus on Tall Tales**
Assessment Tip: Total **8** Points

Teacher's Book, page F109

Key to California Standards in Focus on Tall Tales

1.0 Word Analysis, Fluency, and Systematic Vocabulary Development

R1.1 Read aloud narrative and expository text fluently and accurately and with appropriate pacing, intonation, and expression.

R1.2 Use word origins to determine the meaning of unknown words.

R1.4 Know abstract, derived roots and affixes from Greek and Latin and use this knowledge to analyze the meaning of complex words (e.g., *controversial*).

R1.5 Understand and explain the figurative and metaphorical use of words in context.

2.0 Reading Comprehension

R2.3 Discern main ideas and concepts presented in texts, identifying and assessing evidence that supports those ideas.

R2.4 Draw inferences, conclusions, or generalizations about text and support them with textual evidence and prior knowledge.

R2.5 Distinguish facts, supported inferences, and opinions in text.

3.0 Literary Response and Analysis

R3.1 Identify and analyze the characteristics of poetry, drama, fiction, and nonfiction and explain the appropriateness of the literary forms chosen by an author for a specific purpose.

R3.3 Contrast the actions, motives (e.g., loyalty, selfishness, conscientiousness), and appearances of characters in a work of fiction and discuss the importance of the contrasts to the plot or theme.

R3.4 Understand that theme refers to the meaning or moral of a selection and recognize themes (whether implied or stated directly) in sample works.

R3.5 Describe the function and effect of common literary devices (e.g., imagery, metaphor, symbolism).

R3.6 Evaluate the meaning of archetypal patterns and symbols that are found in myth and tradition by using literature from different eras and cultures.

R3.7 Evaluate the author's use of various techniques (e.g., appeal of characters in a picture book, logic and credibility of plots and settings, use of figurative language) to influence readers' perspectives.

1.0 Writing Strategies

W1.1 Create multiple-paragraph narrative compositions:

W1.1a. Establish and develop a situation or plot.

W1.1b. Describe the setting.

W1.1c. Present an ending.

2.0 Writing Applications

W2.1 Write narratives:

W2.1a. Establish a plot, point of view, setting, and conflict.

W2.2 Write responses to literature:

W2.2a. Demonstrate an understanding of a literary work.

W2.2b. Support judgments through references to the text and to prior knowledge.

W2.2c. Develop interpretations that exhibit careful reading and understanding.

continued

Written and Oral English Language Conventions

1.0 Written and Oral English Language Conventions

LC1.1 Identify and correctly use prepositional phrases, appositives, and independent and dependent clauses; use transitions and conjunctions to connect ideas.

Listening and Speaking

2.0 Speaking Applications

LS2.1 Deliver narrative presentations:

LS2.1a. Establish a situation, plot, point of view, and setting with descriptive words and phrases.

LS2.1b. Show, rather than tell, the listener what happens.

LLS2.3 Deliver oral responses to literature:

LS2.3a. Summarize significant events and details.

LS2.3b. Articulate an understanding of several ideas or images communicated by the literary work.

LS2.3c. Use examples or textual evidence from the work to support conclusions.

Tall Tales

OBJECTIVES

During this *Focus on Tall Tales*, students

- identify and define a *tall tale*
- compare different examples of tall tales
- write their own tall tale

Introducing the Genre

R 1.1
R 3.1

Discuss with students what is taking place in the illustration on page 108. (Sample answer: A storyteller is telling a fantastic story.) Then read with students the introduction on page 109, to arrive at a definition of a tall tale: a story in which facts are *exaggerated*.

108

▶ ## Building Background

R 3.1

Invite students to think of a story they might have told or heard in which something was exaggerated, such as catching a fish or giving reasons for being late. Discuss reasons for exaggerating in a story: humor, dramatic effect, or to gain the admiration or sympathy of the listener.

▶ ## Purpose Setting

LS 2.3.b
LS 2.3.c

Encourage students to look for exaggerations in each of the tall tales. Invite them to think about which tall tale character is their favorite, and why.

Journal Writing As they read the tall tales, students can use their journals to note character traits, exaggerations, and other ideas writing their own tall tale.

W 2.2.a

Teacher's Note

Tip for Reading a Tall Tale When you read a tall tale aloud, read it the way a storyteller might tell it to an audience — dramatically and with humor.

California Standards pp. F108–F109

R 1.1	Read aloud fluently	**LS 2.3.b** Understand ideas/images
R 3.1	Analyze literary forms	**LS 2.3.c** Use examples
W 2.2.a	Demonstrate understanding	

Tall Tales

A tall tale starts out like a regular story, but it tends to stretch the facts a little.

Well, actually, it stretches the facts a lot.

Where was the first tall tale told? Probably around a campfire. Out on the frontier of the 1800s, American settlers liked to exaggerate. They created heroes and heroines who were larger than life, capable of amazing deeds. In a big land with wild weather and wild animals, the stories had to be just as big and just as wild.

Tall tales are still being told today. In fact, after you read these examples, you're invited to add to the tradition and write your own!

Contents

Reading — Analyze literary forms (R3.1)
Evaluate patterns/symbols (R3.6)

109

▶ Suggestions for Using *Focus on Tall Tales*

This section can be used flexibly, to suit classroom needs. You may want to use it in the following ways:

■ As part of a classroom project relating to oral history or storytelling

■ When the content relates to a topic being taught in another curricular area

■ In the week before a vacation or exam period, or before starting another theme

■ For a break, or a change of pace

▶ Genre Connection

W 2.2.a

Use **Practice Book** pages 59 and 60 to review and reinforce the tall tale genre.

Practice Book page 60

Focus On Tall Tales
Genre Connection

Name _____

That Could Ne

Each of the four selections
one exaggerated event. Wri
Sample
Paul Bunyan, the Mightiest Lo
Paul Bunyan chops down te
(2 points)
John Henry Races the Steam D
John Henry swings his ham

Sally Ann Thunder Ann Whir
Sally talks the grizzly bear in
he churns her butter. **(2)**
February
McBroom saws chunks of th
them out during the summe

60   Focus on Tall Tales
Assessment Tip: Total 8 Points

Practice Book page 59

Focus On Tall Tales
Genre Connection

Name _____

**You'll Never Believe
Who I Just Met**

Think about characters you might find in a tall tale. Describe five tall tale characters by completing each sentence with an exaggeration.

Sample answers shown.
1. This character is so tall that
   he has to duck whenever the space shuttle goes by. **(2 points)**

2. This character is so loud that
   when she clears her throat it causes an avalanche. **(2)**

3. This character is so old that
   he used to play hide-and-go-seek with the dinosaurs when he was a little boy. **(2)**

4. This character is so fast that
   she can run to the store, buy a quart of milk, and be back with the change before her father has finished writing *milk* on the shopping list. **(2)**

5. This character is so strong that
   when he loses something, he really *does* turn the house upside down to find it. **(2)**

Focus on Tall Tales   59
Assessment Tip: Total **10** Points

Reading "Paul Bunyan, the Mightiest Logger of Them All"
pages 110–113

....

▶ Preparing to Read

R 1.1
R 2.4
R 3.6

■ Have a volunteer read the introduction on page 110. Ask why a giant logger might have been popular as a "superhero" in the United States.

■ Compare Paul Bunyan with other giants in folktales, such as Jack in the Beanstalk. Note that he is unusual as a giant who is a working man.

....

▶ Purpose Setting

Invite students to predict what might happen in a tall tale about a giant logger.

W 2.2.a
W 2.2.b

Journal Writing Invite students to explain how Paul Bunyan might have created Niagara Falls, the geyser Old Faithful, or some other natural wonder.

California Standards pp. F110–F111

R 1.1   Read aloud fluently
R 2.4   Inferences/generalizations
R 3.1   Analyze literary forms
R 3.6   Evaluate patterns/symbols
R 3.7   Evaluate author's techniques
W 2.2.a Demonstrate understanding
W 2.2.b Support judgments

> As loggers changed the landscape of America in the 1800s, they told tales about a giant lumberjack of incredible strength. Paul Bunyan quickly became a folk legend from Maine to the Pacific Northwest.

Paul Bunyan, the Mightiest Logger of Them All

Retold by Mary Pope Osborne
Illustrated by Chris Van Allsburg

It seems an amazing baby was born in the state of Maine. When he was only two weeks old, he weighed more than a hundred pounds, and for breakfast every morning he ate five dozen eggs, ten sacks of potatoes, and a half barrel of mush made from a whole sack of cornmeal. But the baby's strangest feature was his big, curly black beard. It was so big and bushy that every morning his mother had to comb it with a pine tree.

Except for that black beard, the big baby wasn't much trouble to anybody until he was about nine months old. That was when he first started to crawl, and since he weighed over five hundred pounds, he caused an earthquake that shook the whole town.

The baby's parents tried putting him in a giant floating cradle off the coast of Maine; but every time he rolled over, huge waves drowned all the villages along the coast.

110

About the Author

Mary Pope Osborne

The daughter of an army officer, Mary Pope Osborne grew up traveling around the world. As an adult she has lived in a cave in Crete and caravaned to Nepal. Osborne is the author of over forty books for young readers, including several retellings: *Beauty and the Beast, Mermaid Tales from Around the World,* collections of Greek and Norse myths, and *American Tall Tales,* from which *Paul Bunyan, the Mightiest Logger of Them All* is adapted.

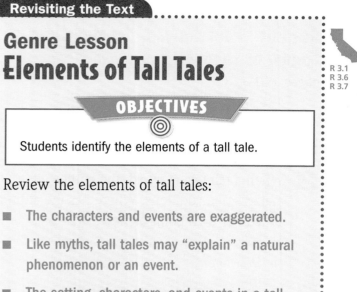

111

Genre Lesson
Elements of Tall Tales

R 3.1
R 3.6
R 3.7

OBJECTIVES

Students identify the elements of a tall tale.

Review the elements of tall tales:

- The characters and events are exaggerated.

- Like myths, tall tales may "explain" a natural phenomenon or an event.

- The setting, characters, and events in a tall tale are often based in fact.

Point out examples of the three elements of a tall tale on page 110. (The baby has a beard; the baby causes an earthquake; the setting is the coast of Maine.)

Have students list other examples of the elements of a tall tale as they read the selection. Allow time for students to share their work.

Reaching All Students

Extra Support

Identifying Settings

Students who are unfamiliar with the geography of the United States will benefit from looking at a map. Point out the locations mentioned in the tall tale: Maine, Minnesota, Michigan, Wisconsin, Arizona, the Grand Canyon, and the Great Lakes.

Reading "Paul Bunyan, the Mightiest Logger of Them All," *continued*
pages 110–113

R 3.7

▶ **Supporting Comprehension**

1 When a tall tale is retold, the author often makes some additions. Where has the author added her own point of view? (She writes: *It would be nice if those trees could have stayed tall and thick forever.*)

2 The author has used understatement in this tale, using a word for something small to describe something much bigger. What are two examples? (The author calls the Grand Canyon a ditch and the Great Lakes ponds.)

3 How does the author give the tall tale an unfinished, "to be continued" ending? (She says that more stories about Paul Bunyan might thaw in the spring and start telling themselves.)

Vocabulary *(page 112)*
pioneers: people who are the first to settle in a region.

So his parents hauled the giant toddler to a cave in the Maine woods far away from civilization and said good-bye. His father gave him a fishing pole, a knife, some flint rocks, and an axe. "We'll think of you often, honey," his mother said, weeping. "But you can't come back home — you're just too big."

That's the story of how Paul Bunyan came to take care of himself in the Maine woods. And even though he lived alone for the next twenty years, he got along quite well.

1 In those times, huge sections of America were filled with dark green forests. It would be nice if those trees could have stayed tall and thick forever. But the pioneers needed them to build houses, churches, ships, wagons, bridges, and barns. So one day Paul Bunyan took a good look at those trees and decided to invent logging.

"Tim-ber!" he yelled, and he swung the bright steel axe his father had given him in a wide circle. There was a terrible crash, and when Paul looked around, he saw he'd felled ten white pines with a single swing.

After that Paul traveled plenty fast through the untamed North Woods. He cut pine, spruce, and red willow in Minnesota, Michigan, and Wisconsin. He cleared cottonwoods out of Kansas so farmers could plant wheat and oaks out of Iowa so farmers could plant corn.

When next heard of, Paul was headed to Arizona. He dragged his pickaxe behind him on the trip, not realizing he was leaving a big ditch in his tracks. Today that ditch is called the Grand Canyon.

When Paul got back from the West, he decided to start a logging camp. Word spread fast. Since all the woodsmen had heard of Paul Bunyan, thousands of them hurried to Paul's headquarters at Big Onion on the Big Onion River in Minnesota to be part of his crew.

"There's only two requirements," Paul announced to the men who'd gathered to apply for the job. "All my loggers have to be over ten feet tall and be able to pop six buttons off their shirts with one breath."

Well, about a thousand of the lumberjacks met those requirements, and Paul hired them all. Then he built a gigantic logging camp with

112

Reaching All Students

English Language Learners

Intermediate and Advanced Fluency   R 1.2

Breaking Down Words

English language learners may find it useful to break large, unknown words into smaller words. For example, *logger* breaks down into *log + ger*. Knowing the smaller word *log* helps students define the larger word.

California Standards pp. F112–F113

R 1.2 Use word origins   R 3.7 Evaluate author's techniques
R 2.3 Discern main ideas   W 2.2.a Demonstrate understanding
R 2.5 Facts, inferences, opinions
R 3.6 Evaluate patterns/symbols

bunkhouses a mile long and bunks ten beds high. The camp's chow table was so long that it took a week to pass the salt and pepper from one end to the other. Paul dug a few ponds to provide drinking water for everyone. Today we call those ponds the Great Lakes.

2

Things went pretty well at the Big Onion Lumber Company until the Year of the Hard Winter. One day Shot Gunderson, the crew boss, complained to Paul, "Boss, it's so cold that the flames for all the lanterns are freezing. And, Boss, when I give orders to the woods crew, all my words freeze in the air and hang there stiff as icicles."

"Well, haul away your frozen words and store them somewhere next to the lantern flames," Paul advised. "They'll both thaw out in the spring."

Sure enough, they did. The only problem was that, come spring, the melting lantern flames started some mean little brush fires. And when Shot's frozen words thawed, old cries of "Timber!" and "Chow time!" started to echo throughout the woods, causing all sorts of confusion. But other than that, things ran pretty smoothly.

Well, there's stories and stories about Paul Bunyan. For many years, old loggers sat around potbellied stoves and told about the good old times with Paul. Those loggers are all gone now, but many of their stories still hang frozen in the cold forest air of the North Woods, waiting to be told. Come spring, when they start to thaw, some of them might just start telling themselves. It's been known to happen.

3

113

Wrapping Up "Paul Bunyan, the Mightiest Logger of Them All"
pages 110–113

Comprehension/Critical Thinking

1 Why do Paul Bunyan's parents move him to the woods as a baby, far from people? (He is too big, and could cause harm to others.)

2 How does Paul Bunyan help to change the landscape of the United States? (Sample answers: He clears the forests; he creates the Grand Canyon and the Great Lakes.)

R 2.3
R 3.6

3 What are some of your favorite exaggerations in this tall tale, and why? (Answers will vary.)

4 How would you describe the author's writing style? Give examples. (Sample answer: She has an informal, conversational style: *Sure enough; It's been known to happen.*)

R 3.7

5 Do you think Paul Bunyan is a good character for a tall tale? Why or why not? (Answers will vary.)

R 2.5
R 3.6

Journal Writing Students can create and write a short description of another larger-than-life character who is a friend of Paul Bunyan. They might use this description in their own tall tale.

W 2.2.a

Using Clues to Define Words

Help students to use context clues to define the word *felled* on page 112. Point out that words like *axe, crash, pines,* and *swing* help define the word as "chopped down." Then point out how the tree stumps in the illustration on page 113 also offer a clue.

Reading "John Henry Races the Steam Drill"

pages 114–118

▶ Preparing to Read

R 1.1

■ Have a volunteer read the introduction on page 114. Note that this tall tale comes from a time when people were worried about new inventions taking the place of human workers.

■ Invite students to predict who might win the race in the title, and why.

▶ Purpose Setting

R 3.1

Ask students to note the point at which they can tell that this is a tall tale.

Journal Writing Invite students to note examples of rhythm and repetition that they think add to the story.

W 2.2.a
W 2.2.c

> **Vocabulary** *(page 114)*
>
> <u>shaker:</u> a worker whose job is to shake out loose rock or other material.

Focus on

Tall Tales

> Stories and songs about John Henry have been around since the 1870s. He became famous as the steel driver who hammered faster than a machine. Did John Henry exist? No one knows for sure. But like Paul Bunyan, he stands for the deeds of many others.

John Henry Races the Steam Drill

Retold by Paul Robert Walker

The Big Bend Tunnel was the longest tunnel in America — a mile and a quarter through the heart of the West Virginia mountains. The C & O Railroad started building it back around 1870. There was plenty of hard work for everyone, but the steel-driving men worked the hardest. And the hardest-working steel-driving man of them all was John Henry.

Now, John Henry was a powerful man — six feet tall and two hundred pounds of rippling muscle. He swung his nine-pound hammer from sunup to sundown, driving a steel drill into solid rock. Little Bill, the <u>shaker</u>, turned John Henry's drill between hammer blows and pulled it out when the hole was done. When there were enough holes, the demolition boys filled them with nitroglycerine and blew the rock to kingdom come. Then John Henry drove more steel — day after day in the heat and darkness and stale air of the tunnel.

114

Reaching All Students

Extra Support

R 1.4

Identifying Superlatives

Tell students that the suffix *-est* turns the adjective to which it is connected into a superlative, such as *longest* and *hardest* on page 114. Have students think of other superlatives that might apply to John Henry.

California Standards pp. F114–F115

R 1.1 Read aloud fluently	**R 3.6** Evaluate patterns/symbols
R 1.4 Use roots and affixes	**R 3.7** Evaluate author's techniques
R 2.5 Facts, inferences, opinions	**W 2.2.a** Demonstrate understanding
R 3.1 Analyze literary forms	**W 2.2.c** Develop interpretations

115

• SELECTION •

John Henry Races
the Steam Drill

R 3.1
R 3.6
R 3.7
W 2.2.a
W 2.2.b
W 2.2.c

Revisiting the Text

Writer's Craft Lesson
Retelling

OBJECTIVES

Students understand what is involved in retelling a
tall tale or other folktale.

Point out that myths and folktales, including tall
tales, were originally passed along orally and
retold according to memory. List some of the
things that an author still tries to do in retelling
a tale:

■   Be faithful to the characters and events.

■   Make the story fresh with action, description,
    and dialogue.

■   Make the story appeal to a new audience.

Remind students of how the author of the Paul
Bunyan tale retells it in an informal, conversational style. Have students look for examples of
action, description, and dialogue in *John Henry
Races the Steam Drill* that makes it fresh to a
new audience.

Reaching All Students

Extra Support

Fact or Fiction?

R 2.5
R 3.6
R 3.7
W 2.2.a
W 2.2.c

Have students decide which parts of this tall tale are exaggerated and
which could be fact. Students can work in pairs to create a fact and fiction chart and then share their work.

Reading "John Henry Races the Steam Drill," continued
pages 114–118

▶ **Supporting Comprehension**

R 3.6
R 3.7

4 Why does the author have John Henry repeat the phrase, "A man ain't nothin' but a man" to Captain Tommy and Polly Ann? (Sample answer: John Henry feels that a person needs to rely on his own natural abilities.)

5 What exaggeration on page 118 does the author use to signal that this is a tall tale, not a true story? (The Polly Ann hammer catches fire.)

Vocabulary *(page 116)*
maul: a heavy, long-handled hammer

John Henry always sang while he drove the steel — and at the end of every line he brought that nine-pound hammer down like a crash of thunder.

> *This old hammer* (Bam!)
> *Rings like silver* (Bam!)
> *Shines like gold, boys,* (Bam!)
> *Shines like gold.* (Bam!)
>
> *Ain't no hammer* (Bam!)
> *In these mountains* (Bam!)
> *Rings like mine, boys,* (Bam!)
> *Rings like mine.* (Bam!)

One day, Captain Tommy interrupted John Henry in the middle of his song. "John Henry," he said, "the company wants to test one of those new steam drills. They say a steam drill can do the work of three or four men. But I say a good man can beat the steam. And I say you are the best man I have."

John Henry rested his nine-pound hammer on his broad, muscular shoulder. "Captain Tommy," he said, "a man ain't nothin' but a man. Before I let that steam drill beat me down, I'll die with my hammer in my hand."

"Son," offered Captain Tommy, "if you beat that steam drill, I'll give you one hundred dollars and a new suit of clothes."

"That's mighty generous," said John Henry, "but don't you worry about that. Just go to town and buy me a twenty-pound hammer. This nine-pound <u>maul</u> is feeling light."

The news of the contest spread through the camp like a strong wind whipping down the mountain. The company men said John Henry was a poor working fool who didn't stand a chance against that mighty steam drill. Some of the working men thought the same. But the steel-driving men knew John Henry — and they believed in the power of a mighty man.

That night, John Henry told his wife, Polly Ann, about the contest. "Don't you strain yourself, honey," said Polly Ann. "'Course we could use that hundred dollars — and you need a new suit of clothes."

116

Cross-Curricular Connection

Music Students may be familiar with "The Ballad of John Henry." For comparison with the prose version, find that song or another tall tale sung as a ballad ("Davy Crockett," "Pecos Bill," from the Walt Disney videos) and share it with students.

Reaching All Students

English Language Learners

Intermediate and Advanced Fluency

LC 1.1

Rewording Dialogue

Explain that dialogue is often written to show how people talk informally. Invite students to reword passages such as "'Course we could use..." or "I ain't worried..." to make them easier to understand.

California Standards pp. F116–F117

R3.6 Evaluate patterns/symbols
R3.7 Evaluate author's techniques
LC1.1 Sentence structure/transition

John Henry smiled and kissed Polly Ann. "I ain't worried about money or clothes," he said. "Don't y'see sugar — a man ain't nothin' but a man, and a man's got to beat the steam."

4

The next morning, the steel drivers crowded into the Big Bend Tunnel. It was hot and dusty, and the air was so foul that a man could hardly breathe. The only light was the flickering of lamps burning lard oil and blackstrap molasses.

The company man wheeled the steam drill into the tunnel and set it up against the rock. It was nothing but a machine — all shiny and modern and strange. Then John Henry walked in and stood beside it. He was nothing but a man — all black and fine and natural.

Captain Tommy handed John Henry a brand-new twenty-pound hammer. "There ain't another like it in West Virginia," he said. "Good luck, son."

John Henry held the hammer in his hand and felt its fine natural weight. In the flickering light of the tunnel, the head of that hammer shone like gold. "Gonna call this hammer Polly Ann," he said.

Little Bill sat on the rock, holding the six-foot drill in his hands. John Henry towered above the steel, just waiting to begin. It was so quiet in that tunnel, you could hear the soft breathing of the steel-driving men.

Captain Tommy blew his whistle. The company man turned on the steam drill. John Henry swung his twenty-pound hammer back and brought it down with a crash like thunder. As he swung it back again, he began to sing:

> *This old hammer* (Bam!)
> *Rings like silver* (Bam!)
> *Shines like gold, boys,* (Bam!)
> *Shines like gold.* (Bam!)

John Henry kept driving steel and the steam drill kept drilling. Pretty soon the whole mountain was rumbling and shaking. John Henry's muscles bulged and strained like they never bulged and strained before. Sweat cascaded down his powerful chest, and veins protruded from the sides of his handsome face.

117

Reaching All Students

English Language Learners

Intermediate and Advanced Fluency

Terms of Endearment

Students may be confused when Captain Tommy calls John Henry "son" and John Henry calls Polly Ann "sugar." Explain that these are affectionate terms, not to be taken literally. Invite students to give examples of terms of endearment in their first language.

Revisiting the Text

Writer's Craft Lesson
Identifying Character Descriptions

R 3.7

OBJECTIVES

Students identify character descriptions.

Discuss with students the ways in which writers can build the readers' understanding of the characters:

■ through the narrator's description

■ through descriptions by other characters

■ through the character's own dialogue

Ask students to find examples of descriptions of John Henry by the narrator. (He was nothing but a man—all black and fine and natural.)

Then ask students to find descriptions by another character in the story. ("The company men said John Henry was a poor working fool who didn't stand a chance....")

Have students work in small groups to find examples of John Henry described through his own speech. Allow time for students to share their work.

Wrapping Up "John Henry Races the Steam Drill"

pages 114–118

Comprehension/Critical Thinking

R 2.4
R 3.7

1 Why does the author have John Henry sing his song throughout the story? (Sample answers: it shows the rhythm in John Henry's work; it shows John Henry's pride in himself.)

R 3.6
R 3.7

2 Does the author convince you that John Henry is "larger than life"? How? (Answers will vary.)

R 2.4
R 3.7

3 Why do you think the author has the tale end with John Henry's death? (Answers will vary.)

4 Do you agree with the company men or with the steel-driving men about the best way to drive steel? Why? (Answers will vary.)

R 3.3

5 Compare John Henry with Paul Bunyan. How are they different and alike as tall tale characters? (They are both super-strong. Paul Bunyan is more fantastic. John Henry is more human.)

W 2.2.a

Journal Writing Invite students to write a verse of two or four lines, like the one John Henry repeats, for an invented tall tale character.

"Are you all right, John Henry?" asked Captain Tommy.

"Don't you worry," said John Henry. "A man ain't nothin' but a man — and a man's got to beat the steam." Then he went on singing:

> *Ain't no hammer* (Bam!)
> *In these mountains* (Bam!)
> *Rings like mine, boys,* (Bam!)
> *Rings like mine.* (Bam!)

5 When they hit the end of the six-foot drill, Little Bill pulled it out and shoved in a longer drill — and then a longer one and a longer one still. John Henry swung his twenty-pound hammer and drove that steel. He swung and drove faster and harder, and faster and harder, until that Polly Ann hammer caught fire. The whole Big Bend Tunnel glowed with the blue flame of John Henry's hammer.

"Time!" shouted Captain Tommy.

"Time!" cried the company man, shutting off the steam drill.

"Time," gasped John Henry, leaning on his hammer. "I need a cool drink of water."

While John Henry drank his water, Captain Tommy and the company man measured the holes. The steam drill had done nine feet; John Henry had drilled fourteen.

"John Henry!" shouted the steel drivers. "John Henry beat the steam!"

"Congratulations, son," said Captain Tommy, slapping him on the back. "I don't care what you say — I'm gonna give you a hundred dollars and a new suit of clothes."

John Henry leaned heavily on his hammer and sucked in the stale air of the tunnel. "That's mighty generous, Captain Tommy. But you give that hundred dollars to Polly Ann. And you bury me in that suit of clothes." Then he slumped to the ground, clutching his hammer in his hand. "I beat the steam," he gasped, "but I broke inside."

As his eyes closed, John Henry lay back against the black earth and whispered, "A man ain't nothin' but a man."

118

Reaching All Students

Challenge

R 3.1

Allegory

Explain to students that an allegory is a tale that works on two levels: as a story and as a symbol for an idea. Encourage students to consider how *John Henry Races the Steam Drill* could be an allegory about the value of people vs. technology. Ask: Does it have relevance today? Why?

California Standards pp. F118–F119

R 1.1 Read aloud fluently
R 2.4 Inferences/generalizations
R 3.1 Analyze literary forms
R 3.3 Determine character traits

R 3.6 Evaluate patterns/symbols
R 3.7 Evaluate author's techniques
W 2.2.a Demonstrate understanding

Focus on

Tall Tales

The Tennessee frontiersman, Davy Crockett, was the real-life subject of many a tall tale. But there is no truth to the story that he had a wife named Sally Ann Thunder Ann Whirlwind. Good thing for Davy, because in her he would have met his match!

Sally Ann Thunder Ann Whirlwind

Retold by Mary Pope Osborne

One early spring day, when the leaves of the white oaks were about as big as a mouse's ear, Davy Crockett set out alone through the forest to do some bear hunting. Suddenly it started raining real hard, and he felt obliged to stop for shelter under a tree. As he shook the rain out of his coonskin cap, he got sleepy, so he laid back into the crotch of the tree, and pretty soon he was snoring.

Davy slept so hard, he didn't wake up until nearly sundown. And when he did, he discovered that somehow or another in all that sleeping his head had gotten stuck in the crotch of the tree, and he couldn't get it out.

Well, Davy roared loud enough to make the tree lose all its little mouse-ear leaves. He twisted and turned and carried on for over an hour, but still that tree wouldn't let go. Just as he

119

Reading "Sally Ann Thunder Ann Whirlwind"

pages 119–124

....

▶ Preparing to Read

R 1.1
R 3.6

■ Have a volunteer read the introduction on page 119. Ask students why they think story-tellers invented a tall tale wife for Davy Crockett.

■ Note that this retelling is by the same author, Mary Pope Osborne, who wrote *Paul Bunyan, the Mightiest Logger of Them All*.

....

▶ Purpose Setting

R 3.3

Ask students to find examples of both real and fictional qualities in the character Sally Ann Thunder Ann Whirlwind as they read.

 Journal Writing Invite students to describe a real person but to exaggerate that person's attributes and abilities until that person could be a character in a tall tale.

W 2.2.a

 Cross-Curricular Connection

Social Studies The real Davy Crockett was a frontiersman, soldier, and politician, born in 1786 in Tennessee. In 1827, Crockett was elected to the first of three terms in the U.S. House of Representatives. When he lost his bid for reelection, he went to Texas where he was killed in 1836 at the Battle of the Alamo.

Reading "Sally Ann Thunder Ann Whirlwind," continued
pages 119–124

▶ **Supporting Comprehension**

R 2.4
R 3.7

6 Why do you think the author chooses to delay Sally's appearance in her own tall tale? (Sample answer: to create suspense)

7 Why does the author emphasize and repeat the word *sweetie*? (Sample answer: Davy Crockett uses the term condescendingly. Then Sally throws the word back at him defiantly, as if to say she is no stereotype of a "sweet" woman.)

Vocabulary *(pages 120–121)*
tiller: a lever used to turn the rudder, or steering mechanism, of a boat

varmint: wild creature

had a reputation for: was known for

---

6 was about to give himself up for a goner, he heard a girl say, "What's the matter, stranger?"

Even from his awkward position, he could see that she was extraordinary — tall as a hickory sapling, with arms as big as a keelboat tiller's.

"My head's stuck, *sweetie*," he said. "And if you help me get it free, I'll give you a pretty little comb."

"Don't call me sweetie," she said. "And don't worry about giving me any pretty little comb, either. I'll free your old coconut, but just because I want to."

Then this extraordinary girl did something that made Davy's hair stand on end. She reached in a bag and took out a bunch of rattlesnakes. She tied all the wriggly critters together to make a long rope, and as she tied, she kept talking. "I'm not a shy little colt," she said. "And I'm not a little singing nightingale, either. I can tote a steamboat on my back, outscream a panther, and jump over my own shadow. I can double up crocodiles any day, and I like to wear a hornets' nest for my Sunday bonnet."

As the girl looped the ends of her snake rope to the top of the branch that was trapping Davy, she kept bragging: "I'm a streak of lightning set up edgeways and buttered with quicksilver. I can outgrin, outsnort, outrun, outlift, outsneeze, outsleep, outlie any varmint from Maine to Louisiana.

7 Furthermore, sweetie, I can blow out the moonlight and sing a wolf to sleep." Then she pulled on the other end of the snake rope so hard, it seemed as if she might tear the world apart.

The right-hand fork of that big tree bent just about double. Then Davy slid his head out as easy as you please. For a minute he was so dizzy, he couldn't tell up from down. But when he got everything going straight again, he took a good look at that girl. "What's your name, ma'am?"

"Sally Ann Thunder Ann Whirlwind," she said. "But if you mind your manners, you can call me Sally."

From then on Davy Crockett was crazy in love with Sally Ann Thunder Ann Whirlwind. He asked everyone he knew about her, and everything he heard caused another one of Cupid's arrows to jab him in the gizzard.

120

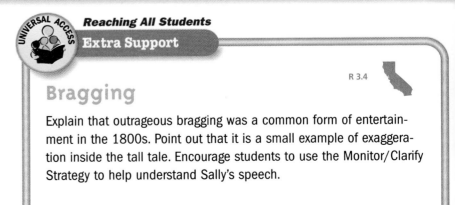

Reaching All Students
Extra Support

R 3.4

Bragging
Explain that outrageous bragging was a common form of entertainment in the 1800s. Point out that it is a small example of exaggeration inside the tall tale. Encourage students to use the Monitor/Clarify Strategy to help understand Sally's speech.

California Standards pp. F120–F121

R 1.4 Use roots and affixes
R 2.4 Inferences/generalizations
R 3.1 Analyze literary forms
R 3.4 Understand theme

R 3.7 Evaluate author's techniques
W 2.2.a Demonstrate understanding

• SELECTION •

Sally Ann Thunder
Ann Whirlwind

R 3.1
R 3.7
W 2.2.a

"Oh, I know Sally!" the preacher said. "She can dance a rock to pieces and ride a panther bareback!"

"Sally's a good ole friend of mine," the blacksmith said. "Once I saw her crack a walnut with her front teeth."

"Sally's so very special," said the schoolmarm. "She likes to whip across the Salt River, using her apron for a sail and her left leg for a rudder!"

Sally Ann Thunder Ann Whirlwind had a reputation for being funny, too. Her best friend, Lucy, told Davy, "Sally can laugh the bark off a pine tree. She likes to whistle out one side of her mouth while she eats with the other side and grins with the middle!"

121

Revisiting the Text . . . .

Writer's Craft Lesson
Humor

OBJECTIVES

Students recognize how the writer creates humor in the story.

Tell students that writers have many techniques for making their writing humorous. Some of these are:

- silly descriptions

- a funny series of events

- exaggeration

- odd coincidences

- nonsensical conversation

Invite students to look for instances of humor in *Sally Ann Thunder Ann Whirlwind*. Encourage them to decide the author's method for making each instance humorous.

Invite small groups of students to try writing a humorous paragraph in the style of *Sally Ann Thunder Ann Whirlwind*. Allow time for students to share their work.

Reaching All Students

English Language Learners

Intermediate and Advanced Fluency

R 1.4

The Prefix Out-

Explain that the prefix *out-* before a verb lends the meaning "to surpass, or be better at" doing whatever the verb describes. Point out the examples on page 120. Encourage students to think of other examples.

Reading "Sally Ann Thunder Ann Whirlwind," continued
pages 119–124

▶ ### Supporting Comprehension

R 2.4
R 3.3
R 3.7

8 What qualities does the author show in Sally during the episode with the Great King Bear? (bravery, cleverness, fun)

9 Why does the author tell about Sally's deeds in the order she does, with the one-liners on page 121 followed by the stories about the bear and Mike Fink? (The examples build from simple to more complicated.)

Vocabulary *(page 122)*
forage: search

✎ **Journal Writing** Invite students to write a bragging contest between two characters in a tall tale, using *Sally Ann Thunder Ann Whirlwind* as a model. Students can use this dialogue in their own tall tale.

W 2.2.a

According to her friends, Sally could tame about anything in the world, too. They all told Davy about the time she was churning butter and heard something scratching outside. Suddenly the door swung open, and in walked the Great King Bear of the Mud Forest. He'd come to steal one of her smoked hams. Well, before the King Bear could say boo, Sally grabbed a warm dumpling from the pot and stuffed it in his mouth.

The dumpling tasted so good, the King Bear's eyes winked with tears. But then he started to think that Sally might taste pretty good, too. So opening and closing his big old mouth, he backed her right into a corner.

8 Sally was plenty scared, with her knees a-knocking and her heart a-hammering. But just as the King Bear blew his hot breath in her face, she gathered the courage to say, "Would you like to dance?"

As everybody knows, no bear can resist an invitation to a square dance, so of course the old fellow forgot all about eating Sally and said, "Love to."

Then he bowed real pretty, and the two got to kicking and whooping and swinging each other through the air, as Sally sang:

> *We are on our way to Baltimore,*
> *With two behind, and two before:*
> *Around, around, around we go,*
> *Where oats, peas, beans, and barley grow!*

And while she was singing, Sally tied a string from the bear's ankle to her butter churn, so that all the time the old feller was kicking up his legs and dancing around the room, he was also churning her butter!

9 And folks loved to tell the story about Sally's encounter with another stinky varmint — only this one was a *human* varmint. It seems that Mike Fink, the riverboat man, decided to scare the toenails off Sally because he was sick and tired of hearing Davy Crockett talk about how great she was.

One evening Mike crept into an old alligator skin and met Sally just as she was taking off to <u>forage</u> in the woods for berries. He spread open his gigantic mouth and made such a howl that he nearly scared himself to

122

California Standards pp. F122–F123

R 2.4 Inferences/generalizations
R 3.3 Determine character traits
R 3.7 Evaluate author's techniques

W 2.2.a Demonstrate understanding

123

Wrapping Up "Sally Ann Thunder Ann Whirlwind"

pages 119–124

Comprehension/Critical Thinking

R 2.3
R 2.4
R 3.3

1 Think about pioneer women in the 1800s. Which of their qualities are exaggerated in Sally, and why? (Sample answer: Pioneer women had to be tough to survive. That toughness was exaggerated in Sally to show that women could be as "super" as men.)

R 2.3

2 What information does this tall tale give you about frontier life in the 1800s? (Answers may include bragging, square dancing, churning butter, and expressions such as *the whole steamboat*.)

R 3.3
R 3.7

3 How does the author use other characters to tell about Sally Ann? (She uses the accounts of the preacher, blacksmith, schoolmarm, and Lucy; she brings up the story about the bear and Mike Fink as friends' reports.)

R 3.3

4 Compare Sally to both Paul Bunyan and John Henry. How are the three characters alike and different? (All three characters perform amazing feats. Sally is a woman and she often shows how she's superior to men.)

death. But Sally paid no more attention to that fool than she would have to a barking puppy dog.

However, when Mike put out his claws to embrace her, her anger rose higher than a Mississippi flood. She threw a flash of eye lightning at him, turning the dark to daylight. Then she pulled out a little toothpick and with a single swing sent the alligator head flying fifty feet! And then to finish him off good, she rolled up her sleeves and knocked Mike Fink clear across the woods and into a muddy swamp.

When the fool came to, Davy Crockett was standing over him. "What in the world happened to you, Mikey?" he asked.

"Well, I — I think I must-a been hit by some kind of wild alligator!" Mike stammered, rubbing his sore head.

Davy smiled, knowing full well it was Sally Ann Thunder Ann Whirlwind just finished giving Mike Fink the only punishment he'd ever known.

That incident caused Cupid's final arrow to jab Davy's gizzard. "Sally's the whole steamboat," he said, meaning she was something great. The next day he put on his best raccoon hat and sallied forth to see her.

When he got within three miles of her cabin, he began to holler her name. His voice was so loud, it whirled through the woods like a hurricane.

Sally looked out and saw the wind a-blowing and the trees a-bending. She heard her name a-thundering through the woods, and her heart began to thump. By now she'd begun to feel that Davy Crockett was the whole steamboat, too. So she put on her best hat — an eagle's nest with a wildcat's tail for a feather — and ran outside.

Just as she stepped out the door, Davy Crockett burst from the woods and jumped onto her porch as fast as a frog. "Sally, darlin'!" he cried. "I think my heart is bustin'! Want to be my wife?"

"Oh, my stars and possum dogs, why not?" she said.

From that day on, Davy Crockett had a hard time acting tough around Sally Ann Thunder Ann Whirlwind. His fightin' and hollerin' had no more effect on her than dropping feathers on a barn floor. At least that's what *she'd* tell you. *He* might say something else.

124

LS 2.1.a
LS 2.1.b

Performing Reader's Theater

The story *Sally Ann Thunder Ann Whirlwind* has plenty of dialogue to make an exciting reader's theater. Invite students to prepare and perform a reading.

California Standards pp. F124–F125

R 1.1 Read aloud fluently	**R 3.3** Determine character traits
R 2.3 Discern main ideas	**R 3.7** Evaluate author's techniques
R 2.4 Inferences/generalizations	**LS 2.1.a** Descriptively establish situation
R 3.2 Main problem/plot conflict	**LS 2.1.b** Show what happens

Focus on Tall Tales

Sid Fleischman has created his own tall tale characters in his stories about farmer Josh McBroom. In this tale, the McBroom family has to cope with unpredictable weather and, as usual, neighbor Heck Jones.

February

by Sid Fleischman
Illustrated by Walter Lorraine

It's not generally known, but I invented air conditioning. I read in the paper the idea has already spread to the big cities.

But, shucks, everyone is welcome to it. Folks around here call it McBroom's Natural Winter Extract & Relief for the Summer Dismals. You can make your own, same as us.

February is about the last month you can lay in a supply of prime Winter Extract.

Wait for an infernal cold day. When the mercury in the thermometer drops to the bottom — you're getting close. But the weather's still a mite too warm.

When the mercury busts the glass bulb and rolls over to the fireplace to get warm — that's Extract weather.

"Will*jill*hester*chester*peter*polly*tim*tom*mary*larry*andlittle*clarinda!*" I shouted to our young'uns. "Bulb's shattered. Fetch the ripsaws, the crosscut saws, and let's get to work!"

Cold? Mercy, it was so cold outside *the wind had frozen solid.*

Didn't we get busy! We began sawing up chunks of frozen wind.

125

Reading "February"

pages 114–118 (excerpt)

▶ **Preparing to Read**

R 1.1

■ Have a volunteer read the introduction on page 125. Tell students that *February* is not a retelling, but was originally created as a written story in *McBroom's Almanac*, a book about the McBroom family over the course of one year.

■ Students may be familiar with other books about the character Josh McBroom and his one-acre farm, by author Sid Fleischman.

▶ **Purpose Setting**

LS 2.3.c

Ask students to find the most outrageous claim made by the narrator of the tale, Josh McBroom.

Vocabulary *(page 125)*

extract: a concentrated form of something

dismal: gloomy

About the Author

Sid Fleischman

Sid Fleischman's eleven books about the incredible Josh McBroom and his ornery neighbor, Heck Jones, include *McBroom Tells the Truth, McBroom and the Big Wind, McBroom's Ear, McBroom's Zoo, McBroom and the Beanstalk, McBroom the Rainmaker,* and *McBroom and the Great Race.* In 1987, Fleischman won the Newbery Medal for *The Whipping Boy.*

LS 2.3.c Use examples

Reading "February," *continued*
pages 125–127

· ·

▶ **Supporting Comprehension**

R 3.3
R 3.7

10 What kind of personality does the author give Josh McBroom? (He gives McBroom a talkative, confiding, cheerful personality.)

11 What does the author's invented language, such as *Summer Dismals, sizzle-hot,* and *scrambly-witted*, add to this tall tale? (Sample answers: humor, exaggeration, folksiness)

✏️ **Journal Writing** Students can write directions for a ridiculous activity, modeled after McBroom's directions for sawing winter winds.

Vocabulary *(pages 126–127)*

skinflint: someone who is very reluctant to spend money.

rustle: to steal, especially livestock

instinct: knowledge one is born with

navigated: steered

10   Now, you got to do the thing right. Wind's got a grain, just like wood. So be positive to use the crosscut saw against the grain, and the ripsaw along with it.

It fell dark before we finished harvesting and hauling that Winter Extract to our icehouse. And there stood our neighbor Heck Jones. That <u>skinflint</u> is so mean and miserly he brands the horseflies over at his place for fear someone will <u>rustle</u> 'em.

"Are you hidin' my left sock, McBroom?" he asked.

"Of course not," I said.

"Someone stole it off the clothesline. My best black sock, too! It only had three holes in it. If I catch the thief, I'll have him in a court of law!"

He loped away, grumbling and snarling.

We finished packing sawdust around the chunks of wind to keep them frozen. "Good work, my lambs," I said. "We're all set for the Summer Dismals."

Well, Heck Jones walked around in one sock the rest of winter, and summer, too.

126

⬤ **Reaching All Students**

English Language Learners

Intermediate and Advanced Fluency

Slang and Colloquialisms

February contains phrases that English language learners may find difficult. Pair English language learners with native speakers to define colloquial passages such as: *That skinflint is so mean and miserly he brands the horseflies over at his place for fear someone will rustle 'em.*

California Standards pp. F126–F127

R 3.1 Analyze literary forms
R 3.3 Determine character traits
R 3.7 Evaluate author's techniques

LS 2.3.a Summarize events/details
LS 2.3.b Understand ideas/images
LS 2.3.c Use examples

As soon as the days turned sizzle-hot, we'd set a chunk of Winter Extract in the parlor. In a second or three it would begin to thaw — just a cool breeze at first. But when that February wind really got whistling, it would lift the curtains!

One hot night I fetched in a nice chunk of frozen wind without bothering to scrape off the sawdust. A few minutes later I saw a black thing shoot across the room. Something had got frozen in our Winter Extract.

"Heck Jones's sock!" I declared. "I can smell his feet!"

He was sure to think we'd stolen it. He'd have us in a court of law! I made a grab for it, but the February wind was kicking up such a blow it shot the sock past the curtains and far out the window.

I could see Heck Jones asleep in his hammock, one sock on, the other foot bare. The left sock hoisted its tail like a kite in the air and started down.

I declare, if I didn't see it with my own eyes, I'd think I was scrambly-witted. That holey black sock had the instinct of a homing pigeon. It returned right to Heck Jones's left foot and pulled itself on. I think it navigated by scent.

What Heck Jones thought when he awoke and looked at both feet — I can't reckon.

11

127

Wrapping Up "February"
pages 125–127

Comparing and Contrasting Tall Tales

R 3.3
R 3.5
LS 2.3.a
LS 2.3.b
LS 2.3.c

Invite students to compare and contrast the tall tales they have read by asking the following:

1 Compare the actions of the main characters in the four stories in the Focus on Tall Tales. (Sample answer: Paul Bunyan, John Henry, and McBroom are working; Sally is helping someone.)

2 How are the endings of the four stories alike or different? (Three are open-ended, but John Henry dies at the end of his story.)

3 Which tall tale did you find the funniest? (Answers will vary.) What did that writer do that made you laugh? (Answers will vary.)

4 How would you describe what makes a good tall tale? Use examples from the four tall tales. (Answers will vary.)

Extending

Before students begin writing their own tall tales, you can teach the following writing lesson.

Writing Lesson
Tall Tales

W 1.1.a
W 1.1.b
W 1.1.c
W 2.1.a

OBJECTIVES

Students write a tall tale.

Review the definition of *tall tales* with students. Discuss some of the choices students will need to make to write their tall tale:

- Who will my main character be? What are his or her extraordinary qualities?

- What is the setting for my story? How is it special or exaggerated?

- How will I make my tall tale funny?

Read aloud "Write Your Own Tall Tale" on page 128. If necessary, give additional prompts:

- Have students refer to their journals for ideas.

- Share other tall tales to use as models.

- Discuss the postcard images on page 128 as ideas for characters and exaggerations.

Have students meet in small groups to brainstorm and outline their tall tale before they write. Then have them follow the stages of the writing process, including drafting, asking "Is this a good tall tale?", editing, and publishing. Allow students time to read their tall tales aloud.

Narrating

Write Your Own Tall Tale

Now that you've read a few tall tales, write one of your own. Think of a heroic main character with amazing abilities. Think of a problem that the character has to solve. Then write a tall tale about how the character solves the problem. The postcard images on this page might give you some ideas for your tall tale.

Tips

- Exaggerate qualities or features of your character, such as size or strength.
- Exaggerate features of the setting, such as the weather, landscape, or animals.
- Have your character change something in nature — for example, end a heat wave or create a river.

128

California Standards pp. F128–F129

W 1.1.a Establish a plot
W 1.1.b Describe setting
W 1.1.c Present ending

W 2.1.a Establish plot, setting
LS 2.1.a Establish situation
LS 2.1.b Show what happens

More Tall Tales to Read

Swamp Angel
by Anne Isaacs (Dutton)
A brave woodswoman in Tennessee saves the community from the dangerous bear, Thundering Tarnation.

The Gullywasher
by Joyce Rossi (Northland)
Leticia's grandfather tells her how a gigantic gullywasher changed him from a daring young vaquero to the old man he is now.

Pecos Bill
by Steven Kellogg (Morrow)
The most famous cowboy in Texas grew up among the coyotes, invented many useful things such as the lasso, and married the equally famous Slewfoot Sue.

The Bunyans
by Audrey Wood (Scholastic)
Meet Paul Bunyan's giant wife, Carrie, and their enormous children Little Jean and Tiny, who helped Paul create many famous American sites.

Cut From the Same Cloth
by Robert San Souci (Philomel)
This collection features tall tales about legendary women from all corners and populations of America.

Presentation Activities

Use one or more of these activities to extend the *Focus on Tall Tales*.

Illustrated Tall Tales Collection

Encourage students to illustrate their tall tales. Collect the illustrated tall tales into a classroom book and donate the book to the library after everyone in the class has had a chance to read it.

Tall Tales Bookshelf

Have students create a shelf or table of books of tall tales that they have enjoyed reading, including the titles on this page. Students can do book talks for one another, describing the tall tales that they have chosen.

Dramatization

Invite students to create a play based on their tall tale. Or students can act out their favorite character from a tall tale and try to stump their classmates.

LS 2.1.a
LS 2.1.b

Glossary

This glossary contains meanings and pronunciations for some of the words in this book. The Full Pronunciation Key shows how to pronounce each consonant and vowel in a special spelling. At the bottom of the glossary pages is a shortened form of the full key.

Full Pronunciation Key

Consonant Sounds

b	**bib**, ca**bb**age	kw	**ch**oir, **qu**ick	t	**t**igh**t**, s**t**o**pp**ed
ch	**ch**ur**ch**, sti**tch**	l	li**d**, nee**d**le, ta**ll**	th	**b**a**th**, **th**in
d	**d**ee**d**, mai**l**ed, pu**dd**le	m	a**m**, **m**an, du**mb**	th	**b**a**th**e, **th**is
f	**f**ast, **f**i**f**e, o**ff**, **ph**rase, rou**gh**	n	**n**o, sudde**n**	v	ca**v**e, **v**al**v**e, **v**ine
		ng	thi**ng**, i**nk**	w	**w**ith, **w**olf
g	**g**a**g**, **g**et, fin**g**er	p	**p**o**p**, ha**pp**y	y	**y**es, **y**olk, on**i**on
h	**h**at, **wh**o	r	**r**oa**r**, **rh**yme	z	ro**s**e, **s**i**z**e, **x**ylophone, **z**ebra
hw	**wh**ich, **wh**ere	s	mi**ss**, **s**au**c**e, **sc**ene, **s**ee		
j	**j**u**dg**e, **g**em			zh	gara**g**e, plea**s**ure, vi**s**ion
k	**c**at, **k**i**ck**, s**ch**ool	sh	**d**i**sh**, **sh**ip, **s**ugar, ti**ss**ue		

Vowel Sounds

ă	p**a**t, l**au**gh	ŏ	h**o**rrible, p**o**t	ŭ	c**u**t, fl**oo**d, r**ou**gh, s**o**me
ā	**a**pe, **ai**d, p**ay**	ō	g**o**, r**ow**, t**oe**, th**ou**gh		
â	**a**ir, c**a**re, w**ea**r	ô	**a**ll, c**au**ght, f**o**r, p**aw**	û	c**i**rcle, f**u**r, h**ea**rd, t**er**m, t**ur**n, **ur**ge, w**or**d
ä	f**a**ther, k**oa**la, y**a**rd	oi	b**oy**, n**oi**se, **oi**l		
ĕ	p**e**t, pl**ea**sure, **a**ny	ou	c**ow**, **ou**t	yōō	c**u**re
ē	b**e**, b**ee**, **ea**sy, p**ia**no	ōō	f**u**ll, b**oo**k, w**o**lf	yōō	ab**u**se, **u**se
ĭ	**i**f, p**i**t, b**u**sy	ōō	b**oo**t, r**u**de, fr**ui**t, fl**ew**	ə	**a**go, sil**e**nt, penc**i**l, lem**o**n, circ**u**s
ī	r**i**de, b**y**, p**ie**, h**igh**				
î	d**ea**r, d**ee**r, f**ie**rce, m**e**re				

Stress Marks

Primary Stress ´: bi·ol·o·gy [bī **ŏl**´ ə jē]
Secondary Stress ´: bi·o·log·i·cal [bī´ ə **lŏj**´ ĭ kəl]

Pronunciation key and definitions © 1998 by Houghton Mifflin Company. Adapted and reprinted by permission from *The American Heritage Children's Dictionary*.

674

A

ab·o·li·tion·ist (ăb´ ə **lĭsh**´ ə nĭst) *n.* A person who felt that slavery should be against the law. *Quakers and other abolitionists believed that owning slaves was wrong.*

a·bun·dant (ə **bŭn**´ dənt) *adj.* More than enough; plentiful. *Fish and game were abundant along the coast.*

ac·com·pa·ni·ment (ə **kŭm**´ pə nĭ mənt) *n.* A musical part, usually played on an instrument, that goes along with the performance of a singer or musician. *Victoria sang to the accompaniment of a guitar.*

ad·ven·ture (ăd **vĕn**´ chər) *n.* An unusual or exciting experience. *Greg thought that sailing to Africa would be a real adventure.*

ag·gres·sive (ə **grĕs**´ ĭv) *adj.* Ready and quick to fight; bold. *The bear cub snarled in an aggressive way.*

am·a·teur (**ăm**´ ə chər) *n.* Someone who performs a sport or other activity without being paid. *You must be an amateur to compete in high school sports.*

a·maz·ing·ly (ə **mā**´ zĭng lē) *adv.* In a way that causes surprise or wonder. *The test questions were amazingly easy.*

ap·plause (ə **plôz**´) *n.* The clapping of hands to show approval. *Adam's speech was greeted with loud applause.*

ap·pren·tice (ə **prĕn**´ tĭs) *n.* Someone who works for another person in order to learn a trade. *The blacksmith helped the apprentice learn how to use the tools.*

arm (ärm) *v.* To equip with weapons. *The rebels were arming themselves as the British troops approached the town.*

ar·ti·fi·cial (är´ tə **fĭsh**´ əl) *adj.* Created by humans rather than occuring in nature. *The zookeepers built an artificial den for the lion to live in.*

ar·tis·tic (är **tĭs**´ tĭk) *adj.* Showing imagination and skill in creating something beautiful. *The dancers gave an artistic performance.*

as·tro·naut (**ăs**´ trə nôt) *n.* A person trained to fly in a spacecraft. *Neil Armstrong was the first astronaut to walk on the moon.*

at·tach·ment (ə **tăch**´ mənt) *n.* A feeling of closeness and affection. *The two cousins have a strong attachment to one another.*

amateur
Amateur comes from the Latin word *amare*, which means "to love." Someone who is an amateur takes part in an activity for the love of it.

apprentice
Apprentice comes from the Latin word *apprehendere*, which means "to grasp." An apprentice is a learner who must grasp what to do in a profession.

astronaut
This word was created in 1929 by combining two ancient Greek word parts, *astro-* and *nautes*, which translate as "star sailor."

ōō **boot** / ou **out** / ŭ **cut** / û **fur** / hw **which** / th **thin** / *th* **this** / zh **vision** / ə **ago, silent, pencil, lemon, circus**

675

---

au·di·ence (**ô**´ dē əns) *n.* People who gather to see and hear a performance. *The audience cheered loudly as the singer bowed.*

B

ban·dit (**băn**´ dĭt) *n.* An outlaw, especially one who robs. *The bandit demanded that the passengers hand over their wallets.*

bluff (blŭf) *n.* A high cliff or bank. *From the top of the bluff, he could see the entire valley.*

braille (brāl) *n.* A system of writing that uses raised dots, for people who are visually impaired. *Angela ran her fingers over the braille letters on the page.*

C

cache (kăsh) *n.* A store of hidden goods. *The bear dug up the campers' cache of food.*

can·o·py (**kăn**´ ə pē) *n.* The highest layer of a forest, formed by the treetops. *Many kinds of parrots and monkeys live in the dense canopy of the rain forest.*

cap·tive (**kăp**´ tĭv) *n.* A prisoner. *The soldiers brought their captives back to the fort.* — *adj.* Captured; held against one's will. *The captive squirrel managed to escape from the trap.*

car·cass (**kär**´ kəs) *n.* The dead body of an animal. *The wolves fed on the carcass of a deer.*

car·go (**kär**´ gō) *n., pl.* **cargoes.** The freight carried by a ship or other vehicle. *The ship's cargo included molasses from the West Indies.*

car·i·bou (**kăr**´ ə bōō´) *n., pl.* **caribou.** A large deer found in northern North America, related to the reindeer. *The herd of caribou swam across the river.*

cau·tious (**kô**´ shəs) *adj.* Careful; not taking chances. *It is best to be cautious when crossing a busy street.*

cel·e·bra·tion (sĕl´ ə **brā**´ shən) *n.* A special activity that honors a person, event, or idea. *I invited ten friends to my birthday celebration.*

cin·der (**sĭn**´ dər) *n.* A partly burned piece of coal or wood. *A pile of cinders lay at the bottom of the fire pit.*

claim (klām) *n.* A piece of land that someone reserves for ownership. *The settlers took a claim that bordered on the river.*

col·lide (kə **līd**´) *v.* To come together with forceful impact. *When warm and cold air masses collide, the weather becomes stormy.*

braille
Louis Braille (1809–1852) was a French inventor who lost his sight at the age of three and as a student of fifteen created the unique writing system that bears his name.

canopy
The Greek word *konopeion*, a bed with a netting to keep out mosquitoes, gave us the word for the covering created by treetops in a rain forest.

caribou
Caribou is the Canadian French version of a Native American word — the Micmac *khalibu*, which means "snow scraper."

ă **rat** / ā **pay** / â **care** / ä **father** / ĕ **pet** / ē **be** / ĭ **pit** / ī **pie** / î **fierce** / ŏ **pot** / ō **go** / ô **paw, for** / oi **oil** / ōō **book**

676

---

col·o·ny (**kŏl**´ ə nē) *n., pl.* **colonies** A territory ruled by or belonging to another country. *The thirteen colonies no longer wanted to be taxed by England.*

com·pete (kəm **pēt**´) *v.* To take part in a contest. *The runners hoped to compete in the Boston Marathon.*

con·cen·trate (**kŏn**´ sən trāt´) *v.* To give full attention to. *It is difficult to concentrate on my book when the television is on.*

con·flict (**kŏn**´ flĭkt´) *n.* A struggle; a war. *The United States had a second conflict with England in 1812.*

con·vinced (kən **vĭnsd**´) *adj.* Persuaded; certain. *They were convinced that the bridge was strong enough to carry their weight.*

cra·ter (**krā**´ tər) *n.* A hollow bowl-shaped area at the mouth of a volcano. *The hikers peered down into the deep rocky crater below.*

crust (krŭst) *n.* The hard outer layer of the earth. *Cracks in the earth's crust help create volcanoes.*

cus·tom (**kŭs**´ təm) *n.* Something that members of a group usually do. *One of the customs of people in the desert is to offer visitors refreshment and shade.*

D

de·bris (də **brē**´) *n.* The remains of something broken or destroyed; rubble. *The bulldozer pushed the debris into the corner of the lot.*

de·but (dā **byōō**´) *n.* First public performance. *The actor made his stage debut as Peter Pan.*

dec·o·rate (**dĕk**´ ə rāt´) *v.* To make festive or beautiful. *We will decorate the room with flowers and streamers.*

dem·on·stra·tion (dĕm´ ən **strā**´ shən) *n.* A showing and explanation of how something works. *The teacher gave a demonstration of how to operate a camera.*

de·scrip·tion (dĭ **skrĭp**´ shən) *n.* A statement that uses words to tell about something. *Debbie wrote an exciting description of the game.*

de·tain (dĭ **tān**´) *v.* To delay; to hold back. *If you detain us much longer, we will miss the bus.*

de·ter·mi·na·tion (dĭ tûr´ mə **nā**´ shən) *n.* Firmness in carrying out a decision. *The team's determination to do better showed in how well they played.*

dev·as·ta·tion (dĕv´ ə **stā**´ shən) *n.* Destruction or ruin. *The floods brought devastation to much of the coast.*

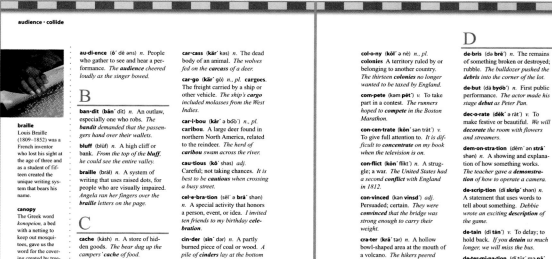

crater

ōō **boot** / ou **out** / ŭ **cut** / û **fur** / hw **which** / th **thin** / *th* **this** / zh **vision** / ə **ago, silent, pencil, lemon, circus**

677

---

dex·ter·i·ty (děk **stěr´** ĭ tē) *n.* Skill in the use of the hands, body, or mind. *The juggler showed great **dexterity** in keeping the oranges in the air.*

di·a·ry (**dī´** ə rē) *n., pl.* **diaries.** A daily record of a person's thoughts and experiences. *Every night Marta wrote about the day's events in her **diary.***

dominance
The root of this word is the Latin word *domus,* meaning "house." The head of a household often had control, or dominance, over a large staff of people.

dic·ta·tor (**dĭk´** tā tər) *n.* A ruler who has complete power over a country. *The **dictator** would not allow any citizens to travel outside the country.*

di·lem·ma (dĭ **lěm´** ə) *n.* A situation in which one has to choose between two or more difficult options. *Sara's **dilemma** was whether to wake up her father or try to figure out the problem herself.*

dim sum (dĭm´ sŏŏm´) *n.* A type of traditional Chinese meal where small portions of different foods are served one after another. *Many Chinese restaurants serve **dim sum** on Sunday mornings.*

dis·ap·point·ed (dĭs´ ə **point´** əd) *adj.* Unhappy because of an unsatisfied hope or wish. *Tanya was **disappointed** when her team lost the game.*

dis·com·fort (dĭs **kŭm´** fərt) *n.* A feeling of mild distress. *Noah always feels **discomfort** when people ask him about his famous brother.*

dim sum

dis·cour·aged (dĭ **skûr´** ĭjd) *adj.* Not hopeful or enthusiastic. *Sam felt **discouraged** when he learned that he had not won a prize.*

dis·mayed (dĭs **mād´**) *adj.* Filled with sudden concern or distress. *They were **dismayed** to learn that the bus had left without them.*

dog guide (dôg gīd) *n.* A dog especially trained to lead visually impaired people. *May's **dog guide** waited until it was safe to cross the street.*

dom·i·nance (**dŏm´** ə nəns) *n.* The greatest control within a group. *Wolves compete for **dominance** in the pack.*

dread (drĕd) *n.* Great fear. *The panther's roar filled the villagers with **dread.***

drill (drĭl) *v.* To perform training exercises. *The soldiers were **drilling** all morning.*

du·o (**dŏŏ´** ō) *n.* Two people performing together. *The sisters performed in the show as a singing **duo.***

E

earth·quake (**ûrth´** kwāk´) *n.* A trembling or shaking of the ground caused by sudden movements in rock below the earth's surface. *The **earthquake** caused buildings to topple.*

å rat / ā **pay** / â **care** / ä **father** / ĕ **pet** / ē **be** / ĭ **pit** / ī **pie** / î **fierce** / ŏ **pot** / ō **go** /
ô **paw, for** / oi **oil** / ŏŏ **book**
678

el·e·ment (**ĕl´** ə mənt) *n.* A basic part of a whole. *Spirals, spins, and jumps are **elements** of a figure skating program.*

em·bar·rassed (ĕm **băr´** əsd) *adj.* Made to feel self-conscious and ill at ease. *Josh felt **embarrassed** when he realized he had called her by the wrong name.*

en·cour·age (ĕn **kûr´** ĭj) *v.* To give support to; to inspire. *Hal's parents **encouraged** him to become a skater.*

en·slave·ment (ĕn **slāv´** mənt) *n.* The process by which one person becomes the property of another. *After years of **enslavement** by cruel owners, the men were set free.*

e·rup·tion (ĭ **rŭp´** shən) *n.* A volcanic explosion or large flow of lava. *The newspaper showed photos of the **eruption** of a volcano in Nicaragua.*

ex·cite·ment (ĭk **sīt´** mənt) *n.* A stirred-up feeling. *The fire caused a lot of **excitement** in our neighborhood.*

ex·per·i·ence (ĭk **spîr´** ē əns) *n.* An event that someone takes part in or lives through. *Camping was a new **experience** for the children.*

ex·press (ĭk **prĕs´**) *adj.* Fast, direct, and often nonstop. ***Express** services promise overnight deliveries.*

ex·tend·ed (ĭk **stĕn´** dĭd) *adj.* Including more; broadened. *Your **extended** family includes your aunts, uncles, and cousins.*

ex·tinc·tion (ĭk **stĭngk´** shən) *n.* The condition of having died out. *No one knows for sure what caused the **extinction** of the dinosaurs.*

F

eruption

fash·ion (**fǎsh´** ən) *v.* To give a form or shape to; to make. *Ralph was able to **fashion** a waterproof cape from a large plastic bag.*

fault (fôlt) *n.* A break in a rock mass caused by a shifting of the earth's crust. *An active **fault** runs through the center of our town.*

fer·tile (**fûr´** tl) *adj.* Rich in material needed to grow healthy plants. *Wheat and corn grew well in the prairie's **fertile** soil.*

fes·tive (**fĕs´** tĭv) *adj.* Joyful; merry. *The party guests were in a **festive** mood.*

fierce (fîrs) *adj.* Intense; ferocious. *The lion gave a **fierce** roar.*

fierce
The Latin word *ferus* ("wild and savage") is the origin of the words *ferocious* and *fierce.*

for·ty-five re·cord (fôr´ tē **fīv´ rěk´** ərd) *n.* A small phonograph record that is played at forty-five revolutions per minute. *The **forty-five record** has one song on each side.*

ŏŏ **boot** / ou **out** / ŭ **cut** / û **fur** / hw **which** / th **thin** / *th* **this** / zh **vision** / ə **ago,**
silent, pencil, lemon, circus
679

funnel cloud

fran·tic (**frǎn´** tĭk) *adj.* Very upset, as from fear or worry. *When she couldn't find her backpack anywhere, Julie became **frantic.***

fright·ened (**frīt´** nd) *adj.* Scared, alarmed. *Billy was **frightened** as he stepped out on the diving board.*

fun·nel cloud (**fŭn´** əl kloud´) *n.* A storm cloud that is wide at the top and narrow at the bottom, often becoming a tornado. *Whenever the settlers saw **funnel clouds,** they hurried toward storm shelters.*

G

gene (jēn) *n.* A tiny part of a plant or animal cell that determines a characteristic passed on to the next generation. *Lucy has blue eyes like her parents because of their **genes.***

H

hab·i·tat (**hǎb´** ĭ tǎt´) *n.* The type of environment where an animal or plant naturally lives and grows. *Sloths and jaguars live in the rain forest **habitat.***

harsh (härsh) *adj.* Demanding and severe; unpleasant. *Winter is a **harsh** season for most animals.*

har·vest (**här´** vĭst) *v.* To gather a crop. *The workers were **harvesting** apples.*

heif·er (**hěf´** ər) *n.* A young cow that has not yet had a calf. *Sally's cow has been winning blue ribbons since it was a **heifer.***

herd (hûrd) *n.* A group of animals of a single kind. *A **herd** of wild horses galloped across the plain.*

her·i·tage (**hěr´** ĭ tĭj) *n.* Traditions, practices, and beliefs passed down from earlier generations. *Yinglan celebrates her Chinese **heritage** in her choice of music, clothes, and food.*

home·stead (**hōm´** stěd´) *n.* A piece of land given to settlers for farming and building a home. *The Andersens' **homestead** lay near Blackberry Creek.*

hon·or (**ŏn´** ər) *v.* To show respect for; to accept. *They will **honor** their mother's request to dress up for Thanksgiving dinner.*

hu·mid (**hyōō´** mĭd) *adj.* Containing a large amount of water vapor; damp, sticky. *The air is often **humid** before a storm.*

I

im·mi·grant (**ĭm´** ĭ grənt) *n.* A person who moves to a new country. *Many **immigrants** from Norway made their homes on the Great Plains.*

å rat / ā **pay** / â **care** / ä **father** / ĕ **pet** / ē **be** / ĭ **pit** / ī **pie** / î **fierce** / ŏ **pot** / ō **go** /
ô **paw, for** / oi **oil** / ŏŏ **book**
680

im·mo·bile (ĭ **mō´** bəl) *adj.* Fixed in one place; unable to move. *He stood **immobile** against the cliff face as the hikers passed by.*

im·pact (**ĭm´** pǎkt) *n.* The striking of one object against another. *The **impact** of the bike hitting the fence knocked the flowerpots to the ground.*

im·press (ĭm **prěs´**) *v.* To have a strong, favorable effect on someone's feelings. *His piano playing **impressed** the audience.*

in·flu·en·tial (ĭn´ flŏŏ **ěn´** shəl) *adj.* Having the power to affect events or sway opinions. *The **influential** Women's League brought the problem to the mayor's attention.*

in·her·it (ĭn **hěr´** ĭt) *v.* To receive something from a parent or ancestor. *They **inherited** their mother's talent for music.*

in·stinct (**ĭn´** stĭngkt) *n.* An inner feeling or way of behaving that is automatic, not learned. *A newly hatched sea turtle's **instinct** is to crawl toward the water.*

in·tense (ĭn **těns´**) *adj.* Very strong; focused. *Patrice put in hours of **intense** study to get ready for the test.*

J

jag·ged (**jǎg´** ĭd) *adj.* Having a ragged or pointed edge or outline. *Jamal cut his hand on a **jagged** piece of tin.*

jar (jär) *v.* To bump or cause to shake from impact. *By **jarring** Matthew, I caused him to drop the ball.*

jolt (jōlt) *n.* A sudden jerk or bump. *When the car went over the speed bump, the passengers got quite a **jolt.***

judge (jŭj) *n.* A person who decides who wins a contest. *The **judges** awarded first prize to my grandfather's pumpkin pie.*

just (jŭst) *adj.* Honorable and fair. *It is **just** to listen to both sides of an argument.*

K

kin (kĭn) *n.* Relatives; family. *Your father's cousins are your **kin,** too.*

L

launch (lônch) *v.* To forcefully send upward. *A powerful blast **launches** the rocket into the sky.*

la·va (**lä´** və) *n.* Hot melted rock that flows from a volcano. *As the **lava** moved down the hillside, it set fire to the trees in its path.*

lava
People from Naples, Italy, near Mt. Vesuvius, used the Italian word *lava,* meaning "a stream caused suddenly by rain" for the molten rock that flowed down the volcano. It became an English word in 1750.

ŏŏ **boot** / ou **out** / ŭ **cut** / û **fur** / hw **which** / th **thin** / *th* **this** / zh **vision** / ə **ago,**
silent, pencil, lemon, circus
681

lay·out (lā´ out´) *n.* The way something is arranged. *The layout of the office building confuses visitors.*

lib·er·ty (lib´ ər tē) *n.* Freedom from the control of others; independence. *The colonists won their liberty from England.*

light·ning (līt´ ning) *n.* The flash of light when electricity builds up in storm clouds. *A bolt of lightning lit up the night sky.*

lime·light (līm´ līt´) *n.* The center of public attention. *Ana's performance in the play brought her into the limelight.*

M

mag·ma (măg´ mə) *n.* Molten rock underneath the earth's surface. *Magma boiled up through cracks deep inside the mountain.*

mare (mâr) *n.* A female horse. *Some of the mares were followed by their colts.*

mas·ter (măs´ tər) *v.* To become expert in a skill or art. *Ramón mastered the violin through years of practice.*

ma·ture (mə tyŏŏr´) *adj.* Fully grown or mentally developed. *A mature dog is calmer than a puppy.*

mem·o·rize (mĕm´ ə rīz´) *v.* To learn by completely remembering. *The hikers are memorizing the landmarks along their route.*

mi·gra·tion (mī grā´ shən) *n.* A movement of animals to a different habitat, especially in response to the change of seasons. *Scientists have mapped the spring migration of the whales.*

mill (mĭl) *v.* To move around in confusion. *The impatient crowd milled in front of the theater doors.*

mis·sion (mĭsh´ ən) *n.* An operation that attempts to achieve certain goals or carry out specific tasks. *The astronauts' mission included bringing back samples of moon rocks.*

mol·ten (mōl´ tən) *adj.* Made liquid by heat. *The molten lava glowed red-orange.*

mus·tang (mŭs´ tăng´) *n.* A wild horse of the plains of western North America. *Joe could not ride as fast as the herd of mustangs.*

N

no·ble (nō´ bəl) *adj.* Showing greatness of character by unselfish behavior. *It was noble of Karen to share her prize money with her teammates.*

no·to·ri·ous (nō tōr´ ē əs) *adj.* Well known for something bad. *Billy the Kid was a notorious outlaw.*

limelight
In the 1800s, theaters used limelights, made by burning the mineral lime. That bright stage light came to stand for the attention of the public.

mustang
This word for a wild horse came from the Mexican Spanish word *mestengo*, which means "stray animal."

à rat / ā pay / â care / ä father / ĕ pet / ē be / ĭ pit / ī pie / î fierce / ŏ pot / ō go / ô paw, for / oi oil / ŏŏ book

682

O

o·be·di·ence (ō bē´ dē əns) *n.* Willingness to follow orders. *Mr. Yee expects obedience from his crew.*

ob·ser·va·tion (ŏb´ zûr vā´ shən) *n.* The act of paying careful attention. *You can learn a lot about nature through observation.*

ob·sta·cle (ŏb´ stə kəl) *n.* A thing that stands in one's way. *The horse had to jump over such obstacles as bushes and fences.*

op·er·a (ŏp´ ə rə) *n.* A form of theater in which the dialogue is sung to musical accompaniment. *The actors in the opera wore beautiful costumes.*

op·pose (ə pōz´) *v.* To be against something or someone. *The neighbors oppose the plan to turn the park into an office building.*

or·bit (ôr´ bĭt) *n.* The path of a spacecraft around the earth. *Shannon Lucid spent six months in orbit aboard the spacecraft Mir.*

o·ver·take (ō´ vər tāk´) *v.* To catch up with. *If we continue at this pace, we will overtake Billie's group.*

P

pan·to·mime (păn´ tə mīm´) *n.* The use of movements and facial expressions instead of words to convey meaning. *Jean used pantomime to show us how she caught the fish.*

Pa·tri·ot (pā´ trē ət) *n.* A colonist who was against British rule in the time of the Revolutionary War. *Patrick Henry spoke as a Patriot when he said "Give me liberty or give me death!"*

peer (pĭr) *v.* To look at with concentration. *Mom peered at Paul suspiciously as he told his story.*

pi·o·neer (pī´ ə nîr´) *adj.* Describing a person who is first or among the first to settle in a region. *Our town was settled by three pioneer families in the 1800s.*

prai·rie (prâr´ ē) *n.* A large area of flat or rolling grassland. *The treeless prairie stretched for miles in all directions.*

pred·a·tor (prĕd´ ə tər) *n.* An animal that hunts other animals for food. *Small lizards must always be on the alert for hungry predators.*

pres·en·ta·tion (prĕz´ ən tā´ shən) *n.* Performance. *Although the actor knew his lines, his presentation was flat.*

pioneer
This word comes from the French word *peonier*, meaning "foot soldier." Those who marched into unknown territory were often soldiers on an expedition.

ŏŏ boot / ou out / ŭ cut / û fur / hw which / th thin / th this / zh vision / ə ago, silent, pencil, lemon, circus

683

---

pres·sure (prĕsh´ ər) *n.* A strong influence or force. *Sandra felt pressure to finish the book over the weekend.*

pri·va·teer (prī´ və tîr´) *n.* A privately owned ship that is ordered by the government to attack enemy ships during a war. *The privateers captured several merchant ships without firing a shot.*

pro·gram (prō´ grăm´) *n.* In figure skating, the routine that one performs in front of judges or an audience. *The young skater spent hours getting his program ready for the competition.*

prose (prōz) *n.* Ordinary spoken or written language, in contrast to poetry. *Most fiction and nonfiction books are written in prose.*

R

raid (rād) *n.* A sudden attack, often with the goal of taking property. *The men brought back horses after their raid on their neighbors' village.*

ra·vine (rə vēn´) *n.* A narrow, deep valley, usually formed by the flow of water. *A small stream trickled at the bottom of the ravine.*

reb·el (rĕb´ əl) *n.* A person who opposes or defies the government in power. *The rebels refused to obey King George's laws.*

ref·u·gee (rĕf´ yŏŏ jē´) *n.* A person who flees to find protection from danger. *As the fighting in the hills grew worse, refugees streamed into the city.*

re·hear·sal (rĭ hûr´ səl) *n.* A session of practicing for a public performance. *The cast needed one more rehearsal before the play opened.*

re·in·tro·duc·tion (rē´ ĭn trə dŭk´ shən) *n.* The process of returning animals to their native habitats. *The zoo's tamarins are doing well since their reintroduction into the rain forest.*

re·ject (rĭ jĕkt´) *v.* To refuse to accept. *The magazine rejected her poem.*

re·luc·tant (rĭ lŭk´ tənt) *adj.* Unwilling to take an action. *Emily was reluctant to get out of the swimming pool.*

re·morse (rĭ môrs´) *n.* A feeling of regret or guilt for having done something wrong. *Jennie felt remorse for the trouble she had caused her sister.*

rep·u·ta·tion (rĕp´ yə tā´ shən) *n.* What others think about someone's character, behavior, and abilities. *Alex had a reputation for getting along well with everyone.*

re·quired (rĭ kwīrd´) *adj.* Needed. *Kayla has all of the training required for this job.*

ravine

à rat / ā pay / â care / ä father / ĕ pet / ē be / ĭ pit / ī pie / î fierce / ŏ pot / ō go / ô paw, for / oi oil / ŏŏ book

684

---

re·spect (rĭ spĕkt´) *n.* A feeling of admiration and approval. *Mr. Garcia won the respect of all his students.*

re·us·a·ble (rē yŏŏz´ ə bəl) *adj.* Able to be used again. *April's family never throws away reusable paper bags.*

rev·o·lu·tion·ar·y (rĕv´ ə lŏŏ´ shə nĕr´ ē) *adj.* Connected with complete change. *The American colonists fought for their independence from England during the Revolutionary War.*

rhyth·mic (rĭth´ mĭk) *adj.* Having a noticeable beat with a pattern to it. *It is easy to dance to rhythmic music.*

ro·tate (rō´ tāt) *v.* To turn around on a center or axis. *It takes twenty-four hours for the earth to rotate once.*

rug·ged (rŭg´ ĭd) *adj.* Having a very rough and uneven surface. *The valley was surrounded by rugged mountains.*

S

sat·el·lite (săt´ l īt´) *n.* A human-made device that orbits a planet. *A weather satellite sends weather photos and data back to earth.*

sen·try (sĕn´ trē) *n., pl.,* **sentries**. A guard who is posted at a spot to keep watch. *Two sentries guarded the gates of the city.*

se·vere (sə vîr´) *adj.* Serious or extreme in nature. *Severe thunderstorms caused flooding in parts of the Midwest.*

shud·der (shŭd´ ər) *v.* To suddenly shake, vibrate, or quiver. *The house shuddered every time a heavy truck drove by.*

siz·zling (sĭz´ lĭng) *adj.* Crackling or hissing with intense heat. *The tree trunk was sizzling after the lightning bolt hit it.*

skir·mish (skûr´ mĭsh) *n.* A small, short fight; a minor battle. *The soldiers galloped away after a brief skirmish with the rebels.*

skit·ter (skĭt´ ər) *v.* To move lightly and quickly, especially with many changes of direction. *The mice skittered across the floor.*

skit·tish (skĭt´ ĭsh) *adj.* Nervous and jumpy. *The cat was skittish during the thunderstorm.*

snoop (snŏŏp) *n.* Someone who tries to find out about other people's doings in a sneaky way. *Maria's brother is such a snoop that she must keep her diary locked.*

sod (sŏd) *n.* A chunk of grass and soil held together by matted roots. *Settlers built houses out of blocks of sod because wood was scarce.*

satellite
In the Middle Ages the French used the word *satellite* to refer to an attendant who waited upon an important person. That same idea is in the modern meaning of a small device circling around a planet.

ŏŏ boot / ou out / ŭ cut / û fur / hw which / th thin / th this / zh vision / ə ago, silent, pencil, lemon, circus

685

Glossary (G3)

sombrero
The name of the broad-brimmed hat that shades the wearer's eyes came from the Spanish word for shade, *sombra*.

shuttle
Shuttle started out as an Old English word, *scytel*, meaning "dart." It came to mean a weaving device that carried thread back and forth, and from that, a vehicle going back and forth over a short route.

som·bre·ro (sŏm **brâr´** ō) *n.* A tall hat with a wide brim, worn in Mexico and the American Southwest. *The farmers wore* **sombreros** *to shade their eyes from the sun.*

space shut·tle (spās **shŭt´** l) *n.* A reusable spacecraft that is launched like a rocket and can be landed like a plane. *The* **space shuttle** *landed safely after a seven-day flight.*

space·craft (spās´ krăft´) *n.* A vehicle designed for travel beyond the earth's atmosphere. *The* **spacecraft** *carried astronauts to the moon.*

spe·cial·ist (spĕsh´ ə lĭst) *n.* Someone who is an expert in a particular field. *A pediatrician is a medical* **specialist** *who treats only children.*

spec·ta·tor (spĕk´ tā´ tər) *n.* A person who watches an event or performance. *The* **spectators** *cheered when Jessie hit a home run.*

splen·did (splĕn´ dĭd) *adj.* Excellent. *The actor gave a* **splendid** *performance.*

stal·lion (stăl´ yən) *n.* An adult male horse. *Lizzie rode a black* **stallion** *at the horse show.*

stam·i·na (stăm´ ə nə) *n.* The strength needed to keep doing something tiring or difficult. *A young child lacks the* **stamina** *for a ten-mile hike.*

store·house (stôr´ hous´) *n.* A place or building where supplies are stored for future use. *The settlers'* **storehouse** *contained dried fruit and hams.*

sub·mit (səb **mĭt´**) *v.* To offer one's work to someone for their judgment or approval. *She* **submitted** *an article to the student newspaper.*

sub·ser·vi·ence (səb sûr´ vē əns) *n.* Willingness to give in to others' power. *Letting the tail droop is a sign of* **subservience** *in a wolf.*

sum·mit (sŭm´ ĭt) *n.* The top of a mountain. *Carolyn and I cheered when we finally reached the* **summit** *of Mount Rainier.*

sur·viv·al (sər **vī´** vəl) *n.* The preservation or continuation of one's life. *Quick thinking is often necessary for* **survival** *in the wilderness.*

sus·pect (sə **spĕkt´**) *v.* To believe without being sure; to imagine. *Scott* **suspects** *that we are planning a surprise party for him.*

T

tack (tăk) *v.* To change the course of a boat. *The sailing ship was* **tacking** *in order to return to the harbor.*

ă rat / ā pay / â care / ä father / ĕ pet / ē be / ĭ pit / ī pie / î fierce / ŏ pot / ō go / ô paw, for / oi oil / ŏŏ book

---

tal·ent (tăl´ ənt) *n.* A natural ability to do something well. *She has a* **talent** *for playing the violin.*

tax (tăks) *n.* Money that people must pay in order to support a government. *England insisted that the colonists pay* **taxes** *on tea, stamps, and many other items.*

tech·ni·cal (tĕk´ nĭ kəl) *adj.* Showing basic knowledge of a complex task. *The acrobat performed the triple somersault with great* **technical** *skill.*

ter·ri·fy (tĕr´ ə fī´) *v.* To fill with overpowering fear. *The angry bear* **terrified** *the campers.*

ter·ri·to·ry (tĕr´ ĭ tôr´ ē) *n., pl.* **territories**. An area inhabited by an animal or animal group and defended against intruders. *The mountain lion hunted within its own* **territory.**

To·ry (tôr´ ē) *n., pl.* **Tories**. An American who sided with the British during the American Revolution. *As the British troops departed, most of the city's* **Tories** *followed.*

tor·na·do (tôr **nā´** dō) *n.* A violent, whirling wind in a funnel-shaped cloud that can cause great destruction. *Many* **tornadoes** *form in Kansas and Oklahoma.*

tra·di·tion (trə **dĭsh´** ən) *n.* The passing down of customs and beliefs from one generation to the next. *There is a long* **tradition** *of helping others in our family.*

train·ing (trā´ nĭng) *n.* The process of learning how to behave or perform. *Guide dogs must go through a long period of* **training** *before they can help people.*

trans·form (trăns **fôrm´**) *v.* To change greatly in appearance or form. *The make-up* **transformed** *the actor into the character of an old man.*

tun·dra (tŭn´ drə) *n.* A treeless Arctic region where very few plants can grow. *Large plants cannot put down roots in the frozen subsoil of the* **tundra.**

U

un·der·stand (ŭn´ dər **stănd´**) *v.* To get the meaning of. *After the teacher explained it again, Ivan could* **understand** *the problem.*

un·du·lat·ing (ŭn´ jə lā´ tĭng) *adj.* Moving in waves or with a smooth, wavy motion. *The* **undulating** *water raised and lowered the rowboat.*

un·sure (ŭn **shŏŏr´**) *adj.* Not certain; having doubts. *She was* **unsure** *of whether to bring her umbrella.*

tornado
Tornadoes were unknown and unnamed in Britain, so Americans borrowed and adapted the Spanish word *tronada*, meaning "thunderstorm."

tradition
Our word for the passing down of customs from one generation to another comes from the Latin verb *tradere*, which means "to hand down."

undulate
The Latin word for a wave, *unda*, contributes the sense of rising and falling in *undulate*.

ŏŏ boot / ou out / ŭ cut / û fur / hw which / th thin / *th* this / zh vision / ə ago, silent, pencil, lemon, circus

---

wilderness

up·heav·al (ŭp **hē´** vəl) *n.* A lifting or upward movement of the earth's crust. *The mountain range was created by a great* **upheaval.**

ur·gent·ly (ûr´ jənt lē) *adv.* In a way that calls for immediate action. *The team* **urgently** *needs someone to take Kate's place.*

V

vol·un·teer (vŏl´ ən **tîr´**) *v.* To offer to do something of one's own free will, usually without being paid. *He* **volunteered** *to make the posters for the show.*

W

war·i·ness (wâr´ ē nĭs) *n.* Extreme caution. *Wild animals show* **wariness** *with people they don't know.*

weight·less·ness (wāt´ lĭs nĭs) *n.* The condition of experiencing little or no pull of gravity. *Astronauts experience* **weightlessness** *in outer space.*

wil·der·ness (wĭl´ dər nĭs) *n.* A region in its natural state, unsettled by human beings. *Grizzly bears live in the Alaskan* **wilderness.**

wound (wŏŏnd) *n.* Injury in which the skin is cut or broken. *The soldier's* **wounds** *were not serious.*

ă rat / ā pay / â care / ä father / ĕ pet / ē be / ĭ pit / ī pie / î fierce / ŏ pot / ō go / ô paw, for / oi oil / ŏŏ book

---

Acknowledgments

Main Literature Selections

A Boy Called Slow: The True Story of Sitting Bull, by Joseph Bruchac, illustrated by Rocco Baviera. Text copyright © 1994 by Joseph Bruchac. Illustrations copyright © 1994 by Rocco Baviera. All rights reserved. Reprinted by permission of the Putnam & Grosset group, a division of Penguin Putnam Inc.

And Then What Happened, Paul Revere? by Jean Fritz, illustrated by Margot Tomes. Text copyright © 1973 by Jean Fritz. Illustrations copyright © 1973 by Margot Tomes. All rights reserved. Reprinted by permission of the Putnam & Grosset Group, a division of Penguin Putnam Inc.

Black Cowboy, Wild Horses: A True Story, by Julius Lester, illustrated by Jerry Pinkney. Text copyright © 1998 by Julius Lester. Illustrations copyright © 1998 by Jerry Pinkney. Reprinted by permission of Dial Books, a division of Penguin Putnam Inc.

Selection from Dear Mr. Henshaw, by Beverly Cleary, illustrated by Paul O. Zelinsky. Text copyright © 1983 by Beverly Cleary. Reprinted by permission of HarperCollins Publishers.

Selection from Earthquake Terror, by Peg Kehret. Copyright © 1996 by Peg Kehret. Reprinted by permission of Childrens Books, a division of Penguin Putnam Inc.

Selection from Elena, by Diane Stanley. Copyright © 1996 by Diane Stanley. Reprinted by permission of Hyperion Books for Children.

Eye of the Storm: Chasing Storms with Warren Faidley, by Stephen Kramer, photograph by Warren Faidley. Text copyright © 1997 by Stephen Kramer. Photographs copyright © 1997 by Warren Faidley. All rights reserved. Reprinted by permission of G. P. Putnam's Sons, a division of Penguin Putnam Inc.

Selection from The Fear Place, by Phyllis Reynolds Naylor. Copyright © 1994 by Phyllis Reynolds Naylor. Reprinted by permission of Atheneum Books for Young Readers, an imprint of Simon & Schuster Children's Publishing Division.

From The Golden Lion Tamarin Comes Home by George Ancona, except photographs of frog, snake and sloth by James M. Dietz and map by Isabel Ancona. Copyright © 1994 by George Ancona, except photos of frog, snake and sloth by James M. Dietz and map by Isabel Ancona. Reprinted with permission of Simon & Schuster Books for Young Readers, Simon & Schuster Children's Publishing Division. All rights reserved.

The Grizzly Bear Family Book, by Michio Hoshino, translated by Karen Collier-Taylor. Copyright © 1992 by Michio Hoshino. Reprinted by permission of North-South Books Inc., New York. All rights reserved.

"James Forten" from Now Is Your Time: The African-American Struggle for Freedom, by Walter Dean Myers. Copyright © 1991 by Walter Dean Myers. Reprinted by permission of HarperCollins Publishers.

Katie's Trunk, by Ann Turner, illustrated by Ron Himler. Text copyright © 1992 by Ann Turner. Illustrations copyright © 1992 by Ron Himler. All rights reserved. Reprinted by permission of Simon & Schuster Books for Young Readers, an imprint of Simon & Schuster Children's Publishing Division.

"La Bamba" from Baseball In April and Other Stories, by Gary Soto. Copyright © 1990 by Gary Soto. Reprinted by permission of Harcourt Inc. The song "La Bamba" adaptation and arrangement by Ritchie Valens © 1958 Picture Our Music (Renewed). All rights for U.S.A. administered by EMI Longitude Music BMI. All rights for the World except U.S.A. administered by Warner-Timerlane Publishing Corp. All rights reserved. Reprinted by permission of Warner Bros. Publications U.S. Inc.

Mae Jemison, Space Scientist, by Gail Sakurai. Copyright © 1995 by Gail Sakurai. Reprinted by permission of Childrens Press Inc., a division of Grolier Publishing.

Selection from Mariah Keeps Cool, by Mildred Pitts Walter, illustrated by Pat Cummings. Text copyright © 1990 by Mildred Pitts Walter. Cover illustration copyright © 1990 by Pat Cummings. Reprinted by permission of Simon & Schuster Books for Young Readers, an imprint of Simon & Schuster Children's Publishing Division.

Selection from Michelle Kwan: Heart of A Champion, An Autobiography. Copyright © 1997 by Michelle Kwan Corp. Reprinted by permission of Scholastic Inc. and Momentum Partners Inc.

Mom's Best Friend, by Sally Hobart Alexander, photographs by George Ancona. Text copyright © 1992 by Sally Hobart Alexander. Photographs copyright © 1992 by George Ancona. Text reprinted by permission of the Author and Bookstop Literary Agency. Photographs reprinted by permission of the Photographer. All rights reserved.

Selection from My Side of the Mountain, by Jean

Craighead George. Copyright © 1959 by Jean Craighead George. Reprinted by permission of Dutton Children's Books, a division of Penguin Putnam Inc.

Selection from Pioneer Girl Growing Up on the Prairie, by Andrea Warren. Copyright © 1998 by Andrea Warren. Reprinted by permission of HarperCollins Publishers.

Volcanoes, by Seymour Simon. Copyright © 1988 by Seymour Simon. Reprinted by permission of HarperCollins Publishers.

Selection from *Yang The Second and Her Secret Admirers,* by Lensey Namioka. Copyright © 1998 by Lensey Namioka. Reprinted by permission of Little, Brown and Company (Inc.).

Focus Selections

"A Patch of Old Snow" from *The Poetry of Robert Frost,* edited by Edward Connery Lathem. Copyright 1939, © 1967, 1969 by Henry Holt and Company, LLC. Reprinted by permission of Henry Holt and Company, LLC. Illustration by Henri Sorensen is reprinted by permission of Evelyn Johnson & Associates. Illustration copyright © 1994 by Henri Sorensen.

"Alex Rodriguez" from *Hit A Grand Slam,* by Alex Rodriguez and Greg Brown. Copyright © 1998 by Alex Rodriguez and Greg Brown. Reprinted by permission of Taylor Publishing Company.

"The Bat" from *The Collected Poems of Theodore Roethke,* by Theodore Roethke. Copyright 1938 by Theodore Roethke. Used by permission of Doubleday, a division of Random House, Inc.

"Be Glad Your Nose Is On Your Face" from *The New Kid On the Block,* by Jack Prelutsky. Copyright © 1984 by Jack Prelutsky. Reprinted by permission of HarperCollins Publishers.

Selection from *Bill Peet: An Autobiography.* Copyright © 1989 by William Peet. Reprinted by permission of Houghton Mifflin Company.

"Campfire" from *A Suitcase of Seaweed and Other Poems,* by Janet S. Wong. Copyright © 1996 by Janet S. Wong. Jacket illustration copyright © 1996 by Janet S. Wong. Reprinted with the permission of Margaret K. McElderry Books, an imprint of Simon & Schuster Children's Publishing Division.

The Case of the Runaway Appetite: A Joe Giles Mystery, by Rob Hale, is based upon a work by Hal Ober. Copyright © by Hal Ober. Adaptation and use is by permission of the author.

"Civilization" from *4-Way Stop and Other Poems,* by Myra Cohn Livingston. Copyright © 1976 by Myra Cohn Livingston. Reprinted by permission of Marian Reiner.

"Dinner Together," by Diana Rivera, from *The Invisible Ladder, An Anthology of Contemporary American Poems for Young Readers,* edited by Liz Rosenberg, published by Henry Holt and Company, 1996. Copyright © 1996 by Diana Rivera. Reprinted by permission of the author.

"Dream Variation" from *Collected Poems,* by Langston Hughes. Copyright © 1994 by the Estate of Langston Hughes. Reprinted by permission of Alfred A. Knopf, a division of Random House, Inc.

"Early Spring" from *Navajo: Visions and Voices Across the Mesa,* by Shonto Begay. Copyright © 1995 by Shonto Begay. Reprinted by permission of Scholastic, Inc.

"February" from *McBroom's Almanac,* written by Sid Fleischman, illustrated by Walter Lorraine. Text copyright © 1984 by Sid Fleischman. Illustrations copyright © 1984 by Walter Lorraine. Reprinted by permission of the author and illustrator.

"It's All the Same to the Clam" from *A Light in the Attic,* by Shel Silverstein. Copyright © 1981 by Evil Eye Music, Inc. Reprinted by permission of HarperCollins Publishers.

"Jane Goodall" from *Talking with Adventurers,* by Pat and Linda Cummings, published by the National Geographic Society. Excerpt copyright © 1998 Jane Goodall. Reprinted by permission of the National Geographic Society.

"John Henry Races the Steam Drill" from *Big Men, Big Country, A Collection of American Tall Tales,* by Paul Robert Walker, illustrated by James Bernardin. Text copyright © 1993 by Paul Robert Walker. Illustrations copyright © 1993 by James Bernardin. Reprinted by permission of Harcourt Inc.

"knoxville, tennessee" from *Black Feeling, Black Talk, Black Judgment,* by Nikki Giovanni. Copyright © 1968, 1970 by Nikki Giovanni. Reprinted by permission of HarperCollins Publishers.

"Langston Terrace" from *Childtimes, A Three-Generation Memoir,* by Eloise Greenfield and Lessie Jones Little. Copyright © 1979 by Eloise Greenfield and Lessie Jones Little. Reprinted by permission of HarperCollins Publishers.

"Árbol de limón/Lemon Tree," by Jennifer Clement, translated by Consuelo de Aerenlund. Copyright © 1995 by Jennifer Clement. Reprinted by permission of the author and translator.

"Ode to Pablo's Tennis Shoes" from *Neighborhood Odes,* by Gary Soto. Copyright © 1992 by Gary

Soto. Illustrations copyright © 1992 by Harcourt Inc. Reprinted by permission of Harcourt Inc.

"Paul Bunyon: The Mightiest Logger" from *American Tall Tales,* by Mary Pope Osborne. Text copyright © 1991 by Mary Pope Osborne. Reprinted by permission of Alfred A. Knopf, a division of Random House, Inc. Illustration by Chris Van Allsburg and book cover of *From Sea to Shining Sea: A Treasury of American Folklore and Folk Songs*, compiled by Amy L. Cohn, are reprinted by permission of Scholastic, Inc. Illustration copyright © 1993 by Chris Van Allsburg. Cover illustration copyright © 1993 by the artists. All rights reserved.

"Reggie" from *Honey I Love and Other Poems,* by Eloise Greenfield, pictures by Diane and Leo Dillon. Text copyright © 1978 by Eloise Greenfield. Reprinted by permission of HarperCollins Publishers.

"Sally Ann Thunder Ann Whirlwind" from *American Tall Tales,* by Mary Pope Osborne, wood engravings by Michael McCurdy. Text copyright © 1991 by Mary Pope Osborne. Illustrations copyright © 1991 by Michael McCurdy. Reprinted by permission of Alfred A. Knopf, a division of Random House, Inc.

"The Shark" from *Fast and Slow: Poems* by John Ciardi. Text copyright © 1975 by John Ciardi. Reprinted by permission of Houghton Mifflin Company. All rights reserved.

"Travel," by Edna St. Vincent Millay from *Collected Poems,* published by HaperCollins. Copyright 1921, 1948 by Edna St. Vincent Millay. All rights reserved. Reprinted by permission of Elizabeth Barnett, literary executor.

"What Are Pockets For?" from *One At A Time,* by David McCord. Copyright © 1974 by David McCord. By permission of Little, Brown and Company (Inc.).

"Whirligig Beetles" from *Joyful Noise: Poems for Two Voices*, by Paul Fleischman, illustrated by Eric Beddows. Text copyright © 1988 by Paul Fleischman. Illustrations copyright © 1988 by Eric Beddows. Reprinted by permission of HarperCollins Publishers.

Links and Theme Openers

"A Thousand Geese," by Joseph Bruchac. Copyright © by Joseph Bruchac. Reprinted by permission of the Barbara Kouts Literary Agency.

"Above Jackson Pond," by Joseph Bruchac. Copyright © by Joseph Bruchac. Reprinted by permission of the Barbara Kouts Literary Agency.

"Blind to Limitations," by Brent H. Weber from the August 1997 issue of *Highlights for Children.* Copyright © 1997 by Highlights for Children, Inc., Columbus, Ohio. Reprinted by permission of the publisher.

"El Niño," by Fred Pearce. Copyright © by Fred Pearce. Reprinted by permission of the author.

"The Eyes of My People," by DaMonique Dominguez, age 11, Englewood, CA. Copyright © 1999 by DaMonique Dominguez. Reprinted by permission of *Skipping Stones* magazine, Vol. 11, No. 3.

"Hands & Hearts" adapted from *American Girl,* Volume 6, Issue 6. Copyright © 1998 by Pleasant Company. Reprinted by permission of Pleasant Company.

"Home on the Range," by Johnny D. Boggs. Copyright © by Johnny D. Boggs. Reprinted by permission of the author and *Boy's Life,* June 1998. Published by the Boy Scouts of America.

Excerpt from *I Have Heard of a Land,* by Joyce Carol Thomas. Copyright © 1998 by Joyce Carol Thomas. Reprinted by permission of Joanna Cotler Books, an imprint of HarperCollins Publishers.

"Into the Deep" from the April 26, 1996, issue of *Time For Kids.* Copyright © 1996 by Time Inc. Reprinted by permission of the publisher.

Quote by Florence Joyner. TM Florence Joyner under license authorized by CMG Worldwide Inc., Indianapolis, Indiana 46256 USA www.cmgww.com.

"Maputo Saturday Craft Market," by Rebecca Beatriz Chavez, age 11. Reprinted by permission of *Stone Soup: the magazine by young writers and artists.* Copyright © 1998 by the Children's Art Foundation.

"Monkeys With a Mission" from the April 1999 issue of *National Geographic World.* Copyright © 1999 by the National Geographic Society. Reprinted by permission of the publisher.

"Nicodemus Stakes a Claim in History," by Angela Bates-Tompkins from Cobblestone's February 1999 issue: *African American Pioneers and Homesteaders.* Copyright © 1999 by Cobblestone Publishing Company. All rights reserved. Reprinted by permission of the publisher.

"One Pair of Shoes and a lot of good souls" originally published in the Winter 1995 issue of *ZuZu* magazine. Copyright © 1995 by *ZuZu Magazine/* Restless Youth Press. Reprinted by permission of the publisher.

Quote from *Pilgrim at Tinker Creek,* by Annie Dillard. Copyright © 1974 by Annie Dillard. Published by

HarperCollins Publishers, New York.

"The Princess and the Warrior," originally published as *"Los novios,"* by Genevieve Barlow and William Stivers from *Leyendas Mexicanas.* Copyright © 1996 by NTC Publishing Group. Reprinted by permission of NTC/ Contemporary Publishing Group.

"Problems," by Kevin A. Zuniga, age 12, Laredo Texas, from the November/December 1998 issue of *Skipping Stones* magazine. Copyright © 1998 by Kevin A. Zuniga. Reprinted by permission of *Skipping Stones* magazine.

"Raccoons On The Shore At Paradox Lake," by Joseph Bruchac. Copyright © by Joseph Bruchac. Reprinted by permission of the Barbara Kouts Literary Agency.

"Robin Hughes: Wildlife Doctor," by Susan Yoder Ackerman, reprinted by permission of *Cricket Magazine,* March 1977, Vol. 24, No. 7. Copyright © 1997 by Susan Yoder Ackerman.

"Swish," by Chance Yellowhair. Copyright © 1998 by Chance Yellowhair. Reprinted by permission of *Skipping Stones* magazine, September/October 1998.

"To Mother," by Aaron Wells, age 11, Eugene OR. Copyright © 1999 by Aaron Wells. Reprinted by permission of *Skipping Stones* magazine, March/April 1999.

"Wind Song" from *Four Ancestors: Stories, Songs and Poems from Native North America,* by Joseph Bruchac. Copyright © 1996 by Joseph Bruchac. Published and reprinted by permission of Troll Communications L.L.C.

"Yankee Doodle" from *Songs and Stories of the Revolution,* by Jerry Silverman. Copyright © 1994 by Jerry Silverman. Reprinted by permission of Millbrook Press Inc.

Special thanks to the following teachers whose students' compositions appear as Student Writing Models: Cindy Cheatwood, Florida; Diana Davis, North Carolina; Kathy Driscoll, Massachusetts; Linda Evers, Florida; Heidi Harrison, Michigan; Eileen Hoffman, Massachusetts; Julia Kraftsow, Florida; Bonnie Lewison, Florida; Kanetha McCord, Michigan.

Credits

Photography

CA5 (hat) The Purcell Team/CORBIS. (astronaut) © 2001 PhotoDisc. (Liberty Bell) Leif Skoogfors/ CORBIS. (flag) Owen Franken/CORBIS. (Earth) Reuters NewMedia Inc./CORBIS. **7** NASA. **10** Independence National Historical Park Collection, Philadelphia. **17** Jeff Greenberg/RAINBOW/ PictureQuest. **18** Claus Meyer/Black Star/PictureQuest. **20** (inset) NOAA, Colored by John Wells/SPL/Photo Researchers, Inc. **20–1** Keith Kent/SPL/Photo Researchers, Inc.. **27** © Kevin Schafer/Allstock/PictureQuest. **45** (t) Jeff Reinking/Mercury Pictures. (m) Courtesy Phil Boatwright. (b) image Copyright © 2000 PhotoDisc, Inc. **48** ©Vince Streano/CORBIS. **49** (t) Mauro Andino/AP/Wide World Photos. (m) Topi Lyambila/AP/Wide World. (b) Geoff Spencer/AP/Wide World. **51** Library of Congress (LC-USZ62-11491). **52** Digital Vision/PictureQuest. **54** (t) image Copyright © 2000 PhotoDisc, Inc. (b) © Johnny Autery. **55** L.M. Otero/AP Photo. **56** (t) Christine Kramer. (b) AP/Wide World Photos./Lennox McLendon. **58–77** Warren Faidley/WeatherStock. **79** (tl) National Center for Atmospheric Research/University Corporation for Atmospheric Research/National Science Foundation. (tr) National Climactic Data Center. (bl) ©Peter Jarver/Wildscape Australia. (br) ©Mark C. Burnett/Photo Researchers, Inc. **80–1** (bkgd) © Bill Bachman/ Photo Researchers, Inc. **82–3** Dr. Peter W. Sloss/NOAA/NESDIS/NGDC. **82** (b) Photo by J.D. Griggs/U.S. Geological Survey. **83** (tl) Photo by Lyn Topinka, U.S. Geological Survey. (tr) ©Nik Wheeler/CORBIS. (b) © Stephen and Donna O'Meara/Volcano Watch International. **85** National Park Service, Hawaii Volcanoes National Park. **86** Terraphotographics/BPS. **86–7** Gary Rosenquist/Earth Images. **88** Terraphotographics/BPS. **90** Solarfilma. **91–2** J. D. Griggs/U.S. Geological Survey. **93** Seymour Simon. **94** (t) National Park Service, Hawaii Volcanoes National Park. (b) John K. Nakata/Terraphotographics/BPS. **95** Terraphotographics/BPS. **96** Carl May/Terraphotographics/BPS. **97** Terraphotographics/BPS. **98** Seymour Simon. **99** (l) Courtesy Seymour Simon. (r) image Copyright © 2000 PhotoDisc, Inc. **128** from *Larger than Life: The American Tall-Tale Postcard 1905-1915* by Cynthia Elyce Rubin and Morgan Williams. Compilation copyright © 1990 by Abbeville Press, Inc. **130–1** © Warren Bolster/Tony Stone Images. **136** AP/Wide World Photos. **137** (t)Thomas

Zimmermann/Tony Stone Images. (m) © Agence Vandystadt/Allsport. (b) ©Tim Defrisco/Allsport. **139** Courtesy of the Kwan family. **141** (t) Courtesy of the Kwan family. (b) © Dave Black. **142** © Cindy Lang. **143** Courtesy of the Kwan family. **145** (t) ©Kevin R. Morris/CORBIS. (m) ©Mike Powell/Allsport. (b) Associated Press AP. **146** (l) © Dave Black. (r) ©1997 Gerard Chataigneau. **149** © Dave Black. **151** Momentum Partners, Inc. **154** © 1985 Jose Azel/AURORA. **155** © Photonews/Liaison Agency Inc. **156** (l) © Photonews/Liaison Agency Inc. (r) ©1985 Jose Azel/AURORA. **157** ©Peter Wouda/Persbureau Noordoost, The Netherlands **162** (t) Courtesy Carolyn Soto. (b) Lorraine Parrow/Mercury Pictures. **178** (t) Archive Photos. (b) U.S. Department of the Interior, National Park Service, Edison National Historic Site/Photo Researchers, Inc. **179** (tl) (tc) Brown Brothers. (tr) Popperfoto/Archive Photos. (mr) © CORBIS. (bl) Smithsonian Institution/National Museum of American History (SI #: 69857). **180** (tl) Archive Photos. (tc) Hulton Getty/Tony Stone Images. (ml) Comstock Klips. (bl) Archive Photos/John V. Dunigan. (br) © Bettmann/CORBIS. **181** (tc) Leonard Lessin/Peter Arnold, Inc. (r) image Copyright © 2000 PhotoDisc, Inc. (bl) Courtesy of Sony Electronics, Inc. **182** © Robert Holmgren/Tony Stone Images. **182–3** ©Andrew J.G. Bell, Eye Ubiquitous/CORBIS **183** Stephen Cooper/Allstock/PictureQuest. **184** (t) Dennis Crews/Mercury Pictures. (b) Michael Justice/Mercury Pictures. **185** (bkgd) image Copyright © 2000 PhotoDisc, Inc. **188–9** (b) © David Muench/CORBIS. **191** (b) © David Muench/CORBIS. **194–5** (b) © David Muench/CORBIS. **199** (b) © David Muench/CORBIS. **202** (b) © David Muench/CORBIS. **204–7** Jamie Bloomquist, American Foundation for the Blind. **208–9** (bkgd) NASA/Ames Research Center. **208–9** (inset) NASA. **208** (bl) NASA. **208** (c) Sovfoto/Eastfoto. **209** NASA. **210** (bkgd) image Copyright © 2000 PhotoDisc, Inc. **211–2** NASA. **214–5** CORBIS-Bettmann/UPI. **216–21** NASA. **222** AP/Wide World Photos. **223** Mike Williams/Mercury Pictures. **226–9** (bkgd) image Copyright © 2000 PhotoDisc, Inc. **227** ©1995 Marty Snyderman. **228–9** © Bruce H. Robison. **232** Chiselvision/The Stock Market. **234** NonStock/PictureQuest. **235** image Copyright © 2000 PhotoDisc, Inc. **236** W.A. Sharman/Milepost 92 1/2 /CORBIS. **237** image Copyright © 2000 PhotoDisc, Inc. **238-9** Roy Corral/CORBIS. **240** Craig Lovell/CORBIS. **242** (t) William Amos/Bruce Coleman. (b) Gossi/Bruce Coleman. **243** Gary Meszanos/Bruce Coleman. **245** Telegraph Colour Library/FPGInternational. **246** image Copyright © 2000 PhotoDisc, Inc. **249** image Copyright © 2000 PhotoDisc, Inc. **250** NonStock/PictureQuest. **251** Nancy Ney/The Stock Market. **252** Ron Rovtar/Photonica. **254** (inset) Independence National Historical Park Collection, Philadelphia. **254–5** detail, William Walcutt, *Pulling Down the Statue of King George III at Bowling Green, 1857.* Lafayette College Art Collection, Easton, Pennsylvania. **260** Colonial Williamsburg Foundation. **260–1** The Granger Collection, New York. **261** (t) The Granger Collection, New York. (b) John Singleton Copley, *Paul Revere.* Gift of Joseph W., William B., and Edward H.R. Revere. Courtesy, Museum of Fine Arts, Boston. Reproduced with permission. ©1999 Museum of Fine Arts, Boston. All Rights Reserved. **279** Tom Iannuzzi/Mercury Pictures. **281** Courtesy, American Antiquarian Society. **283** American 19th Century, *General Washington on a White Charger*, Gift of Edgar William and Bernice Chrysler Garbisch, Photograph © 1999 Board of Trustees, National Gallery of Art, Washington. **285** © Bettmann/CORBIS. **290** Colonial Williamsburg Foundation. **291** (tl) Bettmann/CORBIS. (tr) Collection of Mr. and Mrs. Karl T. Molin, photo courtesy Henry Groskinsky. (b) The Granger Collection, New York. **292** (t) Jon Crispin/Mercury Pictures. (b) Tom Spitz/Mercury Pictures. **306–7** ©Lee Snider/CORBIS. **308** Chicago Historical Society. **309** detail, James Peachey/National Archives of Canada/C-002001. **310** (r) The Historical Society of Pennsylvania (HSP), watercolor of James Forten from the Leon Gardiner Collection. Frame from Image Farm, Inc. (l) Friends Historical Library of Swarthmore College. **311** (t) AP/Wide World Photos. (b) Massachusetts Historical Society. **312** (t) Courtesy Walter Dean Myers. (b) Courtesy Leonard Jenkins. **329** (l) Print Collection, Miriam and Ira D. Wallach Division of Art, Prints and Photographs. The New York Public Library. Astor, Lenox and Tilden Foundation. **330** The Granger Collection, New York. **336** (inset) Collection of Dr. and Mrs. Richard Hoffman, courtesy of Kohn Turner Gallery. ©The Estate of Keith Haring. **336-7** New Jersey State Museum Collection, Gift of the Friends of the New Jersey State Museum, FA1973.19. **342** © Skjold/The Image Works **343** © Tommy Dodson/Unicorn Stock Photos **344** (t) Eric

Bakke/Mercury Pictures. (b) Courtesy Nneka Bennett. **358** image Copyright © 2000 PhotoDisc, Inc. **359, 360** image Copyright © 2000 PhotoDisc, Inc. **366** Sonda Dawes/The Images Works. **367** (l) Mark Richards/PhotoEdit. (tr) San Francisco SPCA Hearing Dog Program. (br) Bob Daemmrich/The Image Works. **368** (t) Courtesy Sally Hobart Alexander. (b) Courtesy George Ancona. **369–385** George Ancona. **386** image Copyright © 2000 PhotoDisc, Inc. **388** Dan Helms/Compix. **389–90** Paula Lerner/Aurora. **391** Dan Helms/Compix. **392** Zeva Oelbaum/Envision. **392–3** Ric Ergenbright/CORBIS. **393** (inset) Alison Wright/CORBIS. **407** (t) Courtesy Little, Brown and Company. (b) Courtesy Kees DeKiefte. (bkgd) Jane Dill. **408** image Copyright © 2000 PhotoDisc, Inc. **410–1** ©2001 Bruce Zake, All Rights Reserved. **411** E. Silverman. **412** ©Danny Turner. **413** Wade Spees/first published in *American Girl* magazine. **417** image Copyright © 2000 PhotoDisc, Inc. **419** image Copyright © 2000 PhotoDisc, Inc. **431** (t) Alan McEwen, 1999. (b) Courtesy Nancy Carpenter. (bkgd) image Copyright © 2000 PhotoDisc, Inc. **460** image Copyright © 2000 PhotoDisc, Inc. **462** (inset) image Copyright © 2000 PhotoDisc, Inc. (bkgd) Artville, the Earth's Palette/Don Bishop. **462–3** © Marc Muench, 1999. **468** (l) LH Benschneider. (r) Photo by O.S. Goff, the Denver Public Library, Western History Department. **469** National Museum of American Art, Washington, D.C./Art Resource, NY. **485** (t) Mike Greelar/Mercury Pictures. (b) Jose Crespo. **488** From the Collections of the St. Louis Mercantile Library at the University of Missouri-St. Louis. (bkgd) image Copyright © 2000 PhotoDisc, Inc. **489** (t) Smithsonian Institution/National Anthropological Archives (#83-15549). (b) Mr. and Mrs. Charles Diker Collection. **490** (t) Mr. and Mrs. Charles Diker Collection. (b) Missouri Historical Society, St. Louis. **491** (t) Collection National Cowboy Hall of Fame and Western Heritage Center, Oklahoma City, Oklahoma. (b) Thaw Collection, Fenimore Art Museum, Cooperstown, New York. Photo ©1998, John Bigelow Taylor, N.Y.C. **492** Bettmann/CORBIS. **494** Library of Congress. **496–7** Solomon D. Butcher Collection, Nebraska State Historical Society. **497** National Archives. **498** Roy Inman/Mercury Pictures. **499** image Copyright © 2000 PhotoDisc, Inc. **500** Nebraska State Historical Society. **501** Nebraska State Historical Society. **502–3** photo courtesy Andrea Warren and the McCance family **504** Nebraska State Historical Society. **505** Nebraska State

Historical Society. **506** The Kansas State Historical Society, Topeka, Kansas. **508–9** The Kansas State Historical Society, Topeka, Kansas. **511–2** The Kansas State Historical Society, Topeka, Kansas **513** Courtesy Billie Thornburg. **515** (bkgd) image Copyright © 2000 PhotoDisc, Inc. **516–7** The Kansas State Historical Society, Topeka, Kansas. **516** Charlie Riedel. **517** National Archives. **518–9** Charlie Riedel. **520–1** Steve Kaufman/CORBIS. **521** ©Hulton Getty/Liaison Agency. **522** (t) Courtesy Julius Lester. (b) Miles Pinkney. **523** (bkgd) image Copyright © 2000 PhotoDisc, Inc. **544–7** ©1998 David Nance. **548** Brown Brothers. **549** ©Bettmann/CORBIS. **563** (t) Courtesy Diane Stanley. (b) Courtesy Raúl Colón. **566** (t) Alan Ross/Tony Stone Images, (b) Hawaii State Archives **567** California History Section, California State Library. **566-7** (b) Alan Ross/ Tony Stone Images. **568** (t) Southern Pacific Photo, Union Pacific Museum Collection. (b) Union Pacific Museum Collection **569** Billy Hustace/Tony Stone Images. **572** Jeff Greenberg/ RAINBOW/ PictureQuest. **574** Courtesy HarperCollins Publishers. **575–8** from Childtimes: A Three-Generation Memoir by Eloise Greenfield and Lessie Jones Little. Copyright © 1979 by Eloise Greenfield and Lessie Jones Little. Copyright © 1971 by Pattie Ridley Jones. Reprinted by permission of HarperCollins Publishers. **579** (t) Michael K. Nichols/National Geographic Image Collection. (b) Staffan Widstrand/CORBIS. **580** (l) Hugo Van Lawick/National Geographic Image Collection. (r) Michael K. Nichols/National Geographic Image Collection. **581** (t) Jonathan Blair/Corbis. (b) Gerry Ellis/ENP Images. **587** © The Walt Disney Company, courtesy The Kobal Collection. **588** (t) Bill Frakes/Life Magazine © Time Inc. (b) image Copyright © 2000 PhotoDisc, Inc. **589** (t) Otto Greule/Allsport. (b) Bill Frakes/Life Magazine © Time Inc. **590** Al Bello/Allsport. **591** Doug Rensinger/Allsport. **592** image Copyright © 2000 PhotoDisc, Inc. **594** (inset) image Copyright © 2000 PhotoDisc, Inc. **594–5** Frans Lanting/Minden Pictures. **600** Roy Corral/Allstock/PictureQuest. **600–1** (bkgd) ©Carol Havens/CORBIS. **601** (m) ©Galen Rowell/CORBIS. (b) ©Alissa Crandall/CORBIS. **602** image Copyright © 2000 PhotoDisc, Inc. **617** Courtesy Michio Hoshino. **618** image Copyright © 2000 PhotoDisc, Inc. **619** image Copyright © 2000 PhotoDisc, Inc. **624** CORBIS Royalty Free. **626** Claus Meyer/Black Star/PictureQuest. **627** (t) David Hiser/Tony Stone Images. (b) ©Wolfgang

Kaehler/CORBIS. **628** (inset) Courtesy George Ancona. (frame) image Copyright © 2000 PhotoDisc, Inc. **644** ©Amos Nachoum/CORBIS. **645** ©Raymond Gehman/CORBIS. **646** (bl) Ben Osborne/Tony Stone Images. (br) Art Wolfe/Tony Stone Images. **648** image Copyright © 2000 PhotoDisc, Inc. **650** (icon) image Copyright © 2000 PhotoDisc, Inc. (t) Courtesy Jean Craighead George. (b) Tom Iannuzzi/Mercury Pictures. **666** image Copyright © 2000 PhotoDisc, Inc. **668** Courtesy of Dr. Robin Schlocker. **669** (t) Courtesy of Dr. Robin Schlocker. (b) image Copyright © 2000 PhotoDisc, Inc. **670** ©Lynn M. Stone/Animals Animals. **671** (t) Virginia Living Museum/Photo by Ron Godby. (b) **675** image Copyright © 2000 PhotoDisc, Inc. **676** image Copyright © 2000 PhotoDisc, Inc. **677** image Copyright © 2000 PhotoDisc, Inc. **678** Zeva Oelbaum/Envision **679** G. Brad Lewis/Tony Stone Images. **680** Corbis Royalty Free **681** image Copyright © 2000 PhotoDisc, Inc. **682** Eastcott/Momatiuk/Tony Stone Images **683** Solomon D. Butcher Collection, Nebraska State Historical Society. **684** Tony Stone Images. **685** image Copyright © 2000 PhotoDisc, Inc. **686** Comstock KLIPS. **688** © Carr Clifton/Minden Pictures.

Gary Aagaard.

Assignment Photography
CA1 (t) Joel Benjamin. (b) Tony Scarpetta. **CA2** (t) Joel Benjamin. **CA3** Tony Scarpetta. **CA4** (t) Joel Benjamin. (b) Tony Scarpetta. **CA5** Joel Benjamin. **138** (bkgd), **153, 160–1, 414–5, 624–5** Joel Benjamin. **78, 80–81** Morocco Flowers. **283** Michelle Joyce. **47, 225** (r), **305** (r) Allan Landau. **107, 231, 335, 439, 571, 673** Tony Scarpetta. **409** (r), **433** (r), **487** (r), **543** (r) Ken Karp.

Illustration
6 (b) **108–109** Tim Jessell. **14** (b) Michael Chesworth. **29–44** Phil Boatwright. **102–105** Stefano Vitale. **115** Phil Boatwright. **121, 123** Craig Spearing **185** (inset) **186–201, 203** Paul Lee. **241, 284** William Brinkley and Associates. **314-327, 329** (r) Copyright © 2001 by Leonard Jenkins. **331-333,** Mike Reed. **347-357, 359** ® Nneka Bennett. **394**(i) **396-406, 407**(i) Kees de Kiefte. **418-430** Nancy Carpenter. **434-437** Copyright © 2001 by Vivienne Flesher. **440-457** Michael Chesworth. **549, 600, 627** XNR Productions, INC. **550**(i) **551-562,** Copyright © 2001 by Raúl Colón. **620-623** Michael Rothman. **647** David Ballard. **648-649** Robert Hynes. **652-664**

Index

Boldface page references indicate formal strategy and skill instruction.

context clues, *41, 55A, 64, 81E, 81F,*
83A, 86
dictionary, using a, *55A, 81E*
longer words, **51E–51F, 81E–81F,**
105E–105F, *R14–R15, R16–R17,*
R18–R19
phonics/decoding strategy,
BTS4–BTS5, 27A, 41, 51E, 51F,
55A, 64, 81F, 83A, 86, 105E,
105F, R3, R5, R7, R9
See also Phonics; Spiral Review;
Structural analysis; Vocabulary,
selection.

Details, noting important, related, and
sufficient. *See* Comprehension skills.

Diagrams. *See* Graphic information,
interpreting; Graphic organizers.

Dialogue. *See* Writer's craft.

Diaries and journals. *See* Journal.

Dictionary skills
alphabetical order, **81I–81J**
definitions, **105I–105J**
guide words, **81I–81J**
sample sentences, *105I*
unfamiliar words, *105J*

Drafting. *See* Reading-Writing
Workshop, steps of.

Drama. *See* Creative dramatics.

Drawing conclusions. *See*
Comprehension skills.

E

Editing. *See* Reading-Writing Workshop,
steps of, proofreading.

English Language Learners, activities
especially helpful for
building background, *24B, R3, R5, R7*
concept development, *26A, 39*
key vocabulary, *R3, R5, R7*
language development, *26A, 35, 47,*
50, 105O
literature discussion, *81O*
panel discussion, *51O*

vocabulary support, *105J*
writing support, *46*

Ethnic diversity. *See* Multicultural activi-
ties/information.

Evaluating literature. *See* Literature,
evaluating.

Evaluating writing. *See* Reading-Writing
Workshop.

Evaluation. *See* Assessment, planning for.

Expanding literacy. *See* Skills links.

Expository text, *26A, 48–51, 54A,*
57–75, 78–81, 82K, 84–98

F

Fact and opinion. *See* Comprehension
skills.

Fiction. *See* Literary genres; Selections
in Anthology.

Figurative language. *See* Literary devices.

Fluency
assessing, *41, 67, 93, 107A*
reading, *41, 67, 93, 107A*

G

Generalizations, making. *See*
Comprehension skills.

Genre. *See* Literary genres.

Get Set
Buildup to a Shakeup, *26A*
Photographing Wild Weather, *54A*
The World of Volcanoes, *82K*

Glossary in Student Anthology, *G1–G3*

Grammar and usage
parts of a sentence
subjects and predicates, simple and
complete **51K–51L,** *53E, 105N*
sentence structure
compound sentences, **81K–81L**
sentences, types of
statement, **51K–51L**

question, **51K–51L**
command, **51K–51L**
speech, parts of. *See* Speech, parts of.
spelling connection. *See* Connections.
usage
run-on sentences, **81L**
sentence fragment, **105N**
See also Spiral Review.

Graphic information, interpreting
calendars, *65*
charts, *81,* **105C–105D**
computer generated weather maps, *79*
diagrams, *65*
globes, **105C–105D**
graphs, *81,* **105C–105D**
maps, *24A, 24B, 26A, 50, 54A, 77,*
82K, **105C–105D**
satellite photos, *79*
tables, **105C–105D**
time lines, *87*

Graphic organizers
category chart, *83B, 83C, 85, 90, 98,*
99, 105A
charts, *31, 81B, 81P, 105B, 105E*
classification chart, *97*
clusters, *53B*
diagrams, *61*
event map, *27B, 27C, 29, 34, 44, 45*
folktale chart, *103, 105*
K-W-L charts, *49, 51*
log book, *71*
main ideas-details, *95*
schedules, *71*
selection map, *55B, 55C, 57, 68, 74,*
81A
sequence charts, *95*
story map/story frames, *43*
summarize, *75*
topic-main idea chart, *89*
word webs, *51J, 51P, R19*

Graphophonemic/graphophonic cues.
See Phonics.

Handwriting, *53G*

Home-Community Connections. *See* Home/Community Connections Book.

Home Connection. *See* Home/Community Connections Book.

Home-School Connection. *See* Home/Community Connections Book.

Homework. *See* Home/Community Connections Book.

Illustrators of Anthology selections
Boatwright, Phil, *45, F114*
Lorraine, Walter, *F125*
Spearing, Craig, *F119*
Van Allsburg, Chris, *F110*

Independent and recreational reading
suggestions for, *20–20D, 28, 51B, 56, 81B, 84, 105B, R2–R3, R4–R5, R6–R7*
See also Reading modes.

Independent writing
suggestions for, *51N, 81N, 105N*

Individual needs, meeting
Challenge, *20I–20J, 28, 33, 34, 40, 44, 51, 51H, 56, 66, 68, 71, 72, 74, 81, 81H, 84, 87, 90, 96, 98, 105, 105H, F118, F124*
Classroom Management, *20I–20J, 28, 48, 56, 78, 84, 102*
English Language Learners, *20I–20J, 24B, 26A, 28, 35, 39, 46, 47, 50, 51O, 54A, 56, 59, 61, 70, 77, 80, 81O, 81V, 82K, 84, 101, 104, 105J, 105O, R3, R5, R7, R9, F112, F116–F117, F121, F126*
Extra Support, *20I–20J, 28, 29, 31, 34, 35, 36, 38, 41, 44, 45, 49, 51B, 51G, 51J, 56, 57, 64, 67, 68, 69, 74, 75, 76, 79, 81B, 81G, 81J, 84, 85, 86, 89, 90, 91, 93, 98,*

99, 100, 105B, 105G, F111, F113–F115, F120
On Level Students, *20I–20J, 28, 34, 44, 56, 68, 74, 84, 90, 98*
Special Needs, *20I–20J. See also* Teaching and management.
Strategy Review, *27A, 55A, 83A*

Inferences, making
about characters' actions and feelings, *31, 103, 105*
by drawing conclusions, *51, 81, 100, 105*
by predicting, *27B, 28, 29, 31, 32, 34, 35, 38, 42, 45, R2*
from text organization, *54A, 55B, 89*
See also Comprehension skills: cause and effect; generalizations, making.

Inflected forms. *See* Structural analysis.

Information links. *See* Information skills.

Information skills
collecting data, *51, 81*
comparing different sources, *51, 51D, 105C*
presenting information, *51, 51D, 81, 101*
using graphic aids: maps, globes, charts, tables, and graphs, **105C–105D**
using print and electronic card catalogs, **81C–81D**
using print and electronic reference sources, **51C–51D**
See also Reference and study skills; Spiral Review.

Informational selection, structure of. *See* Comprehension skills, text organization.

Journal, *29, 36, 47, 53A, 57, 69, 77, 85, 91, 101, F108, F110, F113, F114, F118, F119, F122, F126*

Judgments, making. *See* Comprehension skills.

Knowledge, activating prior. *See* Background, building.

K-W-L Strategy. *See* Graphic organizers.

Language and usage. *See* Grammar and usage.

Language concepts and skills
body language, *105O,* **105P**
descriptive language, *62, 66*
figurative language. *See* Literary devices.
nonverbal communication, *105O*
primary language activities. *See* English Language Learners.
sensory language, *52, 53, 53B,* **53C**
word play: jokes, puns, riddles, *40*
See also Vocabulary, expanding.

Language mechanics. *See* Mechanics, language.

Learning styles, activities employing alternate modalities to meet individual, *28, 46, 47, 56, 76, 77, 84, 100, 101. See also* Extra Support Handbook; Individual needs, meeting.

Lesson plans
daily, *22A–23A, 53Q–53R, 82C–82D*
Universal Access Planning Chart, *23B–23C, 53S–53T, 82E–82F*

Lessons, explicit
author's craft, **61**
comprehension, **51A–51B, 81A–81B, 105A–105B**
decoding, **51E–51F, 81E–81F, 105E–105F**
dictionary, **81I–81J, 105I–105J**
grammar, **51K–51L, 81K–81L, 105K–105L**
language and writing, **51M–51N, 81M–81N, 105M–105N**
listening, speaking, viewing, **51O–51P, 81O–81P, 105O–105P**

literary genre, **25A, 31, 50, F111**
phonics, **51F, 81F, 105F**
reading strategies, **BTS2–BTS13, 27B, 55A, 55B, 83A, 83B**
spelling, **51G–51H, 81G–81H, 105G–105H**
study skills, **51C–51D, 81C–81D, 105C–105D**
visual literacy, **63**
vocabulary expansion and skills, **51I–51J, 81I–81J, 105I–105J**
writer's craft, **39, F115, F117, F121**
writing, **51M–51N, 81M–81N, 105M–105N**

Leveled books
Reader's Library, *53H–53N, R2–R7*
Theme Paperbacks, *53I–53J, 53K–53L, 53M–53N*

Library, using. *See* Information skills; Reference and study skills.

Limited English proficient students. *See* English Language Learners.

Linking literature, *See also* Cross-Curricular links; connections.

Listening activities
assessing, *82H*
guidelines
for a literature discussion, *81O, 81P*
for asking clarifying questions, *81P*
for assessing meaning, *24B*
for demonstrating appropriate listening behaviors, *51O, 51P, 81O, 81P, 105O, 105P*
for gesturing to show comprehension, *81P*
for keeping an open mind, *81P*
for listening attentively, *51O, 81O, 105O*
for listening respectfully, *105O*
for making eye contact with speaker, *81P*
in a writing conference. *See* Reading-Writing Workshop: conferencing.
personal response, *25B, 53W, 82J*
prior knowledge for, *24A, 53V, 82G*

purpose
for details, *82H, 82J*
for information, *24A–25B*
for pleasure/enjoyment, *24A–25B*
for tone and expression, *25A*
to analyze and evaluate. *See* Literature, analyzing; evaluating.
to evaluate author, *82J*
to retell a story, *33, 45*
to think aloud. *See* Modeling: think aloud.
to visualize. *See* Visualizing.
to a read aloud. *See* Reading modes.
to an audiotape. *See* Audiotapes.
to creative dramatics. *See* Creative dramatics.
to literature discussion. *See* Responding to literature.
to oral reading. *See* Reading modes; Rereading.

Listening comprehension
categorize and classify, **82G–82J**
fact and opinion, *82J*
sequence of events, **24A–25B**

Literacy, expanding. *See* Skills links.

Literary analysis
classic literature, *102–105*
common themes, *24A, 25B, 26A, 46, 51, 54A, 76, 81V, 81X, 82A, 100*
comparing, *102*
compare to personal experience, *94*
elements of fiction and nonfiction, *25A, 31, 48, 50, 65, 102*
historical eras, *90*
interpret, *46, 76, 81O, 81P, 90, 100, 103*
literary language and terms, *25A, 31, 39, 50, 61*
real life, *94*
role of author/illustrator, *246, 265, 276, 300, 322*
See also Literary genres.

Literary appreciation. *See* Literature, analyzing.

Literary devices
comparisons, *96*

figurative language, *76*
flashback, *28, 34, 38, 40, 42, 45, 51A, 51B*
idioms, *R3*
imagery, *39*
metaphor, *30*
mood, *39*
poetic devices
simile, *40, 70*
suspense, *28*

Literary genres, characteristics of
expository nonfiction, **50,** *65*
folktales, *102, 103*
narrative nonfiction, **25A**
pourquoi tale, *102*
realistic fiction, **31**
tall tales, *F108*
See also Expository text; Narrative text; Selections in Anthology.

Literary skills. *See* Literary analysis; Literary devices; Story elements.

Literature
analyzing, *46, 76, 81O, 81P, 100, R3, R5, R7, F112, F116, F120, F126*
comparing, *F110, F127. See also* Connections, between selections.
discussion. *See* Responding to literature.
evaluating, *47*
linking. *See* Linking literature.
responding to. *See* Responding to literature.
See also Literary devices.

Locating information. *See* Information skills.

Main idea and supporting details, identifying. *See* Details, noting.

Maps, using. *See* Graphic information, interpreting.

Mathematics activities. *See* Cross-curricular links.

Meaning, constructing from text. *See* Comprehension skills; Decoding skills; Phonics; Language; Strategic reading.

Mechanics, language
    capitalization
        proofreading, *53F, 81N*
        proper nouns, *100*
    punctuation
        comma in a compound sentence, *81L*
        exclamation mark, *51K*
        period, *51K*
        proofreading, *53F, 81N*
        question mark, *51K*

Mental images. *See* Visualizing.

Metacognition. *See* Comprehension skills; Strategies, reading; Think Aloud.

Modeling
    blending, *R5*
    student writing, *31, 32, 35, 38, 42, 44, 45, 64, 68, 72, 75, 81F, 88, 90, 96, 98, 99*
    teacher, *27A, 27B, 27C, 31, 32, 38, 51A, 51D, 51E, 51I, 53E, 55A, 55B, 55C, 63, 64, 81E, 81F, 81I, 83A, 83B, 88, 89, 93, 105C*
    think aloud, *27A, 27B, 51A, 51D, 51E, 51F, 51I, 55A, 55B, 81A, 81D, 81E, 81F, 81I, 83A, 83B, 105A, 105D, 105E, 105F, 105I, R3, R5, R7, R9*

Monitoring comprehension. *See* Strategies, reading.

Morphemes. *See* Decoding skills.

Morphology. *See* Decoding; Phonics.

Movement. *See* Cross-curricular links.

Multi-age classroom, *20F, 20K*

Multicultural activities/information
    Chinese and Spanish word origins, *81J*
    early Hawaiians, *85*
    Hawaiian Volcanoes, *92*
    "hurricane" countries, *R3*
    Roman belief in Vulcan, *85*

Narrative text, *28–44, 102–105*

Newsletters. *See* Home/Community Connections Book.

Nonfiction. *See* Literary genres; Selections in Anthology.

O

Options for Reading,
    Deciding About Support, *28, 56, 84*
    Meeting Individual Needs, *28, 56, 84*
    Reading in Segments, *28, 56, 84*

Oral composition. *See* Speaking.

Oral presentations. *See* Speaking.

Oral reading. *See* Reading modes; Rereading.

Oral reading fluency. *See* Fluency, reading.

Oral reports. *See* Speaking.

Oral summary. *See* Summarizing.

P

Paired learning. *See* Classroom management, partners.

Parent involvement. *See* Home/ Community Connections Book; Teacher's Resource Blackline Masters.

Parts of a book. *See* Study skills.

Peer conferences. *See* Writing conferences.

Peer evaluation, *53E. See also* Cooperative learning activities; Writing conferences.

Peer interaction. *See* Cooperative learning activities; Paired learning.

Performance assessment. *See* Assessment, planning for.

Personal narrative. *See* Literary genres.

Personal response. *See* Responding to literature.

Phonics
    digraphs, *27A*
    long vowels
        a, i, e, 81E, 81F
        a-consonant-*e, 81F, R3*
        ai and *ay, 81F*
        eau, 105F
        ee and *ee, 81F*
        i-consonant-*e, 81F*
        i and *igh, 81F*
        o, oo, yoo, **105F**
        o-consonant-*e, 105F*
        ow, oa, and *o, 105F*
        u-consonant-*e, 105F*
        ue, ew, ui, ow, oo, 105F
        y as long *i, 86*
    patterns
        VC, *51F*
        VCCV, *27A, 81E*
        VCV, *81E*
    short vowel syllables, *51F, 81E*
    short vowels, **51F**
    r-controlled vowels, *27A*
    See also Decoding skills; Spelling.

Photographers in Anthology
    Faidley, Warren, *54A, 56, 57–75, 56*

Picture clues, *91*

Plot. *See* Story elements.

Pluralism. *See* Multicultural activities.

Predicting outcomes. *See* Comprehension skills.

Predictions, making and checking
    conforming/changing, *27B, 29, 34, 35, 36, 44, 57, 68, 74, 75, 90, 98*
    from previewing, *27B, 48, R2, R4, R6, R8*
    review, *35, 44, 45, 68, 75, 90, 99*
    while reading, *32, 36, 42, 49, 57, 69, 91, 103*

Prefixes. *See* Structural analysis.

study strategies
  K-W-L Strategy, *49*
  skimming and scanning, *48, 49, 73*
thesaurus, parts,
  definition, *51I*
  entry words, *51I*
  part of speech, *51I*
  sample sentence, *51I*
  subentry words, *51I*
  See also Research activities; Spiral Review.

Rereading
  cooperatively, *41, 67, 93*
  for comprehension, *88, 95, 96*
  to support answer, *51, 65, 68, 81*
  with expression and intonation, *41, 67, 93*

Research activities, *51D*

Responding to literature, options for
  discussion, *46, 76, 81O, 81P, 100, R3, R5, R7, R9*
  listening and speaking, *47*
  literature discussion, *34, 44, 68, 74, 90, 98*
  personal response, *47, 77, 101*
  viewing, *77*
  writing, *46, 76, 100*

Reteaching. *See* Individual needs, meeting.

Retelling
  information, *75, 81O*
  story, *33, 45*

Revising. *See* Reading-Writing Workshop, steps of.

Root words. *See* Structural analysis.

Science activities. *See* Cross-curricular links.

Selecting books. *See* Independent and recreational reading.

Selections in Anthology
  career article
    "Storm Warning," *78–81*
  folktale
    The Princess and the Warrior, 102–105
  nonfiction
    Volcanoes by Seymour Simon, *84–98*
  realistic fiction
    Earthquake Terror, by Peg Kehret, *28–44*
  science articles and features
    "El Niño," by Fred Pearce, *48–51*
  tall tales
    February, by Sid Fleischman, *F125–F127*
    John Henry Races the Steam Drill, by Paul Robert Walker, *F114–F118*
    Paul Bunyan, the Mightiest Logger of Them All, by Mary Pope Osborne, *F110–F113*
    Sally Ann Thunder Ann Whirlwind, by Mary Pope Osborne, *F119–F124*
  See also Teacher Read Aloud; Theme Paperbacks.

Self-assessment
  reading, *41, 67, 77, 93, 101*
  theme goals, *41, 67, 93*
  writing project, *53G*

Self-correcting reading strategy. *See* Strategies, reading, monitor/clarify.

Semantic cues. *See* Decoding skills, context clues; Vocabulary skills.

Sentences. *See* Grammar and usage.

Sequence of events, noting. *See* Comprehension skills.

Setting. *See* Story elements.

Shared learning. *See* Cooperative learning activities.

Skill Reminders, *51Q–51R, 81Q–81R, 105Q–105R*

Skills links
  folktale, how to read a, **102–105**
  science article, reading a, **48–51**
  sequence chart, reading a, **78–81**

Skimming and scanning, *48, 49, 73*

Social studies activities. *See* Cross-curricular links.

Sound-spelling patterns. *See* Phonics; Spelling.

Speaking
  ask questions, *51O*
  describing, *35, 38, 66, 75, 79, 81X, 82A, 93, 97*
  discussion, *25B, 26A, 32, 33, 34, 35, 44, 45, 47, 48, 51K, 51N, 51O, 51P, 65, 68, 74, 75, 81B, 82J, 82K, 90, 98, 99, 103, 105J, R2*
  dramatics. *See* Creative dramatics.
  explanation, *26A, 55A, 81D, 82J*
  expressing opinions, *76, 100*
  giving an opinion, *81O, 99, 105P*
  guidelines
    for a newscast, *47*
    for a panel discussion, *51O–51P*
    for asking clarifying questions, *105O, 105P*
    for asking for others' opinions, *105O*
    for asking thoughtful questions, *81O*
    for avoiding interrupting, *51O, 81O*
    for being clear and concise, *81O*
    for changing volume to make a point, *51P*
    for effective conversation, ***105O–105P***

Greek word roots, *51J, 81J*
scientific terms: geology words, *51J*
specialized/technical vocabulary, *51J, 83A, 86, 96*
word roots. *See* Word roots.
word webs. *See* Graphic organizers, word webs.
words from many languages: weather words, *81J*
See also Language concepts and skills.

Vocabulary, selection
key words, *27A, 30, 32, 34, 36, 38, 40, 48, 50, 55A, 58, 62, 64, 69, 70, 72, 74, 78, 80, 83A, 86, 88, 91, 92, 94, 96, 102, 104, R2, R4, R6*
See also Context clues; Daily Language Practice; Decoding skills.

Vocabulary skills
classifying, *81G*
dictionary, using a, *81J*
Greek roots, *105E*
Latin word roots, *105E*
shades of meaning, *51I*
signal words, *24B, 33, 51A, 71, R2*
special, *24B*
specialized vocabulary, *79*
using a thesaurus, **51I–51J**
word histories, *51J, 81J*
word origins, *105J, R7*
word study, *70, 94*
See also Dictionary skills; Spiral Review; Vocabulary expanding; Vocabulary, selection.

Vowels. *See* Decoding skills; Spelling.

W

Word analysis. *See* Structural analysis; Vocabulary, expanding; Vocabulary, selection.

Word roots. *See* Structural analysis.

Word webs. *See* Graphic organizers.

Writer's craft
character descriptions, *F117*

comparing by shape, *72*
descriptive language, *39*
details, *72*
dialogue, *53D, 74*
humor, *F121*
mood, **39**
retelling, *F115*
sensory language, *52, 53, 53B,* **53C**

Writer's log. *See* Journal.

Writing activities and types
adventure story, *46*
advertisements, *53F*
answer to a question, *53A, 69, 105C*
creative. *See* Writing modes.
crossword puzzle, *51H*
descriptions, *81M–81N*
dialogue, *53D*
drawing with label or sentence, *39*
fact file, *101*
independent. *See* Independent writing.
job descriptions, *76*
news article, **51M–51N**
opinions, *65, 77, 81M–81N*
paragraph of information, **105M–105N**
poster, *81P,*
predictions, *29, 36, 57, 68, 69, 85, 90, 91*
profile of a volcano, *105*
questions, *55B, 57, 64, 69, 85, 91*
rebus puzzle, *105H*
response to a prompt, **81M–81N**
review, *47*
story sequel, *46*
tall tale, *F128*
theme-related activities, *R26–R27*
travel brochure, *100*
word search puzzle, *81H*
See also Reading-Writing Workshop; Writer's craft.

Writing as a process. *See* Reading-Writing Workshop.

Writing conferences. *See* Reading-Writing Workshop.

Writing modes
creative, *46, 53D, 81M–81N, 81P, F128*

descriptive, *81M–81N*
evaluative, *47, 81M–81N*
expository, *81M–81N, 100*
expressive, *81P*
functional, *76*
informative, *51M–51N, 76, 101, 105,* **105M–105N**
narrative, *46, 53D, 81M–81N, F128*
persuasive, *53F, 81M–81N, 100*

Writing skills
computer tools, using,
  dictionary, *51N, 53A, 81N, 105N*
  spell check, *51N, 53A, 81N, 105N*
  thesaurus, *51N, 53A, 81N, 105N*
  See Technology resources.
drafting skills
  answering the 5 Ws, *51M, 51N*
  capturing interest, *51M*
  character's feelings, *46*
  details of setting, *46*
  indenting paragraphs, *105M*
  organizing by order of importance, size, or position, *53D*
  organizing details, *52, 53B,* **53D**
  organizing writing, *51N*
  planning, *51N*
  putting most important facts first, *51M*
  restating a prompt, *81M*
  using a good headline, *51M*
  using comparison for effect, *53C*
  using complete sentences, *52,* **53E**
  using describing words, *66*
  using details, *51M*
  using facts, not opinions, *105M–105N*
  using logical order, *105M*
  using quotations, *51M*
  using sensory language, *52, 53, 53B,* **53C**
  writing a high-interest beginning, *52, 53B*
  writing a satisfying conclusion, *52, 53*

writing a topic sentence,
105M–105N
writing dialogue, *53D*
formats. *See* Writing, activities and
types.
prewriting skills
asking friends for ideas, *53A*
brainstorming, *46*
browsing through magazines, *53A*
carefully reading a prompt, *81M*
choosing a topic, *53A, 105M*
examining printed materials, *100*
jotting down and arranging main
ideas and details, *81M*
planning an answer, *81M*
planning and organizing, *53B, 81N*
surfing the Internet, *53A*
thinking about and writing details,
46
using imagination, *53A–53B*
webbing, *46*
process writing, steps of. *See* Reading-
Writing Workshop.
proofreading,
capitalization, *100*
sentences, *81N*
spelling, *100*
publishing skills
illustrate original writing, *46, 100*
letters to friend or relative, *53G*
web site on the Internet, *53G*
revising skills
adding detail for elaboration, *51N*
avoiding run-ons, *81L*
avoiding short, choppy sentences,
51L
capitalizing and punctuating sentences, *81N*
checking facts for accuracy, *51N*
checking the answer, *81M*
correcting sentence fragments,
105N
deleting unrelated details, *53B,
53D, 53E*
eliminating opinions, *51N*
exact nouns, *105L*

sentence combining: compound
subjects and compound predicates, *51L*
using a thesaurus, *51I–51J*
writing quotations exactly, *51N*
See also Reading-Writing Workshop;
Spiral Review; Writer's craft.